TIGER CLUB

THE EXUBERANT YEARS

VOLUME II: 1967 – 1976

by

LEWIS BENJAMIN

with a foreword by
HRH The Duke of Edinburgh

CIRRUS ASSOCIATES

PUBLISHED BY:
Cirrus Associates (S.W.),
Kington Magna,
GILLINGHAM,
Dorset,
SP8 5EW UK.

ISBN 0 951 5598 8 5

PRINTED IN ENGLAND BY:
The Book Factory,
35-37 Queensland Road,
LONDON,
N7 7AH.

PHOTO SCANNING BY:
Castle Graphics Ltd,
Nunney,
NR. FROME,
Somerset,
BA11 4LW.

DISTRIBUTORS:
Cirrus Associates (S.W.),
Kington Magna,
GILLINGHAM,
Dorset,
SP8 5EW.

To Michael Jones, who made it all happen.

**IN MEMORY OF NORMAN JONES MBE,
WHOSE INSPIRATION FOUNDED THE TIGER CLUB.**

'I had a friend, Monty Grover, a Lieutenant RNVR on minesweepers in the war who told me of an eccentric minesweeper captain he had who used to grow flowers in pots all around the bridge.
"You mean Norman Jones," I said.
He replied: "How on earth did you know?"'

From James Gilbert.

NORMAN JONES DIED IN 1991 AGED 86.

My grateful thanks go to:

Trudi, my wife, for her day-in, day-out typing, her love and support.

HRH The Duke of Edinburgh for contributing the Foreword and for his very real assistance with the Dawn-to-Dusk background, all conveyed to me with an unfailing courtesy tinged with humour by Miles Hunt-Davis and Sir Brian McGrath.

And so many helped. Ambrose Barber, Lauretta Dives, James Gilbert and *"Pilot"* magazine, Kate Grime, Mavis Harriott, Pete Jarvis, Michael Jones (for Appendices 1 & 2), Don & Tessa Lovell, Fred Marsh, John Penfold, Desmond Penrose, David Phillips, Sir John Severne, Keith Sissons, John W.R. Taylor, Robin Voice and, down at Redhill, "Chalky" White.

Last, but not least, my immense gratitude to the book's publisher, Peter Campbell, for his total commitment, careful editing, and his friendship.

'The Exuberant Years' tells the fascinating story of a man and a club. No ordinary man and certainly no ordinary club. Norman Jones, one time naval officer, had the inspired idea of forming a flying club, the Tiger Club, initially for racing Tiger Moths. The idea was unique in that the club was not intended to teach people to fly, it was to give experienced light aircraft pilots the fun of taking part in competitions and public displays.

I first met Norman Jones when he came to me with the idea of running a flying competition to see who could spend the longest time in the air on the longest day of the year. We called it 'The Dawn to Dusk Competition'. The idea was splendid, but all sorts of complications arose as soon as we tried to settle the details. It was eventually launched, with a certain amount of trepidation, and the idea caught on. There was not a mass entry, but a quite sufficient number of willing pilots, as well as navigators and passengers, decided to have a go to make it the popular contest it is today. The rules and conditions gradually evolved with experience, but it has always remained an event in the true spirit of Norman Jones's Tiger Club.

I am quite sure that anyone with the slightest interest in private flying will be enthralled by this lively account of personal aviation in an age of huge passenger jets and supersonic military aircraft..

CONTENTS

FOREWORD by HRH The Duke of Edinburgh

INTRODUCTION 9

1967
700 OF US, KRONFELD, BALLOONING AND EDMUND 14
SAUSAGES, FOX MOTH, ACCIDENTS, PUSSY AND DEV 21
T.H.-T., FATHERHOOD, A SHOT COOKER, OSNABRÜCK 30
AND PARIS
BEAUVAIS, ANTARCTICA, FIREWORKS AND G-ASKP 38
SHOREHAM, PROPS, DUTY PILOTS AND KILKENNY 48
BLACK CAT, LOVE STORY AND OUR AIMS 57

1968
QUIZ, LEGAL FUND AND "BISH" R.I.P. 61
THE ACTIVE, THE BEAGLE AND BOMBING THE NAVY 70
BLAKE'S SPAIN, LAW, GOOD GUYS AND AMBROSE'S RUDDER 75
FRIENDSHIP, INTERPRETING MINUTES, HIGHLAND 87
HERON AND AEROBATICS

1969
MAN LOST, DISPLAY UPSET, MAGIC CHALLOCK AND A 102
MILITARY DETOUR
OTTER TO OTTAWA, HAPPY SNORING, PASSENGERS 111
AND BARRY
TURKISH ADVENTURE, SHOREHAM, PUNCTUALITY 120
AND FARNBOROUGH
MANHATTAN SEAPLANES, DENMARK AND ESSO 128
THANK YOUS, A YEAR'S AEROS AND A XMAS GROTTO 140

1970
MARKERS, PIXIE, COMMITTEE REFLECTIONS AND 146
OVERSEAS NEWS
"BISH'S" SPIRIT, ANNUAL DIN, MANX AND CHOW MEIN 155
BILL'S ROCHESTER, TURB STORY, HAMILTON COMPS 161
AND SUMMER ON THE BEACH
WE MISS FRIENDS, OVER-CONFIDENCE AND 'WET PAPER, 170
TASTES SALT = DITCHED'

1971
16 TYPES, DAVID'S TROPHY, ISLANDER CHALLENGE 175
AND HRH PRINCE WILLIAM
LAFFY'S CONVERSION, FINGER TROUBLE, FAIROAKS 185
AND DOING ONE'S THING
MUSE AT REDHILL, SEA TIGERING AND A BROOM 193
CRUISER TENDER
DAWN-TO-DUSK, TIMID TURBS, TARMAC REVERIE 202
AND FUNERAL À LA MODE

1972

EULOGY, CHRIS WREN, OUR HILTON DINNER AND   212
THE UNEXPECTED

MACRAE'S AEROS, INITIAL CHECKS, FORCED LANDINGS   216
AND NEIL'S WAY

PILE-ITS, TURB FRIGHTS APLENTY, G-BADN AND   220
COLDEST-EVER B.P.

1973

'TOO GOOD' FACTOR, REVITALISED KRONFELD,   227
CASTLE WATER AND PARK LANE DINNER

TIMMIS TOURING, WELCOME SECOND SEA TURB,   231
GOODBYE SEA TIGER AND NEW A/C

TWO-MINUTE WILLOW WREN AND CROYDON   236
CLOSES – ALMOST

1974

MERRY-GO-ROUND, FUEL CRISIS, WRIGHT FIELD   238
AND THE REDHILL BATTLE

GLOSSARY, CONNED BY D.F.B., REDHILL REMINISCENCES   243
AND TRADITIONAL FOLK SONG

1975

REDHILL PATROL, HANGAR, OUR BALL AND MAC'S TROPHY   249

WHIFF OF NOSTALGIA, NEIL'S FLICK AND WHAT THE OLD   255
PASS ON

FAREWELL HUBERT BROAD, PROPS, LEASE RENEWED,   259
AND KRONFELD – LIFE OR DEATH

1976

BREAKFAST HAIR-DOWN, G-AIVW, ARTS CLUB AND   266
CAA TRY-ON

WAC MONEY-RAISING, KRONFELD VANDALISED,   273
PETER VANNECK AND HOME TOURING

DISPLAY EXPENSES EXPOSÉ, FAREWELL "G.B." AND FINALE   277

APPENDIX 1

TIGER CLUB: DISPUTES WITH LANDLORDS (BRITISH AIR   283
TRANSPORT) RE REDHILL AERODROME

APPENDIX 2

TIGER CLUB: AIRCRAFT OPERATED DURING 1967 – 1976   286

APPENDIX 3

TIGER CLUB: MEMBERS JOINING BETWEEN 1967 AND 1976   287

NAME INDEX   296

GENERAL INDEX   302

INTRODUCTION

Do you ever wonder what happened to all those flying friends whose names pop up so cheerfully in records of long-past events? Names that ring bells in the mind but still fail to register a face one can safely put a name to? Disconcerting, or is it the case of the older among us being eased into facing forward, the better to utilise a mind that grows increasingly forgetful? Could be. "Where are they now?" an inner voice questions. Do they still fly, do they still remember, or today, even care? And yet once we all did so much together.

Idle thoughts, but they surface as I struggle to come to terms with another period of the Tiger Club's past all of thirty years ago – perhaps the most eventful decade of my life, let alone the Tiger Club's – and convey some of it to print. Is it important? From an historical point of view there's meat on the bones of light flying during the sixties and seventies. It was a different age, freer, more light-hearted and all past, never to return. So the answer is: "yes." An intriguing thought; then is this not the first history of a Flying Club and its membership ever published? I think it is. If so it warrants a second emphatic "yes."

That's one way to look at it. Another remains pure nostalgia, but it's not a personal vanity. To have lived through those years, to have embraced so much of life's gifts and occasional pains, experiences that have widened horizons, all of which must have granted a more balanced self – or so I reason.

Today the Tiger Club, now based at Headcorn down in Kent, is arguably the world's biggest and best-known all-pilot flying Club.

It gained its unique air sporting reputation in the sixties and seventies when thousands flocked at the weekends to enjoy unforgettable airshows, all performed in open aeroplanes at speeds more akin to motoring; the chance to wave to pilots in their gaily-coloured mounts, and to the pretty girl standing on the wing, and for them to wave back (often overlooked in the fun of the moment); the skill of the pilots, some of the finest in Europe.

The Tiger Club has always attracted a calibre of men and women who sought to extend their ability; a unified company of friends in what was once described as the university of the air, for nowhere else are the arts of aerobatics, formation, display and air racing practised regularly on Club aircraft.

The world-wide membership tends to maintain a low profile, but the Club has pride in admitting that several royal Princes are members, and when in 1988 the Duchess of York joined, we welcomed a royal Princess too.

In 1990 the first book, *"The Tiger Club – A Tribute,"* which covered the starting years 1957-1966, inspired a film, *"A Tiger's Tale."* It featured HRH Prince Philip, a member for forty years, and Christopher Reeve, who flew over from the States to lend his support for this remarkable Club. The adventure that started in 1957 is still going strong.

Before me now lie sheaves of yellowing paper to drag me back to a desk and attempt to offer a breath of continuity to follow book number one, a book I wrote nearly ten years back in sunny Spain. The last paragraphs of that book must serve as an introduction to the new and so establish the direction I was going then and must continue, for continuity is everything. I wrote then:

"In looking back over the year 1966 my thoughts keep returning to Redhill which stealthily had become the centre of our world.

It was the year Dev Deverell finally won his two-year fight with the American FAA, that ended in the certification of the Cliff Robertson Tiger Moth and a lead for the others that followed. His fighting letters won the day. The stupidity of the FAA had stung Dev into action. Surely they must have laughed too at one of their proposed restrictions: "Shall not fly on Sundays." And we heard from Frank Tallman over there. His new leg worked well, he wrote, he'd got his Airline Transport rating back, had flown the P.51 Mustang, F.8F Bearcat and a Boeing F.481 Hot Air Balloon. The last bit raised eyebrows. Sadly he wasn't to be free of trouble, but at the time we cheered his recovery.

It was the year when all our Club aircraft including the Turbs were finally equipped with two lots of landing cards: the Aerodrome Owners' Association one permitted us to land at any aerodrome of theirs for 9/- (45p) and, the best value of all, the Air Ministry card permitted us to land at one of theirs for free – if you could find one. Taffy Taylor's booklet *"Aerobatics as a Hobby"* was a sellout in June at 1/- a time. He ventured a second lot at 2/- a time and they went quickly too; he must have kicked himself. Paul Poberenzy, the President of the American EAA, flew a Turb at Redhill and John Ayres hit the national press twice. The first time when he successfully completed trials in a Lightning – short stops in a gravel pit – and again when he joined the British Antarctic Survey flying the more mundane Pilatus Turbo-Porter in the Falklands. After the gravel pit business we reckoned he went to the Falklands to recover.

Back at Redhill Robin Voice won the Dawn-to-Dusk in a Turbulent: 1,158 miles at an average speed of 88 mph for 38 mpg. And Roy Davis finally got the first lot of Tiger Club car badges sold at 30/- a time. In the August Don Robertson, sailing this time, came second in his beautiful catamaran "Snow Goose" in the Round Britain Race, Brian Healey became Editor of a new monthly, *"Light Aeroplane,"* and John Urmston, flushed with his success at building a Wot, sent everyone stationery headed "Bespoke Aeroplanes and Purveyors of Wots." December, and a record of 1,500 aerotows in one year. "Jacko" Jackson could be, and was, proud. And before the year ended Sheila Scott had confounded us all with her tremendous Round the World Flight. Sheila was on the way . . . and so were we.

The year ended, as all good years should end, with no regrets and an impatience for the year to come. A direction had entered our lives and it showed. It showed in the confidence we had in ourselves and between ourselves, and without being aware of it – for all true confidence comes naturally – we had unlimited confidence in our Boss and his generosity.

And generous he had been. The new aircraft, and the promise of more to come, had given us a taste of a flying experience few outsiders could possibly have known. He widened our horizons, saw that we polished our skills, was forbidding and encouraging as the moment demanded. We relished our time at Redhill, even at times to the point of straining a home life, but Redhill was a home too.

For it was there that we moved and thought freely. It was where the hangar doors and the aircraft were moved at will. It was where we could drink tea and philosophise and no one ever said nay. No one threw us out, then no one let us in. One speaks of freedom as though it's an old friend, but the reality is often an illusion. For real freedom is of the mind, and our minds were at peace at Redhill.

Ten years of the Tiger Club was behind us. Seven hundred members faced the future with a well-grounded assurance. In the years to come few would be disappointed."

Names spring from the pages, some well-known or soon to become familiar to the outside world, and all reappear in the story that follows, a tale of a flying movement that knew no bounds and proceeded to make a history of its own.

However one name is missing: not entirely true but I only referred to him as the "Boss." And he was The Boss; not only did he found the Tiger Club, for many years he *was* the Club, and his name was Norman Jones. His influence in the years now under review was every bit as strong as in the initial decade, but it should make for a better understanding if I offer a sort of refresher, if not of the history, something of the personality of this very remarkable character. And in any case I am convinced that any amount of repetition will not tarnish his memory. Besides, it's by his unforgettable moments on stage that we will remember him, not only as a founding father but for leaving us anecdotes to be savoured again and again.

I have no wish to sound disrespectful, for Norman Jones was a serious man, a natural leader, a man head and shoulders above the crowd; but even at the time (and heaven knows some of the events related were serious, even tragic) Norman would always provide, if not humour (I doubt if he was by nature a humorous man) a nuance perhaps in word or demeanour that brought forth a grin, swiftly to be subdued for one did not laugh at The Boss, but his brusque manner inevitably contained elements of unconscious theatre, providing moments that we instantly relished and then stored away for a rainy day. At times, just to be a spectator was a privilege. If 'presence' is a criterion of a fine actor, Norman had it in spades. His entrances and exits would have brought respect from a Gielgud or Coward.

He was also prickly. A now-legendary encounter with the law way back in 1961 illustrates this point.

Norman had landed his Tiger at a disused airfield down in Hampshire. He had been on his way to play golf and a change of heart or plan necessitated a phone call.

He was over Beaulieu so landed there to look for a telephone. A Ministry policeman eventually arrived on the scene, and in the ensuing exchange the copper was firmly told by The Boss to stand to attention when addressing an officer. That Norman was in civvies and probably scruffy ones at that – for he cared little for things sartorial – is by-the-by.

When the policeman began to splutter, Norman cut in with: "And get your hair cut."

Could it be that our laughter was to cover our admiration for a man who, unlike lesser mortals, never thought twice about saying what was on his mind?

If the presence of Norman Jones is pertinent to the story that follows, so is the Tiger Club itself: the two interlinked with seamless delight for over twenty years and in such a fashion that one could not exist without the other. Hand-in-hand they helped to shape a quickening awareness to a form of flying that had up till then been the sole preserve of the few, very few. Who, pre-Tiger Club days, or after, for that matter, could have flown a dozen types – none of them run-of-the-mill – from a collection of about thirty-plus aircraft, more or less? We never had time to count, so busy were we getting airborne.

If on one hand The Boss provided the hardware with almost an enthusiastic abandon he also expected a degree of pilot responsibility that was breathtaking in its simplicity. In effect we were encouraged to think of the aircraft as our own. Take it, he was saying, use it as if it were yours, land where you like, go where you like, no questions asked, ever. One was merely on one's honour not to let the side down. Norman placed great value on integrity and consideration for others, but within these honourable confines the freedom experienced was to have a revealing effect on the flying movement in the years to come. If expectations and sights were raised, if eyes were opened as new vistas presented themselves, was not the sport of light aviation bound to flower?

One mustn't overlook that the Tiger Club, unlike the conventional Club, didn't offer *ab initio* training. To join, every pilot had to have 100 hours as pilot-in-charge of light aircraft (highly qualified airline and military pilots were at times stymied by this requirement, but to the best of my knowledge not one let it stand in his way and the right hours were swiftly amassed) and were required to pass a comprehensive flying test on a Tiger. Few failed, for if the standards were high so was the calibre of pilots presenting themselves. All in all it led to something of an élite with pilots priding themselves on their skill and airmanship.

The question of where the sport of light flying would be today without this advanced ability suggests itself. The answer must surely rest with both the established flying schools (where, fettered as the instructors were to initial training, they were unable to provide post-curricula to the newly-qualified) and the providential appearance of the Tiger Club. Once a private pilot's licence was issued, the forty-to-fifty-hour pilot originally had little to aspire to and seldom knew where to go for further development, and was so often discouraged by the lack of opportunity to find new fields that he or she dropped by the wayside. A loss all round till the Tiger Club came on the scene. Redhill was to provide the breath of fresh air at the right place at the right time.

Now let's throw a spanner in the works of conventionality. Not only was the Club a natural home for those happy people who others saw as square pegs, but all flourished in a completely undemocratic environment. Full of flexible round holes, the Club was designed to accommodate a delightful collection of instant friends who fell into the scheme of things with natural aplomb. For nearly thirty years the Tiger Club was totally autocratic. The Chairman was Boss, Committees sounding forums, and we cherished every minute of serfdom.

1967

700 OF US, KRONFELD, BALLOONING AND EDMUND

CLUB NEWS: JANUARY 1967
I write this in mid-January. There may not be much to write about in the general sense of things, but a visitor to Redhill this drizzly Sunday would be forgiven for thinking the winter months were event-packed. It was one of Clive Francis's practice weekends. The circuit literally buzzed with activity, scorning the 1,000 yards vis – ignoring the damp chill air and imbibing an atmosphere of *joie de vivre*. Even the spectators looked interested, and not without reason. At one moment in the day I saw Neil Williams, inverted in the Stampe, leading Dave Allan and James Black, both Tiger-mounted and right way up, in a tight formation which was winding itself right inside the airfield boundary. Beneath them, Dennis Hartas was directing a new act. Turbulents were bursting tethered balloons and in and out of the mire all of the other aircraft were weaving. Tiger 'CDC was practising a crazy sequence which so alarmed Michael Jones that he was heard to cry: "Help me push the more expensive aircraft inside the hangar – they're safer there!" These practice weekends are proving great fun and do much to brighten the winter weekends. The next one is on 12th February.

And all this activity in January. I doubt I could have come up with a better beginning than those emotive words written with so much enthusiasm all those years ago. The *"Tiger Rag"* from which this opening paragraph was gleaned was the Club's newsletter. It may have only been three foolscap roneoed sheets stapled together, the typing wasn't too clear at times and odd errors appeared with cheerful abandon, but it was the best Fred could do, it represented us all. Fred was a smashing bloke, honest, ever-friendly, and he ran his little business in Putney with all his heart and he single-handedly produced the *"Rag"* for years and years. I'd go nowhere else, errors and omissions included. He was a Tiger Club man to his core.

If he had another interest it was his unquestioning belief in a God whose Word was the Bible. Perhaps he thought I was redeemable, for ever once in a while he'd urge religious tracts upon me, and with the open face of the truly good beam his pleasure when I sheepishly took them. We both knew I'd never open the one.

I remember once he'd placed some small truth my way and reinforced the message that it was all in the Good Book, for Fred, bless him, was a walking compendium of biblical quotations. To my shame I, who at the end of a busy day and wanting nothing more than to be fed, answered a trifle shortly that I didn't believe a word of it. I watched the light go out. But I'd lost of course. To this day I wish he were still around. I'd even read his tracts.

Clive Francis, who had taken over the previous season from Bill Chesson as display promoter, doubled up as the new display director. As with all new brooms he swept us all up in a flurry of practising our display acts for the

14

coming year. And it promised to be no small series of events. The Tiger Club Sporting Aviation Calendar for 1967 showed no less than six Full Displays, to say nothing of countless so-called participations.

The Full Displays were truly memorable, so all those practice sessions were important, 'sides we flew them at half price. The whole Club rallied to each full show in strength. All the Club's aircraft were placed at the director's disposal, all that is with the barest minimum left at Redhill for general Club utilization, and oft was the cry of those left behind at the scarcity of mounts, although I doubt there were ever less than four to fly. To say we were spoilt was to put it mildly.

December–January has been as romantic a period in the Tiger Club's history as any. No less than four weddings took place. In chronological sequence: Bob Winter married Nicola, over in the States Cliff Robertson married Dina Merrill, John Mimpriss took Lorraine's hand (and we're all telling Tessa Lovell she isn't losing a daughter but gaining a son) and the latest, Tim Lodge and Angela – and Tim got Tom Storey to speak up for him as best man.

So may I, on behalf of us all, wish them all long life and happiness, and may their days at Redhill not be numbered. By the way, John and Lorraine had the good sense to get wedded near the airfield, so it was an easy move to organise a three-Turb flypast. I led Tom Storey and Dave Allan in what we believe is the first occasion the Club has presented a flypast at a Club Wedding.

I'd been the editor of the *"Tiger Rag"* since 1961 and because I seldom missed a weekend at Redhill I was very much in the picture and every issue of the *"Rag"* started with Club News. So I was always on the lookout for all of those personal items that tended to pull us all together. And this was important. Unlike a more conventional Club to which membership flocked from nearby the Tiger Club had a membership that was truly widespread. Of course London captured the biggest population, and it was *pro rata* where many of our members lived. Even so Redhill wasn't that near, being twenty-five miles due south. So the *"Rag"* stood in as the Club's social notice board.

There is a new Mascaret down at Redhill, and, for the first time in a Club a/c, it is one fitted with VOR. The latest Stampe from France is still to be converted – apparently it is awaiting its Customs clearance – and do you want a chance to win a Condor? Well, "Reveille" magazine featured such a prize on its front page in the issue of Jan. 19. A first-class piece of Rollason PR work. A new aircraft to visit Redhill was the Fournier RF.3. This delightful machine with its extraordinary performance on a 39 hp Volkswagen engine, a cruising speed of 110 mph, retractable undercarriage and glider performance was indeed a welcome visitor; the more so since the agents for the Fournier over here, Sportair Aviation of Luton, had the good sense and trust to allow as many pilots to try it as was possible to cram in before dark. I was lucky enough to fly it and endorse all the good things we'd heard about it. A most remarkable machine, and I learn that its successor, the RF.4, is going to be aerobatic too. Should be quite an experience.

It was too. Norman later bought us one and probably regretted the impulse when he saw the space the RF.4's wings took up in the hangar.

It was with heavy heart that we learned of Donald Campbell's death. So many of us knew him from his days flying his Comanche from Redhill. Norman writes: "Donald . . . We are sorry to think that we shan't see you around at Redhill again – but to go out suddenly, in a cloud of spray, travelling faster on water than anyone has before, is a splendid end."

I sorted out my copy of the 1967 booklet and it was big with nearly six hundred members listed. Don't ask me where I got the seven hundred names quoted in December . . . snatched out of the air or poetic licence, sorry.

The Clubroom was always tight. It dwelt over the offices at the back of the hangar up a steep narrow flight of stairs. The room was in effect part of the roof space with sloping ceilings we'd levelled off at about eight feet, first with opaque plastic sheeting – to keep the heat in – and then later with some hardboard. The ancient strip lighting hung from the roof girders. M & S had discarded them back in 1960. I think I paid five bob a unit and some of them were still going strong in the eighties. Even the furniture that had been donated was tired and run down, but we cherished it with all its tattiness, we even called it 'character' if challenged. Smart it wasn't. The extension had come about by removing the partition that divided the bunk room. I seem to recall we kept the bunks but scattered cushions on the rough army blankets. It remained a useful layover for the odd overnight stay.

OUR NEW TOWN H.Q.

On January 19th the Tiger Club held its first open meeting at the Kronfeld. 'Fraid it was sparsely attended, but that could well have been due to insufficient information. Let's put that right.

The Club is situated in the basement of No. 74, Eccleston Square, S.W.1, and the entrance is on the corner of Eccleston Square in Belgrave Road (opposite the Rank offices). The nearest station is Victoria.

The Club is normally open Monday – Friday 6 pm to 11 pm. Wednesday evenings is Club night when a lecture or film show is held at 8 pm.

On their first visit to the Club, Tiger Club members should introduce themselves to whoever is on duty at the bar; they will be asked to show their Tiger Club membership booklet and to complete the Register, and in return they will receive a Kronfeld Club membership card.

The Kronfeld Club is running a special series of instructional lectures for power pilots in the New Year on Mondays at 8 pm. The fee for attending these lectures will be 5/- for a single lecture or 10/- for a course of four or more booked in advance.

There followed a series of weekly talk titles, the last one being: Feb. 1st: – Marx Brothers epic, "Love Happy." You know, every once in a while

16

someone showed a sense of humour there. The Kronfeld Club was to become a serious part of the Tiger Club scene in the years to come, but initially the response was lukewarm. Most of us considered the place really only for glider types and where we, mere powered operatives, were a bit looked down upon.

LET'S FLY

The U.S.A. Piper booklet "Let's Fly" is a gem of a publication. It tells of the pleasures of learning to fly with an irresistible enthusiasm and with the theme, as Max Conrad would have it, "Let's Fly!" The following extract, listed under Facts About Flying, are worth their space, if only to provide ammunition with which to belabour the powers that be – whoever they are – that the air really does belong to everyone. And if the Yanks can do it with over 50,000 private aircraft we shouldn't be hard put to show some enlightenment with less than 500.

* A Private Pilot (the licence discussed here in "Let's Fly") can take anybody anywhere.
* No advance "clearance" or flight plan is required for local or cross-country flights except, of course, under instrument conditions. A 'plane owner is as free to get his airplane and go as he is in his car.
* All civil airports are "open to all" and aircraft are handled on a "first come, first served" basis, even at such major terminals as Kennedy International in New York.
* Only a small fraction of the airports have need for a control tower, less than 300 out of over 8,000 airports in the U.S.A.

Haven't a clue if things have changed much in thirty years, but this extract from *"Let's Fly"* caused a stir over here, and absolutely nothing changed in our own hierarchy.

LIMERICK for "G.B."

The Royal Aero Club Air Racing Dinner on the 23rd January was a great success. It was a 'House Full' affair, and Simon Ames deserves all credit for a great evening. Apart from the odd bread roll to arrive on our table a menu came fluttering in from John Blake's direction with the following inscription:

'When I dined at the Club with "G.B."
It was as I feared it would be.
His rumblings abdominal
Were simply phenomenal
And everyone thought it was me.'

In the December '66 issue of the *"Rag"* I'd promised to report at a later date on a trip I'd made in the Sept. to Holland, and all because I'd attended the inaugural meeting of the British Balloon and Airship Club. My membership card number was 21 and I stayed a member for several years. Heaven knows why, I only went up once. I wrote:

I WON A RAFFLE. Me, the unlucky one. I've been raffling unsuccessfully for years – the born raffle-sucker. And when I do win, it's a free balloon ride. Everybody says I'm lucky. It's everyone's ambition – except mine. I view the coming ride like I view the taxman. I've been flying for years but I've no head for heights. Upside down at 1,000 ft I like. Fifty feet up on a roof and I'm sick. So I feel that balloons are not for me.

Edmund Fane, the British Balloon and Airship Club Treasurer, arranges it all with some people in Holland. The bit I shall like best will be the flight to Holland and back.

Three of us squeeze into the Club's Jodel Excellence light aircraft and I volunteer for the job of flying it, to take my mind off the impending balloon ride. Edmund and our photographer Mike Andrews, both pilots, don't backseat-drive, for which I'm grateful. They clutch maps instead – probably to keep their minds off the water beneath. With one lifejacket and one dinghy between us, I don't blame them.

We pass the time looking for the Varne lightship. Let me be the first to suspect that there is no such lightship in the Channel. In all my rides I've never seen it. We strike Cap Gris Nez on the nose, tear inland behind Calais and scoot around their TCA and back out to sea near Dunkirk. I have two ½-million scale maps of the Low Countries. The first is dated 1950 and shows only a tiny Koksijde danger area; the other, a 1960 map, shows all of Europe carved up with danger areas, prohibited areas and control zones. Don't ask me how the Europeans cope. I take the older map, fly out to sea and mix it with the yachts – it's easier. My companions discuss marker buoys and ditching procedures.

Rotterdam is patient – by now our radio is on the blink – and we pass on to Teuge some 80 miles further east. What a fantastic aircraft the Jodel is. With three up, Edmund's umbrella and loads of luggage, we cruise at 130 mph on only 100 hp. Lympne to Rotterdam in 1 hour 40 minutes isn't bad. At Teuge we are welcomed by the Club's President and the airfield controller. And I do mean welcomed. Every visitor gets the VIP treatment and all in excellent English. Not once during our stay in Holland did we need to speak a word of Dutch. Not that we knew one.

It's a lovely day. Calm, autumnal, ideal for ballooning. Already our mentors, Jan and Nini Boesman, are busy pulling the fabric into position on the ground. We introduce ourselves, then stand by uselessly – moving forward now and then, like nervous schoolboys anxious to be seen to help. Recognising our confusion, Jan hands us copies of written instructions, gives us some food and we thankfully sit down on the grass. "I'll need your biceps later," he says. He isn't kidding.

The huge blue Daf hydrogen trailer stands by. Already there's the bittersweet smell of hydrogen in the air. The smell is to stay with us for the rest of the day, prompting my imagination to work overtime with foolish little thoughts like fire, explosion and plummeting to earth. Unworthy thoughts. I put them from me, until I catch a whiff of the gas again. Don't wear anything metal or nylon, Jan had warned. I nearly left my braces behind.

For all the world like some figment of Quatermass, the balloon begins to rise. Little people hurry around its perimeter, repositioning sandbags – anything to keep this monster earthbound. We help as best as we can, between taking photographs of each other – Mike because he is a photographer, and me because I want something for my wife to remember me by. Edmund, the very personification of an English Guards Officer, which he was, smiles urbanely at everyone.

As the vast envelope fills we're awed by its size. Like the Pied Piper the balloon has drawn a captive audience, who just stare as it rocks gently above them, 20,000 cu ft of it, resplendent in orange and silver, bearing the word 'Nibbo' in massive letters. I think it's a lovely name, but someone says it's only an advertisement.

"Come on," says Jan, "time to get into the basket."

I don't say anything but I can't see four of us getting in. It looks for all the world like a theatrical hamper, good for props and clowns maybe, but not for us. We get in clumsily. Jan stands on Edmund's foot for five minutes.

"Sorry," apologises Jan, when realisation dawns.

"It's all right," says Edmund.

Jan bellows with laughter: "You English!"

With great ceremony Nini supervises the weigh-off, a little bit of time-honoured procedure to ensure we have just the right amount of ballast aboard. I feel nervous. Edmund stands on my foot, and I tell him promptly. I look up at the now open throat of 'Nibbo.' It looks black in there and I think wildly of someone looking inside with a match. Faces crowd around us, laughing, happy and dying to see us go.

Then, imperceptibly, we're going. No jar, just a silent acceleration as we climb out of the airfield. I look down curiously. Already the faces have lost their features – Lilliputian folk alongside Lilliputian aeroplanes. I can hear their animated chatter and quite suddenly I'm excited. I look down to test my nerves and think of rooftops and ladders; no matter how I tease my vertigo I find I couldn't care less. We chatter like children on the first day of holidays and Jan, the accepted master, smiles knowingly.

'Winds light and variable.' And so they are. Around us buzzes a Tiger Moth, weird with its elongated fin, a modification the Dutch insist on. Its pilot is a charming man whose name sounds like Angus Smith, only now I wish he'd go away. We all think the same thing and wave him off. He waves back. We drift slowly at around 1,500 ft. Every now and then Jan consults his height variometer, and whenever we begin to sink trowels out a little sand delicately. Angus has gone at last and we wander on in our silent world. Sound takes on a new dimension. A cow moos; we hear it clearly and moo back. Youngsters follow us on bikes, weaving precariously and waving furiously. Every now and then Jan drops a picture card of 'Nibbo,' to satisfy the entreaties of those below. Mike, not to be outdone, finds a few visiting cards and we watch them spin slowly down. "Might induce some business," he murmurs.

A lot has been written about the silence and fascination that is ballooning. I confirm every word. If ever there was a potential non-starter it was me. Yet I stayed the course, the complete convert, to relish the beauty of the countryside, with its mass of intricate detail, that can be seen only from this, the most wonderful viewpoint in the world. To see the land soften with the gentle evening mist beneath you, and to hear and see its denizens as you drift quietly above, is to enter a new realm of delight.

Jan suggests an intermediate landing. We had been airborne 2½ hours – it seemed but a fraction of that time. Lower and lower we drop, until we are only some 200 ft up and able to converse with the locals; stolid, flaxen-haired people, dressed as I knew they would be, in clogs, faded and patched jeans, and denim caps that in more-fashionable London are known as "John Lennons." The farm animals accept our presence calmly, all except the chickens which, whenever we pass over them, go stark staring mad. "Perhaps they think we're a hawk," suggests Mike.

The retrieve car, superbly navigated by Nini, is beneath us. Jan blows his battered horn three times and the car's klaxon repeats the message. Going to land, it says. We watch with interest. I wind up the slim, bright, thirty-foot House of Orange banner. The slow motion gives no warning, arouses no fear. We lift over a road, then power cables, until the way ahead looks clear: then the wind changes direction playfully, and we start looking again.

"A good spot," explains Jan, "should include a nearby road and a goodly residence; castles are best, the servants always bring out tea."

Now there are dozens of followers, all sensing something about to happen. A photographer stumbles across fields beneath us. With a healthy pull on the valving line, Jan releases some gas and we hurtle down. We stand mesmerised, near weightless. He skips the finesse of the trowel and hastily pours a sackful of sand over the side. We watch wordlessly as the field comes up.

"Hold on," yells Jan.

We land heavily and bound straight back to 1,000 ft.

"Too much," mutters Jan, quite unperturbed. Beneath us, the cavalcade mount their assorted transport and follow us, as best they can, collecting more spectators en route.

"Good," says Jan, "we'll need them."

Again we prepare to land. Edmund releases the trail rope, which thuds to earth beside willing helpers who literally pull us down. We are greeted like conquering heroes. Everyone is shouting "Batman." This I think very funny, being an ardent supporter of his. When we are ready to leave them, and quite unable to think up a word of farewell in any language, least of all Dutch, I shout "Batman!" They fall over laughing.

It wasn't that funny. Jan explains: "It's actually Bathmen – the name of the village where they live."

I'm only too happy to be abashed for long.

Our final landing is a half hour later. Dusk enfolds us as we touch down, light as featherdown, in a field of cows. With superb direction, Nini and Jan organise the willing spectators. Overhead, the gentle giant expires with a woeful whistle, drooping lower and lower until, with a satisfied grunt or two, it surrenders itself to Mother Earth. In a daze we help to get 'Nibbo' folded up and put on its trailer, to fly another day.

Nini and Jan Boesman had come from the Hague to give us the experience of a lifetime; before these two kindly people returned, we wined and dined them. They, in turn, accepted us into the Exclusive Order of Honor Sic Itur ad Astra – the Balloonists' Union – complete with baptism of sand and champagne. We flew back home the next day in even quicker time – if only to spread the word.

Edmund really was a great companion. It was either just before or just after our balloon trip that Edmund invited us both to dinner. He lived in St. James in a penthouse high above the Park. It really was rather grand. The reception room must have spread across the entire building and a gallery ran around an upper floor. The room was sparsely furnished but in considerable taste. A huge golden bird-cage dominated, it must have stood all of seven foot high. I'm sure there was a parrot.

Edmund and his wife excused themselves briefly and Mike and I took in the sights. In pride of place on a very low table stood a very old helmet and visor. Mike circled the artefact a couple of times, then glanced round in case he was overlooked and quickly tried it on. And then just as quickly tried to take it off. He couldn't. We'd already been told in response to a query from Mike that it was both fragile and very, very old. I suspect the answer had been a discreet precaution on Mrs Fane's part against a repeat of others' endeavours. Now a near-panic set in. We just managed to extricate Mike's head and return the helmet to its place when our hosts returned. Mike's red face and glowing ears gave him away. Mrs Fane glanced at her beloved helmet and seemed to give an inaudible sigh.

QUOTE:
Edmund Fane (about to show some transparencies): "I've got an ordinary projector," and added hastily as he caught the glance: "Oh, not so ordinary: it was a present from my wife."

SAUSAGES, FOX MOTH, ACCIDENTS, PUSSY AND DEV
REDHILL AERODROME, REDHILL

SUBSCRIPTION AND FLYING RATES – 1967

(a) ASSOCIATE MEMBER	*£10 10 0*
(b) FULL MEMBER	*£8 8 0*
(c) PASSENGER MEMBER	*£3 3 0*
(d) OVERSEAS MEMBER (all grades)	*£2 2 0*
	(or equivalent currency)
TEMPORARY MEMBER	*£0 5 0*

FLYING RATES TO TAKE EFFECT FROM 1ST FEBRUARY, 1967

TIGER MOTH	£4 10 0
STAMPE	£5 0 0
CONDOR	£4 10 0
JODEL D.150 & DR.1050	£5 15 0
JODEL D.140	£8 0 0
TURBULENT	£2 10 0
SUPER CUB	£6 5 0
HUSKY	£6 5 0
SEA TIGER	£5 0 0
ARROW ACTIVE (restricted)	£5 0 0
COLT (Fairoaks and Rochester)	£5 15 0
OTHER AIRCRAFT IF AND WHEN AVAILABLE	To be notified
(e.g. Puss Moth, Fox Moth, Luton Beta)	

The Tiger Club and its pilots had always led the way in all things aerobatic, and members were accustomed to receiving regular newsletters, often on a monthly basis. 1967 was no exception.

Robin d'Erlanger was then Competition Secretary and he headed up four Tiger Club-sponsored events for the year. They were The McAully, which was usually held at Little Snoring in Norfolk, the Air Squadron Trophy held at Staverton (and this was its first year), the de Havilland at Sandown in the Isle of Wight (this was the big one, for the winner became the National Aerobatic Champion) and the ever popular Esso Tiger, so often held down in Rochester.

Robin wrote in January:

The 1966 aerobatic season saw a number of newcomers to the sport entering very successfully for the competitions, and with a full British team going to the World Championships in Moscow there was a good deal more aerobatic activity generally. There were a record 36 entries in the three competitions organised by the Tiger Club, and it cannot be overemphasised that plenty of competitors for the national competitions makes for a strong British team for future World events.

In order to encourage still more newcomers to take up the sport and also the accomplished old hands whom we know never lose an opportunity to keep in practice, we are publishing the provisional programme of competitions at home for 1967. Brief details are also included for the manoeuvres and limitations of each competition so that prospective competitors can really get cracking on their winter training programmes. Non-Tiger Club members are especially welcomed.

The aerobatic training weekends at Redhill were usually held over the last weekend of every winter month, but it was a rare weekend that didn't sport tumbling aeroplanes overhead. Circuit-flying carried on normally – well, as normally as possible: slightly lower, but take my word for it, we all kept a weather eye open.

CLUB NEWS: MARCH 1967

It's been a mild winter, with days these last two months when spring has been brought forward for our delight. Sunny samples of days to come and every one of them made for our type of flying and never better than flying vintage machines. It all goes together, leisurely biplanes and green grass and early sunshine and the latest arrival – the DH Fox Moth. It is being flown by everyone. This magnificent old-stager has been lovingly refurbished by Rollasons. Neil Williams has written handling notes, and "G.B." recalls his early flights over thirty years ago when he sales-demonstrated this very same aircraft – all can be read elsewhere in the *"Rag."* On a personal note, I found the Fox Moth a joy to fly, not so much for its handling, which is stolid to say the least, but for the extraordinary experience of riding high on its back. To be able to peer in and shout through the window at one's passengers huddled in the tiny cabin at one's feet. Yet another vintage DH is due shortly at Redhill – it's the rebuilt Puss Moth. This will bring the vintage stable there to four, the others of course Tiger 'CDC and the Active.

The Dinner Dance at the Hilton was a great success. I can only speak for my immediate gang – a noisy collection of friends (one of whom regretfully lost control of a string of sausages), but judging from the happiness and noisy revelry all around it could only have been fun. Mike Jolley won the little 1931 MG two-seater – a gift donated by Norman Jones. Mike was last seen trying to get his six-foot-plus frame behind the wheel – the car still in the foyer of the Hilton. Of the more conventional awards Neil Williams walked off with the DH Trophy with Taffy Taylor coming in second. James Black brought off a double with the Esso-McAully Trophies; David Castor and Robin d'Erlanger took second place, respectively. The Dawn-to-Dusk went to Robin Voice. This year the Trophy was a new one designed by Chris Wren – an original concept end superbly executed. Next month we hope to give a detailed account and description of this HRH-inspired award.

Tom Freer of the Seaplane Club took the de Salis Trophy and George Eyston the Clem Pike Trophy. Medallions went to David Timmis for Foreign Touring and to Brian Hickley the Glider Towing award for no less than 400 tows! "G.B." got the Bird Trophy for – as Jack Piercy so nicely put it – the member who has done the least and caused the most trouble! The Bird Trophy was a breathtaking statuette of a featherless bird – naturally.

A photo taken at that Dinner by the roving Hilton photographer shows a happy group of polite-looking, scrubbed-faced guests, modestly showing their smiles to the camera. Wrong. Any headmaster worth his salt would have instantly spotted the aura of incipient mischief that hung there like a thundercloud. It was there alright. After all it isn't every day one is tempted by a long string of fat sausages with nowhere to go. Heeding Wilde's dictum that he could resist everything except temptation, a guest stood up and, cowboy-like, began to whirl the chain above his head to our enthusiastic encouragement.

Just as he was getting into the swing of it a link broke and they flew out of his control to wind themselves around the neck of Bob Pooley's wife who was seated a couple of tables away. The cheers died as a very irate Bob stormed over.

"Who was it?" he yelled. "Who did it?"

A deathly hush descended, no one was prepared to snitch.

To a growing audience, all eyes were now on Yvonne who tearfully unwound the cold clammy necklace, arose and wordlessly deposited them on our table and left. To this day, I am very fond of Bob, but I'm not sure they should have left because it was developing into a great evening. I read this item to Trudi.

"I'd have left too," she said firmly. "It was disgraceful behaviour."

Me, I pass.

"G.B." stood for Golding Barrett, a man of senior years who delighted in tweeds, shooting and hearing us out when we needed someone to talk to. A father-figure, much loved.

The arrival of the Fox Moth was quite an event, and the Handling Notes by Neil Williams was a typical Neil effort. He was a product of the Empire Test Pilots' School and so the task of providing handling notes couldn't have been placed in worse hands. His critical assessment, whilst doubtless the product of much expertise, was daunting. After all it was only a glorified Tiger Moth; Geoffrey de Havilland would have been turning in his grave.

"G.B." wrote in the same issue:

"G.B." WRITES: THE FOX MOTH

An old log book, battered and cryptic, records that a long time ago – Jan. 10th, 1935 – I collected a Fox Moth, either 'ACEJ or 'CEY, it's not clear which, from the hangar at Croydon which is now Rollasons, and set off to demonstrate it at Mousehold aerodrome, to the Norfolk and Norwich Aero Club, of which incidentally I have been a member since it was formed in 1927.

Despite the brief log book entry – *'Demo to N and N AeC – A/c OK – vis bad, snow showers over a snow-covered countryside in lousy conditions of visibility,'* I remember snow sticking on to the pressure plate of the spring ASI fitted to the outboard strut, until the whole gadget snowed up at a reading around 50 mph – and then finding the cockpit ASI was reading zero. Both thawed out after landing, so I suppose the pitot head was full of snow too. And a long slow journey it was there and back – plus a demonstration all in between the daylight hours of a winter's day. It was cold and I landed back at Croydon at dusk frozen. But in the event it seems they liked the aeroplane for "Jacko" Jackson tells me that they subsequently bought 'ACEJ. Neil, who has written a first-class appreciation of the flying characteristics of the Fox, kindly asked me to read them over and I was only able to add a relevant point or two.

So for me today, it was a nostalgic event to fly again, after 32 years, this splendid aeroplane – now lacking the front bench seat – but having gained a T and

B indicator and a modern seat strap, but otherwise unchanged. The Tiger Club will enjoy flying this excellent aircraft.

CLUB NEWS: APRIL 1967

The introduction of the Fox Moth, and especially the handling notes by Neil Williams, produced a spate of correspondence. Typical of the letters was one from an old friend of the Club, Geoffrey Monk. He wrote in a letter to "G.B.":

"I was stimulated into writing to you by an article in the *"Tiger Rag"* giving 'Handling Notes for the Fox Moth.' I read them with interest and some consternation. When I flew them in 1932/33, no one told me of these peculiarities and I cannot say I remember them. We just got in and flew, and incidentally thought it a nice aeroplane to fly. I was at Bristol at the time and I wonder if you came down and sold one to us. If so, why did you not give us a talk, or 'Notes on handling characteristics'? Darn it, we might have killed our passengers, or even worse, ourselves."

Another letter from "Jacko" Jackson echoed those sentiments. His letter, complete with potted histories of two of our latest vintage aircraft, is reproduced elsewhere in the "Rag." The Puss Moth has just arrived at Redhill. Those of us who flew it some four years ago, before its prang in France, will look forward to renewing its acquaintance. Dev Deverell and his team have lavished all their love and care on this complete rebuild. So to those who will fly it – and I don't believe there will be any pilot restrictions – be careful. I intend to be – I don't think Dev could face another four years' labour!

Whilst the Fox Moth was on everyone's lips its initial hours flown proved but a flash in the pan. For some inexplicable reason it never proved a popular aeroplane and towards the end of its days with us became a hangar queen. Always the bridesmaid, never the blushing bride. Then when she was sold some years later for lack of use – and she also took up a lot of hangar space – everyone protested. I told you we were spoilt.

I've been taken to task for indifferent reporting on the Annual Dinner – and justifiably. I was probably too merry, or too attentive to my fair companion; whatever the excuse, I certainly failed to mention our Guest of Honour. It was an unforgivable lapse. To my dear friend, Sheila Scott, my humble apologies. Not only did Sheila make a first-class speech, she also presented all our prizes. Mark you, I wasn't the only culprit. The winner of the Spot Landing Competition, Nick Carter, failed to even get a mention on the night, much less his medallion or his winner's cheque for £5. I'm sure Nick didn't mind in the least, but the record should be put right. So, to Nick Carter, all our congratulations on his success in a hard-fought contest, and I hope the fiver came in useful.

Members will be glad to learn that Tessa Lovell is back in the Club Secretary's chair and in good time to take part in all of Don's Continental visits. Come to think of it, Tessa is practically the Overseas Touring's First Lady. And all our best wishes to James Black, 'bruised and uncomfortable' (his words) and in hospital for what looks like being a fair time. His spectacular prang at Redhill in the late Zlin put him there. It looks like the Stampes will now be worked a little harder. Fortunately there should soon be a third.

The first overseas visit of the year – the ever-popular visit to Berck on the 16th April – was cancelled at the last minute by sea fog off the French coast. This was a great disappointment. The next attempt is on May 14th; briefing 9 am Redhill. Don suggests you book your aircraft quickly. Another early casualty was the cancellation of the Panshanger Display. This might prove a blessing in disguise, since it gives Clive and his team those few extra valuable weeks' practice and polish. '67 is going to be something of a special display year. Never before have so many new faces appeared in the acts, or has more enthusiasm been engendered. It's becoming something of an occasion to be picked to represent the Club. Things seem to come in threes, and the third cancellation – and let's hope the last one this year – was the April practice weekend. It was a bright, glorious day, but with a variable wind gusting to 40 knots it wasn't the sort of weather for formation.

Jack Piercy reports that the Legal Fund is still very much an active one and is there to consider financial appeals from members in an unfortunate clash with the Law. I know from experience it leans over backwards to be of help – so here's a reminder that when the black moment looms you won't be forsaken. The Fund still needs your support though, so if there's any conscience money going, send it to Jack Piercy. Incidentally, he reports that an anonymous Club member who isn't a flying member has been donating a fiver a month now for some time. It's his way, he's reported to have said, of supporting a wonderful Club.

If nothing else this April issue of the *"Tiger Rag"* points up the accepted scope of the Club's activities. To the much publicised display teams with their exuberant flying over the airfield, the better to judge each act's viewability and, more important to the Club's reputation, the safety aspect be adhered to, there were always the other factions to be commented upon. And one of the most interesting was Don Lovell's overseas touring trips. These more leisurely excursions were hugely popular, and scarcely a weekend seemed to pass without TC trips out and we in turn entertaining others from abroad.

If there was a downside to all this activity it was the unavoidable departmentalising of each branch. Each had its devotees. True we all met in the Clubroom as one cheery noisy crowd, but even then there were little groups huddled together thrashing their own subject about, oblivious to another at their shoulder going on in a completely different direction. New members initially found this a bit off-putting getting in on an act and the accusation of cliques was heard. Those of course on the inside accepted the situation with a comfortable aplomb. The aerobatic lot for instance had nothing in common with either the touring, Turb formations or general flying, and it showed. Nothing nasty mark you, it's just that they lived in a different world, flew different aeroplanes and considered themselves very superior.

Don Lovell, who headed up overseas touring, accepted all this with his usual laid-back good humour. His was not the most adventurous or flamboyant team but he had a faithful following who accompanied him and Tessa – they flew their own Jodel – over to the Continent, where with Don's vast experience of the other side, they were guided out of trouble and into some of the most inspired and memorable excursions it was possible to enjoy.

If Don Lovell was calm, a sound pilot, a tower of strength – yet easy-going – James Black was the opposite. Like his talented associates he wasn't so much a *sound* pilot, he probably bordered on the exceptional, but he was above all a seeker of advanced experience. However like all of the aerobatic lot he had a confidence unhampered by fear of the unknown. His coming down to earth was spectacular.

I didn't actually see the prang but became aware of a move out of the hangar and those out there were all looking south. That was ominous to start with. There wasn't a noise, just a cloud of dust where his Zlin had disintegrated. Poor James got really clobbered, a tough lesson that never really got home to any of our aerobatists. They all shared a fascination with low-level aerobatics. I mean low.

It was even considered something of an affront to be asked to complete aeros at 500 ft – as they were at one time – instead of 300. This, I might add, was over the airfield. The rest of us flew around them perfectly happy, after all there was plenty of room. Just don't ask me to clarify the definition of 'plenty of room' in today's terms, but as a rule of thumb then the airfield boundary peri-track seemed safe enough. And it was.

This business of aerobatic accidents was to be the subject of a serious review in the following year, but at the time I don't think we realised the correlation of prangs to low altitude, for the aerobatists were conditioned to competition rules that permitted an aerobatic minimum of one hundred metres, but overlooked was that this was the domain of the very best, and heaven forbid that anyone of the adherents to this discipline should consider him or herself a lesser being, even when common sense should have decreed a much higher cut-off point.

There was one other awful accident in 1967 with tragic overtures when Beryl Saunders lost control of a Club Stampe whilst performing low aeros. The Stampe was written off and Beryl appeared little hurt, but it wasn't so, for her head had suffered and gradually her condition deteriorated until when we visited her she no longer knew us and we inwardly wept for a lovely lady who was once a vibrant outgoing bundle of happiness.

I know, all this should have sobered us, but with so much going on, not only at Redhill but in our hectic private lives as well, such incidents were soon forgotten.

In presenting this – I can't call it a history can I? – this review of the Tiger Club, I've relied in the main on the newsletters, my logbooks, a selective memory and the monthly Tiger Club Committee minutes.

Nowhere, not no how, can there be anything so particular to our Club as those Committee meetings. Norman Jones was firmly of the belief that minutes should be brief and very pertinent – more like seconds. You could count the pithy words per item on the fingers of one hand, he was slipping if he reached two. If Churchill considered one side of a page sufficient, Norman, staunch supporter that he was of our wartime leader, would suffer nothing less.

That thirty years later I can still chuckle at his concise comments – for compiling the minutes was always the Chairman's task – says a lot about The Boss, and the things we got up to. As from January of 1967 our meetings were held at our new centre, the Kronfeld Club. An hour of concentrated attention before we could unwind and go off to eat at our favourite Italian restaurant in Victoria's Vauxhall Bridge Road, a sort of upper class "greasy spoon" where the greeting was friendly, the food good and hot and within reach of poor pockets.

If I digress a little, bear with me as I try to colour a near-forgotten period, for the meals we enjoyed, all crammed together on tables moved to accommodate upwards of a dozen of us, was where we dissected the earlier meeting and held happy court. We encountered the March meeting head-on with Item 5. It read. *'Aerobatics! Min. 300 ft for anybody. Radio for two Stampes. Team Cup by* "Flight."*'* And that covered a month's earnest practice, and the hopes and aspirations of so many for the season ahead.

If ever there was a wealth of significance to be found in fewer words I've yet to see it. *'Min. 300 ft for anybody.'* Wonderfully final, pleads for special exemptions go by the board, for anybody, and that includes you, Neil. Today it seems unbelievable that anyone could contemplate aeros below that height, but there were occasions when it seemed the OK thing. The roll into the inverted run – wasn't that alright? If the argument faltered it was always safe to name-drop a successful Czech, Bezàc was a firm favourite. The discussions enlivened our meals and entertained the other regulars. I think Norman really drew the line at low flick rolls. Although Norman was adept with the Nelson eye, a fool he wasn't. He gave us more than enough rope, but there were limits, and to be pragmatic about it they were his aircraft and so were the bills. I can still recall Neil Williams insisting to me a few years earlier when I was a display director that his low – 100 or so feet – flick rolls from inverted to inverted were safe. He proved the point wasn't valid at the Biggin Hill Air Fair in 1965, and another Stampe bit the dust.

"*Radio for two Stampes.*" Up till then what few radios we had were installed in the touring machines, so it was a big leap forward, but they weren't for ATC ears but aerobatic duos. Smoke now or later.

Have no idea what happened to the *"Flight"* Team cup.

Along with the much-acclaimed Fox Moth, March also saw another beautiful vintage addition to the Club's collection, the DH Puss Moth. Four years earlier Norman had sent the Rollasons lorry and crew over to France to bring back the remains of G-AHLO where a member – no names, no pack drill – had collided with a cow. Silly questions spring to mind, but I'm sure he said a cow. At her reappearance Adrian Deverell wrote a typical 'Dev' letter of praise for his beloved "Pussy." Part of it ran:

Well, our lovely little "Puss Moth" is now at Redhill, all in one piece and ready and waiting. First, I cannot really put into words the many happy hours this little aeroplane has given me at Croydon, and the thrill of seeing this Moth gradually taking shape. The problems were many and large but these facts probably made the project all the more interesting. The second point is that I offer my sincere thanks to Tiger Club members for their extreme patience during the long wait for "Pussy." Yes, it is almost four years, but most members understood the fact that the project was being tackled spare-time – a rare thing, is spare time at Rollasons, – and so, time to work on "Pussy" had to be created, largely by taking some of Rollasons paperwork home. However, it was all worth it and we sincerely hope that members will have as much joy flying her as it has given us getting her airworthy again. Please, please folks, look after these lovely little treasures that the Tiger Club now possesses, "Tiger Moth," "Puss Moth," "Fox Moth" and "Active." Spare parts on the last three do not exist and all four types cannot he replaced; they are museum pieces and their well-being must not be risked in any way. It is with great pride that many of us in the Tiger Club look upon these historic relics as the very symbol of our love for the light aeroplane. Who, who loves ships, can possibly fail to admire the beautiful "Cutty Sark," now happily preserved for all to see, a permanent monument to the pinnacle of Man's maritime creative genius, and to an era when beauty, workmanship and finish were as important as efficiency.

Now my words falter, because all that one would normally conceive of a chief engineer replete with clean overalls and an authoritative manner shrink before the reality. To a stranger Dev could well be seen as a slight, shabby figure who seemed to haunt the cavernous hangar like a latter-day Quasimodo *sans* hump. If he ever wore clean overalls I never saw them, and his old wellies were as part of the vision as his tooth-challenged smile in a cheerful face. He made the tea, swept up, ran a happy ship, the unassuming man he genuinely was. And his love for his charges shone through the hangar's gloom. He checked them in and out with a mother's concern, each received a pat and a kindly word to greet them of a morning and he never failed to say goodnight to those he tendered before he left of an evening. We cherished him.

I've re-read this bit, worried I may have overcooked things a bit. I haven't you know, in fact I've barely scratched the surface of this remarkable man. How to explain for instance that more than once I've seen him in the hangar in the full regalia of a Red Indian chief which he assuredly was – having been to America to become a blood brother – and I happily recall a Wild West weekend down at Redhill where Dev's many friends gave wagon- and horse-rides to wide-eyed children from all over Surrey. Bows and arrows there were, and six-shooters and horse-drawn chuck wagons and cooking food, a genuine tepee and women dressed in settler's garb mixing with squaws, to everyone's delight.

Dev, for all his undoubted affection for aeroplanes, never flew except the once, and it was during the Wild West weekend. He had begged me to take some of his western friends for a trip in the big Jodel you could cram five in: I agreed providing he came too. His joy on this one venture into the blue was for real.

Dev, if you read this, and I hope you will, it's written as a very real tribute to one who deserves to be recognised for a lifetime's devotion to light flying – if only by words from me.

Dev wrote me late in 1997. I reckon his uniqueness has become a collector's item; here's some of that letter:

"I am now 76 but still journey to Redhill every day to keep with my lovely old aeroplanes. In any case why throw away 61 years of experience? Our hangar at Redhill is still as it has always been, full of Tiger Moths, Stampes, Hornet Moth, Moth Minor, Jodels (even your G-ATKX). This is all due to Chalky White who took the hangar on when Rollasons moved out . . .

. . . Due to my travels every day, I am well looked after by the busmen and railway people. Early in the morning (4 am) I am at Sutton Bus Garage where I pre-flight my bus and several others. It is not every bus garage that has a licensed aircraft engineer checking out their buses. At the right moment they run me to East Croydon Station where I am looked after by the Station Staff. When my train arrives I am the guest of the Driver and Guard and they have trained me in Railway procedure and shown me how to drive.

At Redhill Station the Staff take me in hand and have a complementary taxi waiting for me. I then open up the hangar and check over all the little aeroplanes. It is still like the old Rollasons . . . and when Tiger Club people visit us – well, time certainly stands still."

A LIMERICK

"There was a young man in a Zlin,
Who thought he could fit in a spin;
So spin it he did,
And now we are rid
Of that noisy great thing called a Zlin."

(With thanks to J.B., without whose help this verse would not have been written.)

T.H.-T., FATHERHOOD, A SHOT COOKER,
OSNABRÜCK AND PARIS

It was still early in 1967 when a couple of entertaining letters were received from Tony Haig-Thomas. He, the mercenary he was, had signed on for a spell in the Saudi Air Force. The moment he'd signed up the '67 Arab-Israeli War broke out. His timing wasn't too hot.

He wrote:

HAIG-THOMAS from SAUDI ARABIA:

"As you can see, I have arrived and have already had ten Hunter trips without breaking one – is this a record? Taif is a really beautiful spot; it is **4,500 ft** high; the nights are cool and every day the sun shines; the visibility is 100 miles plus and the temperature climbs into the eighties. If you can imagine a perfect summer's day in England, that is what it is like. One wears a sweater until 10 am, shirtsleeves during the day, and a sweater again at 5 pm.

The flying here is superb, although most of our training time in the air is spent in combat flying I versus I, we always have enough fuel left to bore up and down the huge Grand Canyon-like wadis before our landing back. It does, however, have its own peculiarities. I find it difficult to get used to landing with two or three minutes' fuel left and on my first trip out there I was downwind without enough fuel to go round again. So you can imagine my surprise when I called: "Playboy 09 finals three greens" to receive the reply from the Saudi controller: "Roger 09, you are clear to land, there is a dog on the centre-line." Mark you, on the credit side, I think the dog was even more surprised than I was.

We work from 8 am until 1 o'clock, which I also find very congenial. In fact, the only real snag is the food which is not too hot. Goat-knuckle stew is all right occasionally but six days a week is just too often.

Yesterday I went into the local town shopping with my new-found wealth. I bought a she-camel for reasons that I can't put on paper, a Cadillac to keep up with the Abdullahs who live next door, and a Lear jet because I still had quite a lot of my first week's pay left and it seemed a pity not to spend it. Please send the *"Tiger Rag"* here by Air Mail, give my love to the chaps and to more or less any girl you happen to meet.

Yours aye, Tony."

A month or so later another arrived. He must have made a bob or two on his return because the given word was that he'd opened a chain of laundromats. Now all these years later I've just read he's managing things at Shuttleworth. This after a long spell flying heavy WW II machinery. Another Tiger Club man whose life has never proved dull.

FROM TONY HAIG-THOMAS IN THE HOT EAST:

"Dear Michael,

Just a short line to let you know that the Tiger Club's 'Saudi-Arabian Division' is still active, and to give you the news.

But you will see my address is slightly different. I am now at Khamis Mushayt, down on the Yemen border. Politically, it is very quiet and I am absolutely certain that I shall not fire the guns in anger while I am here. However, all our flying is in practice combat and we are now reaching a fairly high standard; we have five Hunters and five pilots; all the aircraft are serviceable and I am getting fifteen hours a month which is much more than I expected.

At the moment I am deputy flight commander and am taking over the flight at the end of this month – a trifle embarrassing as I am the least experienced pilot on it! The other four pilots are very nice with one exception. They all want to join the TC, so please send me four application forms – by Air Mail, or I shall never get them!

Our accommodation is very comfortable and the food is excellent, which makes life quite tolerable. It became even better the other day when my pay for February and March was credited to my Jersey account – £1,666! And thanks be to God Jimmy Callaghan can't touch it.

I am trying to persuade David McWilliam to come and jump on the bandwagon. It is a pity that Neil W. is signed up with Airwork as for fourteen months here he could have bought his Zlin.

My new home here at Khamis Mushyat is 6,500 ft high; thus we really need the 3,500 yard runway just to get the Hunter 7 airborne. However it does make the climate really very pleasant. I saw a cloud today but it was a long way away.

I shall be home around September 8th, just in time for the last display (!) and will be staying around four weeks.

All the best, Tony."

Again in March I'd written:

Another Dinner Dance, this time in Norfolk, and the 10th anniversary of the McAully Flying Group. A close association has long existed between our two Clubs and to mark the occasion Barbara McAully was presented with a Tiger Club medallion on behalf of the Tiger Club. Needless to say, the evening was an hilarious one, and anyone who has ever heard of Tony Southerland's speeches will know what I mean. On the very day of the Dinner no less than three students took and passed their PPL tests. Hats off to instructors Barry Tempest and Mike Watts. Fred Marsh was there, enthusiastic about another scheme to sell sausages – this one offered as a prize a free flight. The aircraft depicted on the handout was a Turbulent. For visitors to the Cambridge area, a welcome from Fred, and there'll be Winton Smith sausages for tea.

To Jimmy and Leslie Hoseason our best wishes on the arrival of a son, James Charles.

There was certainly an easy ongoing relationship with the McAully Group. I doubt a month passed without an excuse to fly into Norfolk and enjoy the happy-go-lucky ways of the crowd at Little Snoring (yes, and there's a Great Snoring, too). The interchange was as comfortable as family. Shared homes, shared meals, shared friends. A more hospitable lot would be hard to find. And we in turn did our best when they turned up at Redhill.

I pause in my recollections. Isn't it strange that so many aeronautical trophies are named after dead colleagues, it's almost a morbid wish to perpetuate a lost friend with a contest in his name. I'm not agin it, but every once in a while I thinks. All this was prompted by the memory that it was in 1960 Elwyn McAully was killed when he lost it in a Tiger doing low aerobatics over Little Snoring, and here we were celebrating. It's a funny old world. The last little item was a hallmark of the *"Rag,"* it kept us all in the picture. Jimmy Hoseason's name is now synonymous with the delightful Norfolk Broads. Good days.

Those letters from Tony Haig-Thomas in the Middle East struck a chord, a memory that still remains. Blame everything that follows on a new experience for me: fatherhood. I took it seriously. In 1967 I was 41, Lollie was 24 and Robin a year old. From a romantic penniless wedding on Fireworks Night in '62 surrounded and supported by all our Tiger Club friends (recorded in the first volume), I'd struggled to survive since then with first a menswear shop in Colindale, North London – which fell on its face – and then the second which I opened on a shoestring in Hanwell, West London, around '65.

Here I fell lucky. It was a tiny shop in a dreary neighbourhood, but next door to a young up-and-coming music shop called Marshalls, whose customers kept wandering into my shop seeking sartorial inspiration for stage-wear. They were often in small groups with names like "The Who," "The Stones," "The Beatles," names which meant nothing to someone weaned on the swing of the 40s and 50s. I was a friendly bloke, the kettle was always on, and in no time at all I was doing business in a new untapped market, and what was once a mundane menswear shop became fashionably "way out." And since I was undercapitalised to the point of no return I tried mail order as a possible angle.

But space, I had none to spare. Behind the shop was a grotty yard to which I had no direct access and the landlord agreed to rent it to me for ten shillings a week (50p). A couple of chaps from an adjoining woodyard built me a shed during lunch hours which, when placed in the yard, became our mail order base. To help access to it without going around the block, they threw in a set of wooden steps over the sink, through a small window, and down the other side into the shed. Lollie, initially my only helper, and part-time at that, was hugely pregnant but she clambered in and out gamely. And so began a business that was to flourish, but that's rushing ahead.

1967 was also the year of a threat to world peace, or so a lot of us believed, and I got it into my head an atomic attack might in turn threaten my small family, and how could I protect them? Fatherhood had gone to my head and my senses deserted me. Witness what followed. I bought an old wooden river-cruiser on the Thames at Windsor which I envisaged would be our survival retreat and personal decontamination centre in one. Moor midstream, load up with baked beans and baby food, and we could fight off the hungry hordes fleeing out of London.

With the help of Charles Boddington, who had been so supportive when I flew into the ground some years earlier, I purchased a ·38 revolver for seven pounds and a new Walther PPK 9 mm pistol with which to defend ourselves. This PPK I reckoned Lollie could handle. She hated guns so I approached the subject gently. As she watched I withdrew the magazine – I'd been practising loading and unloading – and handed the pistol to her.

"Go on," I urged, "it's empty, just pull the trigger to get the feel of it."

33

She took the pistol gingerly; it was now pointing at me.

"No," I said gently, "even when empty never point a gun at anyone."

She moved the gun to one side and shot the cooker. I'd overlooked the one up the spout.

Deafened, she burst out: "You did that on purpose."

There was a cloud in the kitchen for days.

CLUB NEWS: MAY 1967

The Rollason Beta has now completed some four hours flying and we have heard enthusiastic reports on its handling. It was flown on its maiden flight by our Chairman, Norman Jones. It seems especially sad in the light of this first flight to record the loss of its contemporary, the Taylor 'Titch' racer in which John Taylor lost his life. John was a good friend and member of the Club and his reputation for building fine aircraft was second to none. We offer his wife and family our deepest sympathy.

On May 1st, some thirty members in a dozen aircraft visited the Concorde project at Bristol. It was a most successful outing with Nini Fisher showing an intelligent interest in the Olympus engine. Before she left she was being hailed as Miss Reheat. Our thanks to Mike Jolley, our PRO, for arranging things. Two weeks later the Club was honoured by a visit from its distinguished Honorary Member, Prince Philip. He lobbed into Redhill by helicopter and stayed to see an impromptu Turb formation, some Neil Williams aerobatics – with suitable explanation from Nick Carter – and Norman demonstrated the midget racer. Later in the year, Prince Philip is due to head a team of Club members in judging the Dawn-to-Dusk Competition. Those selected are Pee Wee Judge, James Baring, Ian Scott-Hill and Bev Snook. As a matter of fact the Dawn-to-Dusk Competition is really an international affair, for there is already a German entry. There is still time, just, to get into this exciting contest; enter now!

Don Lovell, our Foreign Touring Secretary, is feeling as frustrated as Clive Francis; his Berck lunch was again cancelled through bad weather for the third time. During June the Club is expected at Osnabrück where we (Lollie and I) can confirm that a tremendous welcome awaits our members. Lollie was fêted in a big way for her 'First Time in Germany' Standing-on-the-Wing act on May 4th. The display drew a 40,000 crowd. Whilst flying displays in Germany still have a long way to go to equal ours, what they lack in acts they certainly make up in the way they enjoy themselves. Thousands stayed on at the airfield to dine and dance until four in the morning. Beer gallonage must have been phenomenal. If spectator control at home occasionally needs a little tightening up, one or perhaps two policemen lend a hand. They took no chances at Osnabrück; the organisers hired 200 local soldiers and a British military band which played rousing marches at all the right moments.

Neil Williams must have wagged his tail with glee at the invitation to fly the Historic Aircraft Preservation Society's Avro Lancaster to the 617 reunion at Scampton. If that fine old veteran's appearance was accorded all honours, our humble flying back at Redhill is coming under fire from the locals over the subject of noise. May we please ask that everyone cooperate in giving the village a wide berth, especially on Sundays.

I must say our flying was well received. Lollie and I had travelled by road along with our young offspring to make a bit of a holiday of the occasion. Tiger 'SKP was ferried over there by Robin Voice. We had grown blasé with our act, and were oblivious to the fact that, to improve its long distance cruising, a fairly coarse-pitch prop had been used. I simply didn't think to check. If there was a question hovering around it was that I felt uneasy at the long lines of cars hard by the runway's edge. All I needed, I reflected, was for the wind to move around: it did. No brakes, no steering and my wife on top didn't make me happy, but a firm take-off with wheels well planted and more than sufficient speed, followed by a landing with the wheels again well planted and the tail well up wasn't beyond me. We set off. Osnabrück is set on a hilltop; quite how fortunate that was hit me once airborne. With full throttle we needed that extra height just to stay in the sky, such was the adverse drag ratio, a state I couldn't throw off. We skittered back by the skin of our teeth, and if that hadn't been hairy enough there was still a blasted landing to make.

Everyone cheered, heaven knows they hadn't seen much. We'd dropped off a hill only to reappear when we landed. Lollie on top had waved merrily throughout. I wondered later how one could so easily forget lessons learnt the hard way earlier. That flight was an exact repeat performance of a flight five years back when David Phillips was my pilot and I was sweating it out on top. We swore then never to fly SOW again without a fine-pitch prop and half tanks. "Benjamin," I can hear the good Lord say, "will you never learn?"

CLUB NEWS: JULY 1967

It's early July, the flying is good, the weather fine and the urge to produce a newsletter recedes with every distraction. June went by without a "Tiger Rag." So concerned did I feel at letting the side down, that in a moment of desperation I tried to resign the job, but no one would let me, and instead three members of the Committee proffered their services to cheer me up. As roving reporters they will be known to you as Splurge, Spoon and Plonk, noms de plume you will come to know, if they remember their promises to submit 750 words a month. Splurge writes this month – I haven't heard from the other two yet. This business of getting sufficient copy for a monthly rag weighs heavily – so come on, you other 649 members, write a little bit. Life can't be that dull that nothing ever happens!

We've seen some fine air displays these last eight weeks. Apart from Full TC Displays at Rochester, Sywell, Woburn and Denham, there have been numerous 'appearances.' Down at Lee-on-Solent "Bish" offers 'open house' to members to join them at the Seaplane Club, and fly their seaborne Tiger. Only kit needed, adds "Bish", is "a pair of old trousers, shorts and socks that will not matter if wetted, a helmet with Gosport tubes." A little belatedly we report that they sent a telegram to Sir Francis Chichester: "Congratulations on magnificent effort. The Chairman, Committee and Members of the Seaplane Club are very proud of their Vice-

President." Sir Francis was one of the Club's first members. Most weekends there is a notice in the hangar at Redhill saying 'SEAPLANE FLYING TODAY' or words to that effect. It is displayed after an early morning liase with Lee-on-Solent and is there to encourage a trip to the coast.

The new tiny Rollason-Luton Beta has flown and a fine-looking racer she looks. She had her first public outing at the Sywell display. James Baring·is racing her in the Nationals and a third Stampe has made a welcome debut. After an unnecessary accident to one of the Club's touring aircraft, this ·is perhaps a good moment to remind members to always carry tying-down gear when away from Redhill, and to use it whenever the aircraft is left in the open. Sudden squalls can spring up – and in this case did.

Today I gasp at the simplicity of the statement: "apart from Full Displays at Rochester, Sywell, Woburn and Denham." The work load must have been tremendous. On the ground side alone consider the advance publicity and poster sticking, the fencing off, refreshments for the public and crews, tents, gate-keepers, sound equipment. The flying every weekend we were accustomed to, even so the mind boggles at all the effort we so casually took for granted.

Attendances varied. At Rochester and Sywell, both regular and popular venues, we could reckon on a long crowd-line of several thousand, most of whom were regulars. They knew the aircraft and the pilots, and were always good-humoured. And we knew them. There was little in the way of cordoning off. Little boys sat just our side of the rope and as the aircraft taxied into line in front of them, they accepted the blown dust and grass cuttings in their faces with excited detachment.

We always parked our machines in a long line close to the public. For them the hustle and bustle of handling and procedures of starting were part of the show. And the animation of pilots clambering in and out of cockpits, the yelled commands and the noise – for all good displays have an ongoing noise level – bound us all up in the adventure of flight.

And when the show was over, and a reluctant peace returned to that grassy place, the mums and dads and little children would wander around the aircraft as though we were friends taking our leave, their movements and hesitant gestures conveyed an unspoken farewell, safe journey, a touching reminder that in our small world of flying the minor performers and our public were, for the day, one big family. Their waves called to us as we taxied away: "Please come back." We did, for so many years.

As for those roving reporters Splurge, Spoon and Plonk, only Splurge ever lent a hand. In truth I can no longer even remember who they were. But Splurge, bless him, wasn't without a droll sense of humour. His Paris report was of the iceberg variety, much of the real happenings obviously left unsaid; that's if I can read between the lines, and I always fancied I could.

TIGER CLUB SHOW AT PARIS:
AN ON-THE-SPOT REPORT FROM SPLURGE

June opened with the Paris Air Display at Le Bourget, and the Tiger Club was there in strength. First evidence of this was Pee Wee Judge and Charles Masefield behaving beautifully in the Beagle kennel. Tea was produced and disposed of and then a Pup-pushing programme followed. This involved burning off the energy imparted by the tea in heaving the Pup through a dense jungle of French. Owing to the walking characteristics of the aforementioned French, which closely follow their driving, considerable danger to life, limb and Pup was involved.

Other obstacles to be negotiated on the way were things you come across in books and don't really believe them and which take you a little aback when you actually see one. For example, there was a German straightupthenalongmitlandingdersamewaybackwardsmachine. There was a French mini-jet delta the size of a Turbulent crouching miserably under a mock-up of Concorde. We learned that it was miserable because it had been told not to fly (even if someone could have been found to go with it) owing to its unusual handling characteristics. Then there was an American version of the German straightupandalongflyingmitalongund straightdownlanding machine with four huge propellers and a tilting wing. This flew, believe it or not, on most days of the show; its programme was to spend great tracts of time hovering above the runway under various degrees of control and sounding as much like a washing machine as it possibly could. There were Russian rockets and RF.4s, Jodels and Lockheed Starlifters. Having avoided all these, we ran slap into Mike & Judy Jolley. They too were behaving beautifully and the next day afforded us a magnificent lunch in the Bristol Siddeley camp.

From our plates we could watch the display. Alan Turley shook the cobwebs out of a Lightning and did a beautiful display; then Bill Bedford turned on the Harrier and kicked the earth away as though it were a football. The next act was most original. Someone flew very fast across the field in a jet with a long pointy nose and a lot of flame coming out of the other end looking for all the world like a dragon going backwards. A few moments after this had left the scene a small whirlwind appeared where it had been. This was positioned nicely upwind of all the tents and sunshades. As it drifted lazily downwind, its passage could be traced by the various bits of paper, hats, small boys and other litter it sent whirling into the air. The best bit of all was when it reached the sunshades. First they twitched, then tugged at their moorings, and finally sailed gracefully skywards like Mary Poppins, only coming to earth rather less gently amongst the scattering mob.

Other supporting acts included an amazing display of aerobatics including loops, rolls and a half loop with a roll off the top by the Lockheed 286 rigid-rotor helicopter. An F-111A showed off its split personality in a high 'g' turn and the French, Italian, American and British formation aerobatic teams gave thrilling displays.

By now Peter and Sue Phillips joined us and we all trooped back to Paris and had an evening. Actually it turned out to be most of a morning too and by the time we had revisited the show to say goodbye, found Beauvais, dug James

Baring's Mascaret out of a locked hangar, explained away a dent which had mysteriously appeared in our hired car and had completed all the operations necessary to find oneself outside the hangar at Redhill it was dark within the meaning of the Act.

BEAUVAIS, ANTARCTICA, FIREWORKS AND G-ASKP

All the names Splurge mentions were indeed Tiger Club. Sometimes I think books such as this really need a follow-up. Characters flit across the page like shooting stars in a star-filled sky, a moment of wonderment, the world holds its breath, and then they've gone. But surely not to oblivion, for such stars must have climbed many stairs to have reached that heady moment. Lives don't stop, do they, even if we are no longer watching.

I'm forever asking where are they now. It's no use reaching for a biographical dictionary, for our stars seldom feature there, and memory falters until it meets up with a familiar name in the Personal Column and sharpens momentarily with a feeling of loss. A nod of the head to mark the passing, a wry smile at what was once, and life moves on. Bit sad really, but by golly, whilst they were here didn't they have their day! One such was Alan Turley.

Alan was the RAF's top aerobatic pilot, must have been for he represented the RAF at all the best shows, and his showing in that huge macho Lightning was a joy to behold, for which he earned a well-deserved AFC. An indomitable spirit, a zest for living he shared with Dawn, a most beautiful woman. Together they moved across our paths, joined, and then moved on, ever seeking new fields. Later on Alan and Dawn feature again but tragedy was to stalk this remarkable couple. Later, I promise.

If I am permitted one more 'wonder,' I wonder what we would have made of life if we hadn't fallen under the Tiger Club spell, gathered up as it were in a fellowship that seemed to direct our footsteps. I bet it would have been a lesser life, and I also bet I'm not the first to reflect thus.

Committee minutes: 22 June. Foreign Touring. Beauvais Osnabrück o.k."

A Beauvais weekend was an event not to be missed. We had been friends with them for many years and our two Clubs regularly exchanged visits. Once in a while the reports that came back lacked nothing in the way of reticence to overstate the fun we all had. The following is one of the more sober accounts.

BEAUVAIS WEEKEND: 27TH/28TH MAY 1967
Bernard Simpson reports:
Saturday morning the weather appeared to be completely without promise. However, the Met people were encouraging, offering an improvement pm, together with the usual bait "it's fine the other side of the Channel."

Eventually some 20 heads left the various dispersal points, all having arrived at Beauvais by 1700 hrs.

Awaiting us was the usual most warm welcome from our French friends with champagne to refresh us in their Clubhouse.

The itinerary next provided for our transport by coach to Paris, some 75 km south. Although early evening, it seemed we had at last found summer, blue sky and a soaring thermometer. Jackets were being peeled off and ties loosened as we drove off through Beauvais beneath the shadow of the unfinished 14th Century Gothic masterpiece of St. Peter's Cathedral, and down along route N1 through Beaumont, entering the Capital through St. Denis and Porte de la Chapelle.

Here, the intersections, cloverleafs and flyovers have to be seen to be believed, a really impressive example of highway engineering, so on to the centre of Paris for a rendezvous with our hosts on the Left Bank.

We were entertained to dinner cruising on the Seine 'en Bateaux Mouche'; a most delightful experience. The dinner was excellent and served as only the French can. Our party was seated in the bow of the boat with a clear view ahead and on either quarter. The boats were equipped with powerful floodlights, and dinner is consumed during a kind of mobile Son et Lumière. The river banks with their many splendid buildings present an entirely new dimension when viewed from this aspect. Quite fascinating to anyone with an eye for the architecture of a long-past golden age and the epitaph to the Master Masons and Architects who discovered the secret of the Ogival vault.

The sound element apart from the buzz of our own very pleasant conversation came mainly from a group amidships who were moved to lusty song, possibly by recent achievements on the field of sport and, of course, encouraged by the excellence of the wine. Photographs recording our party were taken at table, and a copy presented to each of us by our host.

All too soon we were back and tying up at the Quay, the clock having raced round to well after 11 pm. Hotel accommodation had been reserved for us at hotels in the Madeleine area. Some went off in the company of French friends to see Paris by night, others opted for their hotels and bed.

The silent hours of night were ungraciously disturbed by violent thunderstorms, to be followed by unsettled conditions the next day.

The arrangements were for us to pick up the coach at the Madeleine at 10.30 am to return to Beauvais. The rain considerately stopped just long enough for us to circumnavigate the Madeleine with a quick look at the well-stocked flower stalls, then off on our return journey.

The countryside between Pontoise and Auneil is very pleasant agricultural land, redolent of parts of Sussex, but with fine Charolais cattle much in evidence. The very heavy rain persisted throughout the journey; the storms of the previous night had left a trail of split and broken trees along the route.

A splendid lunch was given us in the magnificent salon of the President's home, again a most enjoyable occasion in delightful surroundings.

Reluctantly we returned to the aerodrome to investigate the possibility of returning to England. The rain, although moderating, was still with us, but eventually gave up about the middle of the afternoon.

The general outlook seemed to forecast that anything could happen, but possibly would not, so some of us decided to go. As on our arrival, M. Crucifix was dashing around with great speed and energy refuelling the aeroplanes and helping us with the formalities of departure. The usual quick visit to the duty-free shop and then airborne around 17.00 hrs. The flight home was smooth and uneventful, and quite fortuitously timed to miss the worst and meet the best of the weather from the Channel onwards.

A great weekend provided for us by most hospitable and charming people.

From James Gilbert (from a notice in a British Dakota):
"DON'T BE CONCERNED IF YOU SEE THE PILOT DRINKING DURING THE FLIGHT. HE JUST TAKES A LITTLE NIP NOW AND THEN TO STEADY HIMSELF: SOMETIMES HE GETS SO STEADY HE CAN'T MOVE."

John Ayres had been very much a part of our aerobatic scene. He'd captained the Tiger Club Lockheed international side in 1961, hit the headlines in 1966 when he completed a series of gravel trap landings in a Lightning, and we suspected he'd fled to the Falklands to recover. He was no mean flyer.

LETTER FROM JOHN AYERS – BRITISH ANTARCTIC SURVEYS – JULY 1967

"Dear Tessa,

First may I thank you for forwarding the *"Tiger Rag"*; it keeps me in touch with the outside world. Secondly, I would like to extend my sympathy over Donald Campbell's death. Rose gave me a complete run-down on the accident and we were all pretty shattered.

I would have liked to have written something longer on life down here but life has been a bit hectic over the past three weeks writing up reports. As you probably know, I was given the job of introducing the Pilatus Turbo-Porter into operation down here and this task proved most enjoyable. To any pilot who is looking for a job out of the ordinary, I can strongly recommend this one. On a good average day from 10,000 ft you can see for something like 250 miles in all directions. To have an aircraft that can take off with a full payload in under 200 yards at 10,000 ft adds spice to the work; and the fact that you can land on a glacier which has a slope of 25 degrees, complete the equivalent of a ski-jump turn and run off down the slope adds extra spice.

The routine work has been humping petrol, food, coal, sledge, dogs and personnel about. Our main freight task was shifting some 6 tons of stores to Fossil Bluff (71°20'S 68°17'W) from Adelaide Island (67°46'S 68°54'W) in preparation for an extended survey programme next season. Survey flying has been with a brand-new radio echo-sounding device which presents a continuous profile of ice depth. In the ones we worked we went to 400 metres of ice thickness but further south up on the Pole of Inaccessibility, this echo-sounding work required two types of flying; one which was as accurately straight and level as possible at about 3,000 ft above the ice surface, the other required haring around at 15 ft up and down the glacier. This was excellent sport as holding a steady 80 kt achieves a climb angle of 20° on a descent angle between 65° and 70°. This sort of flying could only be done infrequently as the light conditions had to be right so that you could see the ice/snow surface.

One very good maxim dating back to the early days of flying holds good down here and that is "no see, no fly." The Antarctic is somewhat unforgiving if you disobey the rules. There are plenty of places to pop down on skis but there are also many mountains over 5,000 ft and none of us want to repeat the Innsbruck disaster.

Next season should be pretty interesting as, apart from the routine freight humping, there will be a survey from Fossil Bluff going eastwards into the Batterby mountains. Plenty of short trips with the Porter in its natural habitat of mountains and glaciers. This is what the Swiss designed the aircraft for and it does it superbly.

Aside from flying, which takes place roughly on only two days out of seven because of the weather, one rapidly learns to cook and enjoy Penguin breast, real live Notatheria and chips. Our ex-Greenland Huskies present a challenge and skiing is a year-round sport. At Deception we share the island with Argentinians and Chileans, so there's quite some social life. A two-day stay at one of their bases costs a box of tinned pineapple and a bottle of whisky. When they visit us a flagon of wine and boxes of frozen steaks are brought. With our Argentine friends talk is kept off the somewhat touchy subject of football and the Falkland Islands. The last comment I heard from their Base Commander was: "Well, he was a Swiss referee."

That just about sums things up, but may I add that if anyone happens to be around 13 Henley Close, Rose will offer tea and coffee and one young daughter will want to show some slides which I have sent home.

In the meantime, good flying to one and all.

Yours,

JOHN."

John was never a demonstrative man. I think his forte was understatement. His 'required haring around at 15 ft up and down a glacier' must take some beating. Don't ask what prompted the next move, but I couldn't resist the temptation. Perhaps it was a leaning to Rupert Brooke: " . . . and is there honey still for tea?" I phoned Rose. "The number is unknown," said an attractive but automatic voice. I guess I leant too far.

SEAPLANE SECTION: GUIDE TO VISITORS

For those flying in, look out for aero- and winch-launched sailplanes and gliders; get a green from the GLIDER CARAVAN and land along – or alongside – the runway in use. Park on the grass area to the east of the Control Tower. Make sure that you fill in our 'Movements' record.

Members coming by road must enter the R.N. Station Lee by the Main Gate: to get past the Guardroom it is essential to have your Seaplane Club membership card with you. This should also be carried by those coming by air. If you require any information ring us after 1030 hours at Lee-on-Solent 79143, extension 191.

FROM EVERY QUARTER ·

Tessa tells us that the Tiger Club brooches now cost 32/6d, but she assures us they are worth the extra. We quote from a letter from Norway. 'On behalf of some friends I would like you to help us buy an old double-decker which has to be used to uplift non-engined aircraft.' And an extract from the Snag Book. 'Please check for airframe stress, I pulled so much 'g' I've broken the 'g' meter.' – attributed to Robin Blech. The winner of the Rochester Races was Robin Voice in a Turb, with James Gilbert second similarly mounted. James is here from the States again. Be the first to learn the results of the Dawn-to-Dusk Competition. It was won by Paul Herring in a Fournier RF.4 and Hubert Schnabel second in a long-range Jodel Ambassadeur. John Welsh was third in a Twin Comanche. James Black is making a great recovery, but is still in hospital, and I know he would welcome a line from his fans.

Some things never change. Robin Blech, who was a big lad then, and cheerfully still is, still flies a Turbulent. But his warning all those years ago in the Snag Book was correct. At that time we were aware that that delightful but rather rigid airframe didn't take kindly to high doses of 'g.' Aerobatics were out, especially since a fellow had lost a wing over Biggin after doing loops. I think he'd got to twenty. Ever since we'd eyed the undercarriage from the front for signs of squiffiness.

I still have a graphic drawing by the late Maurice Page of gremlins at work down at Rochester in '64. Maurice, who was a gifted artist and one of nature's originals, shunned convention and lived, so the story went, somewhere on the airfield. He had depicted Turbulent G-ASDB losing its port wing after landing. The pilot has his hand over his eyes in a "I don't believe this" scenario. Then in a corner of the sketch there's a magnified view of a grinning gremlin admiring his handicraft – the broken end of a main spar. I think Rollasons strengthened the spar: whatever, the fears have long since gone.

CLUB NEWS: AUGUST 1967

It's mid-August and already most of the Display season is behind us. Michael reports that it has also been a great flying year so far with this year's figures of hours flown far exceeding last. Not such good news is that of Alan and Dawn's crash in their Proctor whilst taking part in the National Races at Middleton. Latest reports indicate that Alan is progressing well and that Dawn is close behind him after a shaky start. We all wish them a speedy recovery. The race was won by James Baring in the new Beta at an average speed of 144 mph. Latest news from the gliding contingent is a record-breaking 1,500 tows by July. And from Fairoaks the second of their Newsletters. All our best wishes on a bright new venture and judging by the controversial tone quickly set it should provide juicy reading for a long time to come. In more gentle mien, Dagmar Heller is doing a great job on the

BWPA magazine now in its 40th issue. Peter Phillips organised a brilliant Air Pageant at Elstree during July, which included among its many 'firsts' the all-time original late-night entertainment of the Army Searchlight Team versus a brave Twin Comanche.

The *"Tiger Rag's"* Club News was always the cream on the top. Whether it was part of my nature or a dollop of wishful thinking I now no longer know. If bad things happened – and they did – I would try like the dickens to see a bright side, for like the simpleton I've always been, I'm a sucker for halcyon endings, so I underwrote the accidents in the hope that everyone and everything would, in the fullness of time, live happy ever after. It didn't always work like that. And it didn't work like that for Alan and Dawn Turley.

Alan and Dawn were both pilots, a true husband-and-wife team, and when their Proctor burst into flames during the National Races, Alan, with a skill that only comes to the very best, literally threw the aircraft into a rapid forced landing for he knew that airborne time and their very lives were counted in seconds. They stumbled from the flaming wreckage, their clothes alight, but it was Dawn who suffered most. Alan soon returned to flying. He was badly scarred, mostly on his hands where he had beaten out the flames that nearly devoured Dawn. Sadly Dawn had her beauty cruelly taken from her, for her exposed face had suffered most. Dawn was to retire from public scrutiny but she was never forgotten. There's one brave lady.

" . . .The race was won by James Baring in the new Beta at an average speed of 144 mph . . ."

The speed seemed a bit low for a Formula 1 racer so I checked with my log-book. The remarks column explained all. "New racer – disliked it. 65 hp." When later the engine was upgraded to 90 hp the little thing became great fun and the top speed shot up to 170.

"Latest news from the gliding contingent is a record-breaking 1,500 tows by July . . ."

Towing gliders into the sky was a well-established Tiger Club pastime that, because it all happened away from everyone's eye, tended to be overlooked. Reality was that the operation was a major part of our flying with several Tigers converted with towing hooks trailing behind the tail skid. Not a very elegant contraption, but the cockpit rope release was useful when the glider proved too heavy – the far hedge was approaching at a rate of knots and the Tiger wasn't getting airborne. At moments like this the pilot would glance back with evil grin and pull the red handle. Anyway, our thinking went, gliders were more used to forced landings.

In reality I doubt the need to cast off happened often. I only did it the once and that was whilst flying out of Detling, high in the Kent hills. I was towing a heavy T.21 with two up. The ground was rising and the pair of us weren't: it was time to pull the plug. The glider crew were quite unperturbed. "Didn't think you'd make it," the pilot said.

There was quite a bubble of indignation when Norman first gave the OK to equip the Super Tigers for towing. I mean, how could they? A special aerobatic mount wasn't a carthorse, was it? 'Sides it'll stretch the fuselage out of shape and bang goes the flying qualities. Norman could be as deaf as the next man: he knew best. Not for a change The Boss was right.

" . . . Peter Phillips organised a brilliant Air Pageant at Elstree, which included among its many firsts the all-time original late-night entertainment of the Army Searchlight Team versus a brave Twin Comanche."

It was all of that. I was there. Now that Lollie and I had a year-old son no way would we be parted from him. Not for us baby-sitters, no, where we went he went, poor mutt. We bought a twelve-foot caravan which towed nicely behind our first new car, a Volvo 144 (yep, the mail order business was picking up and neither of us were the saving type).

The weekend was tremendous fun and when Saturday's flying was over we retreated to the far side of the airfield, away from the noisy celebrations. We cooked a roast dinner and then contentedly watched from folding chairs the evening's flying entertainment. As dusk descended we became aware of activity from another vehicle parked quite near us. It was a big pantechnicon and two men were busy checking things that seemed to be planted in the surrounding area. Curious, I wandered over to say "Hello" to discover they had set up the BIG SURPRISE for the evening: a huge firework display.

"Don't get too close, mate," said one. "On a dry night like this fires can start."

With mounting anticipation – was there ever a more perfect night – we moved our van a bit further along and waited with some glee for the fun to start.

Down at the Elstree Flying Club – where Peter was the Chief Flying Instructor – the evening was becoming a rip-roaring success. Food, drink, happy voices, dancing, the sounds drifted across. And when it was really dark the searchlights made pencil-like white strokes in the sky and when they settled on an aircraft, well, you could almost hear the oohs and aahs. I believe Peter Phillips also went up and did aerobatics in the dark but I don't think anyone saw him.

Eventually the night's flying entertainment closed, the lights went out and everyone retired, the better for the fun, to continue the party.

"When are you going to set it all off?" I asked. They were now mates, they'd shared coffee and cake with us and I had offered to stand by with a fire extinguisher.

"Midnight," one said, "unless they send someone over to bring it forward."

"Or cancel it," the other muttered.

Midnight. With co-ordinated movements these two pyrotechnic experts – which they certainly were – began to light a succession of tableaux, massive rockets thundered upwards, and the most beautiful of colours lit the dark sky to rain down in a flawless glory that left us breathless. It all went on for a good ten minutes and ended with a huge set piece of the Queen and Prince Philip. We clapped our appreciation, the few small fires were douched and darkness settled in again. The crew began their packing up.

A car bumped across the airfield towards the firework chaps and I heard a cheery voice call out: "It's OK, you can start now."

As editor of the *"Tiger Rag"* there were often delicate moments of finger-crossed diplomacy when lengthy articles were submitted that in truth would have bored the pants off even our partisan readers. If nothing else I wanted the *"Rag"* to be very readable. So when a longish article was presented that was not only that, hugely entertaining, but could be read a second time with a growing relish, it was promptly printed.

This business of real characters appearing from out of nowhere to fly with us was a weekly miracle. And there was no bolder character than one Sam Clutton. He called himself Cecil – we knew him as Sam.

G-ASKP TO JURBY

When people have recently flown biplanes to Russia I cannot believe that any Tiger Moth trip in the U.K. can be of the least interest, but "G.B." says I am to chronicle 'ASKP's visit to the Isle of Man, and one knows better than to argue with "G.B."

I don't really regard myself as a going-places pilot as I simply can't be bothered to mug up all that scintillating conversational repartee required for a radio licence. However, the Isle of Man Rally and Race did rather appeal, as I did some very happy flying from Jurby during the war, and had an invitation to visit a friend in the Island; and, anyway, I'd never competed in an air race.

I invited Hamish Moffatt to navigate. Hamish is a fairly new associate member of the Tiger Club, but he is a very well-known member of the Vintage Sports Car Club, where his extrovert and extremely skilful handling of his Grand Prix Bugatti is always an outstanding feature of any Vintage race meeting. I had recently given Hamish a short turn up in a Tiger which he described as the most terrifying exper-ience of his life; I wasn't sure if this was to be taken as a compliment but at any rate we knew the worst.

Hamish had made a nonsense of borrowing John Blake's life-jacket and I refused to take him across the ocean without one. (No, honestly, old chap, take mine – bubble bubble bubble – glub!) So by the time we had rifled John's office it was 11 o'clock before we were in the air; which was no bad thing, since the weather forecast was so stinking that it might get better, on the principle that it could hardly get worse.

It was decided that I would navigate from the half-million air chart and Hamish from a motoring road map, so that what one missed the other would pick up and in actual fact there was practically no point in the trip when we were both lost at the same time. However, communication was not easy as neither of us had the right sort of hat for connecting to that idiotic pipe effort through which it is impossible to hear what the other chap is trying to shout. So Hamish was to point to the right or left if he thought I was off course.

I've never flown in such persistently and fiercely turbulent conditions, and one was fighting every inch of the way to our first scheduled stop of Wolverhampton, with intermittent rain to add to the fun. There was absolutely no question of steering a compass course. Soon after Stratford-on-Avon, I got as lost as a newt and began circling a small town in the hopes that Hamish would do some pointing. However, as it happened that we were dead on track at the time Hamish thought I had merely stopped to admire the scenery, so he didn't cooperate and I therefore imagined he was lost too. So I set off again in the general direction and luckily the Droitwich masts soon loomed up, and in due course the two factory chimneys of Wolves where we landed, being the first time I had landed there since I completed my Tiger Moth training in 1943.

"Is it always like that in a Tiger Moth?" asked Hamish.

The Wolves people were most kind and helpful, but a call to Blackpool indicated that they and the Isle of Man were down to 300 yards visibility and they didn't want to know anything about anyone without radio. Nor did the next five places we rang up, although by five o'clock it was evident that the weather over the coast was clearing. But it was too risky to try to try to make the island on one tankful and things were beginning to look pretty gloomy. At last someone suggested Barton who were most cooperative and said they would wait an hour until we arrived. By this time there was an almost complete clamp at Wolver-hampton, but there was no time to delay and we reckoned that ten minutes flying due north should connect us with the M6. Flying at 600 ft there were fitful glimpses of the floor and eventually the M6 loomed up. At the Manchester Ship Canal I turned right but Hamish (whose map was rather out of date and didn't show the M6) decided we were somewhere quite else and pointed left. My inferiority complex convinced me against my better judgement that I was sure to be wrong and we started swanning around looking for a non-existent Barton.

By this juncture we started an angry exchange of correspondence between the front and back cockpit but as we only had one pencil between us this had to be passed to and fro with each communication. Eventually my temper managed to get my inferiority complex back into its kennel and we made a very protracted landing at Barton (memo: bad tempers make bad landings) to find two very helpful but rather worried types waiting for us. A very quick refuel and we were on our way.

"Follow that railway," they said: "it goes straight to the coast."

Most railways known to me aren't there any more, but the complex that loomed up through the murk north of Barton looked more like a piece of knitting the kitten had been at, and when the coast finally showed up it was too late and in the wrong place. This is put down to dithering between map reading and compass course, but when the Isle of Man began to sulk in exactly the same way I began to wonder if the wind or the compass had gone peculiar. E.T.A. showed no trace of land and only as I was wondering rather forlornly if we had enough fuel to reach Ireland did Maughold Head consent to appear. We finally touched down in Jurby at 8.30 pm.

Race day showed gusts of up to 30 knots and it was clearly impossible to get the Tiger out of the hangar. However, the modern types were able to practise and Hamish cadged a lift off Tom Storey to see what the course was like. It was in doubt until the last deferred moment whether the race could be held at all, but by 6 pm the wind was down to 15 knots and only occasional gusts over 20. This seemed just about fit for a Tiger if manhandled out and if I kept to a reasonable height in the air. Incidentally, it's interesting to learn from "British Aviation – The Pioneer Years," by Harald Penrose, that even in 1910 flying in such conditions was not thought impossible, and by 1912 it was almost commonplace. Stalling speeds were as much as 40 mph despite the low wing loadings, even if cruising speeds were only marginally higher.

I was kindly given dispensation to race without practising in view of Hamish's ride with Tom, and he was to do his pointing act if I got off course; so we were in after all.

Crab across the runway to keep as near as possible into wind and hold down as long as possible. Then Waygood Otis to about 50 ft to avoid embarrassing wing-drops near the ground. At the end of the first lap we were still leading but as we crossed Jurby a sneaky little yellow number flashes past below us at what looks like mini-skirt level; and by the end of the race I regret to say we are last. I had opted for maximum sustained speed of 2,200 rpm but Norman said I was a softie; nothing less than full throttle. Still there was that sea crossing home to consider.

A complication of my staying on two days was that Jurby is only a relief ground to Ronaldsway and was to be completely closed after Sunday. Sunday showed gusts of up to 40 knots and again the Tiger couldn't be got out of the hangar. No, it just had to stay and by Monday morning the only occupants were 'ASKP and the unfortunate pilot who had landed after the race without benefit of undercarriage. All Monday the wind kept up but Tuesday dawned fair and we got permission for the local policeman to see us off. Down to Ronaldsway to refuel, taking the opportunity to fly over the lovely south-west corner of the Island; and so home, with only one stop at Wolverhampton for fuel.

Redhill was having a shower and my attention was riveted on one of those beastly cloppy-hopters so that I suddenly find myself carving up a Condor doing a proper approach, in a simply beastly manner.

Oh! dear; what an undignified ending to a not uneventful trip. Only 'ASKP behaved impeccably throughout.

Sam used to arrive at Redhill in either an immaculate open-top Jaguar 120 or in a most beautiful Bugatti. In another world he was a well-known vintage car man and drove his cars with a total lack of self-consciousness for their variety or value. The very image of the English gentleman, hugely open and bluff, Sam flew Tigers in the same "let's get on with it" manner. In yet another world he earned a crust with a very upper-class estate agency. We liked Sam.

SHOREHAM, PROPS, DUTY PILOTS AND KILKENNY

Committee minutes: June '67
"Any other business: The need to keep all Tiger Club members in touch discussed. L. Benjamin will make a plan to entertain them."

It's no good, I can't make a story of my efforts, I simply can't recall. I only include the cryptic snippet as an example of our Chairman's firm belief that not only anything was possible but anyone could do it.

Committee meeting: July '67
"Item 5 (a) Sywell and Shoreham V.G.I."

What's that, four words? Our Chairman had descriptions down to a fine art. His object was to cast the past aside in one of three conditions: poor, good, and – his top accolade – very good indeed. Wonder sometimes how he arrived at his classifications since nine out of ten he didn't attend. Perhaps if the pilots parked neatly on their return, if all the aircraft came back in one piece, and if the wind was in the west, the show got a V.G.I.

The Shoreham Show was certainly V.G.I.

SHOREHAM – FULL DISPLAY – PART I

Saturday 12th August dawned bright and clear. Ideal for the full Tiger Club display at Shoreham. At Redhill the aircraft drawn up in lines before the hangar painted a gay picture indeed. Around them bustled the pilots and crews, either playing Redhill's favourite game – cushion hunting – or clustered in little groups discussing flight procedures (usually resolving to a single decision, either to fly over or around Gatwick), and who's for whose formation. It may only take 10 minutes in theory to get in an aircraft and go, but in practice the ritual is complex, repetitive and part of the fun, and never takes less than 45 minutes. Conductor, Robin Voice, with tact and patience gets his brood off. Last minute cries "Is there room for me?", and those famous parting words "Don't worry, I'll keep it to 75 knots" become hollow echoes as a peace you can hear returns to Redhill. Jim or John breathe a sigh of relief and stand and watch till their charges bump their way out of sight.

A keen westerly wind cools the sunshine down at Shoreham. Already by midday lines of cars are drawn up in neat rows, picnics and children and rope enclosures, ice-cream and flapping tents and patient police directing traffic. An orderly hubbub of coming and going, joyriding Austers and a dashing Red Dragon, and Clive and Jean Francis everywhere at once – ever smiling. For a couple of weeks the local newspapers have been fed with good copy and photographs. Everywhere posters have grinned down at the passers-by and now the work is paying off and still the weather holds, cross fingers. The growing crowd is a happy one. It isn't always so; sometimes they're restless and impatient – so much depends on the weather. Today we're in luck. The commentator's task will be easier. The boys arrive, neat formations of biplanes and tiny Turbs which fly around town to herald their arrival and remind the populace to hurry out to the airfield. Then land, refuel, and look for food. The Beagle canteen staff break into a teasing round of applause as the first hesitantly enter. Only 30 minutes late. The canteen fills up. Pilots and helpers, local Club pilots, Richard the ATCO. The meal moves naturally into a briefing. . . . Clive Francis calls for order, and momentarily stills our chatter and the clatter of the waitresses. Richard briefs on local conditions and raises the regular derisive laugh as his 5,000 ft wind forecast follows the equally improbable 2,000 ft. Never towards, or over or near the crowd, Clive's warnings are clear, precise, oft-repeated. Go through the pro-gramme, routine questions, routine answers. Synchronise watches, coffee and then the general move for the exit.

The ground boys under the watchful eye of Roy Davis begin their queries. Props positioning? Balloons: 15-second or 20-second intervals? All this from the busy team leaders. The pilots gather around for race briefing and the commen-tators move in and out like newshawks snatching information and committing what they can to paper. And from 2 till 2.45 a peace descends on everyone – the preparations are complete and there's time to look for the first time at the growing crowds, become aware of the commentator as he introduces the pre-display local demonstrations, and mentally prepare for the big show. Time to notice the sunshine and feel the soft grass under your feet. . . .

Next month – The Display!

LETTER TO THE CHAIRMAN

"Dear Norman,   11th August 1967
Thank you and the Tiger Club for the most beautiful bouquet of flowers which greeted me at London Airport after my Capetown to London flight. What a lovely surprise it was after quite a tough time, particularly the bit where we had to pass through the core of a thunderstorm just outside Paris just when we thought home was in sight!

You and the Tiger Club always think up some nice little surprise or else help me in a very constructive way. I would like you to know how much I appreciate it all and that I am very proud to be a member of the Tiger Club.

I do not know if I told you that I had a wonderful salute from a South African Tiger Club member the night I arrived at Capetown. He took his Turbulent up with special permission from Capetown National Airport and saluted "Myth Too" as a fellow member of the Tiger Club which was a great kick for me being so many thousands of miles away from home.

Again, thank you for so many nice things.
Kind regards,
Sincerely,
Sheila Scott."

Sheila Scott was a remarkable woman, slim, attractive, but as a pilot we unfeeling males derided her. Sheila's nervousness was legend, always in need of reassurance. If trouble was in the offing she seemed to instinctively home into its centre, crying "please rescue me." Well, that's what we thought; the Club wasn't over-gallant to women in those days. But that was in the early sixties, yet she was to conquer her fears, meeting her devils head-on to beat them the hard way, and by sheer strength of will became a world record-breaker and an outstanding pilot into the bargain.

She sold her first aeroplane, an ungainly Jackaroo biplane, and bought a Piper Comanche 260B, and in '65-'66 proceeded to shock the lights out of us with a series of incredible flights, culminating in becoming the first British woman to complete a solo flight around the world in the June of 1966, while on the way establishing several new point-to-point records.

The flight she refers to was her homecoming from Cape Town after establishing a new record there from Heathrow in July 1967, beating the Amy Johnson record which had stood for thirty-one years. And believe it or not she was far from finished.

SHOREHAM – FULL DISPLAY – PART II

We've been to Shoreham now for several years. Little changes from one year to the next. Even the programme has settled down into a proven routine. The odd aircraft comes and goes, the odd pilot makes his mark and moves on – another to take his place and his blue eyes will shine for his short span. But the programme remains. A tradition is being made. We start at 3 – and we start with a bang. Once it was the Active, and then the Cosmic, sometimes a Spitfire or Mustang, today it's rightly the Beagle Pup. The sequence is as predictable as a well-loved pantomime and the regulars among the audience relish it and never tire.

From an aerobatic Pup and Pee Wee to the 20 minutes of continual formation – a sequence originally designed by a then relative newcomer to the Club 5 years ago by name of Neil Williams – and used ever since. The biplane V of five – 3 Tigers and 2 Stampes – led high and sedately by John Slessor and closely followed by Clive with his box of 4 Turbs. The Turbs put on a fine display with echelon changes and tail chase and dive under the hoop. I'm the commentator at this point. I don't say it, but I reflect that the acts, which somehow always contrive to look so fresh, are now favourite oldies, and every one of which I have flown in the past. I feel a bit ancient. The act that is new has been thought up by Bill Innes and Pete Jarvis. Their duo in Stampes is a pretty sight with a tight 'over and under' formation they call a 'sandwich.' It is too, a sandwich with a little air between. A mirror circuit and paired loops and stalled turns all crammed successfully into a couple of rip-roaring minutes.

Fellow commentator Mike Jolley flies the Active noisily and well. I sit back and let our third team mate carry on: the incomparable John Blake. This idea of a team of three commentators is a good one. It works well in practice. Glider aerobatics by Glyn Richards of the Kent Club is quiet and easy on the eye. The parachutists fail us at the last moment. This used not to happen and the boys would always jump in winds up to a good 20 kt but of late they've mellowed or something and have cried off in conditions that to a layman seemed passable. Let me hasten to add that this criticism isn't backed by a shred of personal experience. I've long considered anyone who voluntarily abandons a serviceable aircraft needs his head examined.

The interval is for the birds and ice cream vendors and me, to enact, as the programme says, "a warm-up for the crazy flying." "Laughing" John Stewart-Wood hides in the crowd and I call him out on the strength of a fixed programme number which he happens to have in his hand. The act is as old as the hills, yet it never fails to set the crowd going. And John's brand of crazy flying is delightful. Tied-together formation by Tigers and no one breaks the tapes but on the other hand the crowd I know would like the pilot to at least tempt providence once in a while. As in balloon bursting it's the one that gets away that goes down the best. It was in this act that newcomer Ralph Spurrell did so well and in which the Master, Bill Innes, lets his hair down. Tethered balloon bursting on the other hand puts the wind up me. I concede that it is exciting to watch with balloons and cardboard tubes flying in all directions when clobbered by Turb wings, but I can't take the close proximity of the tiny wings to the ground without a dire fertile imagination taking over.

The vintage flypast, on the other hand, is relaxation supreme. The Tiger, the Puss Moth and the Fox Moth lumber by, the very personification of all I imagine the 'tween wars years must have been like. Of the "Standing on the Wing" what is there to say? Vivian Tidmarsh did the honours and John Stewart-Wood did the flying, all to a generous round of applause from the spectators for a brave local lass at her first public performance. Formation aerobatics by Neil Williams, James Baring, Pete Jarvis and Bill Innes was just about the best anyone is likely over to see in a mixed bag of Tiger and Stampe. And then the race. By 5.30 nearly all the Tiger Club aircraft have moved off with no navigational problems at all – the vis all the way home was perfect. Shoreham was a good one. Good to see James Black – still hobbling – but up and about, and even taking over the commentary for Neil's superb Stampe aerobatic spot. To the west heavy cu is building up and as Lollie, a tired Robin and I climb the downs towards our tiny caravan nestling high on nearby Truleigh Hill, we see a formation of five biplanes flying up the valley beneath us into a distant purple and Redhill and tea and suddenly we wished we could join them.

CLUB NEWS: SEPTEMBER – OCTOBER 1967

September was a busy month at Redhill. The weather was goodish, flying good; all in all we're going to miss the summer of '67, but before we go down in pre-winter gloom let me appeal for write-ups on some of those holidays – it'll keep us up in good reading through the cold spell. Probably the biggest and best event in the month was Redhill's At Home to our many overseas friends. As in past years, the organisation was bedevilled by poor weather, even so it was a successful occasion.

Some of the displays too were treated to dubious weather. Blackbushe was a prime example. On the second day the wind blew a fitful 35 kt – so I was told – yet even so a lot of the acts went on. A few weeks after Blackbushe a team of four Turbs, a Tiger and a friendly Condor flew up to Shobdon to uphold the Tiger Club name. They did it, too. The weather was so duff on the way up that a mass precautionary into a field was called for. The show was a success and, delighted, they set off home, to fly slap through the same front which put them down in yet another field. It isn't often a display team can claim a successful outing and include two precautionaries!

Top flying news, though, this month was of course Neil Williams' brilliant win at Dax, which brings home the Leon Biancotto Trophy. It is the first time a British pilot has won a major International Aerobatic Competition. He flew the CSE Zlin. This news must have done much to cheer up "Bish", who is far from well and at the moment of writing is in St. Mary's Hospital, Portsmouth. "Bish" was the leading British pioneer in the International Aerobatic field during the mid-fifties and he is certainly not forgotten by the present team. I'm sure he would welcome your letters, and on behalf of all of us I send our warmest "get well soon" greetings.

An interesting offer and one that is available to Tiger Club members is that of a remarkable car-hire service which rents VWs, taxed and insured, for only £13 a month. The only expenses over and above this sum would be for the petrol, oil and minor repairs. In the event of a major breakdown the car can be exchanged without extra cost. This is an extraordinarily cheap hire-rate and could be very useful. The Editor will gladly put anyone interested in touch with this organisation.

Snippets: Nick Carter has been quietly working away to provide two portable radios for the Stampe – aerobatic types note! The *"Rag's"* roving reporters have apparently roved out of reach. The Esso Tiger Trophy was postponed a week, and there is a new magazine on the way out that should interest TC members. It is called *"Pilot."* Will, if possible, review it next month.

I can't find any review in the *"Rag"* for *"Pilot"* magazine. If I missed writing it, it was a lost opportunity to acclaim what was to become the country's premier flying magazine under the editorship of James Gilbert.

Norman Jones had originally run it, but a little later, in 1972, had the good sense to sell on to James. James, who is mentioned in the first book, was a fine aerobatic pilot, photographer, writer, editor and *bon viveur* – or so I thought – and an out-and-out Tiger Club man.

If 1967 marks the entry of *"Pilot"* magazine it was, within a few years, to mark the beginning of a one-man campaign to fight the injustices of bureaucracy, and James, through the pages of his magazine, consistently struck out at the threats to the freedom of sport flying. He's still in there, still fighting. No one can stop bureaucratic growth, but James sure slowed it up. Good for him, and more to the point, good for us.

AN ODE TO HAND SWINGERS

"When you have a 'prop' to swing
Don't do gymnastics on the thing.
Even with the switches off,
The engine still may give a cough.
"Dead" motors have been known to kick
And whip an arm off mighty quick!

Besides, an engine runs in jerks
And Gavin wrapped around the spinner
Is roughly right for Pluto's dinner.
An aeroplane will not fly better
With Gavin stuffed in the carburettor!"

[The author asks to remain anonymous. – Ed.]

We certainly had the occasional mishap prop-swinging, but few caused serious injury. After ten years of constant practice on the Club's machines not fitted with self-starters – most of them – we were by no means greenhorns and we treated propellers with a lot of respect. In any one day any one member could be expected to swing upwards of half a dozen props, big ones, little ones, ones that went the other way, and the awkward one that liked to be approached from behind.

With so much expertise around anyone who looked likely to mess up was swiftly helped. The men who had eyes in the back of their heads were the weekend Rollason crews, usually the pair Jim and John. To say they were expert in engine starting is to understate reality. Jim, who even in 1967 had been stripping, overhauling and coping with all the Club's aero engines since D.I.s were chipped out in stone, had, along with his airframe side-kick John, a knack unsurpassed. The only tool they ever used on the tarmac was a hefty long screwdriver, the sight of which was guaranteed to quell any rebellious engine at ten paces. There was one other fellow on call and he was known as the Duty Pilot.

In September Michael Jones, who managed the Tiger Club with a resigned tolerance we admired him for, wrote:

DUTY PILOT ROTA

Volunteers for Duty Pilot are expected to forego flying themselves whilst they are on watch. It is reasonable to expect that once in eight weeks a member can stay on the ground for a maximum of four hours, and we ask all on the rota to do this and not suddenly decide that he or she MUST fly; then asking another member to stand by whilst he/she goes off for half an hour. The DUTY PILOT has a number of responsibilities whilst on watch and he/she is EXPECTED to observe these.

There is, of course, no objection to members exchanging duties if they find the day detailed inconvenient. BUT this must be done in advance of the period in question under advice to Redhill, and all are asked not to make more changes than ABSOLUTELY NECESSARY.

The morning duty is from 1000 to 1330 hours, whilst that of the afternoon starts at 1330 hours and continues until 1700 hours or such time as any night-flying which may be organised is completed. If we haven't put you off, contact Michael Jones.

Overheard in the local pub. Time 13.00 Sunday. Sam Clutton: "Think we'd better get back, I'm supposed to be relieving the Duty Pilot." Michael Jones: "That's alright. You're taking over from me."

NOTES FOR DUTY PILOTS (collated by Paul Minton)

[Originally drafted 6 years ago. Believe me, nothing changes. – Ed]

For those who have yet to indulge in the fascinating sport of Duty Pilotage a few notes might help them avoid some of the many pitfalls into which this D.P. has fallen.

Firstly, although you've not got to sign on until 10 if on morning duty, you'll find that if you arrive at 9 you'll just be organised in time to hand over with a smug smile at 1.30. Probably by 9.15 you will have found the fire alarm and reckon you are winning – don't believe it; just try and find the list of doctors and hospitals. Having done 27 vain circuits of the hangar, you'll need the tea and sympathy which should then be available in the workshop.

By now the vagrants in the bunkhouse will have arisen in spite of all your efforts, and be muttering ominously about flying. This is a strange ritual which involves sniffing at the weather in 'RAM. The reason for using this aircraft is that no matter how late it was put in the hangar at night, the following morning the a/c is right at the back. Hence you'll have the pleasure of pushing all the aircraft out to get at 'RAM, but having got them all out it'll start to rain, so you can put them all back again. The odds are you put 'RAM in first. . . .

While on the subject of weather it is essential that the D.P. ensures there is some. For the non-technical it should be pointed out that lack of weather will prevent an aircraft getting a vacuum on top of its wings and stop it taking off. In no time, all the Club aircraft will be rushing around the airfield like Norman about to jump the tape in a Turbulent. You will then have to sort out the traffic jam.

Weather comes out of the telephone from Gatwick where the Ministry of Aviation makes it. Unfortunately on Sundays it gets rather mixed up with the more obtuse parts of the *"Observer"* crossword, but nevertheless you mustn't miss a word, paying particular care to get the data on Oktas. These are aerial octopuses which, during the winter, hunt in packs of five or eight and are very dangerous to pilots. The only known defence is an instrument rating.

In emergencies, such as losing the paper between the telephone and the board, an appropriate quotation, preferably from *"Alice in Wonderland,"* will generally suffice.

Now all you've got to do is line up the 'T,' a simple job requiring the minimum of intelligence, a little strength, and the patience of Job. Once upon a time we had one windsock and everyone knew which way they were trying to land, even if they weren't very successful. Now we've got three which all point in different directions and nobody knows anything any more. Having cast your lot by making

the 'T' point in a suitably vague direction, you'll find that you're not likely to win, for:
a) Pilots who follow the 'T' do a bad landing; blame you.
b) Those who don't follow the 'T' do a bad landing; blame you.
c) Those who do a bad landing; blame you.

The best you can hope for is a draw and a three-month spell for recovery before your next tour of duty.

To this day I don't know who wrote up the Kilkenny stories. They lead a different life over there. Just to glimpse it is a delight.

ANOTHER IRISH WEEKEND

Regular readers of this column will remember that the last Irish party was the Whitsun weekend at Kilkenny. This year the Rothmans Rally was announced as a more sophisticated entertainment, an Isle of Man-style rally and race, good prizes, champagne receptions and a request for dinner jackets. The organising committee included several well-known names, Maurice Cronin, Killeen, Bigger, Wignall etc., so it looked like being quite a party.

Tom and I decided to go by Tiger, which made flight planning difficult, he in 'OAA and me in 'SKP, with our dinner jackets. Problems of range v. Customs availability and lack of radio beset us at every turn. Finally we went through R.A.F. Valley who were prepared to accept us before 8 am. We were made welcome at Halfpenny Green on Friday night and set off for Valley at dawn on Saturday. It was a splendid misty morning with enough low cloud below to keep us interested without being too frightened. The Welsh hills had generated their own cloud cover, so we discussed the "over or round" decision as we flew along. Tom seemed to be suggesting that he should go round, me over, and that if in doubt we should both go under. Finally we both went over, heading for the clear air that we expected over the North Wales coast. Incredibly there was a break in the clouds over the right village, in the right valley with the absolutely perfect railway that ran all the way to the threshold of runway 25 at R.A.F. Valley. The R.A.F. gave us lots of green Verey lights to show us where to land, fuel and coffee. We were impressed by their radar, they could watch the shipping at 30 miles. We agreed not to drop below 500 ft, so it seemed that our lifejackets were to be useful insurance for once. We shaved in the toilet marked 'Ladies and Officers' but weren't quite sure which category we came under. We were surprised to find that both aircraft had used the same amount of fuel, 'SKP at 2,100 rpm, with fine-pitch prop, 'OAA at 1,600 rpm. The dry tank range for 'OAA seemed to be about 1:50 at 70 knots; fortunately we had only a light headwind across the Irish Sea.

Ballyfree gave us a splendid welcome, the only problem was that they arranged for Saturday as well as the Sunday, so I missed out on the champagne. Among the welcome party we found John Blake. It is strange how similar airfields are – anywhere in Europe they look the same; John never changes either. This airstrip is at the bottom of a valley which leads up into the Wicklow mountains; there are trees, houses and small hills scattered around the valley floor and the approach is through a cutting in a wooded ridge. Indeed, the approach is rather like one of those cartoons of an aircraft following a railway into a tunnel.

The airshow was a nice, casual affair, live on Irish television throughout both afternoons, one or two acts being airborne most of the time. They seemed to like W.O.W. *[Woman on Wing, used to be known as S.O.W. – Standing on Wing – Ed.]*, and featured it on the news broadcasts each evening. Apparently, there is some good film of our round-the-trees, over-the-houses circuit culminating in our last downwind run doing a crossover with a glider and tug taking off early; I suppose he had right of way?

The catering was excellent throughout, good airfield lunches and superb dinners. True to reputation, the Irish had not built our hotel, the Rockfield House, so we were scattered over Southern Ireland at night, but they had finished the kitchens and we ate well. Only about half the rally aircraft managed to reach Ballyfree owing to fog on the English coast, so the food was plentiful too. The fog was still there when we came to go home; Tom stayed about a week and finally came home by Aer Lingus. Having flown round the head and plotted its shape, I found myself in the harbour area and became a bit frightened by cranes and ships' masts which appeared from time to time, so we had to climb out and couldn't get down again. We got back to Ballyfree with some fuel left and next day persuaded Liverpool to let us in non-radio to clear Customs provided that we landed first to give an accurate ETA from Harwarden (Chester). The weather behind the coastal fog and hills was perfect so that was no problem until we reached Harwarden to find the wind blowing 45 knots. Fortunately the Customs were kind enough to come out to meet us as we touched down, and helped hang on to the aircraft. They had brought half a dozen policemen along too, but they were only keen to do their duty regarding landings contrary to the Customs and Excise Acts. The conflict of interests and regulations between the ATC who don't want us and the Customs who do is making non-radio touring rather more involved than our thick heads could cope with. But we were back, and more important, in one piece.

. . . A new division of the Club was founded, appropriately enough, on November 5th. It hasn't a name yet but is exceedingly exclusive and ever so slightly sick. It is restricted to those who, during their membership, unintentionally have written off an aircraft. If nothing else, it's good for a monthly dinner out. Each month we will invite a guest. This month's will be the 'man most likely to join the club.' Barry Griffiths has bravely accepted our invitation. Prospective members please write to the Editor and be prepared to submit photographic evidence. I said it was a weeny bit sick.

A new Condor is at Redhill and is the first with 360 Narco radio plus VOR. And our thanks to Arthur Tyrrell – the Club's top Boffin – for providing three new and extremely efficient squawk boxes for biplane intercom. His only plea: "Don't open them; if the outfit doesn't work it's not my box but your duff headset." He is a very confident Boffin, is Arthur. I hear that Barry Griffiths is planning another attempt at a 16 mm film of Redhill activities which, for the time being anyway, will exclude aerobatics overhead. Local pressure has brought this about, which makes me think it's a pity that member Winston Churchill didn't stand for Redhill and Reigate – we could do with him there! Our congratulations to him for a terrific effort at Gorton.

BLACK CAT, LOVE STORY AND OUR AIMS

Unfortunately our choice of Barry Griffiths for our Guest at the inaugural dinner of the Black Cat Club (for that's what we agreed to call our new Club) as the 'man most likely' was eventually to prove all too true. Norman Jones was displeased when he heard of the Club's existence. Whether he imagined he'd have to face prangs in order to join, I've no idea, but from then on the Black Cat Club went undercover, it was too good to disband. We met each month at Rules Restaurant and on each occasion invited a guest – some I fear must have come under a spell for sure enough they too became members. It was uncanny.

The more I consider the founder members, their signatures boldly scrawled across the last page of a most formal and entertaining Constitution of the B.C.C., the more I wonder if Fate hadn't quietly joined up with us. Dick Emery (he was a beloved comedian), yours truly, James Black, Neville Browning, Bill Innes and Neil Williams, because in time two of them had further prangs in which they also wrote themselves off. Which goes to show Norman was probably right . . . it doesn't do to mock the Fates.

Should these words ever inspire a similar burst of lunacy I can offer up the original Aims and Objects for guidance.

NAME: 1. The full name of the Club shall be THE BLACK CAT CLUB but may be referred to for the purposes of euphony and confusion by its initial letters: "B.C.C."

AIMS AND
OBJECTS 2. The aims and objects of the Club are as follows:
(a) By example precept and exhortation to discourage other pilots from following the example of the members.
(b) To welcome into the Club those pilots who nevertheless do so.
(c) In view of their unique experience and knowledge of this specialised branch of aviation members shall use every opportunity to make their views and experiences known to as wide an audience as possible and shall make full use of all means of communication including the mass media for this purpose. In this context it shall be the duty of any member (in this clause referred to as "the Supporting Member") who shall be present when a member is expounding his views to persuade with the use of such force as may reasonably be necessary any non-member of the benefits to be gained by close attention to what is being said. In this context also members shall be allowed

57

reasonable artistic licence in recounting their experiences so as to extract the last ounce of drama from the situation.
(d) To visit sick and injured pilots and their passengers in any hospital or other institution. At least one visit shall be made by one member who shall report to the Committee upon the physical condition of the injured member and the attractiveness or otherwise of the attendant medical staff and upon these considerations the Committee shall base its decision as to the number and extent of future visits to be paid to such sick or injured member.

Item 9 of the B.C.C. Constitution was the Club Motto: "Newtonious Cavit" – "Newton was right."

Arthur Tyrrell was indeed a top boffin but he was endearingly naive. Older than the rest of us, his absent-minded lapses with his Turbulent would have us rushing forward to help. For instance there was his incurable habit of turning the hot VW engine over to listen to each compression. To do this he would put ear to the cowling and pull the propeller through regardless of chocks, aircraft direction or the possibility of a hot-spot starting the engine. Every Club should have an Arthur.

Arthur had a dream. Like all fictional inventors, Arthur in real life was straight out of a book. His home experiments were his very life, but the constant domestic pressure from a house-proud wife to keep tidying up got him down. The dream – a place of his own.

But timing was important, for Arthur was an honourable man. The years went by. He couldn't move whilst the children were still at school or, for that matter, whilst they continued to live at home. Yet when they eventually moved away he still bided his time, forever seeking the right moment.

His children, who fully understood, offered their help, but leaving the Dragon, as he lovingly called her, wasn't something to do lightly. His affection for his wife was real and I know it was returned, it was just that they were incompatible. Put simply: the freedom to invent on the kitchen table agin a tidy house on the other. We in the Club followed this ongoing saga with growing fascination.

Then one day an excited Arthur told us that, unknown to the Dragon, he'd bought an isolated bungalow in deepest Kent. Now it was just a matter of moving, all that remained was to tell his wife. Trouble was he couldn't pluck up the courage to do so. The solution, he assured us, was to leave the house at the dead of night whilst the Dragon was asleep.

The children hired a big lorry in which to coast up to the house in the early hours, load up in silence, and then push the lorry out of earshot before restarting the engine. It all happened as planned except that once down the road they couldn't restart the engine and, not knowing what to do next, humped the lot back. The Dragon slept on. I don't think that Arthur ever tried again. As age crept over him he drifted out of our orbit, another character that brought some colour to Redhill with what I suppose was as true a love story that was ever told.

QUOTES (two from Robin Blech):

Landing at Gatwick, on short finals, a wide-eyed female passenger turned to me and said: "At what point do you put the feet down?"

An inbound aircraft to London accidentally reported himself as at FL 950 instead of 95. Approach controller without hesitation: "Roger Papa Mike, fire retro-rockets, report re-entry, and splash down in Staines Reservoir."

CLUB NEWS: DECEMBER 1967

1967 was a year to forget. A year of strike and crisis enhanced only by grand summer. Yet for the Club it was a successful 10th year. Unheralded, we notched new records. Never before has the Club had more members, or flown more hours or tugged more gliders. But if no one will shed tears for '67, what of '68?

Like the born optimist I am, I see an eventful year ahead for the Club. New aircraft are en route; the hangars are overfull of exotic machines, with many new members eager to fly them. The touring boys had a vintage year in '67 and will better themselves in '68, and the display and aerobatic divisions are cock-a-hoop. It doesn't do any harm once in a while to play a modest trumpet note – it is the world's greatest flying Club and, as editor, I get a constant stream of letters from all over the world assuring me that this is so. If absence makes the heart grow fonder, then the affection for the Tiger Club and Redhill amounts to home-sickness for so many members overseas. So from all of us in the Home Country we send Christmas greetings to all our absent friends, and we can wish them no better for '68 than "return soon." 1968 will be a good year.

Christmas has brought so many letters and cards, and none came further then the one from John Ayres on the Antarctic Survey; or none more touching than "Bish's" letter of regret that, because he is still in hospital, he is unable to send cards this year, but to tell the blokes he is thinking of them, Drop him a card instead – to St. Richards Hospital in Chichester, Sussex.

The social side of '68 begins with a Film Show on the 24th January at Kronfeld. Ken Smith is organising it, and I know he'll welcome every support. Incidentally, the Kronfeld is your Club too. Membership of this comfortable Club for the flying fraternity is an added benefit of associate T.C. membership. It is central, friendly, and one visit will rapidly lead to another. Go along. The Annual Dinner follows closely on the 16th February. The price has gone up a bit to £3.7.6d, but a sceptical Editor took a peep at the accounts for last year and can confirm that that sum is indeed a most reasonable figure for such a superb venue. N.B. Sausages will not be worn this year.

The '67 de Salis Trophy has gone to Pete Jarvis. This fine award goes to the member who, in the opinion of the Committee, has contributed the most to the Club during his or her first year. Pete earned his Trophy the hard way – by aerobatting in the displays.

FROM THE CHAIRMAN

The Chairman is not Father Christmas although he may look rather like it sometimes, but it would appear to our Editor that it is my job to send to all members of the Tiger Club a Christmas message. So here goes:

MERRY CHRISTMAS EVERYONE! And if you break any more aeroplanes in 1968 I will wring your blankety necks, but thanks all the same for a good happy year. I think that the objects we stand for, and the way we want to go about it, were well maintained and the reputation of the Club among those that know us, both at home and abroad, has continued to grow.

When you get your membership booklet early in the New Year, have another look at our objects and our charter. Like Christmas they have stood the test of time and will, I hope, go on for a long time yet.

The original Aims and Charter were probably drafted by Nepean Bishop with Norman's broad hand on the emphasis.

Tiger Club Aims:

(a) To provide the means of meeting for those who take an interest in light aeroplane racing, displays, aerobatics and other forms of competition.
(b) To provide its members with good sporting flying at the lowest possible cost.
(c) To work for improvement in standards of light aeroplane flying, aerobatics and private flying generally.

The Tiger Club Charter:

A member of the TIGER CLUB undertakes:

1. Always to go out of his or her way to assist other members in aeronautical matters.
2. Always to fly with courtesy and with especial attention to safety and comfort of others.
3. Never to use an aeroplane for any disreputable or unworthy purpose.

In recent years someone has added a further item to our Charter:

4. Never to act or to use an aeroplane so as to breach any Law or Aeronautical Regulation.

"Look, Inspector, we've told them not to do it."

Norman, bless him, would not have bowed his head in that direction.

The Club's tribute to Sir Geoffrey de Havilland. St. Albans Abbey Memorial Service, July 21st 1965. This fine photograph, thought lost, emerged recently. Photo: Author's collection.

TOP: Smith's Lawn, Windsor, c.1976, at the start of the Formula 1 racing season. Prince Philip, who took an active part in the formation of F.1, is shown here with FARA Chairman Michael Jones.
Photo: via Michael Jones.
BOTTOM: A characteristic portrait of Norman Jones framed by the Jodel Excellence, Redhill, March 1972. Photo: probably John Blake.

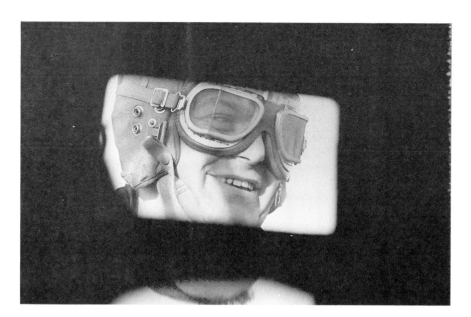

TOP: Michael Jones chauffeuring John Blake in the well-loved Fox Moth, February 1967 (taken from the passenger cabin).
Photo: John Blake.
BOTTOM: A typical bad fly-day at Redhill. Folk gather to chat just inside the rain line. Outside the Fox Moth and Musketeer stoically endure. Photo: Author's collection.

Turbs always needed a firm hand. Norman Jones giving his all at Redhill – a delightful portrait. Photo: via Michael Jones.

TOP: 'The Draw.' Strange photo, this. Probably early 1967, location unknown but it is obviously an aerobatic briefing. Left to right: Nick Carter, Andrew Chadwick, Dave Allan (pulling face), James Black, and there's Frances MacRae's face looking up. Photo: probably John Blake.
BOTTOM: Have no idea what Bill Innes was going on about, but Barry Griffiths was paying attention. Wonderful shot, Redhill, early '70s. Photo: probably John Blake.

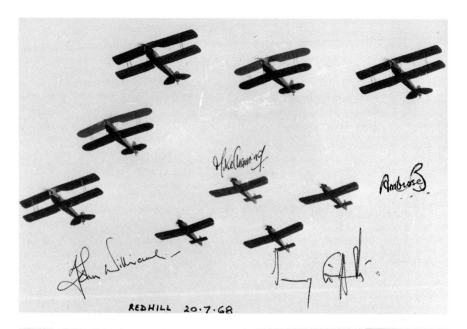

REDHILL 20·7·68

TOP: A magnificent portrayal of a typical Tiger Club opening nine-plane formation. Redhill, July 20th 1968. Photo: via Ambrose Barber.
BOTTOM: A truly hairy happening. Ambrose Barber during his rudderless and very shaky journey back to Redhill (story related on pp. 85-86). Photo: via Ambrose Barber.

1968

QUIZ, LEGAL FUND AND "BISH" R.I.P.

Michael's Xmas quiz – published last month – aroused a lot of interest and indeed the veracity of some of the traditional answers is now in question. Whilst Michael and the Editor get involved sorting out the facts, we are awarding first prize to Barry Griffiths for a valiant effort, and we are printing it word for word, making, as we do so, all the usual disclaimers.

"I cannot give the answers to all of the questions but I can to some of them and in case they may be of use to you, here they are:

Aircraft collides with ILS Mast:
I have no idea but I would like to meet the pilot concerned.
(The aircraft was Tiger G-ASKP, its pilot Tony Haig-Thomas, Hatfield. The occasion, Sir Geoffrey de Havilland's Memorial Service, July 1965. We borrowed a Cirrus Moth at short notice from Panshanger flown by Desmond Penrose and all was well. The diamond nine made a moving sight above St. Albans Abbey.)

Inverted across Channel:
The same, except please read plural for singular.
(It was the late Elwyn McAully in Tiger "The Bishop," G-APDZ, fitted with the successful inverted power system designed by Rollason's Tommy Thompson. The year – '59 or '60.)

All Aircraft bite Fools:
I think that this follows Norman's take-off at Sandown with the fuel off. If this statement is held by the Committee to be libellous, then I emphatically withdraw it.

Turb into Gatwick:
This was Robin d'Erlanger. The reason was that the aircraft was so small that the Controller thought he was undershooting. I recall that he got so frustrated that he made off to Biggin Hill.

Damaged Propeller:
This was James Gilbert and the island was, I think, Stornoway or at any rate one of the Outer Hebrides. He borrowed a hacksaw from a curious native, sawed off the undamaged tip of his propeller, judging the measurement by eye to balance the damaged tip, found that the two balanced perfectly and, after a somewhat protracted take-off, flew the aircraft back in this condition – despite all expert advice to the contrary – to Newcastle-upon-Tyne. The success of this enterprise is usually attributed to Mr Gilbert's noted immunity to the effect of vibration.

Don't interrupt me while I'm crashing!:
This was the Australian member who was invariably equipped with a weather-beaten face and a metallic shirt, the latter usually being attributed to the fact that he once saw Liberace on Television and never got over it. His name was Arthur

Humphreys. The occasion in question occurred, I think, during a return from France where Mr Humphreys was unsuccessfully endeavouring to follow the railway line to Redhill. One of his passengers drew his attention to the fact that he was in a spin – which indeed he was – when he uttered the remark in question which must go down in history as one of aviation's classics. Very shortly after uttering this remark, Mr Humphreys' aircraft – a Jackaroo appropriately enough – finished up in a hop field. Fellow members found it hard to forgive Mr Humphreys, not so much for the damage to the aircraft as for the damage to the hops.

Suspected Assassin:
This, of course, was James Baring who was on his way in his Turbulent to do some skiing in Switzerland. Due to the very limited luggage capacity of the Turbulent, he found it necessary to wear most of his skiing outfit – especially the boots – and thus presented a somewhat curious picture when discovered wandering about a French village after being lost in cloud for some considerable time. Especially as he was still wearing his leather flying hat (which, presumably, he had forgotten to remove) and carrying a flight case. His ultimate destination was, I believe, Geneva, and the General whose life it was thought he was threatening was none other than de Gaulle himself. A full account of this would make a most amusing article in itself but the outcome was that, once it was discovered that James was neither Algerian nor bomb-carrying, he was sent on his way to Beauvais with a tremendous send-off from the local Chief of Police (with whom he had prudently dined on the previous night). He had to go to Beauvais because all unscheduled flights were banned in France at this time and he had to continue his journey to Switzerland in a more prosaic manner.

The Curé:
I think that the aircraft which was to be called "The Curé" was the Tiger Moth that followed chronologically "The Bishop" and "The Archbishop." I did not know that the name "The Curé" had ever been suggested; I did hear that the more practical suggestion of calling it "The Actress" was mooted but was unfortunately vetoed on some quite irrelevant and no doubt puritanical ground. If I am right in this supposition, the eventual name given the aircraft was "The Deacon."

Who was "Tiger Tim"?:
I really can't think unless it was the original children's comic character who, of course, is still very much with us.
(The first Club "Tiger Tim" was Bev Snook – later Chairman of the RAeC. Norman Jones presented Bev with a tiger-skin helmet circa 1958, quite why no one can now remember, but was probably because at that time Bev was a bit of a 'goer' with a record of adventurous delivery flights all over the globe. Bev was certainly wearing it at the 1959 National Races. The helmet was to be an ongoing award but it disappeared. I was suspected of lifting it. Norman, who wasn't without a mischievous sense of humour, had quietly given me one too. Mine disappeared as well.)

<u>Two in a Single-Seat Tiger</u>:
Ah! yes – I know the answer to this one. The passenger was James Baring on his way back from the same trip to Scotland in which James Gilbert flew to the Outer Hebrides. James' Turbulent severed an oil pipe and he landed in extremely remote and hilly country. Neil Williams landed in a single-seat Tiger, onto the wing of which James mounted and, with his head stuck belligerently forward and his beard flowing in the wind like some furious Viking who had had to hitch a lift, was ferried in this improbable attitude to the next aerodrome to organise spare parts. The registration letters of the rescuing aircraft unfortunately escape me but, at a guess, I would say it was 'AA.

<u>A/c Stricken Cow</u>:
I have no idea but I resent the slight to the lady member of the Tiger Club concerned. (It was not a *real* cow, was it?)"
(The aircraft was our Puss Moth, the pilot now forgotten, and it was a real cow . . . or so the story went. The year, 1963.)

CLUB NEWS: JANUARY 1968
I know that during the recent snow there was considerable temptation to put aircraft on some of the skis that for so long have been hanging in the hangar. How many members remember the snows of 1963 and of the 5 Ski-Turbs and Piper Cub that did so much flying during that white spell when all the land was one big flying field? A plea (an association of ideas): just who is it who regularly sends me a copy of the R.A.F. Ski Association Newsletter? It just arrives – anonymously.

1967 saw a record number of Aerotows, no less than 2,500. Our congratulations to Charles Mackenzie, and on a quite different score our congratulations too to Mavis Harriott, our treasurer, on the arrival of a baby son in early December. From Canada we learn that Lloyd Harding is still flying hard and has met member Dennis Culver. Both lament the lack of real sporting aircraft over there. Dave Allen finally made it to Melbourne, and as everybody now knows, James Baring and Tom Storey finally made it to Teheran and back after a series of adventures neither can quite bring themselves to talk about yet. They had successfully delivered a Beagle Husky which they had flown down the Med via Cyprus during the crisis. They were buzzed by MiGs and survived several diplomatic incidents. I'll keep at them to write it up. Incidentally, one version of the MiG story I heard was that they successfully avoided interception for about 30 minutes whilst they listened to Radar directing the MiGs looking for them at around 2,000 ft whilst our lads were overflying them at 6,000. It was only when eventually the MiGs pulled up to go home that the Husky was spotted. The story gets ragged about here but it seems that beaming smiles, military salutes and the Husky on the point of stall did the trick – that or the MiGs were running out of fuel! Visitors to the hangar will know that Tom returned to his latest favourite project, the Wonderplane. It's progressing well.

"Bish" has been awarded the Clem Pike trophy for 1967, and the Club Committee, already numbered in the 20s, has been further boosted with the addition of Tom Storey as P.R.O., G. Crabb (for gliding), Ninny Fisher (House Committee) and Bunny Bramson (as the Hon. C.F.I.) – good luck to them all.

"G.B." reports that Robin Adair, lately Assistant High Commissioner, Nicosia – he flew a Tripacer out there for the Flying Club last year – has been appointed High Commissioner in Brunei (N. Borneo). All our good wishes go with him on his forthcoming appointment.

Of flying there is little to relate for the month of December, but can personally vouch for the re-engined Beta. Its Continental 90 hp gives considerable zip on take-off and its initial 2,000 ft climb is breathtaking. Top speed is a secret. Rollasons and Tiltmans are busy building a further batch of three and are looking for likely buyers. Interested? It is hoped that those fine aircraft will feature in the coming season's displays.

1968 was destined to become a classic year, but even at the years' beginning there were ominous warnings that the Law had its beady eye on us, an awareness if you like that the growing civil aviation departments had begun swotting up on the Air Navigation Acts. Light aviation seems to be enjoying themselves too much, their thinking seemed to go, let's start scratching around. Whatever, Jack Piercy who ran the Tiger Club's Legal fund was alert to the warning. He wrote:

THE LEGAL DEFENCE FUND
The Tiger Club Charter in Action

The Club rules provide for the Legal Fund and set forth its constitution. However, many of those who've joined since 1963 may not be aware of just why the fund came into being, what it has done and is doing, and why it deserves the support of every member.

It all began with the prosecution at Kingston of five of our pilots for an alleged low-flying formation during a display in Ireland. They fought and lost and their costs alone came to nearly £1,200.

The case brought home to us very forcibly three main things. Firstly, the very heavy penalties imposed for comparatively innocuous offences. The tendency is to impose the maximum fine whether or not it is a first offence. Secondly, the formidable costs involved in defending oneself when the full weight and resources of the Crown are brought to bear, which they are in every prosecution. Thirdly, the ill-informed prejudice met with in the Civil courts. I've seen jurors listening with open-mouthed horror to the prosecution's lurid descriptions of such crimes as "near" misses by half a mile. It's been said that in the eyes of the Layman all pilots are 8 foot tall. If so, here is a chance to cut them down to size!

Anyway strong feelings were aroused and we decided to form a legal defence fund, not only to contribute towards the costs of the five pilots, but to provide as well a permanent pool to help other members who might be similarly placed in the future. The response was heart-warming. Over £800 was subscribed in just over two months by a membership very much smaller than it is now. The cry became "give the equivalent of two hours in your favourite aeroplane," and a striking tribute was paid to the popularity of the Turbulent. Seriously, cheques for

£10 and £20 were common and represented a big sacrifice by some young people. The Fund paid £650 towards the costs of its first case.

Happily, we've not yet had to face another case of such magnitude. But we've not been inactive. In 1967 for example, four applications were considered by the Committee and grants made totalled £131. Unfortunately 1968 hasn't started too well; I've had preliminary warning of two or possibly three applications for assistance, and if it is decided to help, more funds will certainly be needed.

Therefore I'm going to make a new appeal to every member who has not already contributed. Please don't leave the burden to part of the membership, and don't worry too much about the equivalent of hours in aeroplanes you can't afford. If every member could send in the odd guinea (or two) we would have little to worry about for the time being. So act NOW.

Finally, a word of warning. Let nobody run away with the idea that the Fund will encourage irresponsible behaviour or bad airmanship. Every application is carefully considered by the Club Committee and I can tell you that cases deemed unworthy of assistance have been and will continue to be turned down without compunction. Put another way, you cannot expect to invoke article ONE of the Tiger Club Charter to cover breaches of articles TWO and THREE.

STOP PRESS – The Editor

It was with great sadness that I learnt of the death of "Bish" – C.A. Nepean Bishop – on 14th January 1968. May I, on behalf of the Club, extend our deepest sympathy to his widow Gladys. "G.B." will write more fully for the next issue.

PILOTS AND THE LAW
"Dos and Don'ts"

The Editor apologises for including here the substance of what was printed in a 1957 Newsletter which still has great relevance today. Jack Piercy, who looks after our Legal Fund, has asked us also to mention that the Fund is still receiving subscriptions. If anyone has a guilty conscience . . . we will say no more.

1) First of all, DO make yourself familiar with the regulations with which you have to conform as a pilot. You will find them all in the latest Air Navigation Order 1966 and the latest Rules of the Air, Air Traffic Control Regulations 1966. Copies of these are in the office at Redhill and can also be obtained from H.M. Stationery Office or the British Light Aviation Centre. You may need a damp towel round your head and a long dry evening to understand them, but they are THE LAW and the basis of any action which may be taken against you.

2) If you do put yourself in the wrong by infringing some regulation, DON'T argue the toss with an exasperated Flying Control Officer or Airport Commandant. Quite a lot of them have been in an aircraft themselves at one time or another, and have not entirely forgotten what it was like. "A soft answer turneth away wrath"; and it's wonderful what a gracious and unqualified apology can sometimes do to avert a prosecution. Play safe with the apology even if you think you were right. You can look up the regulations again when you get home, and if that proves

you *were* right after all, you can still have the fun of writing to him and telling him so.

3) DON'T discuss the case with the police detective who comes to "make further enquiries" or to serve a summons on you. It will be much too late then to do any good; and you can bet your life that anything you say will be taken down and used in evidence against you. If you must have a chat with the nice friendly policeman, then keep the conversation to such innocuous topics as the Cost of Living and the wife's bronchitis.

4) If you do get a letter from the authorities concerning your misdeeds, <u>DO</u> answer it promptly and courteously. If you think it is a hot letter and may lead to further trouble, get advice.

5) If the blow falls, <u>DON'T</u> try to handle the Summons with a Do-it-Yourself Kit unless you are *quite* satisfied that you are a Hitherto Undiscovered Forensic Genius. You may be right, but it's long odds against. It takes five years even to qualify as a solicitor, and a good few years more to learn all the tricks of the trade.

6) So <u>DO</u> take your summons straight to your solicitor. <u>DO</u> get in touch with the Membership Secretary and Legal Fund Secretary, Jack Piercy, as soon as possible. He can give you advice on a good solicitor, but he hates receiving applications to the legal fund, deserving or otherwise, if he has not been put in the picture EARLY.

7) <u>DON'T</u> forget that the maximum penalty for most flying offences is 6 months imprisonment, plus a fine of £200, and the magistrates probably won't have a clue as to whether or not your offence is a bad one of its kind, so even if you are found guilty, your advocate's fee for convincing the Court that that *is* quite a trivial offence after all is going to be well worth the money.

8) <u>DON'T</u> forget that "accident, stress of weather or other unavoidable cause" is a defence to any flying prosecution, but that it's up to *you* to prove it. You can only prove it by giving evidence yourself in the witness-box, so <u>DO</u> take a day off and attend Court yourself, even if the hearing is in quite another part of the country where the incident actually occurred (as it probably will be). Incidentally, in that case your own solicitor will probably arrange for you to be defended by a colleague of his who practises in that particular Court.

9) <u>DO</u> give your solicitor all the help you can about the technicalities of flying, as he may not be a pilot himself. In certain cases he will be glad of some technical assistance, and may ask you if you can produce an expert witness.

Nothing seems to change. The advice – it was certainly written by a very knowing solicitor – is as true now as it was all those years ago, except it costs more nowadays.

CLUB NEWS: FEBRUARY 1968

No sooner had I mentioned the snow in the January issue than it all disappeared and with it the opportunity for many to fly the Ski-Turbs. But for a week members were making Redhill their mecca, just for the chance to try this novel form of flying. It was voted by all a great success. I can't remember now if anyone was towed on skis behind a Turb, but I know the idea was mooted. The latest edition to the fleet is the two-seater Stampe 'AVCO, resplendent in the now-traditional Club Colours. As one great admirer of the Rollason team I take off my hat to a beautiful piece of restoration.

The event of the month was, of course, the Annual Dinner to which Simon Ames, Secretary General of the RAeC, was invited as Guest of Honour. Sally, his lovely wife, presented the awards. It was an excellent evening complete with good food, few speeches and plenty of dancing; in fact a lot of fun. Nini would like to thank all those who helped with the Tombola, both those who donated the gifts and those who helped on the stand, especially Sally Ames, Za Za and Vivian. Tony Haig-Thomas has just got engaged to Julia Wilkinson, and they are getting married on April 25th at what is going to be something of an event in Tiger Club weddings. Tony's words, not mine! Afterwards they will both be returning to Saudi Arabia where Tony is flying Hunters at what is surely the best-paid mercenary job in the business. All our congratulations to them both.

C. A. NEPEAN BISHOP

So "Bish" has made his last 'take-off' – this time into flying history and of him much will be written – more remembered. For me and so many others, another chapter ended – yet not the *book*, for one reads on in the example of his superb flying – reflected in those lucky enough to have been his pupils, or flown under his guidance.

He and I first met in 1930 – at Woodley. He was then learning to fly with his instructor, "Pat" Giddy, at the Phillips & Powis School of Flying, gaining his RAeC Certificate in July and his 'A' licence in August. Since then, save for the war years, we have never lost touch.

His job in a bank precluded all but weekend and holiday flying – but it was not long before he had mastered the basic stuff and was showing a flair for aerobatics.

We flew together frequently – he becoming a leading member of the Reading Aero Club, of which he was at one time Honorary Secretary and Treasurer. He was then putting in around 80 hours flying a year – well above average.

Around 1936 he formed there one of the first "Groups" – called "The Moth Syndicate," with a DH.60 (Cirrus II) G-EBZL – and I'll bet that aircraft spent more time on its back than in level flight.

With the success of the Miles Hawk range of aeroplanes, the old Club changed somewhat in its nature – and "Bish" elected to transfer his energies to Brooklands, where his prowess and enthusiasm were quickly recognised. There he stayed through the prewar years.

When the Civil Air Guard was formed, "Bish" was one of the first to join, and at once got his Instructor's endorsement.

He joined the R.A.F.V.R. in 1940 – and after a refresher course at Prestwick (12 E.F.T.S.) was posted as an Instructor to Sywell (6 E.F.T.S.) and subsequently to Redhill (15 E.F.T.S.).

When this unit was moved to Carlisle, "Bish" went too – and it was there that one October morning he led the take-off of five "Maggies" which, because of frost on the wings, failed to unstick and were wrecked in formation at and around the perimeter hedge. No one was hurt.

About that time I lost touch. He was posted to Southern Rhodesia (25 E.F.T.S.) at Mount Hampden and was instructing on Harvards and Oxfords – though I heard by chance of his enthusiasm and the fantastic number of hours he was flying.

At the end of 1944, he was posted back to England – to instruct on Harvards, Oxfords and Ansons at the Blind Approach School at R.A.F. Watchfield – where we met and picked up the threads again.

He stayed there, becoming C.O. of No. 1547 B.A.T. flight until his demobilisation in 1946 – when back he went to the bank, having clocked up some 5,000 odd hours of flying.

Thereafter he kept his hand in – flying when he could – at Elstree and Biggin, until the Redhill Flying Club re-opened in 1947. He became their Instructor and so returned to Club flying.

And throughout those varied years – from Woodley to Redhill – whenever possible, aerobatics were his love. Dedicated – he was unswerving in his quest for perfection, and those who saw his performances could find neither fault nor equal.

When in 1957 Norman Jones asked him to be C.F.I. of the Tiger Club, he could have chosen no finer Tiger Moth exponent and, quick to appreciate his ability, built for him the first of the famous "Super Tigers," and named it "The Bishop." Subsequently "Bish's" performance on it in the Lockheed Aerobatic Competition will long be remembered.

Soon after he went to the Tiger Club, he asked me to join. Temporarily, circumstances prevented – but not long elapsed before I did join and "Bish" gave me my initial check at Croydon, and thereafter we never lost touch.

Needless to mention his great work over the years in the Tiger Club – nor how much our spirit and fame is due to him.

On his retirement from the bank and move to Bognor, he took on, in its early stages, the Seaplane Club – and to him must be accorded much of the success of this branch of our Club. About that time too his licence lapsed – and I shall never fail to be moved by his letter telling me he was not going to renew his licence as he wanted to decide when to stop, and not be told by the Ministry.

I was with him on the day of his last solo flight on his beloved 'CDC, after which we lunched nostalgically.

Letters galore – that was the form – I had hundreds of them and, if you could read them, there was mostly sense.

He left a vast assortment of Aeronautica: photographs, scrap-books and other material. These are now being sorted and allocated. He wrote prolifically to many aeronautical magazines and, indeed, a book, "Weekend Pilot," which was his biography. This, with a relative scrap-book, he has left to me; and both are, of course, available to the Tiger Club.

Of the several other facets of his life he was reticent. One-time Court Member and upper Freeman of GAPAN, he was too an Associate of both the Royal Aero Club and the Royal Aeronautical Society, and was awarded the Tissandier Diploma for his work in sporting flying.

He had a wonderful collection of old gramophone records – many of which were of brass bands, in which he delighted.

He could tell, on sight, the make, type, year of manufacture and route of *any* London omnibus anywhere. Similarly, his knowledge of railway engines was exceptional and he was, I always felt, the original aircraft spotter. Before he took up flying, his prowess at rowing was notable and to all of those hobbies he brought his unquenchable zest. We shall remember "Bish" – individually and as a Club. His immeasurable loyalty, enthusiasm and sheer hard donkey-work done for us, and sporting flying. His tantrums. His meticulous initial checks. His classic aerobatics. Those early night-flying sessions. The time he got lost leading a formation over Kent, going to a display. When he "landed" 'CDC on the peri-track with one leg of the undercart hanging down broken. Jumping the tape at displays. One could go on endlessly.

And now he's taken off for Utopia (P.P.O.), and I know that when I join him I bet I'll find he'll have all the angels – young and old – practising aerobatics.

"G.B.," February 1968

Hindsight is a singularly useful tool, and nowhere can it be better applied than in our memory of "Bish". "G.B." wrote in his staccato manner of the man he knew whilst "Bish's" presence was still all around him. It's easier to see now that "Bish" was a great deal more than "G.B.," in his immediate sadness, understood.

Legends grow, soaring up into that undisturbed blue of an airman's sky: only the best are remembered. Today I reflect that "Bish" is the only instructor I can think of worthy to join Cecil Pashley to be recalled as two of the country's finest teachers since flying began. They had much in common. Both were short untidy men who were totally dedicated and unassuming, yet brilliant in their ability to convey what's what with the minimum of interference. Please shake your head, it *is* a sweeping statement, set up to be shot down. I hope someone does so. Our instructors, all the thousands of them, deserve recognition.

BROUGHT BACK FROM DOWN UNDER
(From Martin Barraclough – April 1967)

At the airport where I work a private aircraft called the tower.

"Tower, you might inform the Boeing 707 which is about to take off from the north end that the object near my position that looks like a rock is really a turtle on the runway."

707: "Tower, we heard that transmission. Understand one turtle crossing runway."

Tower: "Based on available pilots' reports, turtle's course is orientated south east, heading towards Gate 5."

707: "Tower, can you give us information on turtle's speed and estimated time of runway clearance?"

Tower: "Computer calculations indicate turtle's speed around 200 feet an hour, maybe less in this quartering headwind. If present course and speed are maintained, runway should be clear in 8 minutes."

707: "Unable to wait due to fuel depletion; will employ evasive action on take-off roll."

Tower: "707, cleared for take-off. Be on alert for wake turbulence behind departing turtle."

Continued Martin: . . . "I had to go all the way to the Bush Pilots' Flying Club in Townsville, Queensland, to find this . . . ! Also on a plaque in the Club was the following food for thought: *'Flying, in itself, is not dangerous, but like the sea it is terribly unforgiving of any carelessness, incapacity or neglect.'*

[Editor's Note: By a strange coincidence the same ATC turtle story reached me around the same time via the Condor Group's newssheet, only they accredited it to "Skyliner," the TWA staff paper, who in turn pinpointed the incident at Kansas City Airport.]

Scoop Note: But not only did the Condor Boys run the one story; they also ran the warning – another visitor to Downsville?

THE ACTIVE, THE BEAGLE AND BOMBING THE NAVY

The Club's subscriptions for '68 stayed the same as the previous year, but the flying rates moved slightly upwards.

FLYING RATES TO TAKE EFFECT FROM 1ST FEBRUARY 1968

TIGER MOTH	£5.0.0
STAMPE	£5.10.0
CONDOR	£5.0.0
JODEL D.150 & DR.1050	£6.0.0
JODEL D.140	£8.0.0
TURBULENT	£3.0.0
SUPER CUB	£6.15.0
HUSKY	£6.15.0
SEA TIGER	£6.0.0
ARROW ACTIVE (restricted)	£5.10.0
PUSS MOTH	£5.10.0
FOX MOTH	£5.10.0
BETA (restricted)	£5.10.0

By today's aircraft availability the range on offer for the membership was breathtaking. Those marked as restricted were machines which needed a touch more care and an OK before taking one. To be frank the Active needs a lot more than a touch, but Michael Jones always allowed us to experience the odd fright now and then, something that was always present with the Active.

Of all the aircraft the Club flew, the Arrow Active earned a reputation for being a pig to land: it was. Stories about this much-loved aircraft abound. One member, Howard Rose, really wanted to fly it. (The Active, unlike any other aircraft, was never referred to as a 'she.' Female it was not). He probably saw it as a challenge. It's an interesting fact that few showed an inclination to fly it twice. I briefed Howard as best I could from outside of the cockpit – for it was a single-seater – and with my warnings ringing in his ears, things like "For gawd's sake land into wind and if it bounces on landing don't try and sort it out – go round again," he taxied off. I think I left him a touch worried, reasoning it better he treat with care than relax, especially before the end of the landing run, a moment that the hairy beast awaited with glee so it could groundloop.

Howard's first approach was long and with great care. He wasn't going to hurry things, and perhaps because he wasn't satisfied with his approach – usually around 75 mph – he went around again.

We watched all this with considerable interest. Someone said: "Let's go out and help him." A burst of laughter, and we rushed out to line the grass runway and knelt in a line, hands fervently together in solemn prayer. In shock, Howard made the best landing of his life.

Around this time one of the last British manufacturers of light aircraft was putting everything they had into producing a home replacement for the series of twin-engined aircraft flooding into Europe from the States. The company, based at Shoreham, was Beagle, and their excellent six-seater was the B.206. Every stop had been pulled out to produce a winner, even down to inviting the odd pilot to sit in a cockpit mock-up to comment on instrument and control positioning. Pee Wee even asked *me*. Pee Wee Judge was a Beagle test pilot, a long-time flyer with the Club and a good friend. True it was a bit like taking coals to Newcastle, but his tale of the westward ferry flight was as good as they come.

BY BEAGLE TO THE U.S.A. – "Pee Wee" Judge

I think that it is true that with most of us our flying career is punctuated by a series of 'targets,' the achievement of each of which gives a certain satisfaction of its own. A personal one, until recently ungratified, was to fly the Atlantic – perhaps not necessarily in the pioneering spirit of Alcock and Brown, Lindberg and the Mollisons, but at least in a more enterprising way than as airline passenger.

I recently had the opportunity to make good this ambition by delivering a Beagle B.206S from Shoreham to New York. The aircraft was a standard production one without extra tankage and the only special equipment additions were those mandatory for the route, consisting of a ferry HF radio installation with trailing aerial for use when out of VHF range, a dinghy and an Arctic survival pack.

Jim Jewkes, Beagle Deputy Service Manager, came along for company and to share the goodies in the survival pack in the event of an unscheduled landing.

71

The first leg to Prestwick in Scotland produced what was without doubt the roughest weather of the trip, but after Customs clearance and a very comprehensive Met briefing we were OFF across a very wet-looking bit of ocean, en route to Iceland.

We flew outbound on a suitable radial of the Stornoway VOR until out of range of this aid and then just sat back and waited for the Vestmannaejar MDB on an island south of Iceland to come up on the ADF. We had been asked to report on HF when passing 60° North 10° West and when approaching our ETA we were interested to hear a DC-4 bound in the opposite direction give an ETA for this position within one minute of ours. Confidence in Navigation, Met, winds and compass received a boost when the aforementioned DC-4 was soon to pass a couple of miles away just below us.

At long last Iceland's snowy mountains appeared on the horizon, followed by the lower black volcanic coastline – a rather grim-looking place. Near Vest-whatsisname island was another small islet, unmarked on the map, which turned out to be a recently-emerged active volcano.

We remembered to wind in the trailing aerial after contacting Reykjavik on VHF and being cleared for a straight approach. Yes, there was the harbour and town of Reykjavik . . . but where was the aerodrome? The visibility was reported as 50 kilometres (and looked more) but there was no sign of anything that looked like an airfield. . . . Oh! well, we've got the beacon tuned, and that must be somewhere near the field, so press on. Eventually, on what seemed to be quite short finals, there it was – in the middle of the town! We had been warned that the surface was rough, and they weren't kidding; it was a sort of tarmac Shoreham!

After a nightstop in the comfortable Loftleidie Hotel, we were off bright and early with quite a good forecast (except for the headwinds that dogged us all the way across) for Sondrestromfjord in Greenland. The crossing of the Denmark Strait from Iceland to the east coast of Greenland was over 8/8 cover, but no matter, there was nothing to see but ocean – but was there? Shortly before our ETA for the coast, the cloud broke and to our surprise we found ourselves flying over a mass of islands (and the chart didn't show any there). Then the penny dropped – they were icebergs. I had never seen icebergs before and was greatly impressed by their size and beautiful colouring, shading from the deep blue of the submerged portion through pale blue to whiter-than-white. Greenland itself appeared shortly after, a fringe of jagged black mountains with the towering mass of the ice cap rearing up inland. This extraordinary ice cap is virtually uncharted, but is said to rise to over 11,000 feet . . . we gave it the benefit of the doubt, went on to oxygen and climbed to 14,000 feet. . . . Rather than white the surface of the ice cap is a dirty pale grey colour and wrinkled all over like a prune. Navigation across the ice cap is easy, however, American DEWline stations provide radar tracking and at one point we passed over one of those lonely outposts; it looked like a replica of St. Pauls Cathedral in icing sugar.

A radar cloudbreak was necessary at Sondrestromfjord due to a front over the west coast of Greenland. On emerging from the overcast an unreal scene, rather like a monochrome photograph, presented itself . . . the huge grey runway ahead, flanked by grey mountains, with the icy waters of the fjord in the foreground and the whole lot bathed in the flat grey Arctic light.

A quick refuel, meal (I don't know what it was but it was tasty), charming Scandinavian officials who relieved us of £69.10.0 landing/handling fee (this must be a record), a smile from round Eskimo faces, and Met briefing (better get going before the front moves in over Frobisher Bay), and we were off again for Frobisher in the Northern Territory of Canada. Our concern for the weather of this destination was very real as this was probably the critical leg from the radio aid aspect . . . the beacons at Frobisher are renowned for their weakness and the charts give a sinister warning that compasses are unreliable in this area. However, we arrived there before the front in gin-clear conditions, and on requesting landing instructions a friendly Canadian voice said he didn't mind in which direction we landed – so we took our pick and rubbed our wheels for the first time on the North American continent.

Frobisher provided a pleasant nightstop with the hospitable local airline in their hutted camp, probably the biggest T-bone steak I have ever eaten (well, most of it) and a lengthy delay next morning while we waited for the Mountie to arrive (in a truck, not on a horse) to clear us through Customs. By this time the front had caught us up and we experienced some pretty grotty weather conditions ranging from snow to freezing rain until the weather picked up some 200 miles later over the Labrador coast on route to Goose Bay. Goose Bay is an active R.C.A.F. base but it seemed odd to find R.A.F. erks there servicing visiting V-bombers.

The scenery of Northern Canada has been rightly praised and it was truly beautiful, but on the next leg we were deprived of the sight of the St. Lawrence by a large bank of fog and (due to the Mountie-made delay) we ran out of daylight and arrived at Quebec after dark. The French Canadians of Quebec proved to be just as friendly as their countrymen at Frobisher and just couldn't have been more helpful to transiting strangers.

The final leg of the flight to New York was the shortest, but proved to be one of the most interesting. There can be only one word of description for the American Air Traffic Control System – 'Efficiency.' It is at least ten years ahead of anything in Europe, and with the number of aircraft flying around it has to be! The New York Zone, colloquially known as "The Bird Cage," just has to be experienced to be believed.

We landed at JFK International to clear Customs and then a short 10-minute low-altitude flight to our final destination, La Guardia, with a glimpse en route of the Manhattan skyline.

When he heard our British callsign (and had established that we were not a B.O.A.C. Speedbird) one New York controller said "Say, did you bring that little ship all the way across the Atlantic? Gee, you must be tired"; we weren't.

73

Pee Wee Judge was as smooth and experienced a pilot as one could find. To fly formation with Pee Wee was to have Mr Reliable as a companion. Weaned on the early jets for the Navy as the Rolls Royce test pilot, here was an exceptional operator. He lived in Shoreham and was always to be seen with his little dog, who adored Pee Wee – probably because he fed him – and growled at the rest of us.

Was there ever a better way to nudge one's memory than to open an old logbook? An entry for April stopped me in my tracks. It read: *"21st April. Tiger 'AA (a single-seater) – Redhill-Sandown, Sandown-Portsmouth, Portsmouth-Redhill. Total time 1:35."* The remarks column read: *"via Selsey looking for minesweeper,"* and *"via minesweeper and bombing."* Cryptic wasn't in it. Then it began to come back.

The Royal Navy and the Tiger Club had a bit of a thing going around this time. Quite how it all started is now lost in the mists of history. Perhaps it had all begun with a casually-dropped invitation to drop in and see them sometime that induced the full Turbulent team to accept a visit to land on *"Hermes,"* an aircraft carrier. Everyone got very excited, but the top brass got wind of the escapade and the invitation was modified. Be our guests, but please leave your aeroplanes at home.

Whether it was this link with the Navy or not we got ourselves a second invitation: to strafe a Naval minesweeper that was going to be lurking two or three miles off the tip of Selsey Bill on a certain day at a certain hour. If there had to be a reason for the fun, exercising the RNVR gun crews would sound acceptable.

We gathered early at Redhill. It was a lovely sunny morning. To get nearer to the coming action we decided to station ourselves at Sandown on the Isle of Wight and on the way take a sneaky look for the Navy. Once at Sandown, not having spotted our quarry, we reckoned it was pointless to attack empty-handed so we purchased the local shop's entire stock of one-pound flour bags; plans were agreed, watches synchronised.

The Channel was calm, sunny above a mistiness that restricted visibility over the sea to under a mile. To ensure surprise a decoy was selected to engage first from the direction of the mainland, and whilst the guns were pointing the wrong way the real attack by the other five aircraft led by S/Ldr Robin Voice would come in at wave height from the west. As decoy I set off.

With a minute plus to go I swept out from the tip of Selsey Bill at 500 feet and shortly I spotted a ship's wake and with throttle wide open commenced my dive. The warship – I didn't know minesweepers were that big – loomed large. I'd caught the ship unawares for its guns were still ranged fore and aft.

At a hundred feet I lobbed my first flour bomb, dodged a mast and in a tight turn attacked again. The skipper seemed all at odds. The water boiled at his stern as the ship answered to both helm and power. As he turned I released a second bomb and still the crews weren't at their guns. Puzzled, I scanned the surrounding murk for the others, but they must have missed their way, so I carried on the attack to cover their approach. Out of flour, and a bit put out by the lack of response – the ship was now sailing in a circle – I gained height; I'd done my best to uphold the Club's honour, so I waggled my wings and flew off to our rendezvous point, Portsmouth.

No sooner had I got out to stretch my legs than the others appeared and stream-landed near me. "Where were you, Benjy?" they yelled; "you missed a terrific strafe." When I told them the laughter faded; the question – who had found the right boat? Privately, I think they did.

BLAKE'S SPAIN, LAW, GOOD GUYS AND AMBROSE'S RUDDER

CLUB NEWS: MARCH – APRIL 1968

March wasn't much of a month for flying, beset as it was by the very high winds from the west. It was easy for those sheltering in the lee of the hangar to believe all was well but, as I tried myself, flight out there was indeed a handful. It isn't often a Jodel Mascaret can be seen to fly up wind and make no more speed than 5 mph. At the point of stall it actually began to move backwards!

In the hangar the Beta is having mass balances fitted to its ailerons, and a neat job they are making of it too – the weights completely buried in the wing and new wing tips are going on as well.

Our favourite ferry pilot, Janet Ferguson, writing in modest vein in the 99s newsletter reports:

"I have had two crop-sprayer ferry flights since the last newsletter. First in November a Snow Commander from Rotterdam to Athens (when I was incredibly lucky to have an absolutely cloudless day for the Rotterdam-Graz Austria leg which included crossing the Alps – as the aircraft didn't even have a turn-and-slip this weather was extremely helpful). Then just after Christmas I took a Cessna Agwagon from Cranfield to Asmara in Ethiopia – this also went quite well on the whole, though a complete re-routing was necessary when I was virtually trapped by snow and fog in France."

At a guess I'd say her ferrying experience (remember those Beagle 206s to Australia?) is currently unequalled by anyone, male or female. Ron Jacobs sent me a cutting from the local paper, in which it was reported that member Wendy Cook is now a Pan Am stewardess – and hopping between Seattle and all points west to Hawaii. From a cold and windy airfield in March it all sounds too good to be true.

The comment about aircraft stationary above the airfield would not have raised an eyebrow at Redhill in those days. Whenever the wind got up there was always someone attempting to demonstrate their ability to hover. The accepted method was to fly slowly into wind positioned exactly above the onlookers on the tarmac and reduce power until one was hanging in the air a hairsbreadth above the stall, and then by joggling with the throttle attempt to stay there. From the ground we judged keenly. I never saw an untoward moment, although there was often an incipient stall visible as the aircraft gently nodded, to be caught by throttle or a modest loss of height.

THE LATEST FROM JOHN BLAKE
Tuesday, 19th March, Seville, Spain

This place (Tablad airfield, a Spanish MU south of Seville) is out of this world. We have 27 Heinkel 111 and 18 Messerschmitt Me.109, all in authentic German markings, and the place is swarming with German troops and vehicles. General Milch (a charming man) and Kesselring are here, with Milch's personal Junkers Ju.52 and another one of Lufthansa and Herr Hitler arrived today. All of course, for the B. of B. film – or, as we prefer to call it here, the Batalla de Inglaterra. Anyway that's what the signposts here say.

The Heinkels have been hired from the Spanish Air Force, who use them for transport, target-towing, bombing and so on. The Me's belong to the company. There is a German fighter forward base and mess down by the river and the Heinkels lined up for Milch's inspection look magnificent. We even have some carefully "battered" ones for crash sequences. The camera B-25, loaded with camera mounts and expensive gear, arrived here yesterday and starts air-to-air shooting soon. My particular responsibility is briefing pilots to fly the battle formations we want and seeing that they appear over the cameras in the right place. Our mass of Heinkels is going to look fine in the air, with fighter escort. When Viv Bellamy arrives with a lone Spitfire he is going to be a bit pushed!

From some parts of the airfield, it is often impossible to tell that you are not on a German base; many of the actors are German in fact – the mass of extras are Spanish Air Force personnel. It was quite alarming at first to suddenly find yourself in a mass of charging German troops. The mind retreated 24 years and came abruptly back to the fact that it was tea-break at Tablada.

Tomorrow, I have been warned, I may have to put on a Kraut hat and be a face at the window of the Ju.52 in an air-to-air shot. A lot of the time will be spent on rehearsal in either bombers or B-25, to see the effect of one's work – good or bad.

We have a two-seater Me.109, usually flown by Colonel Santa Cruz, chief test pilot of Hispano Aviacion, the firm that built the Spanish 109s (Merlin-engined like the Heinkels) but the second seat is invariably taken by pressmen and joyriding is strictly taboo. Very much a working place. Perhaps the most fascinating thing here is the noise; can you imagine 50 or 60 Merlins all running together?

There is a local flying Club here, with Cub, Super Cub, Champion (American-registered), Globe Swift and a couple of Jungmann. Those have the original low-powered engine. Two of the Spanish aerobatic team from Bilbao are here with us, Arrabal and Ugarte (the latter also from Moscow). Manuel Ugarte is flying a Messerschmitt for the film; Arrabal had ear trouble recently and is off flying. (Note for James and Neil; practically no one is called Manuel and there is no "vuelo artistic" – not even "invertido." Very disappointing.) Manuel tells me that the Spanish Zlins have been locked away since Moscow, and no one has been allowed to fly them. None of them know if they are even competing in Magdeburg. He sends Neil his regards.

We have several members of the Confederate Air Force working here, who appear alternatively dressed as German officers or as colonels (the only rank in the CAF) in the southern army. Or as bits of both.

Barry would appreciate the photographic service here in Seville. 24-hour service for negative processing and 10 x 8 prints 2s 6d each. There is so much light you only have to think about a shot to over-expose.

Over-exposure is a sin here; one chap was threatened with arrest for indecent exposure for taking his shirt off on the airfield. He was such a puny character I should have thought the only possible charge would have been fraud or misrepresentation. Two of the more nubile wives arrived in miniskirts, but were not encouraged to continue wearing them. All the same, one almost put a photographer in hospital just getting out of the B-25. Curiously enough, a Spanish dancer in an all-enveloping floor-length dress exudes far more sex than any miniskirt.

Went to a Spanish cabaret the other night; four and a half hours of Flamenco and Sevillana dancing and that Spanish singing that sounds as if he has caught something in a mangle, but the whole extremely professional and very entertaining. Only snag was the super-casino prices; 200 pesetas for a beer (162 to the pound, whatever that is nowadays). Normal price for a bottle of beer in my local boozer here is 4½d (true!).

For the touring section, food plentiful, excellent and reasonable in price. The town is superb and in spite of being very much a tourist centre, there is practically no pestering of visitors with pots, pictures and postcards.

Bullfighting starts up shortly; this is a good centre and Ronda, where the whole thing started, is only 50 miles away. John Slessor is supposed to be coming out to see us and I am calling him in the morning to tie up the details. Pee Wee and the Pup arrive, I believe, in April, so the Tiger Club is well represented.

We had a batch of four Pawnees and the Cessna-thing spraying here last week, interrupting shooting badly. As far as one could see they were sousing a minute patch of waste ground behind the aero Club, but there may have been much more to it than that.

Four 88-millimetre anti-aircraft guns have just arrived outside my office, but the Pawnees have left. I have a magnificent private apartment, brand-new, with splendid leather furniture (except the refrigerator) and with beer so cheap housekeeping is simple. I bought an octopus in the supermarket but six of him got away.

Tell "G.B." I'm saving up for a bull for his Gloucestershire estate – very decorative.

I wish you could see the photograph on my Spanish Air Force pass. I look like a bandit with wet feet.

Every once in a while the *"Tiger Rag"* would publish a letter that gave us all a moral lift. The very family aspect of our Club was never more portrayed than by this deeply sincere letter from two utterly selfless folk. In a world so very lacking in kindness to those less fortunate than ourselves this heartening letter gave us a much-needed boost. The question of where are they now lingers.

BETTER LATE THAN NEVER
[A fascinating letter from Michael and Anna Moore]

"Dear Tiger Club Members,

A long and shameful silence from this tiny kingdom in Southern Africa which is, according to the U.N. experts here, the third poorest country in the world. What would we do without Christmas? The season of joy and goodwill, which even the most secular as well as Christian among us uses as a lifeline to maintain the very important contact with friends far and wide. There are those of you who scorn the newsletter as an impersonal and lazy means of communication with friends. On the whole I agree with this, and if only I did not suffer from the terrible Irish affliction known as "I'll do it tomorrow" I would write long interesting letters to each one of our hundreds of friends spread far and wide across the earth's surface.

In so many ways this has been one of the busiest yet most rewarding years of our lives. Despite there being no servant problem, Africa demands much of its expatriates, and being released from domestic chores just means that nearly all one's time is devoted to trying to help the many helpless here, and having survived the severity of one Lesotho winter here in the lowlands (5,000 ft) it is something of a miracle how the mountain dwellers survive at up to 10,000 ft with so little in the way of nutrition to boost their stamina. Mealie meal forms the main article of diet and that is mainly carbohydrate and pretty useless as a sustaining food. Michael's work takes him into the mountains five or six times a week where, among other diseases, he sees the result of malnutrition over the years in such conditions as contracted pelvises leading to difficult childbirth with often fatal results. There is practically no preventative medicine here and our common sense tells us that prevention is better than cure, but it costs money to heal through education, and the cure (sometimes) is all that Lesotho can offer its people yet.

For our own part some things have been achieved in our year here. Two of the mountain clinics, plus the tiny Super Cub aeroplanes, have been equipped with radio through the generosity of private individuals here and in the U.K. and also the British Government. In October the Lesotho Flying Doctor Service received magnificent help from Oxfam with the purchase of a good second-hand Helio Courier aeroplane – ideally suited to the terrain with short take-off and landing performance – a Volkswagen Combi for double duty as an ambulance and supplies van, a hangar complex at the expanding airport here at Maseru, and more radios to bring the other clinics into our radio network. The Government has agreed to underwrite the running costs of the Service, but money for further expansion such as building two more very necessary clinics and equipping them, and the setting up of a teaching programme in preventative medicine, must again be sought through private channels (drugs come from Government). The Government gives what help it can and the Prime Minister, Chief Leabua Jonathan, is sincere in his desire to improve the lot of the people. However, you cannot get blood out of a stone and there is little here to give. If any of you feel like helping in a tangible way, despite the recent devaluation, we would be very grateful indeed. Cheques should be made payable to "AEROMED" and sent to this address.

Now a little about ourselves. We hope to be home in the U.K. for two or three months, and on leave sometime this year. Our home address will be: The Old Rectory, Crittleton, near Chippenham, Wilts, England. We are not yet very sure about exact times and dates, but a letter written to our home address or here will always determine our whereabouts. David, Alison, Justin and Bruce are loving the life here which is perfect for children – riding, swimming and wallowing in the mud when it rains as most roads are unsurfaced. The children are as busily anticipating the arrival of Number Five in early December as their parents, and join us in wishing you a very happy Christmas and New Year."

The Club had a great victory in the Isle of Man Races, with our Chairman, Norman Jones, winning the big prize outright in the Condor. Janet Ferguson came second – also Condor – and Fred 'Sausage King' Marsh came in third. To all three our hearty congratulations and a special bouquet to the Condor on its first big win.

Snippets from around. There is a move afoot to license Redhill, the glider-towing unit have already topped 320 tows – this by mid-April – the Icicle Aerobatic Trophy held at Redhill was won by Neil Williams, James Black was second and John Firth third. I've forgotten why it's so called . . .

On a more serious note, may we remind members who take on the task of Duty Pilot that, should they feel it is necessary, they have the right and indeed the duty to temporarily ground any members they suspect of incompetence. It is difficult to lay down rules for this sort of thing, an easy and obvious case would be excessive drinking. If in doubt advice can always be sought from a senior member. The occasion might occur once in a blue moon, but it is as well to remind members that the job of Duty Pilot has considerable responsibility, and he has the full support of the Committee should such a decision ever be made.

The full support of the Committee was never in question and on the few occasions this veto was applied – never for drink incidentally – the Committee backed the Duty Pilot 100%. In this seemingly carefree Club there was an underlying discipline – thank heavens.

TEN YEARS AFTER – The Editor

After hearing the same grumble three times from three different members in three different days I sat down and pondered on it. The grumble was: "The Club isn't what it used to be." This from members who had been in on the Club since the beginning. Well, so have I, and they're right. But as far as I'm concerned it's not so much a complaint as a statement of fact which must be applicable to every Club which grows up. Look at the facts. In 1958 there were probably around thirty active flying members and at any one weekend the odds were you were going to bang into a round dozen of your friends with instant recognition of the remainder. Ten years later with some 400 flying members the same long-service type will be lucky if he recognises a dozen, much less know them as friends. In fact, to my certain knowledge it's possible to visit Redhill and, outside of the establishment, recognise no one. It's a cold hard truth that unless you are going to spend every other weekend down there you are never going to get to know other members. This state of affairs is off-putting and occasionally too the accusation 'clique' can be heard. Again justified but understandable, because when one of the boys of any particular group sees some friends amid so many strange faces, he would be a queer fish if he didn't make his way over to join them.

The Club has unquestionably the greatest gathering of interesting pilots and characters in a set-up so unique as to be the envy of the remainder of the light flying fraternity the world over. But by the same token its social side leaves a lot to be desired. If I, and I'm as old a Tiger Club lag as any to be found, sometimes feel a stranger, what must be the feeling of the newer members? They have my sympathy and I think it says a lot for the allegiance to the Club to cope as they do. To be on the outside of anything one would rather be on the inside of must be lonely indeed. Now does the original grumble still hold good? True, we no longer feel the collective need to volunteer to redecorate the Clubroom or wash the mud off the Tigers, but I don't honestly think it's the action that's missed so much as the *communal activity*. I've probably got that trite old saying askew but isn't it the people who join a Club, not for what they can get out of it but what they can contribute, that are the best members?

OK. How? Well, think. For every trip you make to Redhill and from which you come away saying "They're a snooty lot, no one spoke to me" you can lay 100 to 1 the others present thought the same thing! Personally I've long campaigned for the introduction of the post DUTY HOST. A 'he' or 'she' happy to spare a day to the Club. Strangers seeing the DH armband won't feel they're intruding if they can go up and introduce themselves, and the DH can spend 'his' or 'her' time not flying but acting as a go-between for the day in an act of friendliness every bit as important to the Club as the Duty Pilot. If you feel as I do, or you're against it or you have a better idea, write to me. And thinking aloud, here are some ideas for that better spirit. Big and joyful gaggles of aircraft up and away early to visit other Clubs for the day. A whacking great picnic on the airfield, a bows and arrows group, there's plenty of room. I remember some years back Norman came up to me and said: "You're the Sports Captain," and I was given a locker full of cricket gear, golf clubs, rounder bat and ball and the aforesaid bows and arrows to look after, and when there wasn't enough money to go flying we had a whale of a time playing instead. Things aren't what they used to be, I agree, but it wouldn't take much effort to improve even on the original.

The storm that was brewing early in the year came to a head with a serious prosecution. The gist of the injustice of the charges and the general indignation expressed in the Club news was but an overture to what was to come.

CLUB NEWS: JUNE – JULY 1968

Talking point this month, and indeed last, warrants top of the page attention. Briefly both the Club, as owner, and a Club member were prosecuted by the Board of Trade, primarily for low flying. On every count the evidence was weak and the accused pilot was completely innocent, in fact he wasn't even in that bit of sky, yet as far as we can see the anonymous powers-that-be trampled on regardless looking for a scapegoat, selected a victim and had a go, secure in the knowledge that win or lose it was no skin off their nose. This in spite of the local police who considered there was no case. Yet to the accused the cost of protesting one's innocence was high and had to be paid for. The Club Committee unanimously decided to give their wholehearted support to the defendant and this, coupled with the help of an American who flew over from the U.S.A. at his own expense to give evidence, tipped the scales of justice in the Club's favour. We offer grateful thanks to Geoffrey McBreen for his selfless gesture and to the Tiger Club Committee who are footing so much of the cost of proving the member's innocence. Naturally the Board of Trade felt no effect and we the taxpayers will pay up for their careless indulgences. If you are in a position to bring details of this abortive case which is so indicative of officialdom's present offensive attitude to private flying, please don't hesitate to contact the Club for chapter and verse.

This is a good moment to make three pertinent reminders. 1. It is vital to complete times of take-offs and landings in log-books and on flying return cards. This is a legal requirement. 2. We earnestly advise that members should not give interviews to investigating police without legal advice. 3. Support the Legal Fund with a contribution now. It's there to help you.

. . . To John and Lorraine Mimpriss all our congratulations on the arrival of a son, and the same good wishes go to Tim and Angela Lodge – a daughter – both apparently born on the same day, June 9th. Margo reports that lunches and teas are now available on Wednesdays in the Clubhouse. There is another new Stampe 'WEF in the hangar. With the recent breakages we never seem to get beyond the total of three. As usual this Stampe is superbly finished and a tremendous credit to the skilful Rollasons team whose plea to pilots would be that we tend these near-vintage machines as if they were their own. Tom Storey's tiny Superplane TSR.3 is nearly ready for its first flight and a joyful sight it is, resplendent with its Union Jack decor across the top surface of the wing.

Tom's Superplane was his very own. He designed it, laboriously built it, and then completed it in the hangar where it was admired by us all. The Tom Storey Racer 3 i.e. the TSR.3 (readers with good memories will appreciate the designation '3') was squat, angular and seemed to hug the ground as if her sole ambition was for ever to live at peace in the hangar. One never got the impression flying was on her agenda. But colourful she was, a proper little butterfly.

The first round of the National Air Races on June 22nd at Goodwood was a literal wash-out. A wet and very windy event at an otherwise admirable venue. There was no racing and little indeed of an Air Display for a public conspicuous by its absence, indeed only fools and pilots would have turned out on such a day. There were bright moments though. Said Norman, pressed at the briefing for a formation of Condors and conscious of the appalling conditions: "You can have three Condors flying in the same direction." And Fred Marsh, who never fails to put his foot in it at least once every year, exceeded himself whilst at the official reception at Goodwood House. To a dear old girl (his words!) dispensing drinks he said, putting his arm around her: "And what's your name, my dear?" "The Duchess of Richmond," she replied.

On the notice board too was the following:

NOTICE

DUE TO CERTAIN IRREGULARITIES IN HORMONE PATTERNS THAT HAVE APPEARED IN RECENT SPORTING EVENTS, IT HAS BECOME MANDATORY FOR CERTAIN QUALIFIED PERSONS, IN THIS INSTANCE THE RACE STEWARDS, TO INSPECT, DETERMINE AND CONFIRM THE APPARENT SEX OF ALL COMPETITORS IN THE 99s RACE.

A TIME AND PLACE FOR THE ADMINISTRATION OF THIS TEST WILL BE ANNOUNCED BY THE STEWARDS DURING THE BRIEFING PRIOR TO THE 99s RACE.

. . . A few weeks back Pitmans gave a cocktail party at the RAeC to celebrate the completion of the Flight Briefings for Pilots series, the last of which I reviewed last month. Guest of Honour was John Cunningham. It was a memorable evening and important guests were of course the authors, Bunny Bramson and A.E. Birch. This makes a good moment to reflect on the Club's good fortune in having Bunny as our new CFI. His qualifications for the hot seat are top-drawer – not only is he a most experienced instructor but he is also a member of the panel of examiners. An extraordinary and successful fellow is Bunny, for when he is wearing his business hat he is also the Managing Director of Nicolsons of Bromley. Add his cheerful sense of humour and we have in him a CFI whose stay we hope will be a long and happy one. So to Bunny and his charming and lovely wife Miriam we say welcome.

Bunny Bramson was to become the Club's last CFI. There were to be only two in the Club's history, "Bish" and Bunny. After Bunny the title became Chief Pilot. If instruction wasn't offered in the accepted sense, there was never any lack of critical comment from every quarter, sought or unsought. It was at best constructive guidance – very useful – and at worse a stage-whispered "call that a landing, a little less haste would have helped," – even more useful. If we were honest that is.

LETTERS

Adelaide/Fossil Bluff, 9th May 1968.

"Dear Benjy,

Had failure main ski pivot during take off 26th February at 70.23 South 66.50 West. Rear undercarriage in process. Field repairs impossible. Attempted salvage flight minus skis 6th March. almost airborne entered soft snow tipped over. Fate confirmed Porter. Other kite would have broken up in first mishap. Joined sledge team and travelled 130 miles to Fossil Bluff (71.20 South 68.16 West), stuck for winter unable to return to base. Joining geological team manhauling in austral spring. Rose very disappointed my non-return this year.

Regards to all.

John Ayers."

"Dear Benjy,

For members' information I give below, extracted from my records, the brief facts of the prosecution of Bob Winter and Michael Jones at Godstone Magistrates' Court on April 30th 1968.

Bob Winter was charged with five offences under the Rules of the Air and Air Traffic Control Regulations 1966 and the Air Navigation Order 1966. The first of the charges related to an alleged flight by G-ACDC on September 24th 1967 closer than 500 feet to a structure. The second related to an allegation that Bob Winter made a false entry in his log book. The third, fourth and fifth charges related to entries in Bob's log book which were incomplete in that the duration of the flight was not shown. Bob pleaded Not Guilty to the first and second charges but Guilty to the third, fourth and fifth above. The second charge of falsifying his log book was withdrawn at the outset after negotiation by his counsel and solicitor with the prosecution.

Michael Jones was charged firstly with being the operator of G-ACDC in connection with its flight when Bob Winter was allegedly the pilot in command and secondly with being the operator of G-ASHS when it was allegedly flown closer than 500 feet to a structure on September 24th 1967. (In connection with this latter flight, no pilot was charged.) Michael pleaded Not Guilty to both charges.

All the charges to which Bob and Michael had pleaded Not Guilty were dismissed after trial. The prosecution's witnesses were a father and son, and a neighbour, all living in a row of cottages at Tandridge; and a member of the Tiger Club. The witnesses for the defence were Bob Winter's passenger on September 24th, who came over from America to give evidence, and an expert witness who was not called.

Bob Winter was fined £10 on each of three charges to which he had pleaded guilty, plus 3 guineas costs in respect of those charges. The prosecution's application for their costs for the other charges was rejected by the Court. The defence's application for their costs relating to the dismissed charges was also rejected. These latter costs amounted to £250.3.0. The Tiger Club Committee agreed unanimously to meet the above costs from the resources of the Legal Defence Fund. It should be noted that the figure of £250.3.0 related only to the expenses of, or incurred by, the defence counsel and solicitors and takes no account of incidental expenses and time lost during the preceding months by the defendants and other helpers. Neither does it include the expenses of the American witness who paid his own fare from California. Those are the bare facts.

As you know, the case has aroused very strong feelings among our members and among fliers generally. Most are agreed that energetic steps must be taken to gain some protection from this type of prosecution and that the proper place to do it is in the High Court of Parliament. Facilities have been provided at Redhill for help and advice to those wishing to take advantage of these facilities.

Yours sincerely,

Jack Piercy."

CLUB NEWS: JULY 1968

July is always a hectic month, not that the weather was up to much but there was a great deal of flying. After the washed-out first round of the National Air Races the Royal Aero Club managed to get the next two rounds in over a long weekend early in August at Middleton St. George. Club members did well. Norman Jones is now well up in the points Championships, flying the racing Condor – he lapped at 128 and Gordon Janney in the Musketeer, racing for the first time, got around at an amazing 152, a speed which won Gordon the race and no doubt radically adjusted his future handicap. Big interest at Redhill is Tom Storey's TSR.3 which is now flying with a decided droopy look, an illusion fostered by the straight wing and the gay Union Jacks painted on top of them. Tom must be very proud of himself – there are few in this world who have, designed, built and flown their own machine. And there is a happy James Baring tearing around the sky in his SIAI-MARCHETTI. It is indeed a beautiful-looking craft and James showed its aerobatic capabilities to good effect at its debut during the Redhill display. As far as I'm concerned it must be the last word in private ownership. Perhaps when we can drag James away long enough we'll get him to write up some details.

Dennis Hartas won the Rochester Air Race in a Mascaret, lapping at 145. His grin at winning became even wider when he received the Kent Messenger Cup and the £50 donated by Bill Chesson. The Rochester 'do' is always a fine venue; for a change the weather cooperated and the accompanying display was a long afternoon of delight. Yet another display was the one we held at Redhill, the first there in several years. The weather again was kind, the flying sound and we hope that local folk who came to see us went away with a better impression than a few regular complainants would have us believe.

The BLAC flying clinic at Halfpenny Green was a great success and we heard that Peter Jarvis (Stampe) and Peter Phillips (Chipmunk) put up great shows with their day-long and hard work giving aerobatic instructions. They were both fully booked up. As I write this the World Aerobatic Team is sweating on the availability of their Zlins, both of which are giving trouble – we can only hope that all will be well on the day, and more, our good wishes go with them to Germany later this month. . .

At a distance of thirty years the happenings during that summer of 1968 have dwindled in my memory to the series of mentions in the monthly Club News round-up. It's strange how little, almost throw-away, items are recalled whilst the substance is a confused blur. For instance I can tell you James Baring only paid £9,000 for that beautiful SM.260 and he didn't confine his aerobatics to Redhill. I recall a time when he, Lollie and I were returning from Dublin and in the Gatwick circuit he suddenly performed a couple of tight barrel-rolls, gave a satisfied grin and turned finals as if nothing had occurred. He was so smooth, no sense of 'g,' it probably didn't happen; except it did.

LETTERS

West Horsley, Surrey 22.9.68

"Dear Benjy,

Our participation at Biggin Hill over, it looks as if another very enjoyable display season is complete in spite of the weather and Shoreham's tragedy. I'm sure that all the participants have enjoyed it immensely and I just thought that you might feel it not out of place to record a thank-you in the *"Rag"* on our behalf, to the helpers etc., and especially to Clive. Certainly his efforts have meant he hasn't had so much display flying himself and he and Jean have put in long hours of work which may not have been all that rewarding due to the weather's effect on the gate. For the sake of the Club, I hope they will not become discouraged.

Incidentally, have you noticed how popular the Club's new car badge has become? It consists of 2 vertical strips of orange paper, 10 in apart, left behind on the rear window after display stickers have been removed!

Yours,
AMBROSE BARBER."

I gave an involuntary grin when I again read Ambrose Barber's letter, and memory stirred.

It was a little earlier, in the autumn of '65 on a lovely evening at Redhill, that I awaited the arrival of some of the slower aircraft back from a display. I'd been up there to commentate and fly a 'Standing-on-Wing' slot with Lollie and now we were observing a trio of Turbulents making an uncharacteristic long and rather fast run in to land. The last of our brood was returning, but something was amiss for they were in a tight line-abreast formation, almost as if the wing men were helping the one in the middle. They were.

They landed fast and successfully but instead of taxying in the two wing men switched off mid-field and hurried across to help the third from his cockpit.

Ambrose looked a mess. He was groggy, shattered goggles, and blood-soaked. His aeroplane looked the worse for wear too. It also lacked a rudder. The story went something like this. The three were flying home in a loose formation at around 1,500 feet when Ambrose eased away and dropped down to overfly a long wood which was directly on course. There was no habitation, just a glorious evening and a wish to relish the sweet joy and warmth of the lower air. As he followed the trees over the hill there was a violent shock (it could only have been a cable) as something struck the windscreen, shattering it, squarely hit Ambrose's goggles on his forehead, proceeded to clobber the top of the fin, and removed the rudder along with the top hinge. It also knocked Ambrose out.

He guessed he was unconscious for about 30 seconds during which the aircraft flew itself – that or in some sub-conscious way the pilot within took over. When Ambrose came to, he felt awful, his wits all at sea, barely able to cope. But cope he did, but in such a bemused state he knew not what to do. Then he went blind. Instinctively he reached for his eyes and in doing so wiped away blood and vision returned. His companions now came down to investigate and by sign language Clive indicated diverting to the nearest airfield, but Ambrose would have none of it. Redhill, his mind instructed; and so began a long, painful journey back, guided and encouraged by his two friends. To be honest that wasn't what I heard at the time, but even cleaned up it is a remarkable tale.

The sequel to this flight had its lighter moments. Once Ambrose had been cared for, the question of where did the rudder finish up became uppermost in the close-knit fraternity of the Turb pilots. All agreed it had to be recovered, it wouldn't do for it to be discovered lying there in the wood like an unaccountable object from space, bright red, and worse, with Rollason's name in white proclaiming they built it. An immediate search was organised. To the best of my recollections they hunted through this remote wood on foot, and maybe from the air too, but it was never discovered.

Ambrose Barber's mention of the tragedy at Shoreham brought me up short. For some reason I hadn't written up the show for the *"Rag,"* perhaps I had been too upset. I had been the commentator and had seen my wife drive a Club doctor over to be first at the scene. From the commentating point of view it was always the rule of the day, probably still is, to play down any accident. Not only was it considered bad form to dwell on mishaps, as if we were appealing to the baser side of human nature, but from the practical point of view, a firm redirection away from the incident did much to prevent the curious from streaming over to get a better view. And they did, given half a chance. More important, the rescue services needed space to operate swiftly. Equally we avoided emergency messages, a runner was usually available – the A.T.C. lads were good at this – so the worst we broadcast was the lost child appeal: "Will Mum please come and collect Willie."

FRIENDSHIP, INTERPRETING MINUTES,
HIGHLAND HERON AND AEROBATICS

It simply isn't possible for anyone to begin to collate the activities of over four hundred individual characters let loose on some three dozen Club aircraft – there were seldom less than eight Turbulents on stream at any one time. Someone that year counted up the members who also owned aircraft. There were seventy-three of them with nearly one hundred aeroplanes to play with. It was no mean air force. The best I can do is to invite you to let imagination take hold and go with the flow, because if by dint of correspondence, articles and memory I've induced a sense of an ongoing adventure, believe me it was all but the fringe of a way of life we all followed with unbounded enthusiasm.

On my desk are letters from that year, 1968. They came from all over the world, keeping the membership in touch with the many journeys and meetings, and all with one aim: to celebrate a Club that had such a charisma it appeared to induce not only an allegiance but a togetherness that transcended nationalities and bound us all together into, I can think of no other word, a family.

Do I exaggerate? I do not. The words "Tiger Club" opened doors abroad and ensured hospitality as surely as if we'd passed through the same portals as regulars for years. For the life of me I can think of no other organisation that contained the same magic.

The philosopher within offers up reasons. The world was coming together after the divisions of war, or, the hand of friendship was extended because the world wanted to be a better place. Both valid, I expect, only that it didn't happen universally. Branches of the Tiger Club opened abroad. The American branch had its own newsletter and visiting British members reported a generous welcome. Others were established in South Africa, Australia and New Zealand. If ever the expression "hands across the sea" meant anything at all, it could well have been coined for this Club.

The following letter from Jurg Weber is just an example of the many regularly received from abroad. Apart from containing an astonishing number of ratings for any one pilot it was typical of that sense of togetherness.

I remember Sheila Scott came back from the States claiming a similar number.

I wrote in 1964:

"She obtained, within the period of three weeks, her commercial seaplane and helicopter ratings plus her multi-engine instrument rating. Sheila also found time to take a High Altitude Course in a pressure chamber and also qualified for jet flying."

In three weeks? If you'd believe that you'd believe anything we said . . .

LETTER

Chicago, August 12th 1968

"Dear Tigers,

I am still a proud member of your Club and I enjoy reading about the activities, even if I am far away and cannot participate in person.

Last year when I came from Switzerland to Canada, I contacted one of our members in Montreal, Robert Gairns. He was very helpful and tried with all sorts of information to make my job-hunt in Canada easier and we also talked about gliding and the flights at Redhill. After all I decided to go to the U.S.A. where I also got stuck, as you see now.

Here in Chicago I got all sorts of ratings being known as: commercial, instrument, airplane and instrument-instructor, multi-engine, seaplane, airline transport pilot license, advanced ground instructor, flight engineer licenses and that all in one year by home studies. Also my airplane and power plant mechanic license. That's a thing that would be nearly impossible in Europe due to tremendous paperwork and slow offices. For example the test results from the written airmen's test are usually back in 4-7 days, properly graded and without charge.

If I have a little more time off I will go back to biplane-flying again, but it looks pretty hard to find a decent plane for a decent price over here; or even start a sort of Tiger Club – there won't be lack of interest you bet, but it will be hard to find good planes.

Many greetings to all the members from the States.

G.J. Weber."

CLUB NEWS: AUGUST – SEPTEMBER 1968

This has been quite a period under review. Some extraordinary activities have been accredited to Redhill's green acres, but few if any can touch Steven Thompson's claim that he has water-skied over them. The Floods of September won't easily be forgotten, not only by the locals but also by the unfortunate visitors from Osnabrück. They arrived, all 18 of them, on the Saturday, never suspecting that by the following morning they would be marooned in their hotels, cut off by the rising waters that swept through so much of Surrey, the same waters that submerged Gatwick's runways and the Redhill hangar floor. Oh! yes, one other oddity. Neil Williams, excited by all that water, fitted the Piper Cub with temporary skis and skated 'RAM around too.

Good news from Dawn and Alan Turley. Exactly one year after their serious flying accident and long sojourns in hospitals and convalescent homes, they have now both been issued with clean bills of health and have returned home to Yorkshire to start breeding and kennelling dogs. Alan's award of the AFC just before he left the RAF was a timely reminder of his prowess as the RAF's solo aerobatic ace. He and his Lightning mount were a highlight at the Paris Show last year.

Down at Lee-on-Solent the Sea Turbulent, after a slight mishap to one of its floats, is again operational and Tom Freer is planning some winter flying. Morton and Lene Olsen flew in from Denmark with two friends especially to complete his initial check for Club membership and Lene fulfilled her life-long ambition to stand on the wing. That's keenness for you. Here's an early reminder to buy your Xmas cards now. There isn't to be a new Xmas card this year, instead Michael is having a clear-out of the accumulation of the previous years . . . at greatly reduced prices. Again this year there will be a spot landing competition organised by Clive Francis.

ROBIN BLECH IN CANADA

"Dear Benjy,

After four months over here in Canada I feel that I owe you some copy, so I thought that I would let people know a bit about aviation in Canada, which is so completely different from back home. Having taken all the necessary exams for the Canadian authorities, I spent a few weeks travelling across the country and taking a good look at general aviation here.

The first great difference, which is very apparent on arrival as a pilot, is that the Department of Transport – equivalent of our BOT – is actually in favour of people flying, whether privately or commercially. Most of the DOT inspectors seem to start on the assumption that one is a responsible individual who has been professionally trained, and that one is not going to fly inverted across the centre of Toronto at nought feet. Reading of the recent legal action against the Tiger Club for supposed low flying made me boil even more than I used to. Here there is no minimum legal height that one has to keep to, except over a city, and nobody worries about that anyhow. I have yet to meet anyone who has ever heard of someone being prosecuted for low flying, or of any local resident complaining about noise from light aircraft. When I first arrived in Vancouver I went to see the DOT inspector about getting an instructor's flying test and on our first meeting he asked me to compile some notes for a new government flying manual that was about to be published. Can you imagine a Canadian arriving in Britain being asked by the gentlemen at Shell Mex House to help them with a similar task? He would have to fly there for at least thirty years accident-free before he was considered responsible!

As one would expect, the size of the country affects many aspects of flying. Most of Canada is uninhabited, which is an easy thing to say, but until one has flown 400 miles without seeing a single sign of life, over dense bush and for the most part out of radio range with VHF, it is difficult to appreciate. In the last couple of months I have been doing general charter and survey work with a couple of Aztecs and occasional trips into the tighter strips with the Cessna Skywagon. Though I have been based in Fort St. John, up in northern B.C., most of my operations have been in the Yukon and the Arctic. Flying in the far north has a fascination of its own, for weather information is unreliable and conditions are highly changeable. Even during the summer large areas of the Arctic Ocean have floating ice, and in another month it will become completely frozen. Then surface temperatures drop to 40 degrees below over most of the country and tyres or skis become frozen to the ground if one leaves the aircraft standing in the open. At the moment, however, we are probably enjoying better weather than you are.

Until one looks at a detailed map of Canada it is difficult to appreciate just how many lakes there are. With the exception of the central Prairies the country is dotted with thousands of them in every direction, which makes map-reading a tricky business on occasions. In places one can quite easily fly for long periods without getting a definite pinpoint, particularly at low level. The obvious answer to the transport problem is to use floats, for most settlements are on the banks of either a lake or a river. Every charter company has its specially-qualified float pilots, and they have perhaps the most strenuous flying of all. They are called upon to fly their frequently-overloaded Cessnas, Otters and Beavers into the smallest lakes, which in the west are complicated by the high mountains that surround them. Frequent downdraughts and hidden obstructions in the water, together with the need for the pilot to care for his own aircraft without adequate maintenance facilities, make the float-pilot's job a highly respected one, and most companies will not take any pilot on without at least 100 hours float-time.

As a commercial pilot here, one immediately realises that there is a fundamental difference in the attitude of both employers and passengers towards aeroplanes and the people that fly them from in England. At home the general public still regard aviation as something unusual, and most pilots think that they are rather special – nowhere more so than in the Tiger Club! Here the aeroplane is as common as the motor car, and the northern settlements are supplied entirely by air, for there are no roads at all. Therefore the approach to flying is highly practical, and one has to sometimes just throw the "book" out of the window, and use one's discretion on loading, fuel requirements, engine limits and other things that one normally takes for granted.

Airway flying is somewhat different from in Europe. Due to the large distances involved VORs are little used and the low frequency Radio Range and NDB are used almost exclusively. At home the nav. facilities are usually not more than, say, fifty miles apart, with the NDBs having a similar sort of range. Here the beacons are usually 150 miles apart but are also very powerful. The last Radio Range at home was Dunsfold, and that was replaced a couple of years ago, if I remember right. A factor which takes a bit of getting used to on airways is that VFR and IFR traffic mix together on airways, and there is no radar coverage to provide separation. However, despite the number of aircraft flying around, the traffic density is very light due to the large area involved. The great exception in the north is Alaska, which the Americans have plastered full of VORs, Tacans and just about anything else that you can think of. It is rumoured that the FAA are bringing out maps one day. . . . Certainly there are American private pilots who come up north each year and get into trouble when they find they are a thousand miles from the nearest VOR.

When one gets up towards the north coast, one is quite near the Magnetic Pole, and the Variation starts to change constantly. You then have the choice of flying on True headings or using a grid system. I personally prefer the latter, but as grid maps are scarce, the True system usually wins, and one simply uses the sun to align the gyro, or an astro-compass which is preferable. This of course presupposes that one can see the sun. However in IFR conditions or during the winter, when there is permanent night, further problems are posed.

Well that's about all for now. For anybody who is interested in contacting me, do please write via my London address in the Club book and it will be forwarded. I move around too much to have a fixed address here. Regards to all, and try to keep at least one Stampe intact till I get back.

All the best,
ROBIN."

Committee minutes: June '68
Any other business: *i. maximum fine increased to £50.*
                     ii. Redhill – P.R. work very important but keep crowd low.
                     iii. Bone domes read good head protection.
Committee minutes: August '68
Reports for month: *ii. Redhill – good show – bad crowd.*

Take my word for it, there's a wealth of significance in our Chairman's comments. For the light-hearted, June's "but keep crowd low" followed by August's "good show – bad crowd" you can safely read Norman didn't want too many to attend, yet when the local populace unwittingly followed his wishes they earned a black mark. I think he feared that if the Redhill Show was a sell-out our touchy landlords would hit us in our pockets the next time. There were also the locals to consider.

The encouragement to wear bone domes was good sense, especially in the open Turb's cockpit with its vulnerability to head injuries whenever they were crashed. And the maximum fine upped to £50 was wryly welcomed by Norman's son Michael who had the job of repairing aircraft via his Rollason team.

For years the Committee was called upon to consider the inevitable incidents that either incurred our displeasure, usually cases of bad airmanship ("I didn't see him Boss, honest . . . ") or something resulting in damage to the aircraft, and in every case the maximum fine we could impose was only £25 – if the pilot got lucky it was only a fiver. Now it was doubled. In vain poor Michael would protest that the cost just to replace a prop was vastly more than the maximum: *ergo* the new figure was insufficent. To all these pleas Norman was deaf.

In his wisdom, and in truth it was also his money, he realised that flying the large number of hours annually – then in the region of four thousand hours – would always result in the bent this or that, so unless the incident was blatant – in which rare case we could ban the member from further flying with us – Norman truly believed we were all redeemable and would not do it again. I say this for the Boss, he had no end of faith in us: if only we had as much faith in ourselves. . . .

There was an established routine. A report had to be submitted which of course was handed around at Committee meetings. The wise offender, and it was amazing how wise everyone suddenly became when the fat was in the fire, would openly admit guilt, with no excuses, and offer profound apologies. If he added contritely that he'd learnt a lesson, that would knock an extra fiver off the fine. Norman, ex-Naval Commander that he'd been, couldn't abide excuses. Own up and he would forgive.

We cost the dear man thousands; I add this sadly as well as honestly. The £50 top fine was to stay for a long, long time.

Committee minutes: October '68

Air racing:	iii. Formula or class racing needed.
	iv. Use American classes.
House Committee:	i. Rota of Ladies being prepared.
	ii. We must keep place tidy.
Any other business:	i. "Tiger Rag" – assistant editor needed.
	ii. Sea Turbulent now flying.

I think it was back in the early sixties when I first heard of the American Formula for one-start racing. A letter to Don Berliner, who was the originator, brought forth an encouraging reply, so I penned an article for *"Flight"* extolling the exciting one-class concept and kicking handicap racing in the teeth for good measure. Can't find the article now, but the story goes it caught the eye of Prince Philip who suggested to Norman that a Tiger Club contest for a single-seater racer might be productive. The competition was eventually won by a design from Luton and Rollason agreed to build the winner – and so the Luton Beta was born.

I didn't do the Royal Aero Club's teeth any harm, for to this day that august body still run the highly successful series of handicap races. We still see a limited amount of Formula One racing, but the problem I didn't foresee was that F.1 required a special aircraft, and a single-seater at that. Costly. Whilst on the other hand handicap races are for any machine and you can share the fun and the cost with others. You can't win them all, all I could claim was a good try.

"Rota of Ladies being prepared," and more ominously, *"we must keep the place tidy."*

In those carefree days it was the done thing to let the women do menial tasks – weren't they always telling us how much better they could do things? – so there was to be a rota of helpers, but it was the lack of consistency that let them off the hook. One weekend we'd be lucky to get a biscuit with our tea: another, the lady prided herself on her cakes and we'd get the lot. In the end we found ourselves a local lady to whom we paid a modest amount. Unfortunately when her back was turned we raided her stores. Oh! yes, and when we remembered we cleaned up after us.

An assistant editor was never found, but we had a new delight, a Sea Turbulent. She had first flown back in '65 but, as I wrote at the time, "had the misfortune to sink." Now dried out, modified, and with a higher compression engine, she now awaited a new future.

I've printed the entire Club News for November/December. The trouble is it's sometime difficult to edit anything out, so much went on. Norman wrote, as he always did after receiving his copy, to offer thanks and to reassure: "I'm not retiring 'ZZ permanently. She is only going into storage until needed in the summer."

All will soon become clear. The Special Tigers weren't just aeroplanes, they'd become our friends and we tended to miss them.

CLUB NEWS: NOVEMBER – DECEMBER 1968

This must be the season for buying aeroplanes. Among the more exotic buys these last few weeks have been Manx Kelly's 1939 Chilton, a lovely single-seater with its Walter Mikron engine, and Adrian Swire has hit the nostalgic jackpot with a Me.109. It's an ex-Battle of Britain film machine with a Merlin engine. We're working on him to bring it into Redhill.

Along with this Newsletter we're enclosing an application form for the Annual Dinner. It is again at the Hilton and destined for the 14th Feb. Bev is asking for suggestions for a cabaret. Will talent scouts report in pronto. The record number of glider tows to date this year is now over 2,500. Gordon Crabb is rightly proud of his team who flew the Husky, the Super Cub and the Tigers 'MZ, 'AA and 'ZZ without incident to complete this extraordinary figure. A sad note for Tiger-lovers is that the Club is retiring Tiger 'ZZ this month, but as one goes into retirement another veteran comes back to Redhill. It's the Puss Moth, and to welcome it back John Urmston flew in with his red and white Puss Moth to complete a unique picture. John is to be congratulated on completing a superb piece of restoration.

As excitement mounts in the London-Sydney Motor Rally, it is welcome news that we have a Club Member to cheer on. Look out for a Volvo 122S No. 25 with Bill Chesson driving.

Frances MacRae has been elected Aerobatic Secretary, replacing Robin d'Erlanger who looks like taking up marriage instead. We all wish Frances a lot of luck in her new appointment and our thanks to Robin for a job well done. Frances is well in the forefront of our aerobatic team and is unquestionably the best woman aerobatist this country has ever had. Ken Smith is again organising film shows this winter and the first of a programme of four begins after Christmas – look out for details on the notice board in the hangar.

News of members this month includes the welcome return of two of the Club's old hands, Sam Key, who co-piloted a Cessna from Singapore, and Robin Blech home for a spell from Canada. Also congratulations to Bill Innes and Linda on their engagement. Morten Olsen, who returned to Denmark a short while back, gave a glowing account to everyone he met of that wonderful aircraft the Andreasson-designed BA.4, and was earnestly recommending everyone to try one. This enthusiasm comes as no surprise to those of us who were lucky enough to have flown the prototype. Peter and Sue Phillips, who now own that first machine and fly it from Goodwood, have obtained the sole building rights, and we wish them every success. The BA.4 must be the most brilliant single-seat biplane ever built. Everyone at Redhill would like to see more of Peter and Sue, especially if they'll bring along the BA.4. *[I'm obviously angling for another ride. – Ed.]*

Sheila Scott's book *"I Must Fly"* has now been released and from all accounts is very worth reading. Our congratulations to her too on her award, for the third time, of the Brabazon Cup for her recent record-breaking flights.

All are invited to a Wine and Cheese party at the Kronfeld on Wednesday Dec. 11th at 7 pm. This is a good opportunity to get to know the Kronfeld better which after all is our London Club and deserves all our support. Look for the address in the Tiger Club Booklet. Do come along.

Your Editors Benjy & Lollie wish all members a very happy Christmas with special greetings to absent friends.

OVERHEARD AT REDHILL

"I won't forget," threatened Nini. "Remind me."

OVERHEARD AT THE KRONFELD

Reg Wise was asked by a pretty young thing what Club his tie represented. Before he could get a word in her boy-friend broke in with: "The Tiger Club, dear, where all the members must have flown 100 hours in a Tiger – all of them upside down!"

RACING NEWS

In view of current excitement about possible class racing next summer, a series of practice races took place at Redhill this month. The weather was not exactly ideal for the stalwarts who turned up – thick November fog. But it did mean that practically no other flying was practical. And the fog eventually lifted to a ceiling of 400 ft with just sufficient visibility across the aerodrome. Three Turbs were lined up to fly a four-lap course round the perimeter track but leaving out the area in front of the hangar. Each lap was 1·75 miles. Three experienced racing pilots volunteered for places on the starting grid and Smith-Thompson Aviation laid on starting and timekeeping facilities. After three races, with each driver changing mounts, it soon became clear that the Turbs were very evenly matched; one pilot won each race on three different machines, which proves something besides the fact that he was also the lightest jockey. The event was certainly a spectacle, in fact I think it was slightly more nerve-racking to watch than the normal Saturday afternoon practice aerobatic sessions. However, valuable experience was gained and speeds established for the course. Not to be outdone the Beta was also exercised with some practice laps over the same course and the corners certainly came up fast. With three more stablemates on the way, and the ribs being cut for Tom Storey's trio of Cassutts, nobody can say that American-style class racing on this side of the Atlantic will lack support.

The name P.D. Morgan at the foot of the following letter made me curious. Could the initial 'D' stand for David, for Dave Morgan who was around at that time, was a test pilot, who not only flew a lot with us, but got his hands on things like Harriers and Spitfires? It didn't, for Dave Morgan was still a member in the late '80s whilst Peter dropped from view in 1970. And that was a pity for both his flying and his writing had an entertaining quality.

HERON IN THE HIGHLANDS
by P. D. Morgan

I hesitate to set pen to paper for the "Rag" as, although a member of the Tiger Club for about two years, I have only appeared at Redhill on two or three occasions and am known to very few of the members.

After leaving Army Aviation we settled in London expecting to join the rat race of 'Europe's Foremost Airline' at Heathrow. It was therefore with alarm, not to say despondency, that we learnt that I had been posted to BEA's Scottish Air Ambulance Flight based at Glasgow/Abbotsinch. Now after eighteen months I feel that a short account of the Heron Flight might help to explain my poor attendance and perhaps atone for it.

The Flight, although an integral part of BEA, is really quite unlike the 'Big Airline' in its operations. The Mk. I Heron is a very pleasant aircraft to fly. It is sometimes said to be like flying four Chipmunks strapped together, although at 13,000 lbs it is scarcely the same in terms of control response etc. The four Gipsy Queens driving constant-speed props are very reliable and the linked throttle/prop system gives a simple single lever per engine. Matters are also simplified by the fixed undercarriage, of which more later.

Our area of operations is bounded in the north by Stornoway and Shetland and in the south by Edinburgh and Macrihanish, with occasional expeditions south of the border on charter and to Harwarden for overhauls. Our main job is Air Ambulance with the crews on twelve-hour standbys for calls to the Highlands and Islands where the Hospital facilities are limited.

In addition, to provide continuity in flying and to serve places whose 'Airfields' are too small for the normal Viscount service, a schedule is run to Tiree and Barra. Tiree has a small but conventional airfield, but at Barra landings are made on the beach. From Tiree onwards it is strictly VFR only, and times of the services are conditioned by the state of the tide and the direction and strength of the wind relative to the six-hundred-foot hill that overlooks the beach. The salty wetness of the sand accounts for the fixed undercarriage as too much of this corrosive mixture would collect in the retraction bays. It is normally quite firm due to the high percentage of cockle shells present (live cockles 5/- a bucket). However the sand did let us down earlier this year, literally, causing a very strenuous and alarming three hours in front of a rising tide. Fortunately, with the assistance of the passengers and some local inhabitants the aircraft was saved from the waves; the fire tender did not fare so well.

The Flight is small, consisting of five two-man crews (no cabin staff) and two aircraft. The Captains vary from very junior to one who has been flying around

Scotland since 1933! The small size and do-it-yourself nature of the Flight allows a friendly and informal atmosphere rarely found elsewhere; you wouldn't catch a London-based Training Captain with his coat off and up to the elbows in the engine changing plugs.

I shall be leaving soon, no doubt to try my luck on some high-speed paraffin stove; perhaps I may be able to renew my acquaintance with Redhill, but I know I shall miss the hours spent VFR around the Western Isles and will be sorry to leave what is undoubtedly the last real flying in BEA.

Frances MacRae, who had just taken on the task of Aerobatics Secretary, began her term with a refreshingly open assessment of the Tiger Club's contribution written in clear unambiguous manner, as befitted a Head Mistress. If her girls admired her as much as we did for her unassuming command of advanced aerobatics she was popular indeed.

AEROBATICS SUPPLEMENT
1968-69 (PART I)

The four open Tiger Club Competitions held during 1968 drew a total of nineteen competitors – down on 1967. Nine of last season's dropped out; there were five newcomers. Most people chose the Stampe, but we saw Chipmunk, Super Tiger, Cooking Tiger and Zlin. At one point Charles Boddington and Barry Tempest were contemplating a dual appearance on a Prentice – one on the throttle, the other with two hands on the stick! Perhaps next year?

SUMMARY OF RESULTS

	McAully Trophy	Air Squadron Trophy	De Havilland Trophy	Esso Trophy
M. Alexander	-	-	6	5
J. Black	-	-	2	-
D. Burbridge	-	6	-	-
A. Chadwick	4	7	-	-
S. Donghi	3	-	-	-
J. Firth	2	-	-	-
A. Haig-Thomas	-	-	-	2
C. Hughes	-	8	-	6
P. Jarvis	1	-	-	-
M. Kelly	9	3	5	3
R. Legg	-	-	-	7
F. MacRae	5	1	4	4
R. Mitchell	6	4	-	-
M. Riley	-	5	-	1
C. Schofield	-	-	3	-
B. Shaw	8	-	-	-
R. Turner	7	2	-	-
F. Williams	-	-	-	8
N. Williams	-	-	1	-

Such sporadic interest is disappointing – as the table shows, only two people did all the available competitions. No one else did more than two, and while the McAully excludes past winners, the other three are open to all. U/S aircraft and the distractions of Magdeburg are only a partial explanation: Ray Turner and Bob Mitchell sat up all night with an ailing Chipmunk, and got there, and Manx Kelly's constant enthusiasm is a cheerful exception. If we are to hold our own in 1969, participation will need to be much more energetic.

THE ICICLE TROPHY, designed and presented by Andrew Chadwick, was flown off on March 23rd. The whole intention was to hold a competition as nearly as possible on the spur of the moment, at the unlikeliest time of the year, for the sheer fun of it. In 1969 we are aiming at holding it when it was truly intended to take place – on a cold February Saturday, to remind us that spring can't be far away. Details later.

PEOPLE

Two who leave a void in the aerobatics scene are Dave Allan and Robin d'Erlanger. In 1967 Dave put an enormous amount of time and trouble into the organising of aerobatics, unobtrusively, but extremely efficiently, both through the Tiger Club and at the Royal Aero Club. After Moscow he went back to Australia – we hope not for good. In fact, we confidently expect to see him leading a strong Australian team in the 1970 World Championships! He left behind a comprehensive scheme for the competitions which I want to acknowledge here as I have every intention of borrowing freely from his ideas.

After three years work as Aerobatics Secretary and a career that took him to Moscow in the British Team, Robin has abandoned aerobatics for gliding, marriage and farming – we wish him happiness in all three!

In the World Championships in Magdeburg this year, Neil Williams captained a team consisting yet again of Tiger Club members: James Black, Carl Schofield, Frances MacRae. This has been written up at length, elsewhere, but the vagaries and oddities of the running of the competition should not obscure the achievement of the men's team. At the end of Group I, before the "technical difficulties" arose, Neil was within striking distance of the top (only 100 points behind the leader) and the whole Zlin group were standing favourites for the team prize – on incredibly little practice. And Carl, unhampered by the crippling attentions of the somewhat dubious "technical jury," flew all three groups without incident, so well that he slid quietly into 13th place, the best we have had so far. He and Neil both qualified for the "finals that never were." By the luck of the draw Carl never flew – an exasperating outcome to so much good work. There is also little doubt that if James had not had engine trouble, he would have joined them.

The Stampe has probably now made its last appearance in a World Championship, but it remains far and away the best machine we have for training, display, and competitions short of the international standard of performance for which the Zlin's extra power is needed. With another coming shortly, perhaps at last we shall achieve a formation of four.

THEN – NOW – AND TOMORROW

1960 BRATISLAVA:
John Ayres, Charles Boddington, Peter Phillips (on Super Tigers)

1962 BUDAPEST:
Nick Pocock (on Stampe)

1964 BILBAO:
Peter Phillips, Bob Winter, Neil Williams (on Cosmic Wind and Stampe)

1966 MOSCOW:
Neil Williams, Tony Haig-Thomas, Robin d'Erlanger, James Black (Dave Allan representing Australia) (on Zlin and Stampe)

1968 MAGDEBURG:
Neil Williams, James Black, Carl Schofield, Frances MacRae (on Zlin and Stampe)

The first aerobatic pilots to put in a British Challenge to the World Championships were adventurous and above all individual. That was appropriate then.

Now we have a team, and a team it has to be, putting all they've got into vigorous and scientific training if they are to take on all comers in the more sophisticated conditions of today. Aerobatics develops fast.

The Tiger Club can be proud of the fact that every pilot who has represented Britain up to now has belonged to it. "Bish," a superb aerobatic pilot himself, engendered the love of it in others and set a meticulous standard. Right up to Moscow, our pilots were joyfully engaged in what was more or less single combat in those days.

The making and maintaining of a team we owe to the leadership and single-minded dedication of Neil Williams, who with Taff Taylor realized the necessity for a new approach. Working virtually on his own, as they all then had to do in the field of advanced aerobatics, he came up the hard way. With what success, we saw in Moscow. With the support of the Taylor/Haig-Thomas Zlin he reached the Finals and at Dax in 1967 he became the European Champion, yet throughout he has given unstintingly of his hard-won knowledge and experience to the point where he sees his own pupils chewing at his heels, and is generously and genuinely glad to see it. That is how a real team is made.

With the World Championships of 1970 in England, there is no reason why we cannot go on to greater heights. It will be very satisfactory if we do. But as a Club we certainly cannot afford to sit back, aerobatically.

FRANCES MACRAE,
Aerobatics Secretary.

Frances MacRae followed up her initial assessment of the Club's aerobatic input with an even more authoritative declaration of the challenge that faced the pilots, not just ours but nationwide. Her clear directives – and I sense the delicate touch of a real leader – are as true today as they were then. A great lady, was Frances.

98

One point she touches on, spinning checks, weren't confined to the aerobatic types. At that time we were all encouraged to offer ourselves for a voluntary check-up. Believe me, as one of the Club's check pilots and with spinning always on the agenda, some of our pilots would have benefited and, if they were honest, would have been glad of the refresher.

Frances once caused grins all round when she burst out with: "If ever I spin in practising over Redhill, I wish to make it absolutely clear now that I do not want John Firth to be allowed anywhere near me."

Everyone knew John – a fellow aerobatist – for an enthusiastic neurosurgeon, always willingly up front when things went wrong.

AEROBATICS SUPPLEMENT
1968-69 (PART II)

CHALLENGE

The enthusiasm we as a Club have fostered, by example and through the National Competitions, has spread. Scattered about are what we hope are up-and-coming devotees with good machines who are going to be a stimulating challenge.

This is all excellent – the more to choose from, the better, we hope, the team and the better the future is assured. We will have to work hard to keep up our record, and that also is excellent.

Just so long as in our seriousness we do not entirely lose the joy of it, or forget that aerobatics is an art as well as a science!

Nor mistake speed for progress. To some extent, in fact, we have to put our house in order, and now is the time.

Along with our growing enthusiasm, perhaps because of it, we have had accidents, causing injury to pilots and writing off of machines. These, combined with other similar incidents up and down the country, have a further effect, equally serious but not so immediately obvious. They damage the reputation of aerobatics as a serious pursuit. They could well provoke more restrictions in a sport already bedevilled with them. And to this must be added the effect on insurance and the cost in repair and replacement.

We are spoilt – we break a machine and our beneficent Chairman in course of time produces a new one – so far. I am not sure however, that he is not in some danger of being regarded as an inexhaustible slot-machine, without our ever expecting to put sixpence in the slot! As for the feelings of the people who have put loving care into the building of the machines – these also tend to be unappreciated and unfairly neglected.

What, then, can we do? First and foremost, simply do not allow enthusiasm to rush us beyond our capacity. And be realistic about our capacity. Aerobatics demands a certain confidence – a very wary confidence, as the real experts know – but over-confidence is lethal.

We must make sure of safe height. At Redhill we have the difficulty of height restriction. It is more expensive to go away to get the height we need. But if we face the fact that we may well be allowing economy to jeopardize survival, the decision makes itself.

A novice, or even more likely, a fairly experienced pilot, anxious to "get on," sometimes equates progress with coming low or doing certain advanced manoeuvres. And, to be honest, sometimes feels there is a particular "kudos" attached. But if he is too low or the manoeuvre is too advanced for this particular stage, he is obviously trying to jump a very necessary part of what is inescapably a logical and disciplined development. Such "progress" is an illusion. And nobody who really knows is going to be impressed.

In view of all this, it has for safety's sake been laid down in the Tiger Club that for aerobatics NO ONE should come below 1,000 ft at any time, excepting certain specified, properly authorized display pilots and competition pilots at international level. No one should be a law unto himself while using a Club aircraft.

At his initial check, or subsequently, a pilot who wishes to do aerobatics is cleared to the height appropriate to his experience and skill and this is entered on his flying card. Most Check Pilots are able to assess and help with basic aerobatics. When he feels capable and the need arises, he applies for another check from which he may be cleared lower. There have certainly been cases, in the last year or so, of these requirements being overlooked.

As spinning is a manoeuvre into which errors can creep unnoticed in the course of time, and is much used in aerobatics, a further precautionary measure is to have a regular spinning check with the Hon. C.F.I. All the present aerobatic pilots do so. Our accidents have shown how necessary this is.

The Tiger Club has very few rules and works on the principle of respect for the individual and trust in his integrity and common sense. Such rules as there are exist because they are absolutely necessary – please comply with them.

What happens to the pilot who needs help, especially in the air? Advice on the ground is always abundant, of course!

The Tiger Club is not an instructional Club. It is composed of responsible pilots already of a certain minimal skill. Nor is it an intensive Aerobatics School, although it provides the comparative rarity of machines capable of advanced aerobatics and the advice and example of people who do them. We are lucky in having a number of the country's most experienced pilots willing to assist. Apply to one of them. That does not mean they will accept full training responsibility – their whole time could easily go on their own very necessary practice. But it means that nobody need be at a loss when he has done all he sensibly can on his own and needs help to proceed.

The great value of this is that no one need clutch at the straw of relying on an insufficiently trained pilot for advice. As he probably isn't aware of his insufficiency, he can be a walking danger. See what may happen: . . .

Enthusiastic "pupil" applies to scarcely more experienced "tutor." The latter is anxious to help, and quite sure he knows all about the manoeuvres – he's "done them lots of times." But he cannot know all the tricks a provoked aeroplane can get up to – the "pupil" makes a mistake his "tutor" never envisaged. Such difficulties can compound very rapidly and he finds it difficult, or even impossible, to correct. This is truly "the blind leading the blind." It is unfair of the "pupil" to ask anyone to accept this responsibility and equally unfair of the "tutor" to accept or offer it.

In this connection, it is good news that Norman is in process of arranging for aerobatics training at Blackbushe Aerodrome, where it is easy to find clear space and safe height. Very shortly, 10-hour courses in basic aerobatics should be available there and it is hoped later to add appropriate facilities for more advanced training. This is just what has been needed and is another example of his enthusiasm and foresight in support of sporting flying. It should help to get the training process into proportion again and under proper guidance and relieve Redhill of some of the pressure.

At Redhill this is the correct proceedure:

1. For basic aerobatic checks, height clearance and help, please apply to any authorised Check Pilot: loop, clover leaf, barrel roll, roll-off-top, hesitation roll, Cuban 8, stall turn, positive spin, avalanche, Derry turn and simple sequences. Those known to be especially interested are Bunny Bramson, Bob Winter, Nick Carter, Pete Jarvis, Mike Riley. Those manoeuvres should be practised until they are really good and wholly familiar.
2. For clearance check to go on to more advanced aeros, apply to one of the above-mentioned five. They will require a demonstration that 1. has been carried out thoroughly.
3. From then on, to Neil Williams, Bob Winter, James Black, Carl Schofield and myself. No one can know everything, but all these have done at least one international competition – they have met most of the possible manoeuvres and many of the snags.

The population at Redhill at any given weekend is unpredictable, but you would be very unlucky if you could not find one of them!

PUBLIC RELATIONS REMINDER

For practice, please find out where the people before you have been, and go in another direction. Take care not to stay long over one spot yourself and make sure you have not drifted over a built-up area. People below do get annoyed by the noise and genuinely frightened, largely because they do not understand what is happening. This is another reason for staying high. Care and communication on our part can minimize disturbance.

FRANCES MACRAE,
Aerobatics Secretary.

1969

MAN LOST, DISPLAY UPSET, MAGIC CHALLOCK
AND A MILITARY DETOUR

1969 started, as most New Years do, on a note of bleary-eyed enthusiasm. Substitute a lively social life in place of flying and everything continued nicely. It was January's par for the course and provided the *"Tiger Rag"* with plenty to go on about.

And statistics. There was now a membership of 625, plus, I like this bit, 'Wives listed: 77' – a total of 702. There were 3 resignations, it's hard to imagine what for. The glider contingent put in 2,662 tows in '68. Read: 2,662 glider pilots, 2,662 tug take-offs and 2,662 landings, and nearly all over weekends . . . it was quite a feat.

CLUB NEWS: JANUARY 1969

Undoubtedly the most notable occasion during December was the Wine and Cheese Party held at the Kronfeld. Arranged by Toni Neilson, aided and abetted by Jean Francis, Jill Southam and Robin Voice, it was voted by all a great success. It was good to see so many familiar faces all conjured up at such short notice. There'll be no such excuse though for missing the Annual Dinner on St. Valentine's Night in February and since there's no limit on numbers it's a heaven-sent opportunity to bring along your friends. This year we will guarantee their safety, providing of course we can dissuade Fred Marsh from bringing along his accursed sausages, samples of which invariably seem to get airborne. It will be the social event of the year, and to those of you who dread long speeches at other dinners there is a pleasant surprise in store – long orations are taboo, the whole time is given over to eating, dancing and laughing.

December flying was practically zero. It was only during the very last week that the weather got off the ground sufficiently for aviating and then all hell was let loose with not one, but two, Zlins letting their hair down. It was quite like old times, that last weekend of '68. For the record, the Club clocked nearly 4,000 hours flying last year, a total fractionally down on '67, but the drop was entirely due to an awful lot of awful weather.

Talking about Zlins reminds me that there are now no less than seven examples in this country and Club Members own four of them. They belong to Mike Popoff, Neville Browning, Ray Turner, and Taffy Taylor and James Black share one (there is one more in South Africa owned by Nick Turvey), and with the Players' mount available at Redhill it means a little aerobatic formation to look forward to.

Michael has been pondering over statistics and has come up with some uselessly fascinating reading. For instance there are 100 Club Members with professional licences, 140 with glider qualifications, and no less than 70 members own their own aircraft, including WWII exotics like Spitfires, Mustang, Messerschmitt; as fine an array of vintage and unique mounts to be found with any group anywhere. I reckon it calls for a Fly-In – someone care to organise it? The latest owner is Winston Churchill with a new Beagle Pup which he hopes to keep at Redhill. Michael is still delving, so with luck there should be more stats. next month including one I suggested, the <u>total light flying hours</u> of the current flying membership. <u>And so to a simple contest to start the New Year with. Here's an opportunity to win a free ticket to this, or if it's too late, next year's Annual Dinner. Send your estimation to Michael Jones at Redhill and the nearest one wins. Entry fee 5/- and all proceeds go to the Legal Fund!</u> It's a painless way of helping a fund that is solely there to help you, so please everyone join in.

Members have been coming in from all over the world to spend Xmas back home. Amongst them Neil Williams from the States where he has been demonstrating the Jetstream, Denis Culver from Canada, and Michael and Anna Moore from Lesotho. Social news includes two weddings and an apology for missing one. To Linda and Bill Innes a wedding last month and not an engagement as announced. Robin and Elizabeth d'Erlanger were married on the 4th January and David Hamilton married James Black's sister, Georgina, a week later. To all of them our warmest congratulations. And to John Stewart Wood, who recently had an operation, all our best wishes for a speedy recovery and a triumphant return to air racing.

I came across the following guide to marriage in the January *"Rag."* No, I can't remember who wrote it, but who ever it was, I doubt they'd had a sober thought.

ANOTHER GOOD MAN GONE
or – some notes on the process of marriage

It all started, the way these things do, with the most ridiculous little incident. All right, Robin d'Erlanger fell in love. Could happen to the best of us – in fact, this time, it did. But the whole thing ended up with the entire Tiger Club galloping off across England, right up at the sharp end, to get to this wedding.

The whole thing was very nearly a terrible disaster, because at the last minute it was discovered that Robin was Duty Pilot and they were just about to cancel the ceremony and send the presents back when Michael persuaded someone to stand in.

Finding a member of the Tiger Club actually asleep in our house, we went down in his car, to save trouble. Unfortunately, *he* made the prompt decision to retire into the left-hand seat and continue sleeping, so we saved ourselves nothing.

Buckfast Abbey, where the action was, was built, or rather rebuilt, by the monks themselves. All the same, one can't help feeling that with the top brass involved in this particular wedding, they could have got a professionally-built job. Anybody who thought Blake was being extra pi during the service, rolling his eyes devoutly to heaven, was up the creek. Blake was keeping an eye on the roof. If there is one thing that gives me the screeching hab-dabs, it's a Do-it-Yourself cathedral. Wedding ceremonies are always too long, but luckily, so was the church, and we had enough quiet at the back to finish several games of noughts-

and-crosses with leader Key on the blank pages for notes at the back of that jolly little book they give you on these occasions.

Two incidents stand out in retrospect, during the service. The organ, which had worked itself up from steam-at-one-hour's-notice to being-in-all-respects-ready-to-burst-into-song and was running throttled back on a rather pleasing carrier-wave effect, suddenly burst into a series of swoops and screeches like a mating call of the Loch Ness monster. "G.B.", who was pumping at the time, explained to me afterwards that he had got the handle caught under his waistcoat and, torn between a desire to save this unique late seventeenth-century garment and a wish to keep things rolling, attempted a fatal compromise.

(Fashion note: the waistcoat is in black bog-oak, with linenfold panelling and has been in "G.B.'"s family – or rather "G.B.'"s family have been in it – for generations. He was approached recently with a proposal that it should be handed over to the National Trust, but finding that it would cost him 2/6 to enter it and it would be closed on Sundays, vetoed the scheme.)

The other oddity was a noise like an axle falling off a car, which turned out to be young Tom Storey and Robin doing the gold-and-silver bit up front. Either they used a tambourine to get that effect or someone's metallurgy is pretty shaky. With Tom building three racers, one hopes the former. . .

The reception was super. A vast sea of respectable wedding guests, with pockets of Tiger Club identifiable by voices, pitched a little too loud, declaiming at intervals: "Actually we were going to fly down but . . ."

Actually, it all went pretty well. Key disgraced himself by busking down the queue with a flute and a top hat and trying to tip the bride's father when we left, but otherwise it was quiet.

I like weddings! Who's next?

CLUB NEWS: FEBRUARY – MARCH 1969

In a month that included in its itinerary a most successful Dinner Dance and some of the most unflyable weather, there's been little else of note to mention. It was great to see the latest Beta, resplendent in navy blue and white, displayed in the Hilton foyer, even better to see a pair of them flown a few days later in formation, and according to Michael there will soon be a third. From a flying point of view the highly sensitive elevators, whilst making the aircraft delightfully responsive, may to begin with be something of a hindrance in tight formation. But nothing can detract from the sheer beauty of its line, even sweeter in the new model now that the undercarriage is no longer so stalky. Whilst on about the new formula racers, the Beta's competitor over here, the trio of Cassutt Racers being built by Tom Storey, are fast coming along and should soon be airborne. Tom returned recently from the States laden down with every conceivable part for the racers. His excess baggage bill must have been quite something. Whilst in the USA Tom attended the Florida Air Races and established a close liaison with the racing fraternity there.

One of the Stampes is now equipped with an exhaust smoke system for forthcoming displays, and according to Robin Voice, its innovator, going successfully. Dick Emery and Barry Griffiths have bought a Turbulent and had it painted pink. . .

TIGER CLUB DISPLAYS

As some of you will know, Clive Francis is ill and may not be able to continue as display organiser this season. It is not clear what will now happen. The operation of displays is part of the Tiger Club charter but this serious activity depends entirely on the enthusiasm of the participating pilots; if people are keen enough to work to maintain and improve our standards there is an enormous field for "participation" flying this year.

For the time being the organisation of shows is in the hands of a steering committee of L. Benjamin, J. Baring and Robin Voice. All these people will be very interested to receive comments and views from the display pilot groups.

For a flying Club that seemed to be flying air displays all the season, this was a hiccup in a big way. On the surface of course the membership accepted the statement with an easy shrug of the shoulders and went on practising as though nothing had gone wrong. There was ever a reassuring belief that if you did nothing about it, the troubles would go away. Backstage they didn't.

Clive had never given anyone the impression that he wasn't working alone, and the knowledge he was working in association with a firm called Land-Sea-Air Promotions meant, not only a review of all the coming season's engagements, but an untoward degree of diplomacy. At this stage Robin Voice took over and with a positive flurry of sensible letters enabled nearly all the promised functions to go ahead and as ever the Club's pilots and helpers rallied round to support him.

I've just taken time off to ponder what I'd written. A few dozen words covers a competence within the Club that, when the chips were down, never abandoned us. Someone always arose, often without being approached, to accept responsibility without question or fuss. In a seamless manner Robin Voice assumed command.

THE CLUB'S ANNUAL DINNER DANCE '69

It's Saturday, and I'm resting up after a hectic night before, the occasion of the Tiger Club's Dinner Dance. It was a glamorous affair, the men gallant and a little unfamiliar in formal attire, and the women folk have never been more attractive. It was a singularly successful evening held in one of London's finest hotels. Of the Dinner, with its exotic-sounding menu, Coupe Miami, Delice de Sole Duglère, the Caneton à l'Orange au Grand Marnier mit Pavlova and tasting every bit as good as it sounded (not that I had a clue what was coming but then I like surprises), what can one say? The dancing was gay and by the time the evening officially ended at 1.30 am it was a bit abandoned too. Everyone had a great time. After dinner we broke from tradition and permitted a couple of speeches. Especially entertaining was our Guest of Honour, Peter Masefield, Chairman of the Royal Aero Club. He is no mean after-Dinner speaker. On the future of the Tiger Club, he reckoned that around the year 2,000 Redhill will probably be known as Joneswick or Jonesrow, still complete with Superduper Tigers and with that 'little place' down the road. His toast to the Club, with its "let's keep this flying for fun," was exactly the sort of thing we too believe in. Peter Masefield is unquestionably the man for us.

Michael had carefully prepared a speech for Norman, and Norman being Norman obviously didn't want to read it. He said: "Fortunately Michael has just suggested that perhaps after all I had better not read it because it will upset too many people," and added, thoughtfully: "We Jones's have a habit of upsetting people!" Prolonged cheers. And heartened by the response our Chairman proceeded to lay down his three ways to enjoy flying in the air. Aerobatics, or dancing in the air, was the first, and for the young. Racing – enormous fun and helps to improve the breed, and finally Touring – fun for everyone. He proudly mentioned our contribution to glider towing with over 2,000 tows last year, the American branch of our Club, and the likely formation of one in Australia. Norman sat down to huge applause. I think perhaps Norman was touched even more when later on he happily received his medallion for Air Racing, to my knowledge the first tangible Tiger Club recognition ever made to our Chairman since the Club's inception. It was well-deserved, for his placing was the Club's highest in the '68 Air Racing Championships.

Mrs Peter Masefield presented the Trophies. The de Salis went to Geoffrey MacBreen – an award for the most commendable service to the Club during a member's first year; Geoffrey rightly earned his by his unstinted help when he flew back from the States to give evidence at the Tandridge Affair. The Trophy was accepted on his behalf by Bob Winter. The hilarious stage whisper: "He's the only person I know who can go low flying and get a Trophy for it!" was attributed to Tony Haig-Thomas. Pete Jarvis took the McAully Trophy home and John Firth, second, earned a medallion. Inevitably Neil Williams carried off the handsome Tiger Club Trophy. I'm not sure but I think it's the fifth or sixth time he has won it. (Isn't it traditional for someone to win a pot outright after winning it three times in succession? I'm not mixing it, just interested.) James Black got the second place award. The Air Squadron Aerobatic Trophy went to Frances MacRae and the Esso Tiger Trophy to Michael Riley with Tony H.-T. runner up. Personally, I think the most outstanding award was the one given to Hubert Schnabel. His 2,000 mile adventure over eight countries and over seven seas within the span of sixteen hours to win the Dawn-to-Dusk Trophy was as impressive a piece of flying as any I've heard of.

Formalities were soon over and then began the round of tables to catch up with friends we hadn't seen in ages. Good to see the backroom man responsible for the Club's fleet, "Tommy" Thompson, and at the same table, vivacious Mavis Harriott, the Club's hard-working Treasurer. There are times when I think it would be a good idea to sport name tags, so that others too could acknowledge those persons they'd otherwise never recognise. Also present, but not formally for a change, was the Secretary-General for the Royal Aero Club, Simon Ames, and Sally his gorgeous wife. We missed Mr and Mrs Frank Hounslow (Frank is Rollason's Chief Engineer) and James Baring – a bit of Asian flu all round – but Nini, James' wife, turned up to organise the Tombola. It was a good evening, a very good evening indeed, even if no one was to win the magnificent Beta racer in the foyer. Someone had hopefully stuck a raffle ticket on it. For the record it had its maiden flight this evening – 24 hours after its much-admired appearance at the Hilton.

Committee minutes: March '69
House Committee iv. Treacle Tart.

After years of Committee experience I can still stop and wonder anew. 'Treacle Tart.' In a meeting that encompassed the doings of a huge Club, to find item iv. is akin to stumbling over the Koh-i-Noor. At a guess it was a straight-faced request that hungry Club members be granted bigger slices of our favourite pud. Big, small, serious or bordering on hysterically funny, our Chairman faithfully treated each item solemnly. Unreal.

CLUB NEWS: APRIL 1969

Well, spring is here and already the visitors from overseas are arriving at Redhill to see for themselves the sort of flying we do. And they're envious. It's of interest to note their comment, and they all say the same thing: "How wonderful to fly as freely as you do, and on these aircraft; the same freedom and aircraft just don't exist back home!" With the line-up of the new and exotic, the vintage and slightly mundane, we are lucky. Even spoilt, perhaps. I wonder our reaction if, ten years hence, someone was to say: "How would you like the chance to fly a Puss Moth, a Fox Moth or a Tiger?" I reckon we'd really go out on a limb to do so, and yet these fine old aircraft are always available – at least they are at the moment. My advice, get flying them whilst they are still around.

Talking about the exotic, I hear that Paul Bannister is painstakingly rebuilding the Cosmic Wind somewhere in the heart of Warwickshire. Michael, who visited him recently, reports a lot of progress but there's probably another two years work there yet. Paul's estimate of cost in material and labour, perhaps £10,000. Paul has built a magnificently-finished Midget Mustang, which again, according to reports, has one of the most beautiful finishes ever lavished on an aircraft.

Elsewhere in the *"Rag"* is more about the McAully Group Fly-In on May 3-4. This is going to be a great get-together and, since everyone who can beg, borrow or steal an aeroplane is invited, it could, and should, turn out to be the event of the year. As I write this though, I have the uncomfortable feeling that no matter how much enthusiasm I engender no one is going to take the least notice. Unfair? Well, consider the scheme we thought up to raise money for that worthiest of funds, and the Club's only voluntary cause, the Legal Fund. Two months ago we planned a simple contest asking members, and there are nearly 700, to guess the total number of light aircraft hours flown by members . . . entry fee a nominal 5/-. Well, we can now report that the contest was won by Major P.F.W. Clarke: his guess 183,000. Not only was his guess the nearest to the actual figure of 343,466 (a figure laboriously extracted by Michael), it was also the *only* one. Why not make amends for previous omissions and make this a memorable weekend? See you there.

By the time this is read it's probable that the second and most unofficial sortie against the Navy has taken place. Remember the first? The flour bombing of the minesweeper and reciprocal gunnery practice? It was great fun. Rumour has it the bombs are going to be lighter this time – eggs. New Members this month include Roy Booth and Ray Hanna, both ex-members of the Red Arrows team. Welcome fellas. I'm dying to find out at first-hand if formation in Tigers is, as some suggest, harder than in jets. Re Displays: Robin Voice has temporarily taken over the Display Director's job, those interested in helping please contact him, or sign their names on the notice board lists at Redhill. This year it looks as though there will be just one Full Display, probably at Shoreham; the remainder of our appearances will be participation acts, and already they include several abroad.

The year under review was to provide yet another record number of aero tows. It's easy just writing those words, but in truth the task was both daunting and refreshingly back to basics. In any normal flight one tended to overlook the little plaque Norman Jones had placed in the aircraft: "All Aircraft Bite Fools." There's a little leeway to precision, an airspeed higher or lower by a careless turn, who's to see; but glider-towing was different, for airmanship had always to be of the highest order . . . it brought out the best in a pilot.

. . . And yet there was, on a summer's day, a magic abroad, the silent flight above, a sharp, almost physical awareness of the sweet sea of grass all around, and the deep satisfaction of real flying in the best of company. 'Mike' captures it all.

CHALLOCK – by a Tug Pilot

Let's imagine the month to be May; the Kentish Weald surrounds me and the windsock hangs, half-cocked, beneath the cotton wool cumulus clouds, amidst a deep blue sky. In front of me, the Tug Marshaller waves his arm below his waist, to indicate taking up slack on the tow rope. I glance at the windsock and gingerly open the Super Tiger's throttle – she rolls gently forward for a few feet then starts to hesitate – slack has been taken! "All out!" signals the Marshaller and I smoothly let forth the full power of our yellow and black Super Tiger. A few seconds pass but nothing happens, the tail comes up but she refuses to move. I juggle with the rudder to keep her straight, then slowly she starts to accelerate. My eyes are fixed on a point ahead – keep her straight – gently hold her down: speed's building up now, 35 kt, and on my left the Clubhouse flashes by. I gently ease the stick back and both tug and glider are airborne. I allow the speed to increase to 45 kt – a quick glance back at the glider to ensure all is well – yes, she's OK and I raise the nose of the Tiger for the climb.

We climb very gently at about 250-350 ft per minute over the trees past the ridge, now the vast panorama of the Kentish scene is ours. To our left Margate and Canterbury, Lydd and Romney Marsh ahead, and last but not least the Sussex forest weald, in the 16th century the very nucleus of the Sussex iron industry; on such a day as today the view is breathtaking! "The Tiger is now overflying the area south of Charing," observes the duty pilot organising the launch area. "Bring up the Capstan ready for the next tow." No sooner is this said than willing hands jump to the next job, and gliding requires great stamina and self-control. How many power pilots would, in exchange for one, perhaps two, flights of 10-15 mins on average, work solidly from 8.30 am till late evening?!

I turn to climb downwind to position the glider in a few minutes about 3 miles upwind of the field. The altimeter slowly creeps past the 3,000 ft mark, then the whole aircraft lurches forward, the glider has released! Now I look behind quickly to make sure all is well; yes, the glider behind is soaring gently to the left. OK. Now I must get down with no delay as I know the other keen gliding types are watching me. In fact, as I roll the Tiger up and over into a near stall turn to the right (I never in fact stall or spin off height in case the rope gets tangled with the rudder), I can almost hear them saying: "There he goes, the Tiger's on his way back." Easing out of the dive at about 1,800-2,000 ft I commence a curved slipping turn to finals over the chicken farm. Balancing the aircraft over the fence, pulling the tow-rope release handle and making a short-field landing almost takes my attention off the tow-rope recovery crew – but not quite.

"Ken" Brissenden and I have been towing gliders since early morning in half-dozen shifts. My day started when one of the instructors (I won't mention his name but I can remember a time when I towed him through a no-return valley of cumulus and just skimmed the Tiger's wheels on the flat tops. Unfortunately, he being lower was not so lucky!) burst into the bunkroom at some unearthly hour in the morning shouting: "Where is that b***** lazy Tug Pilot? It's 8 am already"; the day had started!

The strip at Challock is grass with quite a few interesting potholes. It is situated high on the North Downs just above Ashford. All the Club's buildings were built entirely by the members – a really splendid effort. The only snag being the morning ritual of rounding up the sheep (I once suggested a rapid way or rounding 'em up but became immediately discouraged when I saw the farmer carrying a gun – I don't fancy the Tiger's handling with an aileron half shot off!!). Flying at Challock continues until dusk when everyone mucks in to get the gliders and tug away safely in the hangar. It's only a tiny hangar and requires skill as a hangar-packer to get them all in. No sooner are the aircraft away than all the lads are gathered around the bar in a semi-alcoholic state describing the thermal that got away!

"Come on, Mike!" shouts a nearby chap. "Oh! sorry," I exclaim, "I was just thinking of what I should write if Michael asked me for an article on glider towing at Challock for the Tiger Club." A smile spreads over his face. "What Club?" he shouts back. I smile back and mutter a few words under my breath! I open the

Tiger's throttle again; this time I am going to tow a chap to West Malling where he will set out on his cross-country. Soon "Ken" will take over and I shall be able to lie on the grass watching the tug and glider climbing gracefully over the Kent countryside. But until then I enjoy myself, as I climb over the trees, glancing back to see that all is well with the glider!'

STOP PRESS:
Congratulations to Club Member and Tiger enthusiast Cliff Robertson on his Oscar for his performance in "Charly."

Mention of Cliff stirs memories. As a matter of fact Cliff Robertson had become a good friend to the Club and to Lollie and me in particular. When, early in the previous year, Cliff learnt that Lollie had had a rotten time having our first child (the nuns were angels but immune to pain – at least in others) he urged that she have the next (for Toby was on the way) in America, where they were light-years ahead in birth management. Moreover, he enthused, the babe could enjoy dual nationality.

As it happened Cliff was at that time in a film being shot over here called *"Devil's Brigade"* and he must have suggested my name to the UK division of United Artists. The producer, Frank Bevis, phoned me. Would I be willing to act as the air adviser whilst they were filming over here? Frank, a most civilised fellow, offered me money and mentioned they were also looking for a military adviser. "It's routine," he added carelessly, "nothing much to do, why don't you take it on?" More money. The air side was a doddle. I arranged some flying at Henlow, fixed up a static display and hired things – easy peasy.

They got their money's worth on the military side though. The director turned his nose up at reality, he wanted an imposing Combined Operations HQ. He picked instead of New Scotland Yard a big girls' school in Esher set in magnificent grounds. "That's more like it," he said as the military vehicles I'd hired thundered up and down the sweeping drive to the imposing colonnaded house.

Only one shot was needed on the public highway. Outside the grand entrance gates the police had stopped all traffic as Louis Mountbatten's open Humber (actually it had been Monty's) swept through. The guards presented arms – or tried to. The spectators, it looked like most of Esher, burst into laughter.

The director yelled: "Military adviser forward."

A hush descended. Someone gave me a push. "Go on," they hissed, "it's you."

I was rooted to the ground; inadequate for the task was an understatement. As I resisted the nudges an unknown suddenly stepped out briskly from a nearby group and in no time at all had them presenting arms correctly. To muted cheers from onlookers the C. in C. Lord Louis swept on.

"Who was that?" I asked the assistant producer when my voice had returned.

"He's the *Canadian* military adviser – didn't know he was over here."

Never again, I promised myself – not even for money.

And it was this hard-earned money that enabled us to check out Cliff's claim. America was all he said it would be, and Toby got himself dual nationality.

The Tiger Club was called in again – thanks again to Cliff – to help with some filming in Ireland during the summer of '69 down at a remote airfield called Weston, near Dublin. With several Club members we flew modified Curry Wots made over to resemble World War I SE.5As. There was a rash of first war films around then, probably cobbled together to try and recoup the money these under-powered monstrosities had cost the American film industry . . . and Ireland was the ideal backdrop, green, unspoilt and handy for nipping back and forth from Redhill in James Baring's SM.260.

OTTER TO OTTAWA, HAPPY SNORING, PASSENGERS AND BARRY

CLUB NEWS: MAY 1969

With all the excitement over the *"Daily Mail"* Transatlantic Air Race just dying down it's an opportune moment to congratulate Sheila Scott on her £1,000 win, and to commend Julia Turner, Vivian Wales and several friends of the Tiger Club on their participation and success. Mia Slovak earned a well-deserved £1,000 too for his exceptional endurance and navigational skill in his seven-day trip in a Fournier RF.4. Bill Chesson was instrumental in fixing his final transport arrangements at this end. Nearer home, the Isle of Man Races provided enough excitement for a spell with the Rollason Betas taking the first two places. To Fred Marsh, who temporarily deserted his beloved "Pie in the Sky" Emeraude for a ride in a Beta, first place, and newcomer to racing, Michael Jones, came in second. No more than ½ mph separated their times. Tom Storey expects his Cassutt racers will be flying in a couple of weeks and provide a challenge to the Betas in the new formula races, the first scheduled at Rochester on the 12th July. Already the two Betas are fully booked to be flown by several pilots at every race in the calendar this season. A third is nearly ready to fly, and if I'm not letting a cat out of the bag, the first has already been sold.

Current quote: Norman Jones overheard in the tea room, Redhill: "I remember once when I formated on a seagull. I crept up quietly in my Turbulent behind it and you should have seen the look on its face when it turned round and saw me!"

We reprint a remarkable article, by courtesy of B.W.P.A. Janet is by any standards a superb pilot, and her long-distance ferry trips are becoming legend. This is the story of just one of hundreds made in her typically quiet modest way.

OTTER TO OTTAWA
by Janet Ferguson

I can now find my way with ease to each of Reykjavik's seven or eight cinemas, I know the playing order of the piped music in the airport hotel by heart, and the Icelandic Met Men will probably groan when they next see me . . . all due to an enforced two weeks sojourn in Reykjavik waiting for suitable weather to get to Greenland. This was the longest of several delays in a very protracted ferry flight last November. The exercise set was to take an Otter from Gatwick to Ottawa via Prestwick, Iceland and Greenland; the equipment was one VHF transceiver, one ADF and one HF set. In addition I carried a portable Bayside VOR (which I never used after Scotland) and a Bayside VHF transceiver as a standby, both strapped down on the seat beside me; otherwise the normal flight instruments, but no autopilot and no de-icing, nor, incidentally, a heater as the aircraft had been based in Cairo for most of its life. A ferry fuel system was fitted at Gatwick, consisting of three 44-gallon drums in the cabin with a very simple and effective feeding arrangement.

Unfortunately the aircraft wasn't ready to leave until mid-November – hence the problems of low temperatures and very little daylight on the northern route, making it difficult for a slow aircraft with no de-icing. I planned a couple of days stop at Prestwick while Scottish Aviation sorted out a few snags with the aircraft and then I was ready for the next hop – but the weather wasn't. Five more days passed before I had a good enough forecast for Iceland. Ironically it was then clamped at Prestwick, but that was the least of my worries as there was no problem going IMC with the freezing level a reasonable 5,000 feet for the first part of the route. However, the people at the hotel at Prestwick seemed surprised when I checked out and disappeared into the murk, after spurning excellent (local) flying weather over the previous few days!

I had originally intended to go from Reykjavik to Söndrestrom in Greenland, then across to Frobisher Bay in Baffin Island and south to Seven Islands. Although this route was not the most direct, it did offer the shortest sea crossings. However, when I started my enforced wait in Iceland I realised I'd have to be prepared to go to either Söndrestrom or Narssarssuaq in order to have any chance of making a move. Narssarssuaq is in the south-west of Greenland and provides a convenient midway point between Reykjavik and Goose Bay in Labrador, but it has its weather problems and must be treated with respect. It is surrounded by mountains as it lies at the inland end of a forty-mile fjord and behind it the mountains rise steeply at the start of the ice cap. On each side of the fjord the mountains are 4,000 to 5,000 feet high, so if the ceiling is less than 5,000 feet you have to let down over the sea and then fly up the fjord beneath the level of the mountain tops, being sure to follow the right fjord so that you don't find yourself at a dead end! Needless to say, one has to have a pretty safe forecast for Narssarssuaq before taking off from Reykjavik, particularly as there's no diversion.

Söndrestrom itself is not so tricky – it lies near the west coast of Greenland, just off the edge of the ice cap; but the route from Reykjavik includes about 350 miles over the highest part of the ice cap (topping 11,000 feet in places), which in an aircraft with no heating and an outside temperature of perhaps minus 50°C would be pretty chilly! The real problem with the Söndrestrom route, however, was that when Söndrestrom itself was clear there was usually cloud over the east coast of Greenland and no way of knowing how thick it was or how far it extended inland; and one couldn't risk ploughing across the ice cap on instruments, quite apart from the icing problem. On the Narssarssuaq route, if cloud prevented one from flying across the 90-mile stretch of ice cap direct to the airport, one could follow the coast all the way round, though this adds at least 1½ hours to the flying time. On either route one had to plan to arrive the other end at least an hour before sunset to allow for contingencies (Narssarssuaq is a 'daylight-only' field) and that meant taking off two hours before sunrise, hence another snag if there was low cloud and surface freezing en route as for obvious reasons one didn't want to fly very low over the sea in the dark.

These were the problems confronting me in Iceland, and unfortunately for two weeks there was a succession of Lows moving across the Atlantic just south of Greenland producing cloud all up the east coast, and usually dodgy conditions at Narssarssuaq. Thus my sojourn in Reykjavik proceeded tediously with much frustration (though it could well have been a worse place to get stuck), and as the days progressed, so the hours of daylight grew less and less – a real problem with a slow aircraft like the Otter. Finally the day came when Narssarssuaq's forecast was good, the freezing level *wasn't* on the surface for a change, and there were good tailwinds, allowing extra time for going the long way round the coast if necessary. Another aircraft, an ex-RAF Anson being taken across by an American pilot for sale in the U.S., was going the same day and was about half an hour ahead of me. When he reached the Greenland coast the Anson pilot called back and said he couldn't get on top of the cloud and was going round the coast under low cloud in a snow shower; so I took advantage of his weather report and pointed the nose at the Prince Christiansund NDB on the south-east corner, rather than leaving it to my left for a direct track to Narssarssuaq. I made landfall at the beacon, and started following the desolate icy-looking coastline at 1,000 feet. Shortly before reaching the entrance to the Narssarssuaq fjord another aircraft called me up and asked me where I was. This turned out to be a Dornier Skyservant flown by a Danish ferry pilot whom I had met in Iceland. He was coming the other way and landed just before me, with the Anson about 20 minutes earlier – quite a rush of traffic for this desolate place – and we all compared notes over a cup of coffee.

I was stuck in Narssarssuaq for two days. The first day the fjord itself was completely clamped – it snowed all day with about quarter-mile visibility; the next day the weather was fine locally but the forecast for Goose Bay gave snow with low cloud, surface freezing and quarter-mile vis. The third day I phoned the Met man at 6, only to be told that there was a complete communications blackout. This happens at Narssarssuaq about once or twice a month and means that one can't get any weather information because HF radio communications with the outside world have broken down. This is the most frustrating situation of all, as the weather may be perfectly OK but one has no way of knowing. I packed up for the third morning running and got ready in the hopes that contact would be made, although these blackouts sometimes last a day or two. Eventually signs started to filter through and by mid-morning the weather men had received a surface weather chart by radio and also the forecast for Goose Bay. Although there was the chance of snow showers en route, the Goose landing forecast was good – nothing lower than scattered cloud at 1,000 feet. This was just what I wanted, particularly as I would now be arriving after dark thanks to the delay.

I got the aircraft de-iced and into the air as quickly as possible and set off on a track to the weather ship halfway across. (This was only very slightly off the direct line from Narssarssuaq to Goose and would serve as a useful track and ground-speed check.) I had requested in my flight plan for the NDB on the weather ship to be switched on and had an indication on my ADF after a couple of hours flying. As I was having trouble with my HF radio, I listened out on the weather ship's VHF frequency until I heard an airliner talking to the ship and getting a radar fix. I then gave the airliner a shout and asked him to relay my position report (estimated, of course) and also pass me the latest Goose actual and forecast. When I was within range of the weather ship myself I spoke directly to them, but on this occasion I was only in range for a short time as I was having to fly very low due to the low cloud base in rain and snow showers. In fact my report of my height, along with aircraft type and airspeed, caused some interest both from the ship and the airliner which had been relaying for me, and a little chat ensued between the airline captain and myself about what I was doing "down there"! As I neared the Labrador coast the showers stopped and I started a gradual climb to a reasonable height, just reaching the coast in daylight; for the final hour's run to the airport I was at 6,000 ft (the lowest safe IFR altitude for the area) but only in cloud for about ten minutes, with no sign of ice. This was my third 7½-hour hop, the Prestwick-Reykjavik and Reykjavik-Narssarssuaq legs being just about the same distance.

I felt my troubles were over, having reached Goose, and they almost were – only one day's delay there, when continuous heavy snow prevented any movements. The following day I had planned an early start, with a breakfast stop after three hours flying; but things went awry when my VHF radio packed up on taxying out and the Bayside didn't seem to want to function either. Depression set in, but luckily I remembered an excellent radio man who had come to my help a few weeks earlier when I had trouble with a Beech 18 on route to Los Angeles. I caught him at home – it was Sunday – and he came out and fixed the radio on a temporary basis, enabling me to make a start, albeit two hours late. Breakfast at Seven Islands turned out to be "brunch" – at 2.00 pm – and I was still having trouble with the radio, so I only filed to Quebec to avoid flying after dark in marginal weather with dubious radio. This leg wasn't too difficult navigation-wise – straight down the St. Lawrence river – and I'd filed VFR so that I didn't have to talk to anyone.

After arriving at Quebec I rather rashly booked myself on a 1.00 pm flight from Ottawa to New York the following day and the night flight from New York to London, in the hopes that I could get from Quebec to Ottawa, hand over the aircraft, and dismantle the bits and pieces that I had to take back to England, all before once again the system broke down, though luckily not enough to thwart my return home. Planned schedule: up at 5.00 am, at airport by 5.40; check weather and file flight plan; 6·00 check aircraft, start engine and warm up (a long process with minus 20° temperatures); have breakfast when airport coffee shop opens at 6.30; take off at 7.00. Actual schedule: as planned up to 6.00; I then discover aircraft battery won't cope with low temperatures and so find local airline employee with a view to getting ground power at 7.00 after breakfast. First he says "Impossible" as they're expecting an aircraft in for servicing; after persuasion he says "Now or Never" so I hastily load baggage into aircraft and accept external start gracefully at 6.30 am. It's more important to get started for Ottawa than to eat breakfast, and I had hopes of being welcomed with a cup of coffee the other end.

It was under two hours to Ottawa, but long enough to get extremely cold; furthermore, no coffee on arrival – quite the reverse in fact. As the last straw in a worrying and frustrating trip, the "customer's" comment on seeing the Otter was: "We don't really want this aircraft here, can you take it somewhere else?" I certainly couldn't and didn't, and I firmly handed over log books, papers etc. and got a reluctant receipt for the aircraft. By the time I'd done this I had under two hours left in which to get the equipment out of the Otter and packed into my baggage. This involved taking out the ADF indicator which I'd borrowed from Scottish Aviation to replace the existing u/s one, extracting the crystals from the HF set which belonged to my ferry company, disconnecting the two Bayside radios from the aerials and packing them up, and dismantling all the pipes and cocks in the ferry fuel system, taking with me the taps, hose and connections for use again on future trips. All this with the aircraft outside in the freezing cold and working against time to catch my 1.00 pm flight. My efforts to pack all the ironmongery into the kitbag I had brought for the purpose had to be seen to be believed. If I'd had time, I'd have had a laugh about it; as it was I just got more and more desperate. Eventually all was packed away and I managed to persuade the customer to run me and my baggage down to the other end of the airport to check in for my flight. I saw the airline girls wince as I approached the desk with a large suitcase, brief case, BOAC flight bag full of maps, kit bag full of heavy plumbing, holdall with the overflow, two Bayside radios loose, and an enormous four-man dinghy. However, that was their worry now, as was the journey back . . . which took somewhat less than the 26 days I'd taken for my journey!

LITTLE SNORING FLY-IN AND McAULLY TROPHY MAY 3-4

For the second year running the weather turned up trumps for the McAully folk. Spring seemed to arrive along with the visitors to this lovely part of Norfolk. A gentle breeze full of nature's loveliness caressed us as we began to turn brown – I think most of us spent the entire two days sunning ourselves. Essentially the weekend belonged to the aerobatists, flying their sophisticated sequences against a brilliant sky in a bevy of machines that included at least 4 Zlins, Stampe, Tiger and a beautiful Bücker Jungmeister.

The Saturday started with a misty brilliance that soon cleared. To welcome visitors were all our old friends, Barbara McAully, Tony Southerland, Denis Kirkham and a host of cheerful helpers constantly on the go brewing up tea and handing out locally-made hamburgers, home-made fruit pie and real thick fresh cream. They live well, do the people up there.

It's a memorable airfield, is Little Snoring, with its long ex-USAF runways now somewhat overgrown and nestling between crops; where deep black hangars haunt the skyline and all around dwell the undisturbed ghosts of WW II. A quiet place, I never fail to feel this link with the past, and my own memories are touched and I feel nostalgic. Shades of "12 o'Clock High," I suppose.

The Saturday afternoon we spent lying on our backs in the sun watching the contestants for the McAully Trophy. There's a separate report elsewhere in the "Rag." Lollie and I, accompanied by Sue Phillips and a Swedish visitor, Roger Forss, had flown up in the Jodel Musketeer, more intent on the social side of things, as befitting a Fly-In. It began with a vengeance that evening. Tony Southerland farms up there, and he lays claim to owning Norfolk's second largest barn. I find it hard to conceive there is a larger. Imagine an elongated cathedral twice the area of the hangar at Redhill and, incidentally, twice the length, and you're somewhere near the size of this ancient lofty structure. No one locally seems to care, or know, how old it is; only Londoners living in a modern city would ever ask and wonder. A personal guess is aound 400 years old. In its gloomy timbered heights wing bats, and here Tony had festooned gay fairy lamps, while below the barn's flagstones had been scrubbed in preparation for the dancing. Around were grouped the tables and chairs, obviously from the local church – it's the one that Nelson worshipped in as a boy.

Capture a warm starlit evening, the local band, and lots of good food laid out on long trestle tables, good drink, laughter and friends, and you've an inkling of the fun we all had. The local hostelries cared for most of the visitors but we stayed at the farm where Bridget, Tony's wife, gave us a real farmhouse breakfast and brought us up to date on all the gossip.

Sunday began lazily, sunnily and late. A spot-landing contest was laid on but since everyone seemed happy enough just to sit and eat and watch the flying, it died an unlamented death.

Good to see so many Tiger Club members in that part of the world. Among them Tom Crane, Charles Boddington, Paul Conyers, Roy Legg (the new owner of that desirable Jungmeister), Dawn and Alan Turley – looking very fit and both obviously enjoying the ex-service life – Ray Turner and Mike Popoff, to say nothing of the entire Redhill contingent of aerobatists, their supporters and Judges. We left late afternoon in visibility so good that we got lost.

CLUB NEWS: JUNE – JULY 1969

I may moan about the condition of Redhill at times but when it's been as lovely as it has over these last five weeks I must well and truly shut up. There can be no lovelier place on the face of this earth than Redhill bathed in sunshine, and the opportunity to take out a Tiger to fly just for the fun of getting the sweet wind in one's face is as near heaven as words will allow. Best of all the old Tiger 'CDC is back again with us, magnificently refurbished by the Rollason boys, among whom must number some of the last real craftsmen in wood and fabric.

The third Beta is just about ready and the first of the Cassutt Racers is being sprayed – all this in the Redhill hangar. The Cassutt must surely be the smallest racer made; just where Tom Storey is going to squeeze his six foot plus is beyond me. Incidentally Tom features this month in the Hatches, Matches and Dispatches. He gets married to Vicki Martin later this month. Our congratulations to them both and to John and Jill Anning the same again on the arrival of a daughter, Charlotte, and to Tony and Julia Haig-Thomas, a daughter Hanna. To one and all our best wishes.

F3, the new kind of Air Show sponsored by the Air League, is now only two short months away. If you believe that the youngsters should get a real look in at General Aviation then this is the event to support. Make a note in your diary now: 13-14 September. The theme is flying for fun and all the ways of doing it cheaply. Fly up there for the weekend and take the family. If it's more information you want contact Chris Paul. From Ann Proctor the promise that the Proctor and Minton families plan to bring the Kittiwake into Redhill this month for members to sample. Watch the notice board for the latest gen. This beautiful home-built is fully aerobatic, and Chris Paul in a recent review likened its handling qualities to that of a Mustang. Will try and include a fuller write-up next month.

This may be a bit late to advertise the Air Races Weekend just upon us, but if you're outside the hangar with nowhere to go – and there is an aeroplane left – head eastwards along the hills into Rochester for a full weekend of flying, the likes of which only Bill Chesson can provide. This year the Club is only going to put on one Full Display. Previous years have seen five or six. This one will be down at Shoreham on August 10 and will be a golden opportunity for members who have never seen one of our full displays to turn up and support us. It's a family occasion. Come by car, or plane or even boat – just come. But display flying is by no means dying for lack of activity, indeed the current participation factor is the highest in the Club's history with Club members flying somewhere every weekend. If you're interested in helping, Robin Voice is the man to contact.

A warning. Will members please avoid flying over Nutfield Village at any time but especially during church services on Sunday. To do so is but a common courtesy and anyway the more goodwill we can engender the better. A harassed Michael thanks you. Glider-towing is going strong and by the middle of June had logged over 1,200 tows. Here is an important and much-unsung club activity, and I hear the team is always in need of pilots to help. It's hard and exacting flying but there are few better ways of improving one's skill.

As we go to press exciting reports are coming in of the Dawn-to-Dusk competitors' adventures. Over 20 entries have been received. More next month. Is there a club member who would like a fine unique aircraft to cherish? Brian and Pat Iles are shortly leaving for Malta, and they can't take their beloved Miles M.18 with them. Their main concern is that it goes to a good home and if possible maintained in flying trim. Whilst we'll all miss Brian and Pat – they've been members for years and been through all the fun – it's a scant consolation that they'll be able to set up a Tiger Club cell in Malta; and it is a great place for a winter weekend. From Jill Southam, a plea on behalf of Anthony Smith who had the great misfortune to lose by fire his famous balloon "Jambo." If members have photographs which might prove suitable for the book Anthony is writing, would they please get in touch with Jill.

Was much impressed with the BLAC flying Training Clinic programme scheduled for the end of this month. Not only are the brief courses exactly right but the additional envelope containing a couple of Aspros hit exactly the right note. Where to get an element of planned advanced training is a headache. Our congratulations on a brilliant idea and one that deserves our fullest support. My favourite course? It's for the wife. BLAC ask: Can YOUR wife fly your aeroplane in an emergency and save YOUR life as well as her own? Good question and worth £16!

So much going on. But a niggle was brewing. The Tiger Club membership was graded. Given the necessary 100 hrs and having passed the flying test the new arrival became an Associate Member. If you kept your nose clean for a year or two you could expect to become a Full Member. That was fine for the flying fraternity; it was the "Passenger" classification that didn't go down too well. A letter from a "Passenger" put their point of view succinctly:

TALKING POINT

"Most of the correspondence in the "Rag" flies around between licensed skymen. May I chip in please, as a "Passenger"?

As one who is not accustomed to passengership in its wider sense I am concerned at my inability to rise above the nuisance value of hangar hanger-on. Maybe I'm typical of the species but I doubt it, in no position to take up flying, though keen; too short to reach higher than the propeller boss without a ladder, though otherwise willing; acquainted with no more than two or three members after numerous visits and with a complex about paying for flights. Who said I need a psychiatrist? Unless otherwise engaged on the days of Away Displays, I'd be delighted to come and bang in the stakes and hang out the ropes, or risk my neck tethering balloons, but what about all the other days at home when flying is strictly for pleasure? The whole point of joining a flying Club is to get one's feet off the ground from time to time, but it's the cadging that worries. Say what you will, toting for a lift and bargaining on the apron afterwards is unpleasant. Delay makes a settlement more difficult still, and without one people quite rightly begin to dive for cover when you next appear.

As a local resident I give moral support to the Club. From my garden I can watch every take-off and landing, bar a few feet, and admire the skill of the upside-down men (and Frances), but from an active point of view I'm out of my depth. Conversation on the field and correspondence in the "*Rag*" is mostly of the 'in' variety – how can it be otherwise? What guest from Beauvais wants to fly to Redhill and then stay with someone who can't swap flying chat? Despite the enormous numbers on the books, effectively the Club is run by and for the nucleus of experienced flying members. To me, the puzzle is why you have permitted so many "Passengers" to join. I would have expected the bar to go down several hundred before me. But now that you've got us, what would you like us to contribute – apart, that is, from the annual cheque? I can't help wondering if it isn't a mistake to join what is, at heart, an exclusive Club unless one is (a) a pilot or (b) a pilot's relative.

When, helmet and goggles in hand, you spy an unfamiliar figure, hesitate and then approach across the grass, do you think: "What joy! Another candidate to introduce to the freedom of the skies – and share the cost." Or is it rather: "Oh, hell! Another scrounging beggar come to be sick in the cockpit."

This grouch, albeit composed with the most kindly intentions, sounds bitter and self-pitying no matter how I rephrase it. It's not meant to be either – just an expression of disappointment at a sterile relationship. Airing it may bring forth a few ideas to our mutual benefit. Or, conceivably, I'll be shot down as an unsociable Jonah. What offers?
R.E.W."

Barry Griffiths wrote a sensible and sympathetic reply, a part of which I reproduce, and I do so with a sense of sadness. I'll explain later:

". . . The question is, what can be done about it? First, I would suggest that the term "passenger member" be dropped; people who join the Tiger Club are not by nature passengers, but people who want to do things, and the term suggests one who does not pull his weight and it is, therefore, far from attractive. This may seem a minor point, but I know that a lot of would-be non-flying members are discouraged by this term. The non-flying members could do something themselves by attaching themselves to a group whose activities most interest them (e.g. aerobatics, formation flying or foreign touring) and sitting in on discussions. I feel quite sure that, far from being excluded, they would be welcomed and given any information they want. There are very few people who do not enjoy discussing their pet subject and expounding at length upon it.

The most important aspect of the problem, I think, is the shortage of passenger-carrying aircraft. I recall that in the early days, when we had mostly two-seat Tigers, we took our ground helpers with us to the various airshows. Without them, any air show would look pretty sick and as members of a flying Club they are surely entitled to expect to travel to the show and back by air and not undertake a long and often gruelling road journey on summer weekends when the roads are choked with holiday traffic. This facility is now sadly lacking and it seems to me to be asking a lot of ground helpers – however keen they may be – to drive to and from some distant aerodrome and to work very hard when they get there. I think that there is an urgent need for the Club to possess some large, passenger-carrying aircraft, preferably twin-engined and capable of getting in and out of small fields. Apart from the transport of ground helpers, this would encourage a lot of people to get their twin ratings and would provide a marvellous opportunity for more people to go to lunches at Berck, the weekends at Beauvais and the other cross-channel functions which are tremendously enjoyable. We have plenty of pilots on the Club who are qualified to fly such an aircraft and it seems to me that such an aircraft would not be likely to suffer from under-utilisation.

It is my earnest hope, in writing this letter, that something positive may be done to assure the non-flying members of the Club that they are not only welcome but needed and that they are an essential part of the life of the Club. Yours sincerely."

Barry was a solicitor with a practice in London's Baker Street and it was there we sought his advice over coffee and he, good man that he was, heard us out with warmth and understanding that did credit to his profession. Now I hasten to add I can't confirm my belief that the pressure we put upon his willing shoulders had any part in his death several months after this letter to the *"Tiger Rag,"* but surely taking on board others' troubles must have weighed heavily on this uncomplaining fellow pilot.

An ever-popular member of the Turb team, Barry was seen to leave a Turbulent formation display up at Barton near Manchester, make no attempt at recovery, and crash. His passing was sad indeed for his family but also for us, for we had lost a constant friend whose good humour and practical wisdom had supported us all. The inquest wasn't conclusive. It didn't appear to be a fault in the aeroplane, yet the question remained among ourselves: had he harboured so much of everyone's problems coupled to those of his own that the pressure had proved too much? Death was no stranger in our world of flying; we mourned, and then, in the way of the young, put it behind us. But Barry was to fly with us for a long time, looking over our shoulders with a worldly concern, his presence a real thing.

TURKISH ADVENTURE, SHOREHAM, PUNCTUALITY AND FARNBOROUGH

CLUB NEWS: AUGUST 1969

The big event for August, as I write the month has barely begun, is the Shoreham Display. It was a great success, and there's a write-up elsewhere in the *"Rag."* One aircraft was missed and that was Tom Storey's Cassutt Racer which is now making its initial flights. Tom and Vicky were away on honeymoon. Incidentally their wedding was practically a Tiger Club affair and pews were full of members stiffly unfamiliar in formal attire.

TOP: Neil Williams test-flying the new Rollason Beta "Blue Chip" at Redhill in the late autumn of 1969. Photo: probably John Blake.
BOTTOM: A rare photograph of Tiger 'RAZ attacking a balloon.
Photo: Author's collection, possibly by John Blake.

TOP: A truly remarkable shot of 'NZ in the act of flour-bombing. Prince Philip flew this particular Turb in 1960. Location, pilot, year and brand of flour unknown! But it's still a great picture. Photo: via Michael Jones.

BOTTOM: The Sea Tiger, moored off the Thames Embankment just above Blackfriars. Pilot Keith Sissons, 1969. Organised by Ron Jacobs to commemorate 60 years of *"Evening News"* deliveries by air.

Photo: via Michael Jones.

TOP: Suggests the John Blake touch: Stampe and a misty Redhill. John Taylor (shirtless) and Brian Smith – the shape of the third eludes me.
BOTTOM: Fournier RF.4D G-AYHY viewed from Stampe 'WEF over Redhill. Photo: Jim Alderton.

TOP: Hangar piece. Pete Jarvis (L), Brian Smith (R) and Stampe. Redhill May 1971. Photo: Author's collection.
BOTTOM: Seaplane 'IVW at the Oulton Broad Regatta, August 1971. Superbly flown by Keith Sissons. Photo: Author's collection.

TOP: Don Lovell at Redhill welcoming guests from Osnabrück to an "At Home" in June 1971. Photo: Author's collection.
BOTTOM: If ever there was an evocative memory of a typical Tiger Club air display it's this one. Happy spectators, little boys squatting our side of the rope, St. John's Ambulance, cameras and a windswept commentator, Mike Jolley, holding the action together. Early seventies, no idea where. Photo: via Michael Jones.

TOP: Fairoaks. Lollie, Toby and Robin with Za Za Barraclough aboard the trusty Jodel Musketeer. Probably 1970. Photo: Author's collection.
BOTTOM: The old and new at rest. Beyond 'CDC is the Wassmer (ex-G-BADN). A photo from 'Chalky' White who is carrying on the Club's traditions at Redhill to this day.

The Seaplane Club is now well under way down at Lee with a Sea Turbulent available for experienced Turb pilots. Extraordinary light-weight, the Turb. It has flown on skis as well. Surely as an all-rounder it has no equal in its class. Man to contact: Tom Freer.

Two members, James Black and Charles Boddington, have been flying for an American film company over at Weston, near Dublin. They have just finished a two-week stint flying replica World War I aircraft including a Triplane, Fokker D.7s, Pfalz and SE.5s, for a film directed by another member, Cliff Robertson. It's hoped that before the unit disbands there'll be a chance for some other members – including myself – to fly some.

Entries for the London-Sydney Air Race this coming December are rolling in, and several members are entered. Norman is entering a Condor and is aiming to fly solo. Speaking about our Chairman reminds me of a typical Norman adventure that occurred recently. He encountered some awful weather and made a precautionary landing in a field full of cows. The cows' curiosity knew no bounds and Norman was forced to sit in the Super Cub starting the engine every now and then to shoo them away. Docile cows may be, harmless they are not, and aircraft have been known to be wrecked by these lumbering beasts. I have seen an Auster, its skeleton stripped bare by a happy herd of fabric-munchers. His vigil was a long one. Unable to move aircraft or isolate his companions, he stayed in the cockpit all night, only fortified by bread and cheese brought over by a kindly farm labourer. On the following morn the weather cleared and a weary Norman resumed his flight. There is a precedent in the Club's history of a similar overnight vigil. Several years ago a new and most conscientious member was caught out by bad weather and lobbed into the Lec field at Bognor. And he stayed with the Jodel 117 for three nights – without food or drink. He had no money, had notified the police, and although offered shelter, elected to stay with the aircraft. Three of us in a Jodel D.1050 eventually got through the fog on the third day and led him home.

If the year was to prove one in which we were short of Full Displays, '69 must surely have been the year we discovered film flying. The Tiger Club's activities had caught the notice of several influential Americans in that industry. Up to now there had been a tendency to bring American pilots over to Europe, but producers were quick to realise there were experienced pilots over here too, and some of the best were flying with the Tiger Club – witness the unequalled standards shown at displays, large or small, over nearly every weekend. A clincher, if one was needed, was that it made financial sense. A film pilot spends 90% of his expensive time on the ground. Some of our experiences were eye-openers. At the time I wrote:

Charles gave me a ring. "Do you want to make some money?" he said. The way he said it made my skin creep. Charles is a deep one and full of fun, but he never jokes about money.

"OK," I said, trying to sound casual. "How much and what for?"

But Charles wasn't to be rushed. "Got a passport?" he asked. "Licences all current, and can you take about ten days off inside 24 hours?"

I did a mental run-down. It took five seconds. "Yes, yes, yes, and I suppose at a pinch, yes."

"Good, you're going to Turkey," and he added: "tomorrow."

"Ye gods," I groaned as I hung up, and mentally began rehearsing an improbable story. A film company, namely Columbia, wanted two pilots in Turkey immediately to fly a couple of SE.5As for a film. Don't ask me why the hurry, I still don't know. Presumably they'd had the script for ages and had been filming for weeks; even the aircraft had been organised. I suppose someone forgot they needed pilots as well. Anyway I was to fly one and Derek Piggott the other. Charles Boddington would join the team in about two weeks.

As I boarded the BEA flight to Frankfurt I had a feeling that this wasn't going to be any routine flying assignment. I had had 24 hours of pack and rush in which to arrange time off from my business, chat up my wife and children, and get jabs. I felt edgy and a 50-minute delay on flight 604 didn't help, especially when I calculated that it left me only 15 minutes to catch my Turkish connection.

I'll say this for BEA: the skipper was most helpful and radioed ahead to hold my connection. He needn't have bothered. I was to sit for an hour in that brand new unmoving DC-9 and helplessly watch my Trident make a complete turnround before we even started the engines.

I spent my time watching the hostess. She was absolutely beautiful, but even she was getting hot under the collar at the delay. We made Istanbul in fair time, but it was the extra 200 miles further on into Turkey that piled on the agony.

They began by practising putting us on and taking us off no fewer than three aircraft — two Friendships and another DC-9. We were too tired to raise more than a hollow cheer when we finally re-embarked on our original DC-9 which, according to the knowing, had in the meantime been out on a lucrative charter. The Turks fly their jets well. They'd had them only a matter of weeks and already were vying with each other for the shortest landing.

On arrival, it didn't take long to catch up with the gossip that is part and parcel of film work. The boys met me at the airport and promptly began to put me in the picture. There was Derek and Ben and Bushy and Ted, our interpreter and our driver. Ben, the chief engineer, was a lovely Irish character. With Bushy and Ted, his Irish sidekicks, he had been assembling the two SE.5A replicas in a vast empty hangar at Ankara Airport, and now they forlornly awaited an air test. How to get permission was the rub. It took us three days before we could get our feet off the ground.

Ben and his boys had done a great job of rigging and we taxied out happily along miles of concrete. Ted trotted along by my side, keeping one eye on direction (no brakes) and the other on the fast-diminishing tailskid. Airborne and above the airport, Derek and I turned and chased one another like boys let loose. Below, officialdom breathed a sigh of relief that our tiny mounts flew at all. It was evening, and the cool air and the security of long runways gave us an optimum performance we were never to experience again.

The Slingsby-built SE.5A looks remarkably like the original, but its looks belie a performance that would have been suicidal in World War I. Top speed, and that with the 100 hp Continental going flat-out – normal throttle setting – was around 80 mph. The best climb was in the region of 200 ft a minute. The trouble lay, of course, in the extra equipment we carried. To our parachutes could be added the drag of two external machine-guns and the weight of the heavy gas cylinders and batteries used for their firing. Several coats of matt khaki paint and the radio didn't help. Considering the altitude of 4,000 plus and a working temperature in the nineties, it was surprising that the little replicas flew at all. In fact, that's what a lot of the fuss was about – no one thought they would.

It's hard to convey the effect that our two 'old' aircraft had on everyone who saw them. The populace, unfamiliar with aircraft of any sort (for there's virtually no internal flying except for the remote military and airline) treated us like heroes, especially since we sported Turkish colours. The further we flew into the hinterland the more the inhabitants goggled.

The following day we were all ready to go at first light. The boys had got the aircraft out by 5 am and nicely warmed up, but it was some time before we were cleared for action. We finally got off for the 200-mile flight to the film location around 7.30 am. Together we hung precariously in the still air, making a steady 70 mph as we overflew a sleepy Ankara at around 1,000 ft, unable to climb any more, sweating slightly with the effort even to stay there, and all the while seeking the one road that led across the desolate hills to our destination, Nevsehir. Turkey has no railways in this part of the country, no airfields and no air maps later than 1942; so we used a free road map issued by the Tourist Board and it worked a treat.

As the sun rose, so did the temperature. There were times when we staggered above that lonely road at no more than 100 ft, skirting for 30 miles the world's largest, incredibly beautiful, salt lake. Turkey must be one of the most awe-inspiring places in the world over which to fly. It's a land of breathtaking arid purple landscapes, with the sort of visibility that's endless. To see Derek's SE suspended to one side of me against a backdrop of such rugged grandeur was a sight no airman could ever forget.

The film people had laid out a narrow wiggly runway on a vast level plateau some 4,500 ft above sea level. It hadn't taken them too much effort to construct it. Some money to a farmer ensured that it was raked clear, and it was supposed to be visited twice daily by the film company's water cart in an attempt to lay the dust.

We descended heavily after three hours, at the end of our fuel, into this world of dust, clouds of which billowed angrily out behind us, and into which our wheels sank deeply. Our ground-crew had yet to arrive, and only a few people awaited us, one a bearded Englishman holding a two-way radio. He'd been listening out for us, hoping to be able to guide us to the site by the sound of our engines. We never did hear his call, or he ours, as our three-channel radios were on the blink.

Then a miracle happened. One minute we were alone in the wilderness; the next we were surrounded by hordes of dusty travellers for whom our arrival was the event of events. They, and the hundreds who were to follow, squatted good-humouredly around us for 24 hours a day, asking only that at the end of each sortie we went a little berserk overhead. They were poor folk, practising farming much as their forebears did 2,000 years ago, and getting no more from the barren soil.

We got a lift to the film set a dozen miles away and were immersed immediately in a self-contained township of instant Coke, instant food and instant flap, where costly equipment and primitive conditions went hand-in-hand. The set was constructed by the waters of a natural dam, and crouched in the lee of towering 500 ft cliffs. It represented a tented encampment (*circa* 1922, the year of the Greek-Turkish Wars) and was complete with artillery and field kitchens. The local Turks were having a field day, earning what must have seemed to them a fortune just to lay around all day as Greek soldiers. There were hundreds of them, with a fitting complement of mules and lively Arab ponies, and our job was to 'strafe' the lot.

Flying for the films is a specialised business. It requires a lot of technical know-how and a nicely-balanced awareness of just how much is possible and how much isn't, if only to counter over-ambitious direction.

"Can you fly at the base of that cliff face and up the side of it?"

Above all else you need the patience of Job. "You're paid to do nothing – the flying's for free," had been Derek's words. Spectacular flying by itself is often pointless if the camera angles chosen by the director fail to give scope; so a considerable amount of camera liaison is necessary before the start.

Derek is a perfectionist, probably best in that small team of film pilots. His now-famous *"Blue Max"* stunt, when he flew under the viaduct arches, is well remembered. What isn't so widely appreciated is that the clearances shown were no camera trick. There just wasn't more than two feet on either side of his wingtips, and he did the sequence no fewer than 17 times before the cameras were satisfied. He's a cool customer to follow. I should know.

As usual, our radios were playing up. Whereas I could receive and transmit 75 per cent of the time, poor Derek could only receive me for about the same period. It was under this additional handicap that we began operational flying.

Everything was OK once we were airborne; it was getting off that was fraught. The heat of the day with the sun well up, unquestionably the best time for maximum light, was purgatory to us. Every inch of that dusty runway was used; and we tottered off, to fly a further mile at the point of stall before we dared begin a shaky turn with our heart in our mouth. Later, with speed under our belts, we were as happy as sandboys and beat hell out of the camp.

To be well-paid for a beat-up is exquisite; but there were hazards, not the least of which was the over-enthusiasm of the effects team, who detonated explosions under us to simulate our bomb-bursts. Their favourite and most spectacular bang was produced by a charge of explosive in a buried tube of sifted earth (a hard-won concession to our safety) above which they'd place a plastic bag of petrol. A fraction too soon with the countdown and we flew through a wall of fire, earning a scorched face and plaudits from the director.

It was extra tough on the following aircraft, which invariably ran into the lot. But if the solid thump of explosions under one's tail was thought-provoking, so was the climb-away to have another go. We escaped low over the water of the dam, hesitant to fly up any of the gently-climbing valleys in case we ran out of height; so we were forced into time-consuming circles before we could scuttle back over the cliffs.

The only time we ever got our panting mounts 1,000 ft above that forbidding terrain (by this time we had discarded our parachutes) was when, during a long, long wait for the film crews to set up another noisy shot, Derek spotted some soaring eagles. Intrigued, we made in their direction and snuggled under them, and for 25 minutes three eagles and two SE.5As circled happily together, oblivious to all but the sweet joy of soaring. I don't believe I've ever been more eager to stay aloft, or have ever been so content, as during those stolen moments.

If the film "You Can't Win Them All" ever comes your way, take time off to think of the pilots nursing height and engine, for if the cameras captured a fraction of the excitement of it all, it'll be worth seeing. Watch, too, for a sequence filmed in that weird volcanic wonderland of Gerome, with SE.5As slithering down steep 1,000 ft cliff faces between rocky pinnacles – although just where that situation appears in the script no one knows or cares. Put it down to sensation-seeking poetic licence.

That mention of flying in Gerome's volcanic wonderland and slithering down a 1,000 foot gash in a cliff face fails to mention that the attempt was made at dawn before turbulence made the endeavour too dangerous. Nor was there room for the two of us to drop together as originally requested. Even nosing over the rim solo and to drop vertically was hairy enough with rock faces pressing in on you as your aircraft fell into the abyss.

The director radioed, could we drop slower? I pondered this as we laboriously climbed for height. With no flaps and pointing downwards, even with engine throttled back, no way could we avoid speeding up.

Derek broke in. "I've an idea," he said. I watched as he slipped over the rock rim. The sun was rising and conditions were worsening. It was now or never.

Derek Piggott is an exceptional pilot. Period. What I witnessed him do was a one-off in sheer nerveless audacity. He boldly fell down that narrow cliff face in a series of falling-leaf stalls, each step marked by a nose-high hesitation that appeared to brush the cliff sides. No way could I have emulated that. When we got back to film city the director and his team were ecstatic, a touch saddened but by no means put out by the news the cameraman had missed it.

FULL DISPLAY, SHOREHAM – AUGUST 10TH 1969

For the first time in nine years the Tiger Club has only offered one full traditional display within a season instead of around five. And what a great show it was. It was quite like old times. The crowds were vast, the weather beautiful, if a little hazy, and Bill Chesson had laid on a very well-organised affair indeed. Even the food was noteworthy. I always think a good meal before a display strikes the right note – at least with the pilots. The Display Director was James Baring who, as far as I could see, organised the whole thing overnight, although it went so smoothly I must surely be doing him an injustice.

John Wilkinson opened the proceedings at three sharp with a spirited showing of the Beta, looping and rolling with abandon. The Turbulent slot that followed put on a masterly piece of formation flying. They were led by Mike Channing, and wing men were John Williams RN and Robin d'Erlanger, with Barry Griffiths in the box. I must say it was good to welcome a completely new act to the show, Pat Lindsay's parasol Morane 230. It was extraordinarily well displayed by Manx Kelly who flew a winner of a sequence in that 37-year-old. His leisurely inverted and looping performance was a sight to behold and, in fact, I rated this act something of a highlight and one we must contrive to keep in future displays. Tied together, a Super Tiger paired by two Stampes gracefully presented themselves. It wasn't so long ago that the act always had three Tigers. It's a sign of the times that at this display there were only two Tigers among the many aircraft present. I never did ascertain who flew what – shame on me and I was the commentator too – but Pete Jarvis, Martin Barraclough and Tony Haig-Thomas were the drivers.

In my humble opinion there is but one really great demonstration pilot in this country and his name is Peter Phillips. It's a pilot's opinion and one shared by many, and at Shoreham he showed his fantastic BA-4 off to perfection. This diminutive biplane flew as if possessed, and Sue Phillips' breathless commentary as she tried to match Peter's lightning manoeuvres lent wonderment to a remarkable performance. Balloon bursting was exactly the item to follow Peter, a competitive fling to encourage spectator participation. At an earlier briefing James innocently asked Tony H.-T. if he'd be able to see the balloons – Tony has an undeserved reputation for short-sightedness – but all three gave the balloons hell. Co-attackers were Robin Voice and Pete Jarvis. Pete also featured in the solo Stampe aeros that followed and brought to the end the first half. Not that there was any respite, for the show continued unabated whilst Charles Masefield did some great flying in the Pup and locals demonstrated their captive Parakites.

The parachutists, The Falling Stars, did OK for themselves except that one inadvertently contrived to switch off 'CDC's front switches as he dived overboard. The pilot, David Hamilton, did an unobtrusive dead-stick landing. Another first-time act was the Brian Stevens and Neil Jensen duo in two RF.4s and as pretty a bit of near-gliding I've seen in a long day. Especially noteworthy was the courage displayed when Brian switched off his engine and stopped the prop – at about 50 ft – to demonstrate how easily the RF.4 re-starts. An act that in my eyes is as valiant as leaving a serviceable aircraft by parachute. Carl Schofield put up a sophisticated display in the Zlin and the Turbs returned for their repeat performance. Martin Barraclough demonstrated the Active noisily and well, and Carl and Pete did some admirable dual aeros in the Stampes. Incidentally they only had some 20 minutes prior practice, for regular team member Bill Innes wasn't able to get along.

The big finale was the standing-on-wing act. David Phillips flew Tiger 'OAA with Georgina Hamilton (Hickey aside: David Hamilton's wife and James Black's sister), and Robin Voice flew 'CDC with Philomena Delany on top. They gave a delightful performance that left the crowds laughing, waving and contented after one of our happiest airshows. To those many stalwarts who helped on the ground, among them Roy Davis, John and Steven and of course Frank and Bob Hounslow, all our thanks. A Tiger Club Display has always been, and always will be, a real team effort.

Committee minutes: July '69
House Committee: Mouse and bird trouble reported. Control tower room is in bad condition and must be ready for entertainment. Regular night charge to be paid for sleeping.

Such mementos of thirty years ago are priceless. Presumably if we stayed awake we'd be entertained for free. I suspect our Chairman had taken a look into the first floor room the Club retained for itself – there was no Air Traffic Control in those days – and pronounced it in need of a clean-up. Earlier we had used the room as a lounge-cum-sleeping room. Ancient iron beds doubled as settees and old armchairs littered the place. But it was never popular, we continued to pack into the hangar rooms. Eventually it was closed, but every once in a while we'd open it up and attempt a film show or party up there, then stay over to fly into the dawn. A noisy beat-up was an effective way of getting us up and about. Bleary-eyed, we'd go out to a greasy spoon breakfast, I think the place was called Sam's – it was on the old A23 Brighton Road near Salfords. Sam never showed surprise, never smiled, and never seemed to close. Perfect.

The mouse and bird bit is quite beyond me now. Birds certainly dwelt in the old hangar, but never a mouse can I remember.

Committee minutes: Sept. '69
Displays: i. Punctuality is as important as good flying.

This coming from our Chairman was a bit rich. Once upon a time when he was the MD of Samuel Jones his chauffeur wouldn't dare be a minute late, but once released from the City Norman did have less than perfect timing. Speaking personally he once hugely embarrassed me. The Club had been invited to give a display at the big Farnborough Show, not the Trade Days, mark you, but the Public Days, Saturday and Sunday, and we were given a slot just before the display proper; after all 150,000 people didn't attend Farnborough just to see us, but we were to be the light entertainment before the big noisy affair. And a great honour it was. For some reason our favourite commentator – John Blake, later to become a regular at Farnborough – couldn't make it. Would I stand in?

Sure, I had now commentated on many many occasions and I wasn't in the least stage struck with the 3,000 or so. They were easy going, nearby, and were there to be entertained. Not so Farnborough. To say it lacked the personal touch was putting it mildly. Charles Gardner, from whom I took over, gave a sympathetic smile and cheered me up with his estimate of the numbers present. "Um, possibly 150,000, give or take a few. You'll get used to the echo of your voice. . . ." Then he left. I was alone.

I looked out from the commentary box in its lofty position, then looked up from the packed masses that lined the vast runways to seek the Turbulent Team that was due on in about two minutes time. I looked in vain. Alone, a live mike and oceans of expectant faces, I started to chat. A syllable behind came the boom of a mighty echo. I listened to myself finish a sentence and attempt another. The hesitant bellow reflected my bewilderment.

Bright blue sky, visibility perfect, Norman proudly led the Turbulents in twenty minutes late. By that time I was giving the life histories of each pilot. I think in an attempt at humour I credited Pete Jarvis with at least six daughters – for he and Pat were ever hoping for a boy. Under-impressed, Farnborough didn't invite me back.

MANHATTAN SEAPLANES, DENMARK AND ESSO

PER PEN AD NAUSEAM
from Taffy Taylor O.C. 208 Sqdn. Bahrain

"While scouring through the May "*Rag*" to see if Norman Jones had recently released any new flying secrets, I found myself trapped by our Editor's plea and my conscience. There is a subtle difference between "I'll almost publish anything" and "I'll publish almost anything," but in the heat out here it is difficult to concentrate on such a fine point so here I go.

It is almost three years since I was a regular eater of raisin bread and sipper of hot tea, but I still have fond memories of a howling wind banging the hangar doors and the rain flooding the southern end of the airfield. Allah being willing I hope to savour it all again in July '70.

In theory I am now running No. 208 Squadron, sometimes based at Bahrain, but in fact the situation is usually reversed. We have trusty Hunter 9s (best cost-effectiveness aircraft ever?) which carry almost anything and can drop it almost anywhere. We usually do. For historians RAF 208 started life as RNAS 8 and so we held our 50th Anniversary before the RAF started planning theirs. The Squadron has battle honours in both World Wars, firstly on the Western Front and then later in the Desert Campaign.

For any aviation enthusiast in the Club the weather in the Gulf is interesting, with two seasons competing to be worst. I have a good idea where I shall end up in the life hereafter, but I am not amused by being acclimatised in this one. For a large part of the summer the isobars are not on speaking terms and the air stagnates. When they do get together occasionally we all get covered in sand; as you old hands will know, this is the second worst thing you can get covered in. In winter we watch a massive battle for air superiority between forces from the Mediterranean (?) and the Indian Ocean. We then have the resultant fall-out which means we paddle around in a great warm lake getting the brown washed off our knees.

For those of you sitting near the fire, with the girl friend in the kitchen and Wales thrashing England on the telly, quietly enjoying the "*Rag,*" just think what it means to the likes of me. Please keep the Editor editing and lest he starts on me I close wishing you all luck and cool flying.
TAFF TAYLOR, O.C. 208 Squadron."

Committee minutes in September encouraged us to believe the glider contingent were on their way to new heights (sorry about that) with a total of 2,666 tows to date. But the entry in October's minutes said much for our Chairman's belief in the viability of operating seaplanes. In two words he neatly expressed his relieved optimism: "*Seaplane: still flying.*" He was also in effect unwittingly expressing his misgivings at the entire venture. It was one thing to operate off of inland waters, quite another off unsteady salty runways. Norman was never one to oppose such a press-on venture, but a touch of the reality was reflected in the cost of mounting maintenance, and with the difficulty of launching and retrieving the hours flown were always going to be minimal i.e. uneconomic.

Eventually the quest to establish freshwater bases was successful, but in the meantime this hardy operation of Britain's only seaplanes struggled on in a brave but doomed attempt to resurrect some of the country's earlier maritime traditions. For that was what it was all about. Our Chairman, firmly supported by "Bish" and by so many of that early Tiger Club seaplane crowd were still living in the past. And what a magnificent host of names were in on the venture, men like Oswald Short, Lankaster Parker, Hubert Broad, Chris Paul and George Eyston; they were all pioneers of that time between wars when the future for seaplanes looked so bright – wasn't most of the worlds surface one large natural landing area? A glorious failure, but I, in company with many others in the Club, count ourselves lucky to have met such outstanding men and to have shared their enthusiasm.

CLUB NEWS: SEPTEMBER – OCTOBER 1969

Suddenly the new formula racers are all the talk at Redhill. To join the three Betas are three Cassutts, and scattered about the country are various other contenders; include in that list the potential Cosmic Winds, both of which could be flying next year. 'RUL, the well-loved "Ballerina," is now well into its rebuild, and its owner has another complete Cosmic, less its 250 hp engine with which it was recently fitted, giving it a reputed 5,000 ft a minute climb. That may have been gilding the lily somewhat but the combination must have been a very potent piece of machinery indeed. Tom's Cassutts fly well, so reports every pilot who has flown them, and currently they are some ten mph faster than the Betas, but development on both mounts will certainly produce a lot more performance. If ever there was a moment to contemplate a racing syndicate it must surely be now.

Hard on the heels of that filming stint in Ireland comes one in Turkey where Charles Boddington and yours truly helped to recreate the skirmishes between Turk and Greek flying woefully underpowered SE.5 replicas. Definition of 'underpowered': a maximum rate of climb in favourable conditions of 100 feet per minute. Altitude and heat weren't exactly on our side. Whilst there our Irish engineers were able to give a helping hand to Janet Ferguson (mag. trouble) passing through Ankara on one of her numerous ferry trips. I should think Janet must by now be the most experienced and successful ferry pilot in the land. The "Rag" regularly gets word of her from all over the world.

There followed the usual third of the page with news of social events, babies, engagements, new honours, welcomes and congratulations. Sugar and honey, that was me. Of injury and demises I wrote little. Could be there weren't any of course, but I did like to conceal unhappiness. A happy childhood probably.

On the home front Michael Jones has asked me to declare an amnesty during which members can return the following:

2 microphone-cum-oxygen masks (one's mine! – Ed.)
1 tropical helmet plus electrics
The wings of Brian's M.18
Two pairs of goggles

In the Share Department the following – Peter Treadaway writes:

"Dear Benjy,
Would it be possible to mention in the next "Tiger Rag" that there is a share available in the two-seat sailplane (Ka.13) which has flown at Redhill on several occasions this year? The machine is based at High Easter, a farm strip near Chelmsford, where, incidentally, if anyone is interested in flying a tug over and doing some aerotowing, the Group will pay half the ferrying time.

Conversion from power to real flying is no problem as we have three instructors!

Many thanks."

And your Editor seeks someone, perhaps a family man, to share the care of a magnificent 28 ft river motor-cruiser, all mahogany and comfort, moored at Windsor. Like an aeroplane its utilization is hopelessly low with its owner trying hard to give both loves a fair run ("Flying, darling, but of course I love you as well.").

No, no one answered my plea to join me in keeping *"Purple Broom"* utilised. Sure they came out onto the river willingly enough, but helping to maintain her, no way. Couldn't blame them really, she was then some thirty-five years old and leaked like a sieve, but she had character, yes sir! If she was tired of going along the engine would stop . . . I swear the engine was so old it knew when it needed a rest. The Thorneycroft engine block had a number which I was assured by the engineer was made in 1911. I eventually sold it to a Frenchman who was going to sail her home across the Channel. I tried to keep my incredulity out of my eyes, but perhaps he made it. She'd reputedly been on the Dunkirk run, so maybe she had confidence even if I hadn't.

One of the best and most remarkable letters the *"Tiger Rag"* ever printed was the following. I can't believe such a ferry service could still exist, but if it does then it's hats off to real pilots, for if the Tiger Club's seaplanes couldn't find the right niche in 1969 here were some that fitted the need like a glove.

COMMUTING IN STYLE – 1969 NEW YORK:
MARTIN BARRACLOUGH REPORTING

If you work in downtown Manhattan (New York "City") and have a country house in Suffolk County on Long Island, there are four ways of commuting in the summer; by train, which takes two hours and is hot and stinks; by car, which at its rare best takes one hour and at its more frequent worst takes 2½ hours; by motorboat, which takes 40 spray-whipped minutes of sea and river time in a twin-engined Bertram and 10 minutes in a taxi (if you can get one in the rush hour) – or by seaplane, which takes just half an hour.

Having had ten years too much of London Transport and London traffic, and having tried the motorboat on a previous visit, I accepted an offer to sample commuting in the style to which I could happily become accustomed, and at 5.20 sharp on a Wednesday evening took my briefcase and overnight bag and left the office in Battery Place with Per, my Norwegian host, an erstwhile visitor to the Tiger Club who I once, to my enduring shame, made very very sick in a Stampe. A brisk 10-minute walk and we were at the East River end of Wall Street where two Cessna 185s on floats were waiting at a landing stage. Two minutes later I was strapped into the right-hand seat of N2215T; the pilot cast off, jumped in, and with the back-seat passengers already engrossed in the contents of their briefcases, we taxied out into the East River. One minute later and pointed downstream towards Governor's Island – half flap, trim, full power – and we were airborne over the Staten Island ferries, arcing left to fly up the East River at 500 ft with the compass having St. Vitus's Dance on the windscreen bracing that rattled like the exhaust of one of Norman's VWs. Sole navaids consisted of a Narco Com/Nav, the only frequencies needed (La Guardia Tower & VOR) being stuck to the panel in dymo tape, simplicity itself. As we crossed the Queensborough Bridge we tuned into La Guardia Tower, the field being some 4 miles ahead and to starboard. An almost unbroken and quite unintelligible stream of patter came over the loudspeaker, and our pilot, mike in hand, looked like a gasping fish as he tried again and again to break in to make contact. When he did, it was brief, as was the reply from La Guardia; no more than an acknowledgement of our identity, position, height, route and destination. Flying past the red, white and blue chimneys of the East Side power stations, we had a fantastic view of Manhattan, Queens and the Bronx; the weather was perfect – choppers, mostly Jet Rangers, fizzed past us, jets and other aircraft were all over the sky, being fired off and landed onto La Guardia in a continuous stream. As we approached the Triborough Bridge, just 2 miles from La Guardia, we dived down until we were flying only 10 ft above the water, two more Cessnas ahead of us down on the deck and passing right under the take-off path of the La Guardia traffic, wingtips whipping past the islands and piers (shades of Peter Vanneck at Brighton) until the mass of the Bronx Whitestone bridge loomed ahead and, pulling back on the pole, we soared up over the traffic to regain 800 ft; well clear of La Guardia, and on a course of 070°, we headed out over Long Island Sound to Oyster Bay. Ten minutes later and with a gentle left-hand glide – fully fine pitch, full flap – pick a path between the yachts anchored at Seawanhaka Yacht Club – hold off with the wind soughing through the cabin vents, giving as good an indication of airspeed and attitude as the A.S.I., and we were down on the water and taxying to the beach. As the motor chopped and we drifted in, Per and I got out onto the float, jumped ashore and gave a quick shove on the tail cone; press the tit, half flap, full power, and in a flurry of spray 215T was off to drop the third passenger a mile further up the Bay, and Per and I were in his swimming pool 38 minutes and 35 miles from his office (by which time in London I would still be changing platforms at Earls Court waiting for that bloody Wimbledon train to come in).

Next morning the pilot telephoned at 7 am to announce the morning schedules and allocate seats. Per took the 8 o'clock flight and I had to wait for the 9 o'clock shuttle. Promptly at 8 the drone of a Lycoming announced his arrival from the east with the first passenger already aboard and again at 08.55 he touched down from the west to collect me. (We don't seem, in English, to have an expression for landing on water: the French have those lovely expressions, "faire l'atterrissage" and "faire l'amerissage" which so aptly fill the bill.) At 08.59 we took off westwards, skimmed the water for no more than a minute and slapped down at another beach to pick up a stockbroker. Stockbrokers, as Tony H.-T. will know, are no respecters of schedules anywhere in the world, so I had a few minutes to chat with the pilot (never did get his name). He reckons to operate the service with two Cessnas from March to November getting 3 hours a day utilization per aircraft, 5 days a week, weather permitting, which is officially VMC, but is in practice down to 1 mile vis. and a few hundred feet ceiling. As we finished discussing the hapless fate of a one-winged seagull whose other wing was hanging forlornly from the float bracing wires, the stockbroker finally wandered down the beach putting on his tie, with his Wall Street Journal under his arm, and at 09.08 we were off again and flying south-west at 800 ft to the Bronx Whitestone bridge and the skyscrapers of Manhattan with other floatplanes converging on us all the way. Down to 10 ft over the river again and we curved past the wharves with a 727 passing right overhead at 200 ft on finals to the threshold of La Guardia's Runway 22, only 1,000 yards on our port beam (how about that, Southern Division?); if the vortices hit the plane it sounds like a crate of Coke cans being dropped. One quick call to the Tower and then up again and over the Triborough Bridge and the mass of traffic pouring into the city. The seaplane ahead of us does a 270 left and slides onto the East River at the 23rd Street base. Past the green glass slab of the U.N. Building and we put the nose down to fly under the Manhattan and Brooklyn Bridges – half flap, full flap – touch of right rudder to avoid a tug and barge – touch of power to take us under the stern and over the wake of the giant tanker *"Esso Nurnberg"* pulling out of the East River for the Persian Gulf, and with a series of slams we're on the churned-up water sharing our quay – time 09.24 – flight time 16 minutes. 12 minutes later at 09.36, and just 28 minutes after leaving Oyster Bay, I make my first telephone call of the working day. Cost? $12.50 each way, which in our devalued money comes to a princely £5.4.0! Justification? To the high-powered American executives, an extra two hours in the office a day, which means that much salary saved, that much more business concluded! Verdict? A grand example of the American "can do" attitude to marine aviation and everyday life.

NOTICE TO MEMBERS STAYING OVERNIGHT AT REDHILL

It appears that a number of members staying overnight at Redhill are forgetting that there is a charge of 4/- per night. So, will all members please remember to sign their name in the book in the bunk room, and put 4/- in the drawer. The same procedure applies to members staying in the Tower. Please also make sure that you tidy up after yourselves, and that you pay for any coffee, tea etc. that you may have. 4/- is not an awful lot of money, so please try in the future to remember, and remind other people who may be staying there as well.

Q. "Why do control zones extend from ground level?"
A. "Aircraft do not wish to fly below ground level, sir."

Committee minutes: November 1969

Glider Towing:	*3,313 tows to date*
Australia Air Race:	*75 firm entries*
Seaplane Section:	*12 hours on Seaplane Turbulent – more encouragement needed*
House Committee:	*Sausages and mash OK for lunch*

If words fail me on "sausages and mash" (was there ever a more evocative suggestion?) then the opposite was true in November. Just contemplate the scope of the Tiger Club's activities in every direction at the end of that year.

CLUB NEWS: NOVEMBER 1969

If ever there was an occasion to write with poetic grace of Nature's loveliness down in Surrey at this time of year – and I'm told I've laboured the point for years – it's now. Unfortunately I've not been down there enough to savour it, so exiles abroad must this time be content with a second-hand report that the continuing fine weather has made flying a joy and the airfield has had a parched hard surface that would do credit to a tropical clime. It's interesting to note the big increase in pilot membership from that sophisticated strata, the big airlines – especially from the States. It's obvious that our sort of flying goes over big, and as one put it: "It's good to fly real airplanes again." Still on the flying side there have been a lot of long jaunts this summer to far-away places, including two to Corfu – both trips in the Mascaret. One such trip took Neil Harrison on his honeymoon, and there were a couple to Malta as well, where Don Lovell led four members to attend Malta's first Air Rally, and I hear Pat Iles was there to welcome them.

Perhaps the best recent flying occasion though was the Esso Trophy held at Rochester. Everyone relates how successful it was and all echo the same sentiment – how much we owe Esso for their support. For the record, not only did they provide free fuel, but starting money for everyone and big prizes too. I hope the Tiger Club members of that great organisation who read this will convey everyone's appreciation to the right quarters. It is gestures like this that keep worthwhile sporting flying going in this country, and directly help our aspirants to show the flag in the world contests.

The British team did well at Dax, France, where the International Leon Biancotto Aerobatic Trophy was held. The winner was Peter Kahle of East Germany with James Black coming fourth. Neil Williams won the contest two years ago, incidentally; Neil has temporarily forsaken competitive aerobatics to concentrate on test flying but doubtless he'll be back for the next World Contests – to be held here for the first time. Clive Rose has just finished a forty-hour sight-seeing tour of Britain in the Husky, pilot for a photo recce by Anthony Smith – an exercise in preparation for a new book of his.

Air Racing has been going great guns with a happy Robin Voice the victor again in a Turbulent. He's just won the Strongbow Trophy at the Shobdon Races and earned the Club and himself £250. He also deserves a pat on the back for a season's hard work organising participation displays. I believe there are now several hundred pounds in the kitty for next year's display practising. That news should stir some of you to start practising. Telegrams and urgent calls direct to Robin. One sight I missed, and I'm sorry, was the latest modification to the Condor. It's a 45-gallon external tank to Norman's possible mount for the Australia Race. If he names it for that occasion he should call it the Pregnant Condor – everyone else does.

This year's Xmas card is a beautiful reproduction of Michael Turner's painting of three Tigers over Goodwood. (I think I was number three, in which case I apologise in advance for being a bit high. – Ed.) They cost 1/6d each and the time to get them is <u>NOW</u>. Miss Reed, who so efficiently ran the teas in the Clubroom for so long, has left us, and is now married – news which will please everyone. And Mike Riley has got engaged to Jackie. All our best wishes to them all.

A sad thought for so many of us is that the Puss Moth has been sold. As a financial proposition it was always a bit hard to justify, for its utilization was ever low, but it has gone to a good home – in fact to Father MacGillvray over in the States, where her stable mates will be a Tiger and Hawk Major.

Whenever space permits in successive "Rags" I'm using some 'funnies' gleaned from Air Traffic Control. We are indebted to John Reynolds for their collation. They can't be such a bad bunch you know, and their sense of humour is nothing if not broad – so much so I can only use about half those proffered. Never mind, those I use are worthy indeed. The next Annual Dinner date has been fixed. No less than Friday 13th February – and again at the Hilton.

There was barely concealed anticipation of our Dinner at the London Hilton on St. Valentine's Day. I can't say it was a tradition to hold the big event on that day, but we'd always tried to do so. In the misty past the idea of a fling very early in the new year was, we thought, the very best way to counter bills and wintery weather. And a Beta racer in the foyer, it always looked good, but Michael took great care to empty any fuel first; there was always some joker unable to resist swinging the prop, but not before a glamorous floozie had been crammed in the cockpit with instructions on how to operate the switches. . . .

Roy Booth was the Red Arrows leader at this time. I can't say he was converted to our way of aviating but he gamely gave it a go.

EN ROUTE DENMARK
by Roy Booth

I don't know what I expected when I took the opportunity to fly one of three aircraft to Karup, Denmark, for a Royal Danish Aero Club display. After numerous trips abroad with the Red Arrows I expected this trip to be quite different and yet I was surprised to find so many similarities, and the difference often came from the least-expected quarter.

With barely enough space in the Gnat to carry a toothbrush, our luggage always followed in the Argosy with the ground crew. So it was with a little apprehension that I taxied the Stampe out for take-off, a pile of baggage roped into the front cockpit. Watching Robin Voice take off with the WOW stand upended in the Tiger's front cockpit, and looking for all the world as if he had taken it away before the builders could remove all the scaffolding, made me feel better. For ground support we were taking Brian Smith, who flew in the other Stampe with Charles Boddington, a small toolkit and a lot of enthusiasm.

To cover the greatest distance we always flew the Gnats at high level and any country we did see was a long way down. More recently I had flown many low-level sorties in the Phantom so speed was obviously going to provide a big contrast. It took just eight hours flying to reach Karup from Redhill, a distance I had covered the day before we left in an hour and a half. It took time to adjust to the twenty miles I usually covered in under three minutes now taking a quarter of an hour, but figures cannot tell the whole story. I found it unreal for a train to match our speed on the way to Maidstone and, with visibility clear enough to see the French coast from Folkestone, the Channel crossing seemed to last an age. Yet even here the situation has its familiar touch when that anonymous and slightly disturbing vibration peculiar to all sea crossings (and dark nights) put in an appearance halfway across.

The real contrast, however, was the amount of time available to study the detailed landscape below. On close inspection the countryside assumed a surprisingly different national character as we crossed each border. The most obvious example of this was Holland. Incredibly neat and clean and with its many waterways so precisely laid out, it might well be an engineer's model. Having recently done some reconnaissance training I could not resist practising my new-found skill by trying to identify and categorise each bridge and lock. By the time we reached Seppe, our first stop after Lydd, I had a headache – the result of two hours flying or, more likely, my mind being fully boggled after all that mental exercise.

In my experience of jet low flying, if you see someone on the ground with his arm raised the chances are he has a rock in his fist. So to see so many people waving at us came as a very pleasant surprise. This was especially so as we flew low along the Belgian coastal resorts but on many subsequent occasions I spotted people waving in fields, farmyards and streets.

One aspect peculiar to an open cockpit came when we flew over a bakery and for several seconds the air was filled with the smell of freshly-baked bread. As it was late and we had had no lunch it was most tantalising. Subsequent incidents were less enticing, such as the farm we passed which had just celebrated muck-spreading. I suppose if nine red aircraft pull up into a smoking, looping bomb-burst before landing then someone is going to notice. Crowds gather curiously around and they all think you get more money. But just as we took our red Gnats for granted so we took our bright biplanes for granted. Everywhere we landed people came to stare and photograph – "Please can you line then up?" Young air taxi pilots, weaned on Cessnas and wearing the firm's smart blazer and badge, leaned into the cockpits and talked of their boss starting in the old days, ten years ago, with three Tigers. As I had been based only fifteen miles away (in the old days) I appreciated that remark – thanks, kids! A surprised controller telephoning the arrival of "drei Englischer Doppelganger" to the local Customs post – you could almost see the exclamation marks coming from the other end. "There are no more aircraft like these in Germany." It made us aware of how lucky we were.

The Team Manager made sure that all domestic problems were sorted out. Unashamedly we left Robin to organise meals and accommodation and very smoothly he did it too. I think that, had we landed in Kurdistan, he would have produced the local currency. The problems we encountered in Denmark were out of his control and very reminiscent of the Arrows. I don't think Robin believed me but the way the organisation – at home and abroad – used to go awry became the team's biggest and longest-standing joke. I think that anyone who has spent an afternoon sunbathing in a monsoon drain on a French base has learned to be philosophical about these things

Our groundcrews were the most dedicated men I have ever met. They would work all night if need be and politely but firmly refused any offer of assistance from us. At first I felt rather spare when it came to turning round the Stampe. But gradually I picked up picketing techniques and found out where the oil went and almost crippled myself trying to lift the Tiger's tail as nonchalantly as everyone else. Looking after the aircraft gave me a great deal of pleasure and satisfaction. We had several small snags at Karup but the base workshop was most co-operative; Brian and Robin worked hard to fix the smoke system, and Pete Jarvis and Bill Innes, who had flown in via BEA and a Cook's tour of the Danish hinterland, spent an afternoon trying to make the radios work.

We had a short morning display and a half-hour slot to fill almost at the end of the programme. As always, the programme was very tight and adjustments impossible, while the actual display was somewhat slack. "Under no circumstances would aerobatics be allowed below 1,000 feet" – hearts sank – "with the exception of the 'Air Circus.'" As the Arrows always seemed to be the exception, so was the Air Circus – us!

We had been invited primarily at the instigation of Morten Olsen and his wife Lene, both Club members from Copenhagen. Lene flew on the Tiger's wing and, just as the two solo Gnats always attracted the crowd's attention, so the sight of Lene standing on the low-flying Tiger, long blonde hair streaming in the slipstream, brought the crowd to its feet. During our stay in Denmark we became very grateful to Morten and Lene for their generous hospitality.

My own small participation did not go unnoticed either although not through any skill on my part. During the tied formation take-off I lost ground steadily and only the leader's throttling back averted what promised to be the shortest tied formation trip ever. In the afternoon, as the Tiger stubbornly refused to start I sat feeling rather foolish while the crowd, including Crown Prince Henrick, looked on with bated breath. At the last second it fired and I was off to hit my one and only balloon just after take-off.

I confess that, not having seen a Club display, I wondered what sort of reaction three biplanes would get. Certainly the rest of the show was flat but the many RDAF and RAF pilots I spoke to were obviously impressed. The one moan came from an RAF pilot who did not think it right for an aircraft to top its loop at his lowest height clearance! Certainly it was one in the eye for the elegant officer who, hearing what we had flown across in, commented: "Good heavens, how dreadful." The return journey proved far from boring. My most unsettling moment came as we crossed Germany. I expected the area to be full of low-flying aircraft and I was right. Sitting at 75 knots I felt very exposed as fighters flashed past in all directions – and my nerves were not helped by the Starfighter which overtook us (from directly behind and about 200 feet above) with a scream that drowned the noise from my own engine. Robin's worst moment must have been when we landed in gathering dusk at Ghent to find that we had picked the one Belgian airfield which closes on Monday!

Why does it always rain on the last day? After a two-hour delay, and a one-sided conversation with the airfield commandant, we took off for what proved to be the worst leg. In heavy showers, a low cloud base and strong headwind we reached the French coast. As we buffeted our way over the rough sea at 500 feet and a ground speed of 50 knots, steering an approximate heading on an uncertain compass, I began to understand Blériot's problems. But despite Charles' comforting remarks about water in the petrol we made Lydd and, after all the superb food of the previous week, the tinned salmon sandwiches were a change.

When Redhill came into view after a total of seventeen hours flying I for one was disappointed. My week's holiday which I had enjoyed so much was ended. A rush to the station and I was headed north and home. The next day we were blasting down the runway to unstick at a speed higher than the Tiger's maximum. Three weeks later I was back in Germany flying low-level over some of the route we had used and, as I scanned the sky for other aircraft, I half expected to see two Stampes and a Tiger come droning out of the gloom.

Incidentally another tale of a Squadron Leader member was entertaining us around then. Clive Francis used to keep a Club Turbulent in his Squadron hangar, through which one day he flew the Turb. In one end and out the other. When asked at the subsequent enquiry why he had done this, he replied: "To improve Squadron morale." I suspect it was shortly after this he became a civilian.

THE ESSO TIGER TROPHY 1969

The "Esso" is unique. The only predictable thing about it is the weather – whatever September Saturday it's held, there will be sun, great piles of cloud and a fairly formidable wind – this time dictating an axis not quite parallel to the M2, and drifting the unwary downwind right into sun. The alternative would have been to ask the Judges to camp out in the woods on the other side of the valley. There's no doubt Bob Winter, "G.B." and Angus Eggleston would have done it for us, but we reckoned it was really a pilot's problem. Positioning was, in fact, good.

There were 13 competitors – more than ever before. And more supporters and spectators, beyond the usual gathering of our perennially welcoming Rochester friends. This is partly that aerobatics is a growing sport, partly that this competition is fun. The entry is unrestricted, it's the last of the season – let's enjoy ourselves! All this adds up to valuable experience of a kind none of the other competitions quite match.

And undoubtedly the Esso Company's far-sighted generosity is a stimulus in itself. Perhaps the Club in general has not realised quite how much we and aerobatics owe to them. They provide liberal prize money, free fuel and even starting money for all. No wonder the pilots look more cheerful than usual. This year's line-up was impressive – Morane 230, Jungmeister, Stampe, Zlin, Falco, 2 Chipmunks, and 3 valiant Tigers, all tackling a competition for the first time.

Two sequences were required – compulsory known and unknown, all simple basic manoeuvres. Everything depended on pilot skill – and the standard was high. The spot-landing was frankly abysmal, even though Don Henry and David Hamilton laid out a Brobdingnagian mark. Only two people scored at all!

Manx Kelly's winning Morane was a joy to watch and Tony Haig-Thomas came a good second in the Stampe, on infuriatingly little practice. Roy Legg's Jungmeister has done well all season.

Results

1.	M. Kelly	Morane 230	438
2.	T Haig-Thomas	Stampe	433
3.	R. Legg	Jungmeister	418
4.	P. Meeson	Stampe	416
5.	D. Gaster	Zlin	408
6.	A. Chadwick	Stampe	407
7.	R. Turner	Chipmunk	389
8.	R. Mitchell	Chipmunk	381
9.	C. Hughes	Falco	370
10.	J. Firth	Stampe	349
11.	W. Goldstraw	Tiger	322
12.=*	P. Benest	Tiger	282
12.=	R. Stenhouse	Tiger	282

* Scored in spot-landing

Do you ever reflect where those Esso pilots are thirty years on, and reflect too with a touch of sadness that some are no longer around – for aerobatics was ever to prove a more dangerous form of flying than any other. On the bright side I know Tony Haig-Thomas is currently running Shuttleworth, Phillip Meeson an airline, and John Firth is the country's leading brain surgeon. Unlike boxing aerobatics doesn't seem to harm the grey matter.

The first Aeroflot Schedule to Paris was shortly due when the company representative visited the control room.

"We have only three pilots qualified on this route," he said. "The first speaks very good English but his visa has expired. The second speaks fair English but has a bad cold. This leaves the third and his English is very bad. Would you like me to stay with you and when he calls ask him to speak Russian and I will translate?" The offer was gratefully accepted.

A little later the aircraft called, the message from the loudspeaker sounding complete gibberish. As soon as he heard and recognised the voice a beaming smile spread over the rep's face.

"Gentlemen," said he, "you have no trouble – he has renewed his visa!"

QUOTE: Standing watching Michael Jones put tape over his Oil Temp. Indicator.
Self: "What's that for?"
Mike: "I won't have to worry if it's too high."

THANK YOUS, A YEAR'S AEROS AND A XMAS GROTTO

CLUB NEWS: DECEMBER 1969

As I write this, snow covers Redhill, and if it looks like staying there will soon be skis on some of the aircraft. There are, I believe, sets for four Turbs and the Piper Cub. Not that I'm over-keen on a white Christmas – although the children are – but it does have its consolations, and one of them is the chance of flying off skis, it's quite an experience. And getting experience is what the Club is all about. For instance, Michael reports that that hot racer, the Beta, has now been flown by no less than 115 pilots. There are no restrictions on it, and it is hoped that many more members will try her out. All being well there will be four Betas for the next year's racing season. The first, 'ATLY, has been called "Forerunner" and is currently away having a modded cowling fitted in an attempt to add speed, and the blue 'AWHV, now known as "Blue Chip," will stay flying at Redhill. over the winter. For the record, someone has already claimed 20,000 feet in her – not bad on 100 bhp. There are now two Stampes at Redhill with a third in reserve back at Croydon. A welcome returnee to Redhill will soon be the old Fox Moth. As a confirmed vintage pilot I can't wait to fly her again, and I hope others will feel the same urge, because if we can keep up her flying hours we'll perhaps be presenting a sound case for her retention when, in the fullness of time, the economics of low hours plus precious hangar space force the inevitable decision to sell. It happened to the Puss Moth, a fate which might never have occurred had each member put in no more than 45 minutes a year. It's a sobering thought, and it's being wise after the event, I know, but knowing could save the Fox Moth. And from Michael Jones, will the member who removed the fuselage and returned the wings of the M.18 please contact him.

The Air Race to Australia is but a week or so away. Whilst the handicappers clobbered any serious entries in the real light aircraft field, Norman, Sheila Scott and Carl Schofield are the only members I know of to have a go. We all wish them loads of luck. Redhill is again going to be open over the Xmas holidays – Xmas day excepted – and volunteers to help out with the teas and to run things will be needed. Do give a hand if possible, phone Michael.

Big event for the New Year is the coming Annual Dinner and Dance at the Hilton, and on, of all days to pick, Friday 13th February. Tickets available now. Let's make it the biggest and most successful evening ever with everyone of the 600-plus members present. Well, it's a thought anyway. Air racing, both Formula and Class, will be big events as well, with confirmed meets at Isle of Man, Goodwood, Tollerton, Rochester, Halfpenny Green and Shobdon. John Blake, the RAeC Racing Manager, would welcome members who'd help out at any one of these meetings.

There's a great Xmas Party coming up at the Kronfeld on Tuesday 16th December, immediately after the Committee meeting there. It's timed for seven and Nini Baring promises there'll be lots to eat and drink, and she'll not charge more than 10/- a head for it! All members are invited. Let's make it a great get-together.

It's Xmas, and this *"Tiger Rag"* is a seasonal, light-hearted *pot pourri* of old and new. . . a chance to remember absent friends both over here and abroad. The Tiger Club is now far-flung, but every year at this time our thoughts centre on the activities and beliefs that draw us together. To everyone, wherever they are, go the Xmas wishes of each one of us, and the hope that 1970 will be as full of good flying and friendship as in past years.

And a few thanks wouldn't go amiss. To our friends, John Sarrett and Jim Ellis, the cheery engineers who keep us operational at Redhill. To the boys back at Croydon who, although unseen, support John and Jim's efforts with an unsurpassed standard of aero-engineering. To Mavis our Treasurer and her small team. And one last thank you: to Jill Southam who volunteers for the long job of collation needed to produce the new Club Membership booklet.

The BEA Vanguard was slowly letting down the Paris stack when at FL90 he was startled to see another aircraft whistle past his wingtip. Complaining bitterly to the approach controller he was not much reassured by (after a very long pause): "Ah! do not worry monsieur – he is working airways."

If there's one thing that is guaranteed to cheer up a poor historian – and in this case one who was never too hot on aerobatics – it's to come across a neat resumé of that sport for the past year, which even ends on an optimistic note with a taster for better things to come. How could I therefore, in deference to the aerobatic crowd, fail to reproduce it? Frances MacRae had gathered together the reins in a firm yet unobtrusive manner, and if there was one thing she excelled at, it was a delightful yet feminine touch of command that didn't upset the sport's macho fraternity, for in those days she was the lone woman to take aerobatics seriously.

Sadly this cheerful lady and serious competitor is no longer with us, but in her time her pioneering spirit contributed a great deal and I for one remember her with some affection.

AEROBATICS NEWSLETTER
DECEMBER 1969

COMPETITIONS 1969

The number of competitors remains almost constant year by year – newcomers neatly fill the spaces of those who drop out. This year 22 pilots competed – slightly up on 1968. Six more entered but did not compete. Total entries were 62, well up and including 4 from abroad; 42 materialized. There were more people doing only one or two of the competitions rather than having a go at them all.

The number and variety of aircraft used increases encouragingly. This year there were seven: Chipmunk, Falco, Jungmeister, Morane 230, Stampe, Tiger, Zlin. We have not seen the Beagle Pup competing yet – perhaps next year? There certainly seems the possibility of others coming forward in 1970 which, with the World Championships being held here at Hullavington, promises to be a very exciting year all round. Altogether there is a general atmosphere of growth and enthusiasm.

	Icicle Trophy	McAully Trophy	de Havilland Trophy	Air Squadron Trophy	Esso Trophy
M. Alexander	Disqual.	-	-	-	-
P. Benest	-	-	-	-	12=
J. Black	1	-	1	-	-
A. Chadwick	7=	3	-	-	6
J. Firth	-	1	-	-	10
R. Forss	-	4	-	-	-
D. Gaster	-	-	7	-	5
W. Goldstraw	-	-	-	-	11
A. Haig-Thomas	-	-	-	-	2
C. Hughes	-	5	-	-	9
P. Jarvis	5	-	-	-	-
M. Kelly	4	-	-	-	1
R. Legg	7=	8	-	4	3
F. MacRae	3	-	4	3	-
P. Meeson	6	2	5=	2	4
R. Mitchell	-	6	8	1	8
M. Riley	2	-	3	5	-
B. Shaw	-	7	-	-	-
C. Schofield	-	-	5=	-	-
D. Stenhouse	-	-	-	-	12=
R. Turner	-	-	-	-	7
N. Williams	-	-	2	-	-

J. Black thus became the British National Champion for this year.

The British Team for the European Championships at Dax were all Tiger Club Members.

Results: J. Black (4), C. Schofield (8), D. Gaster (14).

John Blake was the British Judge. Team Manager: David Hamilton.

The airfields we use are dotted about the country. Competitors – and judges – often travel a long way to take part. So do the other people who help: judges' assistants, timekeepers' assistants and, of course, Smith/Thompson and John; Roger Forss came from Denmark for the McAully; Madeleine (Delcroix that was), the Women's World Champion, and her husband Andre Cottelarda intended to take part in the de Havilland but they, and Pierre Bonnet, who entered for the Esso, were plagued by unserviceable aircraft. We hope to see more foreign entries soon.

Unlike Display techniques, which cater directly for the crowd, competition aerobatics is not in itself a good spectator sport, except for the initiated, but it is interesting and encouraging to see that the number of people coming to watch is growing steadily – while a few, such as Norman and his umbrella, are constant and faithful supporters. There is a lot to be said for combining a competition with a Fly-In, as the McAully Flying Group did very successfully in May.

Failing a central national 'pool' of professional judges, which is very unlikely to emerge, the general principle has been to draw from four different sources, if possible, for each competition. One from the organizing body, the Tiger Club; one from the Royal Aero Club, associated with the organising and whose support is invaluable; one representing the sponsors of the individual competition; and one from the Central Flying School, R.A.F., which has become a regular and valuable contributor to the Judges' Pool.

AEROBATIC SCHOOL

This time last year we announced the provision of aerobatic instruction in a planned course of ten lessons at Blackbushe, away from the height restrictions that bedevil us at Redhill. 'WEF was based there from March and two qualified instructors laid on. This was in response to the many requests for casual instruction that were made to the practising aerobatic pilots at Redhill, and to explore the potential demand for a national school such as other countries have. In these nine months no one has made use of the opportunity. So the project has been cancelled; 'WEF is back at Redhill and we must thankfully presume that everyone is well able to look after themselves, which is a very satisfactory state.

BASICS

Why do competitions? To win? If that is all, then only five people could find it worthwhile each year!

To measure your present skill, in the best machine you have available, against other pilots – possibly in better machines, possibly more experienced, and possibly simply better pilots? Surely! To come 10th in the de Havilland is as real an achievement for a man with less experience or a more difficult machine as it is for an experienced man with a good machine to win it.

Why compete? Aerobatics is a strongly individual sport and certainly flying for flying's sake is best of all. But it is also an art and as with all arts, it is not all sheer pleasure pursuing it – it is hard work, demanding unremitting attention and presenting considerable challenge. Most of us find that the fact that you have just got to be able to do this "impossible" manoeuvre in just two weeks from now is a stronger and more urgent stimulus than any we can provide from within. And every competition pilot knows that by some magic a five-minute competition sequence teaches him something that no practice session achieves.

But it remains individual. The approach is as varied as the number of pilots – you can see quiet confidence, nail-biting apprehension, cheerful abandon, the grim pursuit of mathematical exactitude according to diagram, the sweeping delight of sheer artistry. The only thing they have in common is the conviction that each is the only way and the judges "don't understand." Outside that, take your pick – or invent your own !

FRANCES MACRAE,
(Aerobatics Secretary).

It's unlikely I could stumble upon a more delightful way to close a chapter than to include Bunny's 'Xmas Grotto.' Today Bunny Bramson is renowned for his books on flight instruction and his lively authorship on testing out the sort of aircraft we'd all love to fly, a vicarious pleasure but none the less enjoyable. In those days he was a departmental store manager yearning to get out from under in order to fly. It's good for us he made it.

THE XMAS GROTTO
by "Bunny" Bramson

Convention dies hard in all walks of life. The principal male in Panto is played by a girl while her mum is always a man. In departmental stores, like it or not, at Xmas time you are expected to have a Grotto.

"We must," I said at one display meeting, "do something quite different next year."

"Like what, Sir?" said my Display Manager.

"Well," said I, "well, er – we, we could, er – put them in a jet plane and take them on a flight – to Brighton – that's it, to Brighton."

Fool that I was, the Display Manager took me seriously and as Christmas drew near I was faced with having to back out or take the plunge. Now I have never been very good at backing out so with the help of B.E.A. who loaned us some airline seats and literally gave us the old trim out of a Vanguard my maintenance chap started to build the fuselage. He had no knowledge of aircraft so that I spent most of my time discouraging him from turning it into a Trolley Bus.

Then there was the problem of getting the illusion of flight. At first I thought of having moving scenery but the mechanics of the thing were out of the question. It soon became clear that it had to be ciné, but how do you get an 18-foot picture when there is not much more than nine or ten feet between projector and wall? Snag number one. Bounce the film through one mirror and you certainly get a bigger picture but left becomes right and the plane appears to fly backwards. So you do a double bounce on two mirrors but here is where the trouble really starts – we needed a second mirror ten feet long by four and a half feet high! Now these are not in everyday use in most homes and when I obtained a quote for a new one the price was like the national debt.

So came the great day when Jack Piercy clambered into the right-hand seat of a Cessna 150 armed with a 16 mm Bolex and a box full of spare bits. I had written a script down to the last second so that it was necessary to fly with one hand and use a stopwatch with the other. The landing at Gatwick at 120 mph must have impressed the controller but remember this was supposed to be a jet flight. We even took the flying shots in slow speed so that when the film was run through the projector it wouldn't look like a Cessna 150 at 85 knots.

Then there was the business of sound. The film had been striped with the usual magnetic tape and Ken Smith kindly offered to let Miriam and me record on his machine. A device made by our radio department for the purpose of creating jet noises went up in smoke halfway through our recording session but Ken managed to produce an industrial vacuum cleaner – a monster affair some four feet in diameter with three separate motors which I used as 'throttles' (did I tell you the plane is supposed to be a Trident?).

So now it is finished and last Saturday the kids were queueing up to 'Fly with Captain Santa in a Jet to Brighton.' They walk up the stairs into the fuselage where our air hostess (ex-linen department and the living image of Margaret Rutherford) relieves them of three bob. One parent only is allowed to stand in the fuselage while the children sit in their Vanguard seats looking out of the oval windows while clouds drift by (projected on the far wall), then the lights go out and Gatwick Air Terminal appears complete with those little yellow vans dashing about. A jet engine starts, the buildings disappear as we taxi and the voice of the hostess (Miriam) says: "Hello, Boys and Girls, welcome aboard B.E.A. jet flight to Brighton. Your pilot today is Captain Santa (4,000 hrs. on reindeers!)." Then with a "get ready for take-off" the runway flashes past to the accompaniment of the loudest industrial vacuum cleaner you have ever heard. Actually it really does sound like a jet. Soon we go into cloud, then burst into blue sky. "This is Captain Santa speaking (yours truly); we have just climbed through cloud and now we are descending over Brighton where we shall fly along the front at 400 mph."

By now Rottingdean is in view and you can clearly see the waves breaking against the cliffs. It was a rather rough day and at 50 ft above the water the Cessna took a bit of a beating. Jack Piercy had his straps undone so that he could twist around to the window with his camera and on occasions Brighton Pier shoots from top to bottom of the picture. Any day now I am sure one of our young customers is going to be sick. A steep climbing turn over Brunswick Square is followed by another word from the flight deck: "We are now approaching Gatwick and after landing the engines will go into reverse thrust," followed by the air hostess inviting the children to "join Captain Santa on the flight deck where he has a present for you." The lights go on in the fuselage, clouds roll past the window again and the children walk forward onto the flight deck complete with lighted instruments and windscreen covered in ice. Father Christmas gives them their dolls and plastic swords while 'Margaret Rutherford' is busy filling her up for another flight.

One thing is certain, Nicholsons have a grotto with the highest stalling speed in the business.

1970

MARKERS, PIXIE, COMMITTEE REFLECTIONS AND OVERSEAS NEWS

... In some ways these cold January/February days are the good times for visiting Redhill. No crowds, a complete range of hardware to choose from, and to fly in lonely clean crisp skies ...

This was how the Club News opened the new year. A new decade was opening, the seventies beckoned with a solid assurance things can only go from very good to even better. True to a point. I went on:

... Mark you, from the flying point of view there are hazards, the worst of which is probably one of condensation, so quickly induced in cabin aircraft. Although I mention this in light-hearted vein, one minor mishap did occur a few weeks back and was attributed to misting up. Another, and not so easily avoidable, hazard is the area slap in the middle of the airfield which is believed too soggy to operate over. If I question the validity of the markers that litter the area, I don't underestimate the menace to aircraft of those big metal obstructions. Clobber one of these and there's going to be damage aplenty. One day someone is going to replace them with a safer plastic version, but not, I suspect, until there's been the most almighty mishap. There's a mystery here though, because for the life of me I can't think where all these markers keep coming from. For years now I've heard recurring rumours of surreptitious dusk sorties that have gone out to 'lose them' – the local drainage ditches must be full of metal – yet still the markers keep reappearing. Must be the work of gremlins in the pump house. I've always suspected that place.

The markers I mentioned were clumsy metal elongated red/white triangles which quite unnecessarily lined the N/S and E/W runways. Unnecessary because Redhill Airfield was a generous expanse of grass with loads of room to land into wind without disturbing other flyers. A signals area was clearly visible and windsocks did the rest. But now we had 'landlords,' those mysterious beings who were then starting to make themselves a nuisance. There was still no air traffic control, just an awareness big brother was watching, and big brother had a name, Kerridge. To be honest, a big brother he wasn't, at least not at that early stage. Major Kerridge was a short, dumpy, bristling man, and was the first airfield manager we'd encountered, and we took the rise out of him whenever we could. The real big brothers came later, but if we'd have known how nasty our landlords were to become perhaps we'd have treated the Major better on the 'better the devil you know' principle.

These early signs of interference with our precious freedom were at this stage quite ignorable, it was just that at times we felt that a modest show of resistance wouldn't go amiss. There were the odd sorties to move the hated markers, either by opening up the width of the runways when suddenly overnight they'd reduced it, or by that final sanction, removing them to the ditches. And, strange as it may seem, no one ever witnessed either side's action. An early example of stealth technology.

On the aircraft front there's a lot brewing. First to reappear will be the ·beloved Fox Moth. Suddenly this old aircraft has an historic aura about it. Rightly so because it's a rare bird, but more so because members are becoming aware that to retain it, it must pay for itself on the economic front. Hence the target of every member putting in one hour's flying a year in it. To be honest I can't say it's particularly sensational to fly – indeed it's bus-like – but even so there's a remarkable fascination in moving it about the sky. To sit high up above one's hapless passengers like some Hansom cabbie, and to every now and then open the little flap to the cabin and smile benignly on the occupants is pleasant indeed. I might even put in two hours. Keeping aircraft like this in the family is one of the attractions of our Club over others.

In the hangar Tom Storey is pressing on with the Cassutts, improving his mounts as fast as he can, for the racing season will start with no less than six of the new Formula I racers ready. Half will be Cassutts – the others Betas. Michael Jones is equally busy, a bit of competition does wonders for the breed. Currently he's making a smooth new cowling for "Blue Chip" (yes, it's been nicknamed that as well). It'll be the Beta with the mostest. The new profile is mean and long. I heard Michael mutter: "God knows where the C. of G. is going to be." It looks a hot ship all right. For the first time the public will see close-circuit one-start racing, with machines rounding the course at a snarling 200 mph plus, and the calibre of the pilots will count as never before. Indeed I believe the success of these crucial first races will depend more on the selection of top drivers than on their exotic mounts. To catch on, the racing must be tight and fierce, and absolutely nothing like the dreamy flying that has helped ring the death-knell for the handicapped race – a perfect description.

This Formula 1 racing was catching on, and I, firm advocate that I was, began underlining my words in an attempt to push what I saw as the inevitable. As usual I was completely wrong. "Death-knell." I can't read it now without a modicum of embarrassment.

Some new and some strange aircraft have visited Redhill's hangar recently. There's Winston Churchill's new Arrow, a gleaming new Luton Minor Michael has been invited to test-fly, a Nipper, and for one week only a wingless stubby grubby fuselage with tired wings alongside, the lot labouring under the name of "Pixie." I don't know how much of the story to believe but it's too good to keep to myself. Once upon a time an owner-builder of an ultra light (sic) felt people weren't treating his new design with the recognition it deserved, so he wrote to the Duke of Edinburgh. Philip didn't sit on the problem for long, and gleefully passed the buck in a return letter suggesting that Norman and the Tiger Club had the right sort of sympathy. So early one morning this character appeared unannounced at Redhill with this red Pixie all tied up on the back of his lorry, which he then proceeded to unload, all the while waving his Royal letter like an enclosure pass to

Ascot. Anyway, it impressed Michael long enough to let him deposit it in the hangar, and for him to return happily to the other end of England, confident that the Tiger Club would evaluate and fly his plane. One by one members gathered around the ungainly Pixie, and one by one they laughed and declined to touch it. I admit to offering to taxy it, and that, it seems, was the best offer received. Anyway, I question whether the main spar would have tolerated more. The next week it had gone. And only then did I feel compassion for that unknown little man who would have to go back to the drawing board, and although he'll never know it, I felt sorry I laughed.

There are two good aeroplanes for sale in the hangar. Only one is mentioned officially, the other I know is thinking seriously of a touring Beta, so if your taste goes to a Jodel Excellence, and a beautiful example at that, let me know and I'll point the letter in the right direction. Arthur Tyrrell is looking for a good home for his Turbulent. Now, as everyone knows, this machine must surely be the most cared-for Turbulent in the whole world, and with just about every conceivable extra. Ladies and Gentlemen, one owner from new and perfect – offers to Arthur.

Glider towing had a record year in '69, the Tiger Club team putting up a total of no less than 3,427 tows. 3,427 careful take-offs and landings and all without incident. Is there a Club in the wide world with a like total of aero-tows? It's a guileless question inspired by the stark modest and factual statement of 3,427. I tell you, I'm impressed.

As with every start to a new year Michael would drag up statistics. His endeavours began in January with the number of members, and he continued with a stream of facts until about March, by which time there was so much to do the figures dropped by the wayside. I personally think this happiness with statistics can be blamed on a deeply embedded guilt feeling that his perfectly good economics degree wasn't being adequately reflected in his managerial task of running the Club.

1970 begins with 646 members:

Founder	4	Members	277
Honorary	28	Members O/S	102
Associate	73	Passenger	120
Associate O/S	42	(51 with flying qualifications)	

SOME MORE USELESSLY FASCINATING STATISTICS FROM MICHAEL JONES

From 400 members who returned membership renewal forms we have:

39 Instructors' ratings	42 A.L.T.P.'s
50 I.H.C. ratings	131 Glider ratings
181 R.T. ratings	55 Instrument ratings
99 Night ratings	5 Helicopter ratings
37 C.P. L.'s	Plus of course 525 P.P.L.'s

92 aircraft and 9 gliders are owned by Club members, the most numerous type being – you will never guess – the Tiger Moth!

To the figure of 646 members the realist used to add the number of listed wives, which at the time stood at 73. To Michael they hadn't paid, *ergo* how could they be members? To the countless 'wives' who stood spells of duty – minding children, feeding the Club's hungry hordes, and spending weekends in the cold at Redhill, their exclusion was an affront. With Lollie in mind, who did all the aforementioned plus Standing-on-the-Wing slots as well, I always counted them in. For 646 read 719.

QUOTES:
"When I was flying for a living . . ." – our C.F.I., in expansive mood.
"Good old British Tigers – set the flying movement back years." – Michael.

Without searching back over what I've written so far, I offer the following comment on the Club's legendary Committee meetings, and ask that you forgive any unintentional repetition. I still think of those monthly occasions and find it impossible to conceal a grin.

COULDN'T WE JUST HAVE A COMMITTEE MEETING?

John Blake's spontaneous suggestion – it was during a discussion in Committee on the absence of cabaret acts at the coming Annual Dinner – prompts me to write a few words on this unique body and enlighten members who must at times wonder what on earth goes on every month. Accused James Gilbert once: "This Committee isn't democratic." Well, let's put that hoary old misconception out of its misery to start with. He's right. The Tiger Club Committee also has a huge complement, it's more like an inner Club. This follows, for Norman our Chairman was once a sea captain and to all sea captains big complements are right and proper. Nor is it hard to get on the Committee, it's only necessary to think of something to head. For instance, I was once a Sports Captain, a position I invented before I thought of the *"Tiger Rag"* (and that one could be resurrected, couldn't it?). My sole qualifications at that time were the huge indoor archery target I had built from cake boxes, and that I'd donated an old set of cricket gear – still in the old sports locker – and on the strength of that I was in.

Actually I can still recall all that early sporting activity with delight. You know we really should behave like children more often – it was great fun. We used to play a lot of bows and arrows between flying. The only rule was: not too often at passing aircraft. And there were favourite variations on the Robin Hood stuff. Filling balloons with hydrogen was one, and then releasing then to float to the roof of the hangar and then to try and burst them. I can still hear the clatter of arrows in the roof and the anguished cries of aircraft owners as spent missiles bounced willy-nilly below. Then when we'd been chased out of the hangar we'd try our hand at seeing how far we could send an arrow. The record stands at five yards short of the far peri-track from the hangar entrance. I digress.

"Why don't you resign?" We are all asked this at some time or other, when a matter of principle has arisen, and we remain guiltily in office. Speaking personally, I'm always about to do so, but by the time I've got the paper in front of me and begun: 'Dear Norman,' visions of all the awful formal rubbish usually written floats before me, a grin wreathes my face, and I screw up the paper. Trouble is, there's nothing in the book that quite covers this Committee. To put down the irresistible draw of this monthly performance to entertainment value is to underestimate a remarkable institution. For although I agree that there are times when our Chairman will waive a decision by vote, its members somehow retain their individuality in the face of each *fait accompli* and do so without trace of rancour. Don't ask me to explain this phenomenon. The only criteria is: does this body contrive to do a good job? And the answer is unquestionably 'yes.' The reason can lie either in the members' understanding, wonderful, selfless selves, or the very competent Chairmanship. I lean to the Chair, and no one can accuse me of bias, I've more incipient resignations to my credit than the rest put together. But oh! the monthly value, for at times the chat is priceless. This month, for instance.

Item I on agenda – Membership:
Chairman: " . . . he's an Irishman, that's the only trouble." He spoke kindly.
Bunny: "I'd like to think we are going to be choosy about new members." He spoke reprovingly.
Muttered Bev: "We haven't been in the past."

And then ten minutes later:
Chairman: "I think you might say he's got to an awkward age." – pronouncement on a youngster of 75.

I ask you – would you resign?'

Committee Minutes: January '70
Total tows for 1969: 3,427.
Glider towing: Award for year – Glyn Richards.

There are times I'm lost, not so much for words, but for the gift of clarity. To express my memories of thirty years ago only through *"Tiger Rag"* generalities is to offer but a fraction of the picture. On one hand I've no wish to bore readers with what at times might seem trivia, but if I fail to cover more of the canvas once in a while I'll be failing to embrace what being a member of this Club once meant.

For instance, in the first weeks of 1970, I received many letters. If I was a sort of magnet for the news of our overseas membership, then so too was Michael Jones as the Club's Manager. Speaking for myself I never seemed to stop writing, so how can I fail to mention these arteries of friendship just once in a while? The simple answer – I cannot. It also begs the question: where are those good friends now who from far afield shared their flying moments with us? Let's share a prayer that their recollections be as warming as ours, all these years later.

LETTERS

"Dear Benjy,
Your newsletters of Aug., Sept., Oct. '69 have just caught up with us via South Africa. After performing a do-it-yourself one-man flying circus act as the Lesotho Flying Doctor Service, I spent six months practising in the Cape before returning to the U.K. So for your information and the benefit or all Tiger Clubbers, we are at home at Church House, Grittleton, Nr. Chippenham, Wilts, – right next door, in fact, to the Neald Arms which those of you who ever flew from Hullavington will doubtless remember. Hullavington is nostalgically silent (It soon won't be! – Ed.).

Workwise, I am at I.A.M., Farnborough, and for sheer convenience I have become airborne from Blackbushe. If I can find somewhere to land near home then I've got the commuting problem licked. Martin Barraclough has challenged us to demonstrate the British "can do" attitude too.

Barry Griffiths' suggestion that the Tiger Club should invest in a light twin receives my unstinted support. I hope the efforts of people like Barry will persuade Adrian Deverell and his dog to come back to Redhill. My dog is still in quarantine.

Now that I'm back for good I hope to spend much more time at Redhill and get to know many more people. Again, a light twin would make it much more tempting for Anna and our five fledglings, with the odd trip to Le Touquet thrown in. Or is that too parochial these days with the forthcoming air race to Australia? I'm backing the Tiger Club to win it.
Yours sincerely,
MICHAEL MOORE."

Johannesburg, South Africa.
"Dear Sir,
After my visit to your Club 2 years ago I was so impressed with the effort the Tiger Club had undertaken to resuscitate these aeroplanes that we formed a similar Club in South Africa. There are a few photos enclosed of some of our best machines (they are excellent photos. – Ed.). We have 12 Tigers at our aerodrome – the Johannesburg Light Plane Club – and according to the present register, there are still approximately 50 that are still flying in various parts of South Africa. The red Tiger is my own aircraft, and as you can see it is in practically "brand new" condition having been completely rebuilt, chromium-plated, baked-enamelled, and a new propeller from Rollasons. The two Tigers standing with the registration 'F' have come recently from the Portuguese Air Force of Mozambique E.A.; they were stored for 20 years and were completely rebuilt – the blue and white Tiger came second in the National Aerobatic Championships on Saturday. This was won by Mr Nick Turvey in a Stampe; the Trener Master that is normally used in the championships was damaged when the engine failed just after take-off, so that left just the Stampe and the Tigers to battle for the honours – and as you know the

Tiger has a problem on the outside loop, so far nobody has worked out an efficient fuel system to sort this one out – so it went to the Stampe.

Most of the best Tigers have been rebuilt by Mr C. Strecker who has been at this for about 40 years, having worked on SE.5s as an apprentice in the 1920s, and this he does for a living, each one passing a strict D.C.A. test with flying colours, and as you can see by our weather conditions, (these pictures were taken in mid-winter), our Tigers will still be flying when the Cessnas etc. etc. have been phased out.

Yours sincerely,
ALAN HINDLE."

Extract from another letter from South Africa

". . . I have made supreme efforts in South Africa, all to no avail, to get anyone to teach me to fly a Tiger Moth. If you have any suggestions along this line I would appreciate it but most of the Tiger Moths here are privately owned and guarded very jealously.

On July 11th this year, myself and another member of the Tiger Club – who shall remain anonymous at his own request – entered the Star Air Rally, finishing 13th out of 60, having pre-posted an average speed of 103.5 mph which is not as difficult as it sounds as it is 90 knots, to which a Cherokee 140 can perform quite nicely. One demerit point was taken off for each second over or under your E.T.A.s and we finished 1 minute 13 seconds out, after 200 miles. The course was given to the Navigator 15 seconds before take-off in Longitude and Latitude, it comprising of five checkpoints. Three of the checkpoints were manned but no one knew which three. Approximately 5 minutes after take-off, after having received an immediate, commendable and very accurate compass heading, I heard my Navigator softly swearing to himself in 'Oxford.' As it is not his nature to swear softly I queried him and he tearfully asked me what our take-off time was. It seems that he had forgotten to start the stopwatch on take-off, being so involved in computing a compass heading. We tried to compute it mentally but were 1 minute 13 seconds off at the end of the 200 nautical miles. It was interesting in that there were no height restrictions and it was made quite clear at the pre-race briefing that it was incumbent upon the pilot to see that his plane was easily identified. This encouraged very low flying and was a sight to behold indeed. We, incidentally, entered as Tiger Club and it was our intention that one half the prize money, which we were completely confident of winning, would go to the Tiger Club Legal Fund. There is a bigger and better race scheduled for next year and we'll see what we can do in this one.

The Star Air Show was completely successful including a balloon ascent, parachute jumping, and a demonstration in aerobatics by the inimitable (no offence, gentlemen) Nick Turvey – South Africa's finest. I was unfortunately not able to introduce myself to him but Peter Liversage managed it. . . .

Very truly yours,
PATRICK O'ROURKE."

"Gentlemen:

Although I have not personally had the opportunity of visiting the Tiger Club for several years, the Tiger Club News Bulletin makes me feel still a member of the happy band.

I would like to take the opportunity of extending an invitation to any of the Tiger Club members who will be visiting the Hanover Air Show this year to come and see me at the Piper stand to try out all our range of aircraft.

Yours very truly,
JOHN R. DOYLE,
Sales Manager,
PIPER AIRCRAFT INTERNATIONAL S.A."

Norway

"Dear Michael and all other friends in the Tiger Club,

I thought I would write and tell you all that we are now living very happily in the new house we bought near Oslo when we managed to raise the cash required. I can best describe the location as very close to the Outer Marker to 06 at Fornebu, Oslo. I have, however, refused to join the local committee against aircraft noise.

We have plenty of snow, and many aircraft owners have just this permanently on their planes ready to break the undercarriage – I mean land on any of the many frozen lakes. The effects of a strong wind on the snow can prepare a very unfriendly reception for an innocent airplane, something you probably avoid when you occasionally can use skis on Redhill.

I have not had much time to think about flying over here yet, with the short daylight period, moving and all that. I was in for a mental shock, however, when I wanted to renew my Medical Cert. The attitude was nobody above 40 could possibly be fit for flying and they put me through a big test. You should have seen me madly pedalling a stationary instrument-solid bicycle while clever electronic devices measured my heartbeats. All this for a P.P.L.!! I made it and should probably be grateful for all the prop-swinging and plane-pushing at Redhill.

Let me also mention that every year a big get-together of Club pilots and planes takes place during the Easter week at Fagunis in the centre of South Norway. Gliders also come here and soaring in waves from the mountains is sometimes possible. The big lake serves as the airfield and usually the snow soon gets hard enough for planes on wheels also. Some TC members may be in this corner of Europe at that time and should not lose this opportunity to meet fellow Club pilots.

I will be back in London on a business trip before long and if it is at all possible I will fit in a trip down to Redhill.

Best regards from ARVE CASPERSEN."

CLUB NEWS: MARCH – APRIL 1970

It's raining, and through my head runs the silly jingle: "April showers bring forth May flowers." Outside there's a steady downpour and even without being down at Redhill I can envisage the damp and forlorn huddle of aircraft within the hangar and members aimlessly looking out at the dreary curtain of rain pattering on the tarmac beyond the heavy doors, doors which now and then clang and grumble as the wind tugs at them.

And even so I yearn to be at the airfield to see the latest aircraft to shelter there. A real live Spitfire it is, all decked up, I'm told, in black and gold. It belongs to Adrian Swire and I hear that Ray Hanna also flies it and handsomely, in a lazy effortless Jeffrey Quill way. And more, people in nearly Nutfield are already grumbling. We try hard to keep aircraft noise away from their sleepy village, and at the worst the sound can be than a fraction of a 707 at two thousand feet yet still they cry "noise." Speaking personally, I shall continue to steer clear of all local habitation and urge all members to do likewise, but at the same time I can't help thinking that if people buy houses near an operational airfield – and I shouldn't wonder the airfield was going strong before most, if not all, of the locals moved in – what on earth are they on about?

. . . The two Betas are now out and about a lot and occasionally seen flying as a duo with Ray Hanna and Roy Booth practising for displays. Their cross-overs should gladden Norman's heart – and I hear that their formation loops off the deck would weaken mine. The new cowling on "Forerunner," the first Beta, has, if it hasn't provoked much speed, added something to its looks. It's now positively a mean spiteful Beta and every inch a racing plane. There's been a predominance of single-seaters at Redhill lately. On the first weekend in April someone counted no less than 19 single-seaters in the hangar at one and the same time. To start with there were eleven Turbulents. Can't help thinking it's time someone organised a Turb Rally, for there must surely be enough of them to do so. What with the Cassutts and the Arrow Active, the Stampes, the Spitfire – all single-seaters, the airfield is becoming something of a bachelors' paradise . . . but then it always was.

I hear that Manx Kelly, now a bit ex-RAF, has a job getting up an aerobatic display team for the Rothmans' five Stampes. I know he's on the lookout for full-time display men. I must be mightily out of touch. I didn't even know Rothmans had one Stampe, much less five. . . . The Tiger Club display participations have begun well despite the weather. There was a good outing at Lydd over Easter Sunday. For those interested in helping please contact Robin Voice.

Everyone will be sad to learn that Frank Hounslow has been ill and been abed in the Redhill General Hospital. Frank is Rollason's engine expert and everyone's friend, and the news that he should be back after a month's convalescence will relieve those of us who'd feared he'd finally gone mad trying to get Gipsy spares. By the way, it's about time the Governors named one of the wards in the Redhill General after the Club, enough of our members have been through it.

. . . It's time I added a Club postscript to that Race to Australia last Xmas. Several of our members competed and all deserve our hearty congratulations on individual and epic performances. To Sheila Scott, Carl Schofield, Tim Phillips and Mike Somerton-Rayner, our doffed caps of approval. Mike, who was flying solo in his Auster 9, did the trip in fourteen days with 141 hours flying . . . a valiant feat if ever I heard of one. I'm not sure whether Terry Kingsley and Peter Evans flying James Baring's SM.260 are now Club members or not, but they deserve to be included in. Talking of James Baring, we've just heard the wonderful news that he has become a father – a son, Alexander. I've forgotten the weight bit but it was seven stone something-or-other. Our happiest good wishes to James and Nini.

. . . Bill Chesson wrote me after my exposé on the Tiger Club Committee enclosing a cartoon. Unfortunately I can't use it, but the caption runs: "Gentlemen, there are two sides to this question – mine and the wrong one!" Thank you, Bill. Incidentally, he is going on that mammoth driving rally to South America. You will recall his last rally – the one to Australia? It ended with a kangaroo on his front bumper!

. . . It's early April and I'm all too curious that the best part of February and all of March went without a Newsletter and I regret it. Michael has been phoning every other day nervously chatting about this and that, too polite to simply say: "pull your finger out." Yet to get the *"Rag"* out isn't just an exercise in finding 4,000 words a month – that in itself isn't difficult, but because it's the voice of the Club it should have something relevant to say. But who's to say it? The Editor? He's just another member like you with his share of family bliss and graft, and weekend visits to Redhill squeezed between trips to the zoo and distant parents, so he can only report on so much. Have the 600-plus members anything to say? Occasionally yes, something like a dozen squeaks a year. Tell me, am I, as Editor, wasting my time keeping the *"Rag"* going? Be honest.

As you can guess the job of Editor was ever a love-hate relationship, but what was more revealing, now seen from afar, was that I'd unwittingly become something of a workaholic. Consider the casual comment "4,000 words a month in itself wasn't difficult," but at the time I really meant it. Not only was I in regular practice, what with the *"Rag"* for ten years, but I was also by then writing for a weekly trade paper for menswear called *"Style Weekly"* and was churning out the same amount for them. It was a tough discipline, especially when it was added to a pair of growing businesses. Happy days, probably because there was never time to think. Back to aeroplanes.

"BISH'S" SPIRIT, ANNUAL DIN, MANX AND CHOW MEIN
TALKING POINT

As is customary the conversation got around to flying and Tiger Club flying in particular and someone said: "If only we had another 'Bish.'" "Bish" was our first CFI in a Club that, even as late as 1963, was still a smallish movement. Most flying members knew all the others and we still flew Tigers as the norm. But "Bish" wasn't just CFI – a title that was very much a misnomer anyway – he was more of a guiding spirit, a leader to channel our efforts. Our weekend flying for instance was planned days before. He'd phone around in the week and leave cryptic messages: "Redhill 9 am. Bring sandwiches and your girl friend if you must. You're in 'OAA. 'Bish.'" And sure enough by 9.30 we'd be airborne in a gaggle en route perhaps to the Isle of Wight. And once there we would break formation to land in strict turn and taxy up in line astern to park correctly, a yard between wingtips, very tidy, was "Bish." And then later over a picnic we'd plan a race or spot-landing contest and when the day was done we'd fly home to Redhill into one of those lush old-fashioned sunsets. Flying had point to it.

Perhaps the Club is now too big for such a man, too informal or too full of strangers for whom we haven't time to chat or haven't the inclination to get to know. There's now air touring, and aerobatics, and lots of visiting firemen. Yet the ghost of "Bish" is still with us. Has our flying become aimless? Because if it has, the question "Do we need another 'Bish?'" is a valid one.

FOR THE RECORD

In the January issue of the *"Rag"* I innocently asked if the Club's 3,427 aero tows in '69 wasn't something of a record. Roy Proctor has written and put me to rights:

"Lasham did 5,455 aerotows last year on our own site. Doesn't include those done for others! However it was a bad year. In 1967 the figure was 7,986 tows!"

(But isn't Lasham a professional gliding centre with full time staff? – Ed.)

A postscript from "G.B.": "Have James and Nini so named their child as to placate a certain body if occasion arises in the future? A.R.B."

The Annual Dinner Dance, 13th February 1970

The Annual Dinner is now a memory of many weeks back but it was very much a successful evening and well-remembered. The evening was set off in high fashion with the excellence of the Guest of Honour's after-dinner speech. I've been to every Annual Dinner since the Club's inception and I concede no speaker to excel John Hunt MP. Even James was moved to exclaim: "He can come again," and as an afterthought add: "He must come again." If Bunny Bramson can talk him into attending next year he'll earn his keep with that one achievement. The prizes and trophies were presented by Capt. Bill Bright, the winner of the Air Race to Australia, to an accompaniment of ribald comment and applause – as ever. Philip Meeson earned the de Salis Trophy for the member who has done the most for the Club during the preceding 18 months. For aerobatics John Firth received the McAully Trophy, James Black the de Havilland, and Bob Mitchell the Air Squadron Aerobatic Trophy. Michael (Manx) Kelly took the Esso. The Icicle Aerobatic Trophy – so named because it's held in freezing weather in January – went to the joint winners David Gaster and Michael Riley. The Dawn-to-Dusk Trophy went to the late Hubert Schnabel, and the Icarus Trophy to Mike Bialkiewicz. Tiger Club Medallions went to Fred – of the sausages – Marsh for his Air Racing. The Foreign Touring one to Freddie Fox – a most popular win this – and the Glider Towing Medallion to Glyn Richards.

I thought the new Tiger Club Medallion a vast improvement on the original and I believe credit for the design, a close-up of a Stampe, goes to Andrew Chadwick.

It was, as I have said, a great evening, but it could have been an even better event. There were probably 200 members and guests there out of a membership of several hundred. It struck me that if we home members extended hospitality to the out-of-towners, a lot more would want to come along. It's a very expensive business spending a night in London and I for one would warmly welcome a couple of members to stay over – I'm equally sure every other London member would want to do likewise. What about it, Bev?

Manx Kelly, of happy memory, was a flamboyant product of the postwar air force and he revelled in aerobatics. He was ever in competition with Neil Williams, Neil himself being a similar RAF extravert. Their flying did much to enhance our time at Redhill. They flew together, but friends they were not, yet they harboured a considerable respect for the other, but at a distance.

When Manx could he persuaded to write it was always worth reading.

MANX DOES HIS THING!

". . . Frances MacRae said to me this evening that I should send you aerobatic news so here goes – out of date and on the first scrap of paper to hand.

The ICICLE Aerobatic Trophy. Well, it was appropriately cold, cloudy and windy when this was flown at Redhill on February 7th to see who would win what I think is the most beautiful trophy – Andrew Chadwick's splendid design in perspex depicting a few aerobatic manoeuvres. The sealed envelope was duly ripped open and a formidable unseen sequence designed by Neil Williams reared its angular and largely inverted features.

Somehow it has to be flown between 2,000 and 1,000 feet and three pilots managed this without breaking to regain height – Dave Gaster and Mike Riley, who were joint winners, and Philip Meeson who was placed fourth. Philip screwed up his rolling circle which was probably what enabled me to pip him for a 3rd place I didn't feel I deserved. Everyone used the Stampe. Dave did remarkably well to place first as he hadn't flown a Stampe for months, being a Zlin man now. In fact he'd probably have won outright had he not used a Zlin-timed recovery for the finishing flick roll. It was good to see two new faces amongst the nine competitors: John Neumeister from the USA, who came sixth, and Ian McCowen who has started aerobatics on a Stampe of his own which lives at a lovely little private field – Bighton Farm near Alresford.

Ian and Philip Meeson have just set up in business with a firm called SAUSA – the best guess as to what these letters stand for can have my longest cigarette butt.

Saturday and Sunday 21st/22nd March was rehearsal day for Charles Boddington's Barnstormers at Sibson airstrip near Peterborough where the organisation is in Barry Tempest's aerobatically-minded hands.

Bob Mitchell made his first 'public' appearance in his KZ-8. What a beautiful aeroplane – it really swings – and seems to maintain an almost constant speed. Bob did a double horizontal flick for us – most impressive. "Though I haven't quite learnt to land it yet," he says.

Roy Legg's Jungmeister performance is becoming very polished. His one-and-a-half-flick from knife-edge to knife-edge looked good though the aircraft is a bit short of speed at the end to keep going level. He also seems to carve round the outside manoeuvres pretty well in an aircraft that I believe Neil said wasn't very suited. I was supposed to be the speed merchant in the Cassutt though Clem Hughes' Falco possibly went a knot faster. Now I've got used to the former it really does seem a marvellous machine – an aerial mini – tuned for racing of course.

On the subject of minis, two aerobatic girls were at Sibson. Caroline, a friend of Bob's who is warming up on a Chippy but didn't show us, and a girl from Blackpool called Jane who drinks a yard of ale very neatly and can demolish pints inverted – a manoeuvre none of the lads were checked out on. She also flies a Stampe. Help!

Mike Coburn's had his Jungmeister repainted in a very pretty scheme. Unfortunately he didn't give his low low show which impressed at Stapleford last year. Talking of Stapleford or thereabouts – that old bold pilot Neville Browning has a Jungmeister for sale. Any sensible young lad with 4Ks+ to spare would do well to contact Neville as, contrary to reports in Air Progress, they are not likely to be starting producing them again.

QUICKIE TIME:

DISPLAY PILOT at party prior to German airshow: "This is a great party, but why, oh! why BEFORE the show?"

DEUTSCH LUFT ORGANIZER (or something): "We haf it alles worked out. If you crash tomorrow you don't miss the party."

INTERROGATOR TO CAPTURED SUICIDE PILOT: "Name?"

S.P.: "Chow Mein."

INT.: "Age?"

S.P.: "48."

INT.: "Bit old for a suicide pilot?"

S.P.: "Yes. All boys on Squadron call me 'Chicken Chow Mein.'"

FLIGHT SAFETY: Some Stampes around – not Tiger Club ones – have rather unevenly-tuned bracing wires. This is NOT a good thing if they are used for aeros. Correct tensioning of Stampe bracing wires is v. important. Secondly – I've flown one aircraft and possibly two where a French type 'sucking' pitot was connected to an English ASI. By crossing pitot and static lines you can get the system to give a reading, but it's up the creek and could lead you into flicking the aircraft at too high an airspeed. So watch it if the stalling speed is absurdly low or you hit max rpm at low airspeed.

Pay a visit to Sibson. It's a good grass strip 2,000 ft in two directions, no, four. Easily found by road or rail. Mind the H.T. cable. The airfield offices, conveniently situated in a film set 10 feet port of the main runway, provide an excellent view of any beat-ups. The bar is 30 yards from the offices and hangar. Don't try to fly halfway up the windsock between the bar and the hangar. The post is only 10 feet high.

Message Ends – MANX.

Committee minutes: April '70
Any other business iii: 20 Japanese pilots at Redhill.

I only put that in because an irreverent thought crossed my mind (blame Manx): "Was Chicken Chow Mein there too?" Methinks I'm getting nationalities mixed up, and no, I can't remember the occasion. At the previous month's meeting there were no less than twenty-one displays and participations listed for the coming season.

The usual routine for the would-be participating pilot was to initially get the Committee's approval for an away show; big or small, an OK was the form. Once the 'thumbs up' was given the team leader would finalise arrangements directly with the outside event organiser. Questions like: can we land there, refuelling facilities if necessary, how long display, how often and a rough map of the location, and eventually how much. The dibs to be shared out between the pilots. At no time did the Tiger Club management interfere, all they requested was the flying times per aircraft and subsequent payment. Sound airmanship, respect for others and the safe return of the aircraft on time was taken for granted. The last point could be a stumbling block. The odd mishap, caught out by bad weather or an unavoidable delay needed an instant notification, for others may have booked the aeroplane. But here the rule was firm: "You took it away, you get it back" was taken seriously. And sometimes the doing needed real-time initiative. Dull our flying wasn't.

CLUB NEWS: MAY – JUNE 1970

It's flaming June all right – the heat shimmers off the wings of the parked aircraft and I crouch away from the sunshine in the cool embrace of the hangar. For years now this column has reflected the seasons at Redhill, mainly for those members overseas whose dream of home is as much for the vagaries of the British weather as our sort of flying. I'm all too aware that I last wrote of April showers and two months is too long to leave a Newsletter.

The news that shocked us all in this interim period was the death of Barry Griffiths in a flying accident. I'll write at another time of the Barry I knew, let it suffice at the moment to extend the heartfelt sympathies of every Club member to his widow Elspeth, his son and daughters. This sad occasion brought me a flood of letters as never before from his many friends in flying, all anxious to pay a last tribute. His funeral was a moving moment attended by so many of the Club and the theatrical profession and presided over in the most natural manner possible by John Blake.

. . . The forthcoming World Aerobatic Contest is bringing a lot of old friends to this country eager to take the opportunity of renewing acquaintance. Among them count Dave Allen and Nick Pocock. Welcome fellas! Unfortunately the DH Aerobatic Trophy has been put back till the 22nd of August. Murmured Michael, half joking, half relieved when the decision was made: "The thought of that mob getting on to our last remaining Stampe horrifies me." More names in circulation are those of three Club members standing for election to the House – probably past tense by the time you read this – John Wilkinson, John Firth and Winston Churchill. Let's hope they all get in, regardless of politics.

Dicky Reid is engaged. Dicky must be one of the last of the genuine bachelors left in the outfit. Let's hope his wife-to-be will tolerate his unique brand of joie de vivre, his beloved Tiger and impossible landing strip. Our best wishes to them both. And Pete Langstone has reappeared after a long spell in North Africa. He claims 5,000 hours of desert flying and to have covered a million kilometres.

I clanged good and proper in the last *"Rag"* when I raved about Adrian Swire's Spitfire being in blue and gold. Hearsay was wrong – I've now seen it. It's immaculate in service camouflage, and how I secretly yearn to fly it. Currently it's at Rolls Royce for C. of A. Neil Williams is an exceptional pilot, an accolade I reserve for few, but recently whilst flying the Zlin he saw a wing begin to shake – 'flutter' is too mild a word. He was at 1,500 feet, no parachute. I hear he kept his head and promptly rolled the Zlin onto its back to ease the main spar load, and only rolled out at the last moment before touching down into what must have been the forced landing of all time. He was quite unhurt but furious with himself for damaging the aircraft.

The EAA visited Redhill on the Saturday before Whitsun and were greeted by a great Club turnout. There were vintage aircraft to please the most ardent of our visitors. But the backstage preparation of these successful 'At Homes' needs a lot of help and the House Committee urgently asks members willing to give a hand, either on the Committee, or in the field, to join them. And why not?

Here's a great opportunity to do something for the Club, and the chance is open to either sex, flying or passenger members. Michael Jones will direct volunteers to the right quarter. The Dawn-to-Dusk Competition is now in full swing – there are 23 contestants from Clubs all over the country. But even before the contest began there had been several very long flights recently and all within the span of daylight. One by John Firth made it to the Shetlands and back . . . flying a Musketeer. I couldn't help recalling a trip I made to John O'Groats in a Tiger – only that took a long, long day for the one-way trip with our cruise limited to 65 knots. I carried the Standing-on-Wing rig clamped on top and a fine-pitch prop up front. Jill Southam writes from Scrabster today to say that no one up there has forgotten that Tiger Club Display back in '63 – the most northern the Club has ever attempted. How much further could we have gone? Jill is with Operation Seashore on their round-Britain trip.

There's a hotted-up version of the Condor at Redhill. It's got a 140 hp unit and is used for glider-towing; it's reported to be very potent. It's a little-known fact that 36 Condors have been made and the production continues. Incidentally, if there is anyone anxious to buy a Harvard will they please contact me. Philip Meeson has located some good ones in Holland. The King's Cup is going to be something of a tough one this year, what with its 300 mile circuit. It's all a bit sad really, for the distance cuts out all the fun machines. No Tigers, no Turbs. Maybe that's what the organisers want. Not so down at Rochester though. Down there Bill Chesson is noted for laying on fun races.

Committee news this month includes the appointment of Bill Goldstraw to Membership Secretary, and a firm vote of thanks to Jack Piercy for his long term in the office, during which time the Club has grown to its present strength of nigh-on 750 members. Jack continues to guide the Legal Fund and prudently reminds members that this unique fund is solely there to assist members who come a cropper with the law, and those who have encountered this expensive business will confirm the good this fund can do. It's not there to pay your fines but to help you in deserving causes to defend yourself in a proper manner. I urge you to support it. Perhaps by donating prize monies, conscience monies, or just the occasional cheque. One day you may be grateful it's there. On the gliding side we've already had a record innings with no less than 1,565 tows, and all by the middle of June. 300 up on last year. Gordon Crabb, who is so successful running this side, is looking for a volunteer to do a week's free flying for the Nationals up at Doncaster during the last week in August. Interested? Get in touch with him now. This would seem a good moment to remind members that it is essential to have the correct aircraft type on your flying card before flying off into the blue. One member who failed to do this and added to the omission with some other carelessnesses was this month suspended from flying for three months . . . we only pass on the gen.

BILL'S ROCHESTER, TURB STORY, HAMILTON COMPS AND SUMMER ON THE BEACH

Bill Chesson certainly laid fun races on down at Rochester. That the big grassy airfield there was in some way a part of Norman Jones' unofficial empire we never questioned. I can't recall if he rented the place from the local council or in some typically Norman stroke of assumption 'took it on.' Whatever, the venue was always a very popular one. Absolutely divorced from any airways or other such restrictions there was always a delightful air of slight neglect about the place. No one came out of the woodwork to reproach or frown; it was smiles and a warm welcome all the way, and it was Bill Chesson's base and happy hunting ground.

The airfield sat high on a hill, closely skirted by a busy local road along which we seemed to have hordes of supporters; our noisy presence so close to their houses and everyday life in no way put them out, indeed they waved greetings as friends whenever we taxied near. How could we not enjoy Rochester?

Bill's idea of racing had nothing to do with racing – real racing that is. Oh! sure, we called it 'racing' and we did our best but the reason for the race – any race – was pure entertainment. No one took it seriously in a competitive sense; it was always serious fun. H.E. Bates would have relished Rochester, a would-be Kentish man in whose eyes and memories the sun always shone . . . it was always 'perfick' there.

I still envisage the sweet joy of piloting a Tiger there, the warm air buffeting my face as I gently bumped my way eastwards along the Kentish escarpment, every sense alert with pleasure. And do I imagine I once smelt that evocative tang of rich greenery arising from the garden of England 1,000 feet below: I like to think I could.

The Rollason Turbulent was always so very much a part of the Tiger Club story, her presence a colourful passage through so many adventures, and yet only one owner-pilot ever really conjured up the magic of flying that little machine and that someone was the late Barry Griffiths. I can vouch for the veracity of his tale for Lollie and I were at the Beauvais dinner when a dishevelled Barry finally turned up. If ever there was a case of utter determination this was it.

The story he hesitantly told was unbelievable; and how we cheered the telling. It joins another epic Turbulent flight – James Gilbert's journey from the Orkneys back to Redhill in '63 – in the Tiger Club's hall of legend, tales which were often larded with glorious failure, a generous touch of lunacy and a consistent courage that only lingers with the best.

Here is what Barry wrote:

"This story is about an aeroplane – to the everlasting credit of that aeroplane. If it reflects rather less credit upon the pilot, I still think it should be told for reasons which will appear.

It is a short story. It would have been longer, but after two thousand words, when I was halfway through, I rang the editor, who said fifteen hundred at most, so I'll leave out all the exciting bits about how I got lost in the murk over France and shouted "the b****y coast must be there," only there was no answer and it wasn't.

I had started out in my Turbulent for the Beauvais thrash in company with assorted Club aircraft crammed with dedicated aviators (one had twelve pencils, all sharpened) licking their lips in anticipation of the orgy to come, but the beasts rushed off and left me flogging along on my own, which I didn't really mind as I didn't have to worry about keeping them in sight and after all we private owners must draw the line somewhere.

Now there are those, I regret to say, who regard Turbulents as under-powered, unreliable, fragile and generally unfit to be taken out of sight of the aerodrome. It is to these dribbly-nosed beasts (if I may be forgiven a technicality) that this story is directed. To the rest, may it confirm their faith.

Late on Saturday afternoon I found myself – and my Turbulent – sitting in a field on a French farm. The field was 150 metres long with a barbed wire fence at each end; it had been formed when the earth was in torment – it was not a smooth field, you understand.

I know you would love to hear the gripping story of how I came to be there in the first place, the excitement, terror and pathos of it all, but the editor says he cannot spare the space so now it will cost you a drink to hear it. After a thrilling battle with the cows – who bitterly resented the intrusion – some rough but effective men appeared who chased them away and got me some *essence super* from a garage.

It had been difficult to get into that field, so any attempt to get out of it seemed to me quite hopeless; however, my new friends were so obviously looking forward to seeing me try (they had brought, with the petrol, some village children to see me fail) that it seemed churlish to refuse. Furthermore, the alternative was the dismantling of the aircraft (for no one but a desperate owner would try to fly it out), endless explanations and colossal expense. If I could just get the wheels over that fence I could get to Le Treport before dark and the whole picture would change.

What wind there was came out of the sun. There were also some trees. With my heart in my mouth, I strapped myself in, started the engine and taxied back down the abominable field. Four times I rushed up that field with the sun in my eyes, dodging the cows as they loomed up; the poor little Turbulent bounced and rattled over the tussocks, lurching like a drunk, but the wheels would not unstick, and with never more than 20 on the clock, each time I had to slew violently away as the fence came up in front of the nose. I could not understand how the undercarriage was still in one piece but it was. I determined that the next attempt would decide the matter, one way or the other. As the fence came into view a few feet ahead I dragged back on the stick and – glory be – there was air beneath the wheels. Wallowing impossibly, I thought I'd just scraped over when there was a terrific bang and down came the Turbulent on her nose in the next field. I had acquired thirty feet of barbed wire but lost a spat, the pitot head and some canvas. This really did seem to be the end, but we were in soft earth, the prop was whole and the engine started. The little lads were clearly delighted with this performance, if a bit disappointed at the lack of blood, and willingly helped me manhandle the Turbulent through the mud. They pointed to stubble some distance away and said it was "plus dur." They were getting the point. *"Plus long?"* I asked, no doubt with pathetic eagerness. They shook their heads. *"Le même. Cent cinquante metres."* Oh! well.

This time I taxied over a deeply-rutted cart track for about 200 yds. When I got to the stubble the wheels, incredibly, were still turning. I abandoned the negligible wind for the advantage of going down sun. Once more I opened the throttle, felt the wheels dragging in the soft earth, banged into a sharp dip and out again; still no feeling of buoyancy but here comes the fence so here goes. Once more, back on the stick; again that feeling, as the Turbulent was dragged off the ground, of going against all one had ever been taught. I didn't dare look at the fence but simply waited for the bang and braced myself for the crash. But nothing happened. I can't tell you what the speed was because I had no A.S.I. but, Glory Hallelujah, we were airborne again, flopping about like a drunken duck, but flying. Nothing came off and I landed 15 minutes later at Le Treport where they took one look at my dishevelled, mud-covered clothes, another at the aircraft and poured me a vast brandy. After a hectic interlude at Beauvais – oh! I got there, by car, to a welcome I certainly didn't deserve – I flew the Turbulent back to Redhill the next day.

Don Lovell, considerate as ever, hovered up-sun of me in the Ambassadeur, just in case. But the Turbulent behaved beautifully, and I have never crossed the channel with more confidence. An aircraft that could stand up to such appalling treatment and still perform normally was, to say the least, to be relied upon.

And _that_ is the point of this story."

I got me a letter, part of which read:

". . . here is something about the competition I propose to run for the Club in October."

It continued:

"The object of the competition is that of a fun contest, basically for those members of the Club who do not compete in aerobatic or air racing competitions. Over the last year I have heard a certain amount of muttering that there are no general competitions for aviation apart from the Dawn-to-Dusk and it was with this in mind that I proposed this contest to the Committee. I enclose a set of rules which you will see is divided up into a number of events, including Nav exercises, forced landings, instruments flying etc. I do hope a reasonable number of people will enter and my spies tell me that you will be guaranteed to win it.

Yours ever,
DAVID HAMILTON."

Basic Rules for Competition

GROUP I

Navigation: A course of not less than 100 miles and not more that 150 miles will be selected with one turning point and one airfield on which the competitors will be required to land in order to obtain a signature from the Air Traffic Controller witnessing their visit. Pilots will be required to identify the turning point in their report. One hour before the start, pilots will be briefed on their course and turning point and they will be required to submit a time for this exercise before their departure. In the competition they will allow 15 minutes in the total time they require for the exercise for obtaining the signature at the landing airfield. This Group is intended to test the skill of exact time by competitors and it is not intended that it should become a race. The aircraft are expected to complete the flight at the recommended cruising speed of the aircraft.

Points: The maximum number of points for a perfect exercise will be 250. Competitors missing the turning point or wrongly identifying it will lose 100 points. In addition, 10 points will be deducted for every 30 seconds early or late the competitor is over his specified time.

GROUP 2

Spot Landing: Pilots, solo only, will be required to position themselves over the centre of the airfield at 1,500 feet. After a suitable wing-rock, they will then stop engine and make a dead-stick landing on to the target area which will be a number of concentric circles placed in the centre of the airfield. The competitors will be permitted to make a power-on practice attempt followed by an overshoot and a re-climb to position before attempting the dead-stick landing. The circles and points pertaining to it are as follows:

Centre: 5 ft radius = 250 points
          10 ft radius = 200 points
          15ft radius   = 150 points
          20ft radius   = 100 points
          25ft radius   = 50 points
          30ft radius   = 25 points

GROUP 3

Instrument Flying (C.F.I.'s benefit): This group will comprise a short instrument training flight where each competitor will be required to achieve a straight and level flight at normal cruising speed of the aircraft after the instructor has placed the aircraft in an unusual attitude. Three attempts will be permitted in respect of this group. It is suggested that the C.F.I. be the examiner as he is likely to be a non-competing pilot. Consideration in awarding marks should be given to those competitors who hold any form of instrument rating. Those pilots will be expected to achieve a higher standard.

Points: The maximum mark for three perfect attempts will be 100. The mark actually awarded to each competitor will be at the discretion of the examiner.

GROUP 4

Balloon Bursting: Each competitor will be permitted three attempts. One balloon will be released from the centre of the runway as the aircraft crosses the boundary. The competitor will attempt to burst the balloon as he passes but without turning back. The competitor will attempt to burst three balloons and will be awarded 50 points for every balloon he bursts.

GROUP 5

Flour Bombing: Three concentric circles will be placed in the centre of the airfield with the bull having a 5 foot radius, the inner having a 10 foot radius and the outer having a 20 foot radius. Each competitor will be permitted three individual attempts to put the flour bomb in the bull.

Points: Bull   = 75 points
         Inner = 50 points
         Outer = 25 points'

And so was mooted a contest that was to run for many a year. The appeal to 'have a go' was certainly there. If today an adventurous CFI wanted to lift his (or her) Club out of the mundane, he (or she) could do no worse than to benefit from David's highly original fun.

CLUB NEWS: JULY – AUGUST 1970

It's mid-summer and Redhill remains a green and peaceful haven, one of the few places I know where one can unwind amid folk with the same idea. This thought occurred to me whilst I sat around one quiet Sunday hoping no one would recognise the fact that I was the Duty Instructor – sic. It wasn't that I was anti flying, it was just that I was deeply engrossed in observing people moving around in that faintly bemused state of wonderment, unable to believe that such a place existed in 1970.

An American member put the case in a soft voice. "I've travelled many thousands of miles just to be here – it's like coming home." He stayed in England seven days and didn't move beyond the airfield. Fact. Ask Michael.

Perhaps Michael can help me a little by recording some of the details of all the races that are going on practically every weekend. Everyone is so busy, I can't get anyone to put pen to paper. It's all happening. I do know that Hilary Trice won the Isle of Wight race and, if you didn't already know it, Hilary is Michael's secretary, and that pleasant voice that answers your phone queries. Of the racing at Rochester however, I can comment. The *"Kent Messenger"* Race was won in convincing style by local man and Club member Harry Foulds in his Chipmunk, and the Formula One race was a pointless exercise around a course that was far too tight. All this I know because I was there, and I was there to witness some of the most senseless and dangerous flying a hardened commentator could ever dread to see. Another observer, and himself a top display pilot, put it bluntly: "Unpractised, unrehearsed showing off." I know the pilots read this *"Rag"* and, if only for the sake of their next-of-kin and the very future of private flying, I hope they'll take this warning to heart and that I won't have cause to write the obituaries of good friends.

Comments off the top of my head usually come easily, but as I re-read those words of mine written on a summer's day all those years ago I fumble. Is it perhaps that I can now perceive an innocence, a happiness, an aura perhaps, that settled about those bewitched, on that grassy corner of Surrey. It was there all right. Redhill was at times a magic garden where nothing, be it voice or demeanour, marred the spell that could settle on anyone at any time. The thought warms me today.

Yet, with the '180s' one accepted on a day-to-day basis, the events at Rochester showed another side of a coin. For me to have written "to witness some of the most senseless and dangerous flying a hardened commentator could ever dread to see," I must have been well and truly shaken. But here's the funny thing. Whilst I can recall a summer's day at Redhill with all the warmth and clarity an old man could wish, I can't remember that awful flying or that group of pilots misbehaving down at Rochester. Nature, with its selective memory, can be kind, can't it?

"Dear Sirs,

On Saturday, while carting off bales of hay here at High Easter in the afternoon, I was disturbed by the familiar friendly drone of three biplane engines cruising in my direction north-eastwards. They were two red and yellow Stampes and a Tiger. The sun was very hot and not a cloud in the sky and, working "miles from anywhere" I can only describe as bliss the scene as the two Stampes, flying at about 500 feet line-abreast formation, lowered their noses with gaining speed and revs, proceeded into a perfect formation loop right over my small airstrip, and then chugged on their way as if having simply fulfilled a manoeuvre to remove the dust from their top wing-planes.

Please will you thank the three pilots for me as I find it a real pleasure to see real pilots flying REAL aircraft.

Best wishes to your Club.

M. LUCKIN."

A copy of this *"Tiger Rag"* has gone to Mr Luckin and with it our warm invitation to be our guest at Redhill one day. The pilots were Pete Jarvis, Carl Schofield and Robin Voice, who no doubt breathed a sigh of relief no one else was about.

Ian Scott Hill was a most delightful chap. He was a director of BEA and larger than life. He and his charming wife would arrive at Redhill over a sunny weekend and proceed to lay out a scrumptious picnic on the grass before the hangar, to which they would invite all and sundry. Ian, a born raconteur, would pour the wine and regale us with gossipy snippets, and all the while his wife, a gracious Lady Bountiful, would hand around food to her appreciative guests. His contribution to the *"Rag"* was every bit in keeping with his special charm.

From Ian Scott Hill comes this delightful story all about our Fox Moth G-ACEJ – the carefree pilot and author is Jack Newbury.

"I think that one of flying's more pleasant experiences is to sit in the open cockpit of a light aeroplane, on a summer's day, in shirt-sleeves, doing circuits and bumps. To get paid for it adds to the pleasure.

This is just how I spent my summer holidays some years ago. Through an advert in *"Flight"* I met S/Ldr Giroux MBE, who ran a small company at Southport which owned two Fox Moths. He was a veteran of the first World War and flew one aircraft himself. The other was flown by miscellaneous chaps like myself, who had a few hours to spare and needed the money.

The Squadron Leader was a wonderful character. He no longer flies but still lives at Southport. He kept his aircraft in the municipal bus garage. Every day he would arrive at the garage with his little dog. He used to talk about the dog and the aeroplanes in almost the same breath, and in the same terms. "I think 'EJ would like a little more oil this morning, and see if Graham will take some water!"

When satisfied that yesterday's technical snags had been cleared, he would tuck his travelling rug and a few spare parts on the baggage rack of the aircraft, put the dog on the seat in the cabin and proceed, with a mechanic on the wing, past the buses and down to the beach. He usually took 'CB (G-ACCB), which he always felt was rather sloppy, and therefore a little more tricky to handle. I would follow in 'EJ (G-ACEJ).

At the entrance to the beach there was a ramp which used to accumulate seaweed. You had to taxi quickly over this to avoid the main wheels sinking in. If that had happened of course the aircraft would have turned on its back. Somehow it never did, although the tail left the ground on several occasions. Part of the vast beach was licensed as an aerodrome. You simply picked a path for take-off clear of weed and pools on the driest sand you could see. I never met any holiday-makers on the beach on those summer mornings, although the horses drawing the shrimp carts from Morecambe Bay often used to plod along at the water's edge.

After take-off you set course inland for the centre of Southport, sometimes climbing as high as 500 ft! From there you flew to the coach park or the railway station, depending upon where the greatest number of trippers could be seen arriving. You then proceeded to make a series of shallow dives pointing the way to the main beach aerodrome. On some days we did the dives in formation, always with S/Ldr Giroux in the lead, always with the ball of the turn and slip indicator hard over to one side as he instinctively edged away from the other aircraft!

On arrival we went to the booking hut, cleared out the debris from the last high tide and opened for business. Small lads acted as linesmen, guarding the roped-off boundary of the sand aerodrome. They worked for a few shillings a day, plus the occasional aeroplane ride. I always arranged with them to let the rope droop to the ground at the far end of the "runway" in case the aeroplane failed to lift off. More than once I was glad of this unofficial runway extension.

On the fence we erected a long sign advertising the flights and the aeroplanes. The message ran: "Built by the firm that built the Comet." The local wits suggested that "Built by the fathers of the men who built the Comet" would be more appropriate, since the Fox Moth dated from the 1930s.

The Squadron Leader knew his market. He wasn't allowed to tout for business, but he would stand in front of the hut in his leather coat and talk about flying to likely groups of four – the capacity of the cabin. It was one such group – they turned out to be all-in wrestlers from an act on the pier – who gave me the fright of my life. They so overloaded my aircraft that not only did I go through the rope but, by the time we got to the Ainsdale Hotel a few miles further down the coast, we were still no higher than the second floor windows. I'm sure that I bent the throttle trying to get that little extra power from the tired old engine.

There were short trips and a long cross-country across the river estuary and around Blackpool Tower. Once we had got a booking for Blackpool the remainder of the load went there too, regardless of what they paid. However, one US serviceman with blonde girl friend booked the long flight (8 minutes) and said they wanted the cabin to themselves. Now, although the cockpit was outside, there was a small window in front of the pilot, so that he could pass messages to the passengers and keep an eye on them. I looked forward to an entertaining quarter of an hour. As soon as we were airborne, however, a hat was promptly stuffed in the window and I spent the rest of the flight busily adjusting the trim.

The pre-flight briefing was meticulous. On a typical occasion it went like this: "Now the wind is coming from the north so you are taking off towards the Big Dipper. If you can't get the height, arrange to cross it where it curves downwards. Don't fly over the Winter Gardens until the open-air band concert finishes. If your engines fails aim between the white pillars of the pier, the others have still got their bracing struts. Get round the circuit quickly, there will be a queue today because the cold wind will stop them settling on the beach."

As the tide came up the aerodrome got smaller and smaller, so you were eventually landing on a narrow strip with dunes on one side and the sea on the other. In these conditions there always seemed to be a crosswind and it wasn't unusual to end the landing by running into the sea. The aircraft was then pulled unceremoniously backwards onto dry land; the passengers got out, and you taxied back for the next lot hoping that by then they hadn't lost their nerve. At low tide the sands at Southport go out some-mile-and-a-half. People drive their cars as far as they can and then have a picnic or simply doze off in deck chairs. From the air you could see the rising tide creeping round the slightly raised patches of dry sand where the cars were parked. Every day someone got cut off and the local amphibious vehicle (DUKW) owner would circle around them haggling over the price of a tow. It was a very one-sided bargain with the water rising steadily by the minute.

The customers were delightful. For most it was their first flight. One chap gave me 2/6 as he climbed into the cabin and asked me to do a loop to "frighten the Missus"; he didn't know that she had previously climbed in on the other side and had implored me to make it a nice, smooth ride. I compromised on a rather steep turn, which was about all that the Fox Moth could do anyway, and they both seemed satisfied. There was a spring-operated air speed indicator on one wing strut, visible from the cabin. Age had weakened the spring so that it read about 25 mph faster than the authorised ASI in the cockpit. Only the smallest and brightest lads seemed to have doubts about the 100 mph we achieved on the circuit. One chap complained that the total flying time was only 2 minutes 37 seconds; but, as the Squadron Leader explained, "4 miles for 5/- in a taxi of the air wasn't bad." Still, we gave him another ride for nothing.

One year, when I got back to London, I read in the papers that 'CB ("the sloppy one") had fallen into the sea with a heavy load aboard (I immediately thought about my all-in wrestlers). They all escaped with cuts and bruises. But with only one aircraft left the Squadron Leader didn't need any help the next season. So ended a very happy encounter with one of the characters of the aviation world."

WE MISS FRIENDS, OVERCONFIDENCE,
'WET PAPER, TASTES SALT = DITCHED'

CLUB NEWS: SEPTEMBER 1970

September has been one of the saddest months in my life. In quick succession I have lost two close friends, and the Club will long miss two of its oldest and most active members. Just what made this summer so regretfully unforgivable I shall never know, but as the fatalists among us gain scant solace in their belief, I, no fatalist, can only echo shocked disbelief at the tragic deaths of Pee Wee Judge and, a few days later, Charles Boddington.

Pee Wee was a superlative and sensitive pilot, a kindly gentle man who was everyone's friend. And Charles, a skilled and practised pilot, who leaves behind him the memory of a trusted and good companion in a hundred adventures, and worse by far I mourn for those these two men leave behind. It is in the tradition of those of us who fly that the passing of a fellow pilot be the occasion for no more than the paying of respect, and then, as though nothing has happened, we get on with the game. But for one lone pilot, and I suspect many others among us, the game will never seem quite the same again.

In time honoured style, I humbly offer to Pee Wee's mother, to Charles' wife Diana and children, and to all the bereaved, the Club's heartfelt sympathy and compassion in the moment of their loss.

Pee Wee was killed flying a small gyroplane at the Farnborough Air Show. It was thought he'd reacted as a conventional pilot in a stick-forward manoeuvre, resulting in a fuselage flexing that permitted the main blades to strike the tail assembly. Whatever the cause the tragedy was seen on countless television screens to aviation's sorrow.

Charles also died flying, but in his case whilst on film work in Ireland. He crashed his SE.5A replica reputedly off a tight turn near the ground. What a sorry film set that was: no less than five deaths – and a serious injury – marred the filming. Apart from Charles one incident caused the loss of four in a horrific crash. A replacement pilot (in fact he was the C.O. of the Irish Air Force base at nearby Baldonnel, and had volunteered his services) flew into the camera helicopter's blades. And so we lost the pilots, the cameraman and the producer Burch Williams. An ill-fated project if ever there was one, my sadness compounded by the knowledge I'd been flying with them days before. The story at the time was that the coming together had been filmed from the ground, and the film hastily sent over to the States before investigators could get their hands on it.

Haven't a clue who won the ESSO Tiger Trophy on Sept. 26th, but its mention is a good lead into a success story down at Shoreham with this year's sole Full Display by the Tiger Club. I can't remember a better or happier display at Shoreham in all the ten years we've been flying there. I heard that Norman was so delighted he immediately threatened us with four or five Full Displays next season. I hope he will settle for a maximum of three, for they take a lot of effort to do the job properly and Shoreham was above all else a proper job, with a magnificent degree of timing and every act performing to the second. To Peter Phillips, the organiser, the Bouquet of the Month. I reckon Michael earned himself a Green endorsement some weeks ago when he successfully pulled off a faultless forced landing in, of all things, a propellerless Beta. He put it down in several fields. I say 'several' advisedly, that thing has an approach speed in the late eighties.

The Towing contingent, under Gordon Crabb, has now recorded (late August) a total of 3,111 aerotows – the highest number to date. All our congratulations on a terrific and still largely unsung achievement.

Every now and then a wise old head would arise and attempt to guide us into the ways of the safe. Of course we nodded sagely and murmur "he's right you know" but such warnings were for the other fools – as nice a case of tunnel vision as ever there was. The wise head in this case was Surgeon Commander Roger Vaughan, a long-standing Club member whose words should be repeated annually if it would do any good.

"I remember flying as a passenger in a Service Tiger Moth a good many years ago. The morning was sunny with billowing cumulus, the grass might have been even greener than Redhill, and the pilot was a popular officer with a good many thousand hours and several medals besides his campaign ones. I considered him rather elderly because he had three grown-up daughters.

After a pleasant hour over the sparkling waves, he turned onto finals at a thousand feet or so, looped and then rolled to bring us out flat and level over the hedge in time for a delicate "three-pointer." A beautifully judged and executed piece of flying.

Shortly afterwards, in the bar, Commander (Air) approached my friend and expressed himself thus (white with emotion in the knowledge of the large audience and his victim's seniority): "I knew you were a good pilot. I didn't realise until this morning that you were a B.F. as well. As I consider it my first responsibility to ensure the safety of the aircraft on this station and the crews who fly them, you'll do no more flying from here while I am in command." And so I believe it was, and a happy morning ended in grief and woe.

Some might think this reaction to a little ebullience by a professional somewhat extreme. There was no doubt but that a sombre and cautionary note had been struck, but equally no doubt that a margin of safety had been laid down which neither skill nor seniority would allow one to transgress.

I cannot help remembering this episode sometimes when I read issues of the "Tiger Rag," especially the last one. It is full of youthful and enthusiastic accounts of mishaps and dangers passed, but rarely any mention of safety factors, of risks taken which should not have been taken. Relish, not regret, is the theme.

I believe that, with the ever increasing numbers of young members, some balance should be given to the "Rag" in the way of serious comment. Remember the mythical and inimitable Dilbert in another flying magazine. He recounts similar hairy episodes in humorous fashion, but his tales are followed by pungent comment. "Well, there we are, folks. Another exciting adventure by your favourite pilot. It only remains for me to add that no one but a corn-chewing ding-a-ling from the sticks, such as Dilbert, would ever have got himself into that situation in the first place."

I believe that there is a growing over-confidence among some pilots in the Club, which is reflected in contributions to the magazine which suggest to me a lack of insight which will prove their undoing, sooner or later. Flying, like the practice of Surgery, is not inherently safe, as some people mistakenly "quote." It is inherently dangerous, but by a calculating approach, designer and pilot have used their experience to minimise that risk. Pilot and surgeon provide themselves with an escape clause, a let-out, a Wilsonian option: "If such and such were to happen at this moment, what would I do?" If the answer to that question seems to be "There's nothing you could do," then it is the mark of the true professional that he will withdraw from that situation or preferably avoid getting into it. He considers it no reflection on his skill and courage to admit that the weather is "strictly for the birds" and that is why people will trust him with their safety. This professional requirement for an alternative rests on the fact, as any statistician will tell you, that the chances of any two unconnected failures occurring simultaneously are absolutely minuscule compared with the chance of a solitary failure. The risk of aerobatting an aeroplane at 3,000 ft, compared with 500 ft, is not just a matter of 2,500 ft more room, but lies in the proven fact that spin recovery within 2,000 ft of sky is almost certain, whereas within 300 ft it is extremely doubtful. Thus, at 3,000 ft, you have, in a sense, two chances compared with one at 500. Your safety factor is not merely doubled, but enormously increased. If you pull a Turbulent into a high-speed stall around a pylon, there is no escape clause even though you have 3,000 hours and an ALTP. If you lose radio contact after you elect to go IMC in fog across the channel (and light aircraft radios are notoriously unreliable) then you and your passenger are immediately placed in extreme peril. You have put yourself right out on a limb and if Chance should choose to saw off that limb, then you have little further control over events.

Tales of dangers survived with the help of skill or luck make good bar-room chat, but let me tell you this. Your BOAC chum may appear to be laughing with you, but inside he is laughing at you.

A final word. Beware acting up to an image. Light aircraft pilots, especially when flying open biplanes, tend to obscurely identify with 1914-18 military flying ("real pilots in real aeroplanes"). When the chances of survival are inevitably small it is more comfortable, and more human, to ignore statistics and laugh in the face of Chance. Such an attitude in peacetime flying for pleasure is not only inappropriate but reprehensible; unfair to yourself and more especially to your family or dependents.

I should be sorry if the older members of the Club considered this article contrary to the spirit of Redhill. I don't think that they will. To the younger members I admit that I have less right to advise you than you have, to fly as you

172

see fit. But, from what I have heard, and read, recently, I do think it might be timely to urge you to see the situation clearly, whatever you do, and to hear a less light-hearted view point, as I did twenty years ago."

Extracts from Committee minutes: November 1970
Displays: Country to be split. Fairoaks. Shoreham. Rochester.
Foreign Touring: Irish tour discussed - whole emphasis to be on Irish touring – not drinking or showing off.

This was typical Norman-speak. He knew what he meant, but at this stage we sometimes got lost. And then in his eyes the Irish were letting the side down, what with all that drinking and having fun. Worse, I suspect, was the knowledge that we were using his aeroplanes in our haste to get over there to join in.

CLUB NEWS: OCTOBER – NOVEMBER 1970

Every year around this time the *"Rag"* becomes a seasonal war-cry urging this and that upon members. "Buy your Xmas cards from us" asks Michael, or "For heaven's sake mention the Annual Dance." Well, it's on the 12th February, and now is a good opportunity to extend some hospitality to members from out of town. Will you Londoners and near-Londoners please act as hosts for that night? Write and let me know how many you can accommodate, and perhaps those from far-off will get in touch with me too. I will gladly do the necessary. I'm sure everyone will agree the Dinner Dance is expensive enough without adding hotel bills, and it's a great chance to get together in true Tiger Club manner.

The flying side hasn't been overactive. October and early November were too boisterous. Odd snippets though. The seaplane Tiger has been flying from Rye (I think Keith Sissons was the pilot) all revamped to look like Francis Chichester's Gipsy Moth. For a film. And for commercial TV the Sea Turb has been skating around at Aldburgh, down in Suffolk. Would you believe Manikin Cigars? On the social side it's all been happening. Of news to reach me I reckon we owe good wishes to Vicky and Tom Storey – a daughter Eleanor – and Robin Voice and Philomena got married. To them all our warmest congratulations. By the way, do let me know such little items, we all like to know what's going on, so don't keep it to yourselves.

The Hamilton Trophy was a great success and elsewhere in the "Rag" I've published the results. One thing is certain, the event is going to become a popular annual occasion. As an added inducement to visit our London social centre, the Kronfeld, there's an excellent aviation art exhibition on at the moment, nor can there be any excuse this time for failing to make the Tiger Club's Xmas Party there on the 15th December.

METEOROLOGICAL NOTES FOR PILOTS – From Roger Keith Barnes

Observation	Interpretation
Paper dry, crisp, easily held and easily read without artificial light.	VMC
Paper limp and damp.	Humid
Paper wet, ink runs and words smudge.	Rain (precipitation)
Wet paper, tastes salt.	Aircraft ditched
Print is blurred.	Haze, mist or fog
Print may be read with artificial light.	Night
Paper blows away.	Wind
Paper stiff.	Ice

Norman was trying to sell Turbulent display flying.
"Do you know the definition of a salesman?" he asked Robin Voice.
"No," replied Robin tartly. "I'm a buyer by profession."

1971

SIXTEEN TYPES, DAVID'S TROPHY,
ISLANDER CHALLENGE AND HRH PRINCE WILLIAM

Our Chairman, Norman Jones, sent all the membership a letter early in January, as indeed he did each year, asking that we settle our annual subscription ASAP and regretting that the flying rates had to go up a little. The excuse had a new flavour:

". . . also to take account of decimalisation they present a slightly different appearance because the rates have to be divisible by 12. . . . I would like to put in a special reminder about the Dinner Dance on 12th February at the Hilton. . . . Prince William of Gloucester has accepted our invitation to be our guest of honour.

With regard to our flying at Redhill, I would like to take this opportunity of emphasising again the need for courtesy and the strict observation of circuit procedure and runway direction. Our neighbours Bristow Helicopters are now a great deal more active . . ."

I couldn't resist the opportunity to illustrate not only the flying rates for that year but the variety – no less than sixteen different types.

SUBSCRIPTION AND FLYING RATES 1971

(a) ASSOCIATE MEMBER	£10.50	(£10-10-0)
(b) FULL MEMBER	£8.40	(£8-8-0)
(c) PASSENGER MEMBER	£3.15	(£3-3-0)
(d) OVERSEAS MEMBER (all grades)	£3.00	(£3-0-0)
(e) TEMPORARY MEMBER	£0.30	(£0-6-0)
(f) JUNIOR MEMBER	£0.60	(£0-12-0)

FLYING RATES TO TAKE EFFECT FROM 1ST FEBRUARY 1971

TIGER MOTH	£6.30	(£6-6-0)
STAMPE	£6.60	(£6-12-0)
CONDOR (100 HP)	£6.30	(£6-6-0)
CONDOR (130 HP)	£6.90	(£6-18-0)
JODEL D.150 & DR.1050	£6.90	(£6-18-0)
JODEL D.140	£8.10	(£8-2-0)
TURBULENT	£3.60	(£3-12-0)
BETA (restricted)	£7.50	(£7-10-0)
SUPER CUB	£7.20	(£7-4-0)
HUSKY	£7.20	(£7-4-0)
SEA TURBULENT (when available – restricted)	£4.50	(£4-10-0)
SEA TIGER (when available – restricted)	£7.50	(£7-10-0)
ARROW ACTIVE (restricted)	£7.50	(£7-10-0)
FOX MOTH	£7.50	(£7-10-0)
NIPPER (available through Rochester Flying Club only)	£3.60	(£3-12-0)

COLT (available through
Fairoaks Aero Club only)   £6.60   (£6-12-0)
CURRIE WOT (available through
Fairoaks Aero Club only)   £3.60   (£3-12-0)

Club members could now also fly at Fairoaks, Rochester and Blackbushe Flying Clubs at published Tiger Club rates. We were spreading our wings in no uncertain manner.

Our royal connections had now grown to three: Prince Philip in '59, Prince William ten years later (both of whom had flown from time to time at Redhill) and now Prince Charles joined us. Sadly Prince William was to lose his life a year or so later in an air race, but in '71 it was a great start to the year to entertain him at the Hilton.

Membership had risen to 751 and the 4,064 glider tows for 1970 was a new record.

CLUB NEWS: JANUARY 1971

This year's white Xmas was celebrated in style at Redhill with a spell of Turbulent skiing. Three Turbs were so equipped and were thoroughly operational, at least whilst the snow hung around. There's something invigorating and very special about flying an open Turb over a gleaming white landscape. Incidentally, the Super Cub wasn't put on its skis but, given another fall of snow — and the chances are there will be — then the fun can begin, and fun it is, for then there's room for a passenger to enjoy the beauty of it all.

STOP PRESS:

Challock Hangar collapsed under weight of snow, seriously damaging several gliders, some beyond repair. Miraculously the Club Tiger 'SKP (which with 'OAA put in a record 2,400 tows at Challock in 1970) survived unscathed but had to be dismantled completely to be removed from the wrecked building. Can you beat it!

If the following report on the inaugural Hamilton Trophy contest lacks a known author, it lacks nothing in the telling.

FUN FLYING, OR HOW I LEARNT TO STOP WORRYING
AND TO ENJOY COMPETITIONS

The weekend of October 24th/25th was scheduled as being the date for the Hamilton trophy. This competition is the last in the Club's calendar and is held purely for pleasure before pilots' hibernation begins.

Much to everybody's amazement the weather was acceptable — the organisers privately hoping for a total clamp. Saturday's main exercise was a triangular navigation course. At briefing, faces proceeded to get longer and longer when entrants were told they must first obtain a signature at Headcorn before proceeding to a point in Essex, just south of the Southend Arterial. This was to be a timed exercise. Maps and sketches of Headcorn were provided, and Andrew Chadwick announced that the Southend Arterial Road was not shown on his map. An increasing number of members are aware of the problems Andrew has with navigation when departing from the Redhill circuit. However, his comment required careful investigation and it transpired that the only map he possesses and has used for years was an extract from a pocket diary dated 1904. Rest assured, Andrew was provided with a modern up-to-date map.

Shortly after 14.00 Norman Jones led the field away en route to the second turning point which was Ford's Experimental Centre. Eleven starters disappeared down the railway line and the judges relaxed to await their return. Some 5 minutes before Norman was due to land he was spotted carrying out Rate 1 turns some two miles east of the airfield. This applied to most of the other contestants, the rules being slightly too easy and allowing more time than was necessary.

The contestants arrived back, having identified Ford's, and the times were particularly good, the best results being from Norman Jones (0.05 of a second late), Roy Legg (0.15 of a second late), Ralph Hart (0.75 of a second late). Andrew Chadwick delighted everybody by being no more than 15 seconds late, hence the value of his new map.

The navigational exercise was followed by spot-landing and, as was to be expected, the efforts varied enormously from a 200-yard undershoot to a 100-yard overshoot. Terry Eggett split the bull on practice on his Hornet Moth but failed to be consistent.

Sunday morning dawned again with the weather being acceptable, but due to the steadily-rising wind, it was decided that the exercise on instrument flying would be abandoned. (N.B. The organisers have the right to alter the rules at any time, irrespective of protests and waved £5 notes.)

John Blake kindly consented to judge the bombing and balloon bursting. Balloon bursting had started late, unfortunately, due to Gavin Dix's staff releasing most of the balloons while the contestants were still on the ground. These were last seen heading for Biggin at a rate of knots. During the exercise eight balloons were definitely destroyed and there were a number of very close misses. It was entertaining to see the various techniques being used, from trying to frighten the balloon to death by sheer speed, to Dennis Sole's slowly stalking them downwind in a Tiger before pouncing. Varying shouts of 'left a bit' and 'right a bit' flowed freely from the other contestants who clustered around the judges' pitch.

Flour bombing followed immediately and again the other contestants' cheers, boos, laughter and rudeness were a source of great amusement. Nobody actually achieved a bull, but some of them were very close. John Nurse's first bomb did a full vertical flick and was pierced by the Stampe's aerial, where it remained for a while.

It appears that everybody involved, from judges to contestants, thoroughly enjoyed themselves and the entry list for next year already stands at nine. There will, of course, be modifications to the rules and it has been suggested that bombing is done in pairs. The team member to the pilot endeavouring to catch the bomb to qualify for extra marks – I hope it rains. Credit must be given to all contestants whose enthusiasm made the competition a great deal of fun. Many thanks also must go to the judges – John Blake, Frances MacRae and Iona Radice

(Staverton Aero Club) – for their efforts, and to Norman Jones, whose encouragement and enthusiasm both before and during the contest greatly cheered the organisers.

The Britten-Norman Islander was, in '71, the talk of the town. At £20,000 – its first published cost – this small airliner was designed for STOL strips the world over. Peter Phillips was the company's chief pilot and the challenge he issued to me was a genuine one.

"It's that straightforward to fly," he said, "anyone could cope. If you'll write an article on your experience I'll put an aircraft at your disposal."

He did, I did, and Air BP published.

"It was raining – what else? – and believe me there are times when Gatwick can look like a showman's nightmare: all wind and rain. This was such a time. Inside the warm General Aviation Terminal wet clusters of would-be aviators huddled around, looking self-conscious; reassuring themselves that it wasn't really worth the candle to ring Met every few minutes. It seemed as if they hoped that their prayers, mingled with those of the Met man, would dispel the warm front passing overhead; to say nothing of the cold one that was threatening in its wake.

"All cancelled?" I asked hopefully, as Peter Phillips came back from the telephone.

"No," he said, grabbing his briefcase and hustling his six-foot frame past lesser mortals. Opening the door, he let all hell loose as the weather tried to get in out of the cold. I followed him out. All I could think of as the rain devoured us was a half-forgotten line from "As You Like It"; something like "creeping like snail unwillingly . . . "; that was me.

We fetched up alongside a Britten-Norman Islander.

"This is Dick Millward," said Peter, as brightly as he could in the circumstances. "He's coming down to Bembridge with us."

We shook hands in the rain.

"Benjy's going to fly it. OK by you, Dick?"

Dick grinned and climbed unprotestingly in ahead of us. I was practically speechless. My idea of a first-ever go in a twin would have included a quiet, isolated field where, in my own time, I could browse through the unfamiliar panel and fathom out, by trial and error if needs be, what all the knobs did.

Anyway, what did he think I had, an Airline Transport Pilot's Licence? If I said I'd flown 10 hours during the last year I'd be pushing it: heaven alone knows what my 15-minute trips every other blue moon add up to. At the Club's average charges of £8 an hour I'd become an enthusiastic circuit shooter, and a smart one at that: yet here was I . . . a sudden thought occurred.

"Hey, I haven't done an outside check," I bellowed at Peter's departing figure as he clambered in.

"I have," he shouted back.

I was stuck with it, and followed him in out of the rain. The door slammed shut and a little quiet reigned; all I could hear was the rain drumming gently on metal and my heart getting worked up on my behalf.

"It's all yours," said my ex-friend. His hands were all over the cockpit controls in a rapid *legerdemain* that produced the quickest pre-start check, engines start and post-start check I'd ever witnessed. The whole performance was accompanied by a ritual chant, the words of which I understood but couldn't for the life of me associate with reality. Peter was by now well into his Training Captain's stride, so I let confusion ride over me and mentally changed the subject. I looked back over my shoulder at the rows of empty seats. The biggest thing I'd flown previously had only a bench seat behind to throw things on. I could get a football team, the ref and goal posts into this lot.

Dick sat quietly behind us, hands in lap.

"I should have bought a newspaper," he murmured politely. It was as if he hadn't heard Peter's triumphant declaration, once the door had locked me in, that I'd never flown a twin before, much less a junior airliner. I gave Dick his due. A lesser man would have excused himself at that point and found the nearest exit.

Peter was busy with the radio.

"Golf Tango, clear taxi runway . . . " the ATC chattered on.

"Off you go," said Peter.

I released the brakes and gingerly pushed the throttles forward. We moved off. Sidling towards a magnificent Swiss jet, I eased on the rudder to get out of the way: nothing happened.

"It's a bit stiff," said Peter, obviously unaware of the enormity of his irresponsibility.

"If it breaks, it's their fault," I thought vindictively as I stood on the rudder bar: by this time I was actually off my seat to exert sufficient pressure. I had a bright idea – differential throttle. As the expensive-looking jet slid past unscathed I breathed a sigh of relief, and we moved in ever-decreasing wiggles to the holding position.

"Well done," said Peter.

"You must be joking," said I.

"Clear take-off," commanded some fruity voice from heaven, and there was the most massive runway you ever saw stretching out forever in front of me. It was all lit up as well.

I opened the throttles steadily; a push in my back and 50 knots came up. I pulled back as the handbook had said, and not only did we promptly unstick but we climbed almost vertically as well: at least that's what it felt like. Up flaps; 1,500 feet and on into the clag.

Consider. First big aircraft. First twin. First take-off with same: in fact, first flight in same. Throw in bad weather and immediate IFR at one and the same time. Yet here was I, a rusty pilot with only single-engine experience, managing safely – if not skilfully – *without any prior instruction or dual.*

"How's that, Dick?" Peter queried over his shoulder, and leaned back with a smug look.

"What's it like as an aeroplane?" I had asked Peter.

The question hadn't seemed important, more a conversational gambit on my part. Rather like saying "Good morning" to the boss who's just arrived in a filthy temper. But if, on my part, I'd asked the question automatically, it made sense to someone so completely immersed in his job as Peter. To him, and to me for that matter, there are aeroplanes and aeroplanes. All aeroplanes fly, or are supposed to; but in common with another mutually agreeable subject – birds (female) – they come packed differently.

Some aeroplanes are good and some are bad, flying-wise that is. Too many are puddings with control columns to stir; a means of getting from here to there with little encouragement for you to enjoy yourself. But a few, very few, have character: they are pilots' aeroplanes and you know them by the way they fly. But I digress.

As I said, the question got through and he eyed me speculatively for a moment.

"Ever flown twins?" he asked suddenly.

I shook my head.

"Well," he continued, "the Islander is that safe and remarkable that you could fly it with no more of an aid than a brief look at the handbook."

"Call me guinea pig," I said.

We flew on. To each side of me the 260 horsepower engines roared away in as near a synchronised beat as I could establish, and I settled back, content to maintain height and course over a grey, broken layer of cloud through which occasional glimpses of the ground could be seen tantalisingly. Down there was my scene, for over the past few years I had become something of a fair-weather pilot.

By my side Peter was chatting amiably to the controller at Thorney, establishing traffic and Met conditions.

"200 feet at Bembridge," Peter relayed to no one in particular.

"Don't forget the rain," I said rudely.

"I think," he continued, "you'll have to land on the STOL strip."

It sounded like "stall strip."

"What the devil's that?" I asked, my voice rising a pitch. "What's wrong with the grass?"

"Probably under water by now," replied Peter.

Not easily ruffled is Peter, and anyway he knew what he was doing – him with his professional licences with every known form of rating.

The Islander felt good to fly, notwithstanding its size, and everything came nicely to hand. Someone had done a good job thinking out that cockpit. As we left the mainland the clouds temporarily relinquished their hold and to the left I could see Thorney; Portsmouth, to the right, was in the clear too. We flew on, over a submarine. Suddenly the spell ended. Peter pointed a bit to the right.

"It's over there."

TOP: How John and Jim ever got 33 aircraft into Redhill's hangar will ever remain a mystery. Pure nostalgia c.1975. Tom Storey's Cassutt looms large. Photo: probably John Blake.

BOTTOM: Another view of Redhill's hangar. Occupants suggest the early '70s. In the foreground a visiting Moth has folded its wings. Photo: probably John Blake.

TOP: Two of our best: Neil Williams (L) and Manx Kelly (R) at Redhill, c.1974. A Pitts aerobatic biplane the common denominator.
Photo: Author's collection.
BOTTOM: The Club's original Sea Turbulent arises as new. Cranfield PFA Rally, 1995. Photo: Author's collection.

TOP: John Blake greets Cliff Robertson at Redhill, c.1975.
Photo: Author's collection.
BOTTOM: Where else but Shoreham? There were two separate crowd-lines
at this display, each with its own commentator. Probably 1975. The Active
and Beta grace the foreground. Photo: John Blake.

TOP: "G.B." en route to a wedding c.1962 – suspect it was to Sue and Peter Phillips'. Norman also went in a Turb similarly attired. Photo: Arthur Humphreys.

BOTTOM: Sue and Peter Phillips. A delightful shot of these popular members recorded at an air show. The year probably 1975.
Photo: Author's collection.

I took his word for it and wheeled around. All I could see was a misty foreshore with a bank of cloud rising like dirty meringue above it. I throttled back and we slipped through the mire into reasonable visibility at 800 feet.

Said Peter: "That's better than 200 feet."

A voice from Bembridge welcomed us – there was no other traffic – and it had to be the STOL strip.

"It's going to be a bit difficult, in fact it's hard to imagine worse conditions for your landing," mused Peter. "90-degree cross-wind; might even be a slight tail component."

"You expect me to land it?" I asked; "and where's the strip?"

It was still raining. All I could see was a tiny extension to a road that led to the hangars. It had a dumb-bell end and was quite obviously a compass-swinging base. It looked about 50 yards long and five across. I discovered later I'd got the five right.

"I'm landing this on that?" I cried when Peter pointed it out, and stared back in disbelief as the wet strip dropped astern and faded into the mist.

We flew base leg, close-hauled past the Foreland, at the rocky feet of which lay a half-submerged steamer pounding itself to slow destruction in the merciless surf. For a moment I thought the tragedy had only just happened, so clean and shiny was the superstructure and so bright the red funnel, and half-turned to Peter.

He guessed my question and shook his head.

"It's been there a month."

Out over the horizonless grey sea, to turn finals at 600 feet and point reassuringly again at land.

"Aim to just miss that clump of trees, and you must be over them at no more than 50 knots because you're going to have to descend fast."

I gave the engines a last dose of carb heat and dropped full flap. To my dismay the nose didn't go down as I'd hoped. Being a short fellow my visibility was getting decidedly sticky. At 50 knots the Islander still felt nicely controllable, only she was sinking like a brick. I opened up hastily, wallowed over the trees and there before me was the strip.

It was the first time I'd seen it properly and even at 300 yards it looked ridiculously small. I craned forward to assess the score. The aircraft rocked in the disturbed air that funnelled from every direction around the valley threshold, and I drifted off to the right. I hastily booted on rudder and flew towards the edge of the strip like a drunken crab. Then everything happened at once. The tarmac was rising to meet me, so I naturally hauled back to get out of its way, desperately kicking off rudder en route. Between us we arrived at a compromise, a solid no-rubbish no-bounce arrival. Forward went the controls – that in itself must have been an involuntary movement, for I usually fly tailwheel aircraft. I stepped on the brakes and we stopped just before we ran out of strip.

My descent was greeted with delight by Peter and Dick. Both clapped me on the back and made sounds of approval. I was speechless for the second time that day. The best I could do was to put on my special face, one of instant composure that I reserve for wordless occasions like this, plunge unsteady hands deep into my pockets and stride off with them for lunch, as if it were all part of a normal day's work.

But the drama was far from over. It was still raining when we plodded back through the mud to have another go. There still remained the uneasy feeling that the first landing had been a fluke.

"I'll soon dispel that," Training Captain had said.

Upstairs amid the low scud and weeping cloud we essayed stalls; the sort of stalls you do in a Tiger Moth, stick hard back and eyes clamped unbelievingly on the ASI as it winds itself back. Without engine and full flap I got the needle down to 25 knots, and when the stall did come the Islander fell forward gently like a timid old lady and needed but an easing of the wheel to come under control. I looked a bit disappointed.

"Try it with engine then," Peter said encouragingly.

With the engines roaring heartily and the nose pointing to heaven we hung suspended with the ASI barely registering. It was something under 10 knots. Peter had a go and I think he got the needle back to zero. He would, of course.

While we tossed the aircraft around like demented men, another Islander surreptitiously joined the circuit, and together we watched with interest as the pilot prepared himself for the STOL strip from the opposite direction to that we'd taken.

"He's probably as much in the wind that way as the other," conceded Peter. "Close the throttle and we'll try the single-engine performance."

I have tried not to make this sound like a flattering test report, yet that must be how it will read. It's not my fault. After I'd flown the aircraft in every conceivable configuration, I'll accept Peter's statement that the Islander is in a single-engine performance class of its own.

He told a good story to back it up. During a short-landing competition somewhere in the USA the Islander came first. The win met with a howl of protest because the aircraft was twin-engined and all the other contestants were singles. Believe it or not, the protest was upheld. This so incensed the pilot that he took off again, this time on one engine, flew the circuit and landed it on one, and did even better than the first time! The win was conceded.

I took another 50-knot stab at the STOL strip, made it, and then in the innocent belief that the grass could not be in *that* bad a condition, was allowed a conventional approach and landing at 65 knots. It was a greaser. As the wheels settled into the mud, for mud it was, it seemed we'd taken a dive into a fish tank. All forward vision went completely as earth and water enveloped the Islander, and we decelerated so rapidly it was as if I'd touched down on deck arrester gear.

"Hell," I muttered into the darkness, "we're in it up to our necks," and instinctively opened to full throttle to keep her rolling. It was that or sink. We staggered across the field, throwing up mud and spray with every lurch. If I needed a dramatic demonstration to round off the day I'd had it.

Back to Gatwick and a ride in the right-hand seat. No. 2 to land and then through the cloud appeared the most wonderful sight. The threshold looked like a shimmering mirage, a fairylit playground in the sky.

"Runway in sight," I called to Dick and then we were down, turning off with ease at the first intersection.

The Islander has been flown by a whole lot of better pilots than me: but I wager that none could vouch better for this aircraft's extraordinary STOL capabilities, or say more for its docility and ease of handling. Britten-Norman have sold over 300 Islanders already. May they continue to sell them in their hundreds, not only for the pilots' sake, but for the multitude of happy commuters who, but for this aircraft, might never have experienced the thrill of flight. This unsophisticated airliner possesses an elusive characteristic: it is fun both to fly and to fly in."

CLUB NEWS: FEBRUARY – MARCH 1971

"Now the postal strike is over you'll be getting out a Newsletter?" The way Michael put it was not so much a question as a reproach for tardiness. The strike had been over all of 24 hours.

Perhaps the most important item of interest during the period under review, and certainly the one shared by a goodly number of the Club, was the Annual Dinner Dance in February. It was a most successful affair, considered by some to be the best ever. Personally I couldn't have gone that far because for me the best by far were those less formal occasions during which members would put on an ad lib cabaret. However, I do concede that the food was the best yet. Guest of honour was Prince William of Gloucester; he was in good form, he certainly needed to be especially when he was suddenly called upon to auction a painting of John Blake's. I can't remember how much it went for but I wager it was more than John usually gets for his able work, and it was for a good cause – Bev's longstanding Save the Children's Fund.

As ever these occasions are marked for some by the asides. I can only record those I heard. For instance I heard "G.B." mutter into his fish: "I'm failing fast, I missed a pheasant last week." The Trophies were despatched by HRH in an atmosphere of almost cheerful abandon – nothing went right. Firstly half the recipients weren't there to receive their awards, personally I reckon that was a bad show, and the other half of the awards all seemed to go to the same person – one Roy Legg! The Duke of Edinburgh and Dawn-to-Dusk Trophies went to Mike Bialkiewicz who also collected second place in the Icarus Trophy. To Keith Sissons the de Salis Trophy – it's awarded each year to the member who in his first 18 months contributes the most to the Club – a unanimous Committee decision this for some good work organising the Seaplane section. (Incidentally, members interested in flinging themselves off a rather lovely stretch of water near Rye this summer in Sea Tiger or Sea Turb should get in touch with Tom Freer at once. Season starts May 1st and there's a distinct possibility of a newcomer to fly – a

Volmer Sportsman.) Miss J.M. Brace, the only woman to receive an Award this year, collected the Bonney Trophy and B. Shaw the McAully Aerobatic Trophy.

Neil "Stay-with-it" Williams walked off again with the de Havilland Aerobatic – I can't think why the organisers just don't give in and let him keep it, albeit that's only a personal and very non-aerobatic opinion. The Air Squadron Trophy went to Mike Riley and the Esso Tiger Trophy went to a new and bright newcomer in this aerobatic field, Brian Smith. Brian has been a follower (and later, member) of our Club since his schoolboy days. He began by helping in the hangar and swinging props, learnt to fly with the Rollason group on their black Tiger, and recently entered the Club proper to promptly win a major award. Mike Jones deservedly collected the Air Racing Medallion, Rad Radwanski the Foreign Touring – who else in view of his epic European trips? – and to Gordon Crabb the Glider-Towing one.

Last but not least was the award of the Club's top accolade, the Clem Pike Trophy, to "G.B.", or to give him his unfamiliar full title, W/Cdr. Arthur Golding-Barrett. This was a fitting and popular gesture to the outgoing Vice-Chairman and the man who, among other things, is reputed to have taught Wilbur Wright to fly.

I can't let all this back-slapping go without recording some back-stage Committee chat during the meeting that preceded the Dinner. A modest and embarrassed Gordon Crabb protested at the proposition that he should get the Medallion for Glider-Towing. Said Norman soothingly: "It's only something to give away at the Dinner." To which Mike added: "You've got to have these damn medals – Norman's trying to get rid of them." We jest, but these awards are small recognition for a lot of hard and often unrewarding effort – long may the Chairman go on handing them out. An award that wasn't presented at the Dinner was an RAeC one, the Tissandier Trophy to "Titch" Holmes, and in your editor's humble opinion it couldn't have gone to a more deserving member.

. . . The Dinner and Dance went on well into the small hours. Whilst the postal strike may have hit the numbers able to attend, there must surely have been well over 200 present. Our thanks for yet another great occasion must go to Bev and Pauline Snook and to all their helpers.

. . . Elsewhere there is a long list of coming events. One could if one had the time attend a flying and Tiger Club-oriented function every weekend throughout a long summer, so knowing which ones to support isn't easy. First on most people's lists will be our Full Displays. Turn up by air or car and bring friends and picnic and it's as good a way to pass a few happy hours as any I know. A welcome is due to Peter Phillips on joining the committee as Display Director. Contact him if you would like to help in any capacity. Surely the next on one's list is our 'At Home' – it's the best way we know of returning hospitality to our countless friends in Europe. Our Club isn't a closed shop – please do join in.

The Editor, The *"Tiger Rag."*
Cirencester, Gloucestershire, May 11th 1971

"On occasion in the past I have been described variously in your *"Rag"* as a "Tramp," "Lady Chatterley's Lover" and as an "unlikely dyed-in-the-wool Antique

English Yeoman." But *never*, sir, as a law-breaker – and to this accusation I take great exception. In your last issue you presumed to record that at the recent Tiger Club Dinner I was heard to remark something to the effect that I was feeling my age (a mere 66½ years) these days and "even missed a pheasant yesterday." Which, Sir, is a foul calumny – for which I demand a published apology – and if possible damages (in cash).

For you should know that the date of "yesterday" prior to the TC Dinner was well within the close season for game – which ends on February 1st each year. I am not a poacher.

Only small comfort is derived from your statement that I "missed it" – which might in a court of law be considered in mitigation of a clear-cut offence, tho' the whole story is a fabric of lies.

All in all, I am much put about, and I demand, Sir, that you insert my denial and your apology in an early issue of your obviously unreliable broadsheet.

Yours in umbrage,

"G.B."

LAFFY'S CONVERSION, FINGER TROUBLE, FAIROAKS AND DOING ONE'S THING

I had never intended this volume to become a showcase for others, I wanted to remain on a constant Tiger Club course, but with every firm intention there comes a moment of doubt – and, besides, it makes a welcome break because Laffy's Conversion is as timeless as they come. I reproduce it exactly as I first saw it one afternoon on an Elstree notice board.

PETER LAFFY'S AUSTER CONVERSION

Here we go again. Blasted Ogilvy. Blasted Austers. 'XT. Where's 'XT? Down by the gate, as usual. Blasted route march. Chocks. None around. Jock Russell's fire I suppose. Couple of bricks. Just as good. Do an external. Prop. Wooden. Damn sight safer than metal ones. Sharp as hell. Hated swinging them. "Look – no fingers." Tyre and wheel. Seem OK. Bang wing strut. One damn silly little bolt holding wing in place. Death-traps. Aileron, OK. Elevator, rudder, OK. Just like chunks of flat board. Tail wheel OK, also cheap and nasty spring effort. Aileron. Pitot tubes. Landing lamp. Wheel and tyre. Cowlings. Ogilvy heading this way. He can laugh. Better get in. Left-hand seat. Captain Laffy. Usual contortions, slippery step, damn stupid thing for hauling yourself in with. Success. In. Blast. Want cushions behind me. Feet miles from rudder pedals. Another route march. . . . That's better. Right. Slide window back. Brakes on. Fuel on. Switches off. Throttle closed. Ogilvy priming. Off and open. Blowing out. You do it so well. Throttle closed, set, contact. Still on. Still on. Still on. Still on. Off. Off and wide open. "Any aeroplane will start." Perhaps this one is the exception. Hope so. Blasted Austers. Closed, set, contact. Still on. Still on. Ah! Up with the other switch, oil pressure OK, revs just over a thousand, ready on brakes, wave chocks away. Trying to creep forward. Heave on heel brakes, haul on handbrake. That's better. Ogilvy aboard. Bit out of breath. Good. Dead-cut check. Instruments. OK. Check flaps.

Damn stupid handle. Never know whether to push or pull. Ailerons. Stick to left, look at ailerons. Something wrong. No. Keep forgetting, looks different on high-wing aeroplane. Elevator. Trimmer. Another menace. Compass. Fire extinguisher secure. Nothing floating about loose. "Ready when you are." Right. Throttle back. Handbrake off, bit of throttle. Just moving. Try starboard brake. Nothing happens. Push harder. Nothing. Harder still. Wheel almost locks. Same for port brake. Blasted Austers. Slow down for runway intersection. Heave on both brakes. Nothing. Harder. Harder still. Blimey, nearly on her nose that time. Approach and runway clear. Trundle over runway and on to the grass, grinding halt, facing roughly the right direction. Dead-cut check. Heave hard on brakes, haul on handbrake, open up to 1,600. No alarming mag drop, damn it. Oil pressure OK, slow running OK. Nothing else for it now. Have to go.

Ogilvy's pet remark to me. Blasted Ogilvy, sitting there looking smug. All right for him! Vital actions. T.T.M.F.F. and all the old malarkey. Here goes. Approach clear. Brake off, bit of throttle. Bit more, more still, stick right back, waggle rudder. Move you cow, move. Ah! about time. Still nothing on approach. Runway clear. On to runway. Right rudder. Bit of throttle, right rudder, try to shove right-hand heel brake at same time. Need four feet for this caper. That's about the middle. And so we say farewell to exotic Elstree. . . . Full throttle, keep her straight. Swinging right. Left rudder. Come back, you menace. Right rudder, left, off again, bit more left. Stick forward. Left hand. Feels all wrong. Up she comes. Fight tendency to push stick towards centre of instrument panel. Pound, pound, pound. Keep her straight along the middle. Nose too far down, driving her into the deck. Ease back a shade. Curse it, airborne too soon. Keep her in the air now. Wallowing along like a ruptured duck. That's better. Speed 70. Climb away at that. Throttle back, fair chunk. What a blasted aeroplane. Wing tip drops six inches, move stick six feet to correct. Blasted Austers. 1,000 feet coming up. Turn crosswind. Bags of aileron, bags of rudder, top needle prancing about like a drunken CFI. Wing hides runway nicely. Another charming Auster attribute – can't see when to stop turning – wing in the way. Lift it up, have a shufti. Not a bad guess. Level wings. 1,300 on the clock. Stuff nose down. Speed to 90, throttle back a bit. Fiddle with trimmer. Wrong way. Near enough. Turn downwind. No need for wing-lifting lark on this turn. When the bus repair place is ahead, that's it. Downwind checks. Brakes off, fuel fully on and sufficient, oil pressure and temperature OK, mixture rich, carb air hot, hatches and hammocks secure. Top needle way over to one side. Fiddle around with stick and rudder until it's where it should be. Lucky the air's smooth today. An Auster in rough air must be hell. Altimeter still reading 1,300. Fluke. Shufti around for other aircraft. Nothing in sight. Turn on to base now. Take off bank with bags of opposite everything. No, not far enough round.

About right now. Throttle back, feed on right rudder, hold her level, speed to 70, one notch of flap. Easier said than done. Pull knob out, pull lever down, release. Lever slips smartly back to neutral. Damn and blast. Try again. Got you. Christ, speed down to 50. Stuff nose down. 60. Nothing else about. Turn finals.

60. Another notch now. Struggle. Struggle. Success. Stick heavy. Trim. Stick heavier. Must have been wrong way. That's better. 60. Undershooting. Spot of power. Fine. 60. Runway coming up fast. Round out. Throttle right back. Miles too high. Check and let her sink. About there. Off to left of runway. Never mind. Back gently, back, back. She's going. Right back. CRASH. On three points, anyway. Keep her straight. Almost stopped, turn left on to grass. Mate. "Quite a good one." Ogilvy taking the mickey. No, he means it. Gawd. If that was a good one I should hate to do a bad one. Stop. Brake. 1,000 revs. Flaps up. Loosen friction nut. Rock and roll and clatter back to holding point. Do one myself and don't break it? He's stark staring bonkers. I can't fly Austers. Come back. Gone. Swine. It's all right for him. He'll have a nice pint now and stand outside the Clubhouse with the others and laugh, blast him.

Ah! might be a duff mag. No such luck. Try again. No, both perfect. Oh! well, it's his aeroplane. Can't say I didn't warn him. What about me, though – patter of tiny feet downwind and he lets me loose in this deathtrap. Oh! well, they say only the good die young. But I'm not young. Can just see the next newsletter. "Members will be sorry to hear . . . spun in on finals . . . Committee Secretary for many years . . . sad loss to Club." Hypocrite. Well, let's get it over with. Trim, friction nut, mixture, carb air, fuel, flaps, gauges, hatches and harness. On to runway, full bore. Blimey, nearly on her prop then. Airborne. 70, throttle back fair chunk . . . 1,300, turning downwind. Downwind checks. There's the hangar. Lucky devils over there, safely on the ground, sinking pints and all ready to gloat over my landing. Base leg, throttle back. 70. Two notches of flap straight away. Save a bit of sweat on finals. Success at first attempt. Lucky Laffy. 60 and trim. Wrong way first try. Bloody trimmer. Finals. About right. Just a trickle of power. 60. Lovely. Keep her on the centre line this time. Keep power on until round-out completed. That's it. Chop. Keep her in the middle. Seem to be closer to the deck this time. Now gently back. Secret of success – try to prevent her from landing as long as you can. Back, back, back, back, now right back. Beautiful, a real greaser. Just kissed the deck. Hardly knew I was down. Smashing. Keep her straight. Don't spoil things now. Gang watching. On the grass now. Brake. Revs 1,000. Flaps up, friction nut loose. Now for a pint with good old David. Not bad little aeroplanes, Austers . . ."

Peter Laffy's Conversion – I wonder if he's still around – leads neatly to some words of wisdom from the Committee I was asked to propound. It went as follows:

FINGER TROUBLE

One aspect of Tiger Club flying is always viewed with dismay by the Committee at their monthly meetings and that's the lack of simple common sense shown at times by members. These moments come to light when accident reports are examined, and the inexplicable thing is these lapses in sanity are invariably those of highly experienced pilots. It would seen that hours spent in a big office don't necessarily qualify one to make what to a lesser pilot is the obvious decision and easily summed up in the phrase: if in doubt, don't. So the Committee have asked me to urge members faced with a decision that questions safety that they opt out smartly . . . there's no loss of face in preventing accidents.

To illustrate a point consider this recent accident to a Tiger Moth. The pilot was invited to fly one of the lightweight machines to a narrow strip on a private estate. When he arrived there was a strong 20-25 knot 90-degree crosswind. Beneath him he could see that two other biplanes had already landed (true, but the wind hadn't been so strong when they'd come in) <u>and although doubtful whether it was on or not decided to have a go</u>. At that stage the only possible common-sense answer should have been <u>DON'T</u>. Influencing his decision was the knowledge that people were expecting him and his mount and he had no wish to let the side down. I think that within this oft-heard sentence can be found the cause of so many unnecessary prangs, yet by this very act of loyalty they are doing just that. There can be nothing more to the reply: "I couldn't get through safely" than an understanding acceptance of a pilot's honest recognition of his limitations, and we all have them, no matter how good we think we are! The outcome of this landing was an incorrect crosswind technique, a tail too low, a bounce and an inevitable drift in a semi-stalled condition into the long grass and onto his back. I didn't see the second mishap, it was around the same time, so can only record that flying men who witnessed the accident, this time to a Stampe, were struck dumb by the enormity of mishandling by the pilot. Momentary lapses by otherwise very skilled pilots? We don't know, and unfortunately the Committee also know that nothing they say will stop accidents, but if by airing the occasional instance they induce a fellow pilot to think again, then these words won't be in vain.

CLUB NEWS: MAY– JUNE 1971

It's 5·15 am and I can begrudgingly understand why the earlier aviators got up at the crack of dawn to fly. Outside in the dew-drenched garden of a May morning the air is still and clean, and to fly a Tiger just now would be a sweet moment, just the thought of it makes up for the unearthly hour. You see, I couldn't sleep and the *"Rag"* was crying out to be written. In a few hours time the hangar doors will be opened to commence another weekend of flying. Michael reports a lot of activity and I can confirm the need to book aircraft well in advance. Members are certainly getting afield with their overseas touring. For instance, Robin Voice in a Tiger led two Stampes piloted by Carl Schofield and Pete Jarvis all the way to Göthenberg in Sweden and there put up a superlative performance. (James Baring happened to be there at the time and promptly reported back – good news travels fast.) As a matter of fact were my wife writing this she'd bypass the congrats to the pilots and instead applaud Robin's wife, Philomena, for just being the Tiger's passenger. There can't be much to choose in discomfort between Phil's trip to Sweden and Lollie's epic Redhill-to-Wick ride.

Displays are now in full swing up and down the country – from wee village fêtes to full-blown affairs at big airfields. There's a fascinating story to be told by someone of these so called 'participations.' I think this aspect has never been aired sufficiently, for these appearances must do more for light aviation than all the

Farnboroughs and Le Bourgets rolled into one. Flying from local fields, members are still barnstorming in the traditional manner. There must be a full dozen appearances over any weekend throughout the country and their success is reflected in the increasing number of requests for the boys to appear. Did you not wonder who was flying that Sea Tiger in the BBC film on Francis Chichester? It was Keith Sissons and I thought our machine looked tremendous and so cleverly decked up as an earlier Moth. Sad news though so far on the floatplane front. Tom Freer has been unable to negotiate a site down in Kent to operate the Sea Tiger from, and is now trying for a big stretch of water in Berkshire. We wish this small group of Tiger Club members every success for they are single-handedly trying to maintain the last floatplane as a going concern. I should think such pioneers as the brothers Short will turn in their graves that this maritime island has so completely lost an entire arm of light aviation. To the seaplane section, to Norman who foots the bill, and to the Rollason engineers who spend so much time and care on this expensive project, our encouragement and best wishes for an eventual launching.

The Jodel Mascaret was stranded for a while in the Scilly Isles because of duff weather. When the member returned to collect her he found, to his horror, that the cows had damaged it. I would have added "eaten it," for that's how it appeared, but I'm assuming cows don't eat things, they only munch them. The aircraft had just completed its C. of A. and was wearing a new coat of fabric too. So to members who use the odd farmer's field or airfields on which cattle are let loose: beware. And you can't trust sheep either for they eat aeroplanes too. All right, nibble them. It's not one-sided of course, aircraft can bite back; I know because there's a notice to that effect in every Tiger Club aircraft.

. . . The 'At Home' on May 17th wasn't exactly a success. It would have been, but as usual the weather spoilt it and in the event only one aircraft was able to get through. In all eight visitors arrived, the other four came over by hovercraft and then hired a car to the RAF Club where a dinner was held in their honour. Apparently another car-load of them got lost en route and we never did see them. For determination our German friends from Osnabrück take the cake, the sad thing is the same thing happened last year. One day the weather will shine on our 'At Homes.' The next try is planned for September. Incidentally not one of the 20 visitors from Beauvais got through, so bad was the weather. Some 40 Club members gathered that evening to welcome our guests and I record that it was a good and happy occasion and the dinner excellent. An unexpected presentation was made to us by the President of the Osnabrück club, a beautifully engraved trophy which was promptly filled with champagne and downed by everyone present. We saw our one aircraft off on the Sunday after an excellent lunch which must have taken a lot of time to prepare – apparently no less than 90 sat down to enjoy it. To Don and Tessa Lovell and all the helpers, our thanks for organising this friendly get-together.

Fairoaks was ever separated from our base at Redhill by the North Downs and all too often separated by a bad visibility and low cloud weather system of its own as well. True there were gaps to skate through, our favourites being the Dorking and Guildford ones, but at times even that was hairy. Keep low, hug the road, or rail – heaven help those who didn't find the right one – and ignore all else. Moments like: "Darling, weren't we too close to that building? It looks like a cathedral." "Where?"

(And yes, I did write "Finger Trouble" but as my dear mother was wont to say: "Don't do as I do, do as I say.")

FAIROAKS – FULL DISPLAY 30TH MAY 1971

There's one thing we're positive about and that's the uncertainty of our weather. Let me explain. For those of us standing around the hangar doors that Whit-Sunday morning the show was an odds-on washout. Rain lashed down, and when it stopped for a bit, the clouds came down and settled at 500 ft. Reports of similar weather conditions came in from Robin Blech stuck down at Bristol, from Mike Holtby at Shoreham and from Tony Haig-Thomas to the east. Yet when we rang Fairoaks at 12 noon the weather report was great, so with disbelief we set the system to go. Robin set off at 300 ft in his Stampe, Mike said "I'll come by car" and Tony Haig-Thomas flatly said "No." It must have been bad.

The team pessimistically set off from Redhill beneath a drizzling overcast sky to follow the railway. Yet, once over the hills the weather lifted – would you believe?

At 3 pm precisely Adrian Swire's Spitfire Mk.9 tears in and rolls away into the blue; beneath his slipstream the flypast begins, a cheerful follow-my-leader of about 20 aircraft from which the four Turbulents break away and reach for height prior to beginning their act. We've begun things this way for years . . . and this year must be our eleventh consecutive annual event at this face-lifted airfield. Face-lifted? They've moved the hill – extraordinary but true. The Turbs dance in, a nice tight box led by Robin Voice, his wing men Mike Holtby and Mike Riley. Newcomer Brian Smith is in the box; this, his show debut, marks him out as someone who'll do well. Aerobatics by Roy Legg in his Jungmeister is a riot of movement – his flicks knife-edge to knife-edge never fail to put the wind up me, but it's all beautifully done. Balloon bursting by Robin Voice, David Phillips and A.N. Other brings cheers from the ground, especially when the odd balloon escapes. (I think Robin got his three and must have won.)

The new act this year is a brilliant cameo of duo aerobatics in the Stampes. Pete Jarvis and Carl Schofield put on a super show which must surely put them number one in Europe today. For me, and I know for the audience, it's six spellbound minutes presented in a tight envelope smack in front of the crowd. The near silence and graceful looping of the Sportair Fourniers that follows comes as a sharp contrast. The three, two RF.4s and Brian Stevens in the RF.5, perform a low-level ballet which improves with their every showing. Neil Jensen and David Perrin fly the RF.4s. They've lifted the act a few feet since last year's contretemps – a loop that ended with a sudden landing, – even so these fine aircraft obviously handle superbly, with surely the tightest loops on record.

190

Frances MacRae flies the solo Stampe spot with considerable verve and versatility and the fact that it's a female pilot brings terrific applause. Admiration from the men for something they can't do, and fervent cheers from the women libs on the appearance of a female in an otherwise all-male cast. The fact that Frances is also a top act only adds to their enthusiasm.

Our thanks to Mike Somerton-Rayner for the fill-in spot across the overlong interval caused by the swift descent of two parachutists. Funny, why do we always give parachutists a ten minute slot when we know they'll only jump from 5,000 ft at the best, and must land inside a minute of jumping?

Mike in his Skeeter is a joy to behold, he is here, there and everywhere, bobbing and curtseying before us in his £75 helicopter (at least that's what he's reputed to have paid for it). Robin Blech is billed for the comedy act, a free flight from the winning programme number; a burly reluctant Robin is pushed into a Stampe for his free ride, the commentary pushing the act for all it's worth – and this act is worth a lot, for as a laugh it never fails. He takes off downwind, cavorts and rodeos all over the place with strident vocal help from us all to land. Every year it's the same, every year the act gets more popular. Even the certain knowledge it isn't for real does nothing to mar the fun.

Two SOW (Standing-on-Wing) items are well presented. Two pretty girls, two Tigers and two good pilots will make this a crowd-puller for years to come. And Ray Hanna's Spitfire demo is in a class of its own. For nine minutes he holds the stage as only he can, and for nine minutes we lap up the nostalgia of it all, all too aware that time is running out for such appearances. Neil Williams flies memorable aerobatics in the Stampe. He is unquestionably still the master and it shows. Delightful.

Flour bombing and a Rollasons van left untouched. It's more difficult than it seems to lob 1 lb bags of flour accurately. And then the Race. I can honestly record that this event is unique. I have personally been in, or have seen, practically every Tiger Club race since we started races and this one remarkable moment beats them all. And it is all a misunderstanding. Bill Chesson waves off the slower Turbulents and inexplicably keeps waving so the next wave move off as well, and the next and the next and suddenly everyone is airborne in the most unexpected mass take-off in the decade; 19 aircraft are airborne in the space of eight seconds. It is a breathtaking sight as they jockey for space and then set off. For me, the commentator, it's all hell breaking loose, for the audience the most exciting finish to a perfect day. No, I don't know who won, Indeed the race was scheduled for four laps but by my count most did six. Now you've an idea what a Full Display is all about, and there are two more to go this year – August 15th and September 19th. So come along if you can, even better, join in and help.

A word of thanks to the helpers. It's always the pilots who get the cheers, but never the boys backstage who set it all up. To that stalwart Roy Davis, the Club's tribute. He has been the driving force behind our helpers for so many years, long may he lead them.

It's understandable with hindsight to recognise the spate of warnings from the Tiger Club Committee. It must have seemed at the time that with so much going on, the whole venture was approaching a nightmare of unthinkable possibilities; the question of how to steady things up must have been on their minds.

ON DOING ONE'S THING

Tiger Club Committee meetings are, as so often pointed out, different, but then it's a different sort of Club so it follows, and as a Committee it functions well, for as a sounding board on opinion it does a good job for the Club. One such airing arose over a rebuke the chairman chose to give a member for practising a display act on a Sunday afternoon. His acid comments met with an uneasy silence, the same thought was written across every face: "There but for the grace of God go I." And so we in turn defended a member's action, not because he was in the right but because we might sometimes be in the wrong.

Tiger Club flying is also different, at least it's different in many ways from the big majority of flying Clubs. The prime reason of course, our members aren't *ab initio*. *Ergo*: more advanced flying is practised, but this fact is not always appreciated. A simple example: other flying Clubs are also invariably flying Schools and it follows that a proper example must be shown at all times, because the pilot in the circuit might just as easily be a first solo as a QFI. Now Tiger Club circuits at Redhill can be a sight to behold, but then the pilots in it are far from beginners, though to the uninitiated accustomed to the square search it could look casual to say the least.

We of the Committee have always defended the right of all members to fly their way in the belief that all members are responsible pilots, at least until proved otherwise, and tight precautionary circuits and short landings are every bit as valid in the book as traditional RAF circuitry. Equally, display practice and aerobatics are as much a necessary part of the scene as a sedate cross-country, and provide the sort of experience the advanced pilot needs to improve his skills.

We come to the crunch. When is it right and when is it wrong to occasionally do one's thing? Michael Jones refers to the Rules of the Club, but they are too correct and formal to anticipate every need. To resolve the dilemma pilots sometimes find themselves in, I would refer them to the long-standing Tiger Club Charter wherein are the words: "always to fly with courtesy." It isn't a courtesy to fly low over a hangar or near the village or to blatantly beat the place up, but no one will raise an eyebrow if you pick a quiet corner of the field or occasionally demonstrate a manoeuvre – it's all a matter of degree. Far be it for me to lecture, indeed that goes for any one of us, but the Committee have asked me to try and put over a view. Let us do our thing by all means, but for heaven's sake pick the right time and place, and believe me teatime on a Sunday is no time to make the Chairman spill his tea.

LETTERS

"We most certainly enjoy reading the *"Tiger Rag."* Some of the true experiences written by your wonderful members are a riot. We love your British humor; it's so subtle yet hysterical! In fact, I think it takes a person who IS hysterical to fly a Tiger Moth. Of course, I am speaking for myself only – as a Passenger Member. I have approximately 130 hrs in the front seat and my teeth marks on the instrument panel and doors prove it. Our friends don't call me "Chicken Jinny" for nothing! My poor husband has begged, pleaded and threatened, trying to force me into at least learning how to land our Insect – oops – Moth. He keeps saying: "What if something happens to me while we're flying?" Well, I wouldn't know about it anyway 'cause my eyes are shut tight from the moment we take off until we land! So why learn to land the "thing"?

But, all in all, I do love to be with my husband and since his second love is his Tiger Moth, it behoves me to see that "it" remains so. Huh!

Warmest Regards,

Mrs Virginia "Jinny" Davidson, Inglewood, California."

MUSE AT REDHILL, SEA TIGERING AND A BROOM CRUISER TENDER

CLUB NEWS: JULY – AUGUST 1971

I write this late one Saturday afternoon and do so as best I can between spells of distraction – the cries of tired children alternating with the fascination of a TV presentation of man's latest visit to the moon. It's all I can do to even envisage Redhill, much less write about it. Yet by dint of yelling and the slamming of doors I've won an uneasy truce . . . and little by little I'm getting tuned in.

I echo the comments of the visitors from abroad, and July has been their month; what a beautiful airfield Redhill is, all green and cool and not a yard of concrete in sight. So much flying has been done there these last few weeks, and so much of it away from the field that there have been times when there has been precious little left to get airborne in. At any given time there must surely be the better part of twenty freely available aircraft based at Redhill, so it doesn't seem unreasonable that a couple be left for visitors – anyway so goes a current grumble and one the Committee agrees with. So, all being well, there will always be a selection of mounts held back and at all times at least one a Tiger.

One restriction I can explain away easily – and that concerns the Betas. Formula racing is so much an up-and-coming thing, and what with qualifying races nearly every weekend flying these single-seaters has been left to the racing pilots. As one who has in the past lavished hours of care over a racing mount, I can readily appreciate the pilot's distress every time we scrounge one to circuit in. A more telling point is the hard fact that if every available F.I racer is airborne the grand total is only six. Just one unserviceable makes a lesser race and two out will scratch it! There'll be more flying by next year. A snippet I picked up from Michael. He tells me that no less that 130 Club pilots have soloed so far on the Betas.

. . . Membership has reached an all-time high with a total of 714 members . . .
but even as members join us we do, on occasion, have to record a resignation or
two. A resignation the Committee found difficult to accept was that of that most
popular of members, Bunny Bramson, a resignation brought about by pressure of
work. Even now I find it hard to believe that Bunny and his charming and lovely
wife Miriam won't be at Redhill at weekends to greet us, for their stay with the
Club has made them known to so many of us, and of course Bunny's contribution
to the Club, both as CFI and Committee man, has been immeasurable. There are
no plans at the moment to appoint a new CFI, and it is quite possible that the
appointment of a Senior Pilot will suffice in a Club of the Tiger Club's nature;
anyway, it's a decision that won't be made until the next Committee meeting in
September.

QUOTE:
We were discussing the possible willingness of induced volunteers making tea at
Redhill over the weekends. Said Tom darkly: "I think you can tell whether a
sandwich has been made under duress or not!"

The following pages may seem familiar to some who've read Book No. 1, but
I'd assembled it again in what was a quiet editorial summer issue in 1971.
It's offered up now as a latter-day reminder of what flying was like in those
carefree immediate postwar years. Mark you, there were moments at the
Tiger Club that varied not one jot from those halcyon days. For instance an
early awakening whilst overnighting it in the hangar Clubroom certainly
prompted the musing that follows. I can remember the culprit too; it was a
youthful Robin d'Erlanger who, irresistibly drawn to aviate, pushed out the
aeroplane nearest the doors and proceeded to beat up the place. At 4.30 am.
When he returned he couldn't face the collective hangover of misery he'd
awakened and hid in a corner somewhere to avoid us.

A MUSE AT REDHILL – by JOE DELL
"I recently caught myself grumbling inaudibly at someone's exuberant flying.
"Twit!" I muttered as he screamed past the hangar, the roar of his engine
reverberating off metal walls. Immediately my conscience awoke and protested: "If
he's a twit, what were you when you were his age?" Touché – acknowledged self
generously.

It was 1947 and I was on a delicious demob leave from the RAF getting brown
on the pebbly south coast beaches, and not too remorseful of my grandmother's
well-timed departure of this life, for in her going she had left me £500. That and
£45 demob pay left me well provided for. In quick succession I bought an
Armstrong Siddeley Coupé '31 vintage; a motor bike; began a hitch-hike to South
Africa (fell in love with Paris en route and stayed long enough to spend all my
money); and started a flying Club. I was twenty-one.

I had taken my 'A' licence immediately civil flying recommenced after the war. It's dated the 7th January 1946 – I was still in uniform. My service flying gave me exemption from the flying test, I only needed to pass the oral examination. With a fellow pilot we presented ourselves at the RaeC. The formidable Mossy Preston glowered at us from behind his desk.

"You," – he pointed to Dicky Richards (what happened to you, Dicky?) – "what's a customs carnet?"

"Well," hedged Dicky, "if you leave the country you'll probably need one."

Mossy looked at me. "And you?"

"I agree with Dicky, Sir," I said loyally.

Mossy's face was a study. "I see you two know damn-all about it!" he shouted. "Here, give me those papers."

He scrawled his signature and dismissed us.

"Is that it?" asked Dicky, visibly shaken.

I nodded. They also lifted 5/- off us for an Aviator's Certificate, a wonderfully copper-plated screed that must have been a hangover from the days when we had an Empire. Indeed it had the words 'British Empire' in gold on the cover, and inside it urged people to aid and assist the holder. It was worth five bob of anybody's money.

The RAF had done nothing if not excite my love of flying, only now I was going to have to pay for it. I joined the South Coast Flying Club at Shoreham and got checked out by the late Cecil Pashley.

"I'll swing it," I offered eagerly when we approached the Tiger Moth for a check.

"You," said Pash, stopping midstride; "you will do nothing of the sort. Never. It's the job of a professional, either a ground engineer or qualified instructor." "It's for your own safety," he added tartly. "Now get in." He looked around for someone to give us a hand, but there was no one in sight. "I'll swing it," Pash decided.

The engine started first swing and the Tiger moved forward smartly. Pash hastily shot out of the way. "Chocks, you must remember chocks!" he panted as he and his leather coat disappeared into the front cockpit.

I suffered the limited freedom of the conventional Club for a few months, then had a great idea. "I'm going to form my own Club," I said one day to Duncan Davis who was boss around there at the time.

"Good lad!" he beamed; "all for initiative."

"Thank you," I replied, and I won't really be in opposition to you over there."

"Over where?" he asked suspiciously.

I pointed to the other side of the airfield.

My bright idea was to find 50 partners with £10 each to begin a community-type flying Club. In those days I had very socialistic views. I put an ad. in the local paper: "FLY WITH US. Newly-formed ENTHUSIASTS FLYING CLUB invites all keen flying types including ladies to FIRST MEETING, Old Shoreham Road, Southwick, Friday 21st November, 1947.

195

15 enthusiastic types turned up and looked to me for a lead.

"Let's form a Committee," I suggested innocently, and since everyone was so helpful I asked each in turn: "And what would you like to be?"

In no time at all we had volunteers to be Chairman, Vice-Chairman, Deputy Chairman, and when we'd exhausted that angle we began on Treasurers and so on down the line. No one left that meeting unhappy, and what's more I had three positive offers of £10 and one wee Scotsman handed me £100 in fivers; more of Danny later.

Rollasons sold aeroplanes, so I phoned them and bought a "Maggie" with a year's C. of A. for £325. I phoned the Air Ministry and they offered us the use of an old blister hangar on the north side of Shoreham, and was a fiver a year too much for rental?

"No," I replied cautiously, "and can we rent the two old sheds there too?"

They came in at £25 a year. Years later I can only look back in wonderment at those negotiations, all of which took place over the phone. I can't recall anyone ever confirming anything in writing. The Civil Service was then of course full of liberated ex-servicemen who were not only civil but wanted to help. Even the police on the gate were cheerfully bribed to our side with bottles of beer and endless cups of tea.

Our Miles Magister arrived early in the New Year flown in by our first CFI, an ex-ATA pilot called Chadwick. Off we went, one after the other, on our first familiarisation flight. On mine I petrified Chad by preparing to spin.

"Not on your Nellie," said Chad firmly, "at least not with me in it!"

I was no sooner down than I planned the deed with an ex-naval pilot. Today it's accepted, at any rate by some, that pupils can learn to fly with never a spin, but for pilots fresh out of the service it just wasn't the done thing. So Baggy Woodward and I took off and climbed to a goodly height and proceeded to spin the poor "Maggie" either way with considerable élan hoping that our CFI would take heart. We soon tired of spinning and decided on aerobatics. I was in the front seat and, wasting no time, promptly went into a full-blooded loop. As we moved over TDC there was a resounding thump, followed by a yell from Baggy.

"Stop!" he shouted, "something big hit me!"

I levelled off, Baggy got out of his straps and began crawling around the cockpit floor. He soon came up, triumphantly waving a huge dry Leclanché cell (we were experimenting with electric hats at the time).

"I think it came from the luggage locker – there's a hole right behind my head – it must have fallen through!"

He did his straps up, gave me the OK, and with Baggy hanging on to the battery I began a second loop. Another and even louder thump shook the airframe. It was followed by a bellow of laughter.

"It's the second one," yelled Baggy; "hang on, I'll get it." And off he went to come up with a second. Now he had one in each hand.

"OK?" I shouted, "then here we go!" And I stuffed the stick forward. It seized solid.

Over the screaming slipstream came a yell of terror. The stick force eased sufficiently for me to level out.

"My straps!" croaked a shaken Baggy, "I'm not strapped in!"

Eight hours solo was all that was needed in 1948 for a licence to be issued – that from a simple flying test during which one didn't leave the circuit. As the Club grew bigger, it was now known as the Brookside Flying Group. Chad began to delegate instruction, and since no qualifications were necessary, I offered to have a go. In no time at all I was hard at it. An ex-flight engineer was my first victim.

"Any previous piloting experience?" I asked grandly.

"Not really," Jack Hamblett said, "although I have on occasion held the controls of a Lancaster."

After three hours twenty minutes I sent him solo. And a jolly fine effort he made of it too (incidentally Jack later joined the Tiger Club).

"How's that, Chad?" I asked proudly when we walked in. Chad sat down on the nearest chair, too lost for words to comment. Perhaps that record still stands for a postwar solo.

Ah! halcyon days – of siphoning petrol out of the "Maggie's tank," for we were granted more petrol coupons for flying than we could ever fly off, and petrol was strictly rationed.

"How much do you fly?" asked the official at the Town Hall.

"I calculated thoughtfully. "We hope to do about fifty hours a week."

The official sucked in his breath. "Hmm," he pondered, "and at ten gallons an hour (that was another of my figures) that's an awful lot of petrol; can you make do with 300 gallons a week?"

"I'll try," I answered.

To this day I can still put my hands on some of those coupons.

Every flying day opened with a low pass between the Worthing and Brighton piers, and once when two pilots flew too low, we bought another "Maggie" with the insurance money and, with the unfeeling spirit of youth, pressed on; like scattering pamphlets all over Brighton drumming up membership: "If you can afford to smoke you can afford to fly" was our platform, and at 30/- an hour it constituted fair comment.

The longest flight I made in the old "Maggie," at least before she was stolen, was to an airfield in Scotland. Danny Taylor, the wee Scotsman I mentioned earlier – he was a fairground showman and had an arcade in Brighton – asked me to take him up there. No sooner said than done and we were off, my only map a half-million of Southern England.

"Don't worry," said Danny, "I've got a map."

He had, too – a pocket diary one – only I didn't know that till later. It was getting dark when we refuelled at Sherburn-in-Elmet but we pressed on. The moon rose and we sailed on into a dark and peaceful star-filled night. Still north we moved over a land that had all but faded from view, and then gradually ahead loomed a softly-shimmering Firth of Forth to welcome us, and we turned left to follow the river until we found the moonlit runways of Grangemouth. I peered down intently for the faint runway numerals, only they weren't figures, they were crosses, white unserviceable crosses. I hadn't expected that. In those days disused runways were often used to store munitions on, and since I could scarcely see the runway, much less anything on it, I hadn't much option but to land on the grass to one side of it.

We descended into a gentle summer night, and as we sank below the tree line the moon hid her face and all became black and still, only the singing slipstream was there to keep us company. Back, back I eased the stick. I could hear my breathing, so quiet was the night. It was like being suspended in space. I could see nothing, hear nothing beyond our little fabric world of wood and whispering engine. By now the stick was right back and I waited in oblivion for the kiss of the wheels on the grass, only I waited in vain. Nothing happened. After a while I switched off the engine and sat back nonplussed. Presently Danny spoke from the back seat.

"Are we down?"

"I don't know," I said.

He must have thought about it for a bit for he said: "Hang on, I'll step down and see if I can feel the ground."

The absurdity of this moment completely eluded us. I stared back into the darkness where I could hear Danny climbing out.

"It's alright," he called, "we're down."

We'd landed in a rich crop of wheat so thick that our landing run couldn't have been more than ten yards, and so gently had we arrived neither of us had been able to discern the transition. Soon lights began to flicker a long way off and as we watched they came nearer and the quiet was broken by shouted welcomes. From the shadows came dozens of Danny's funfair friends.

I turned to him.

"They knew we were coming," he said simply.

I slept that night in a showman's caravan, a sleep that was long, happy and content. I was 22.

I sometimes wonder where you all are, my friends from the past. Are you now all cautious middle-aged family men too, and do you, like me, forget the past and call out "Twit!" at youth? You do? Shame on you."

CLUB NEWS: SEPTEMBER – OCTOBER 1971

Since last I wrote this column – could it have been so far back as July? –the summer has proved so warm and friendly and so very eventful that there just hasn't been the inclination to get down to writing any of it up. Big Club events like the Full Displays – those at Elstree and Fairoaks were among the best ever seen – and our latest and best 'At Home' were tremendous successes, yet not a word has been written. Fabulous Formula One meetings and one very memorable seaplane appearance have also gone unrecorded, and these are but some of the tasty moments in, what is after all, a typical Tiger Club summer. If we mention all this in passing let me appeal to members who were there to jot down a description now for such good reading will be the saving of many a dark chill winter evening to come.

Our congratulations to Manx Kelly for his win in the de Havilland Trophy, an award that clinches for him the British Aerobatic Championship. And whilst on the bouquets let me put one up for Peter Phillips for so ably organising those two great displays. Elsewhere there is mention of a seaplane – well, as one who has now sampled the sweet joy of flying G-AIVW, our Tiger on floats, let me say here and now that you haven't flown till you've handled the Sea Tiger – the experience is in a class of its own. There isn't going to be room in this "Rag" for further seaplane chat – I'll include it in the next issue.

Now that the evenings are drawing in, may I recommend a visit to the Kronfeld Club – after all, you are all members. It's open every Wednesday evening for social get-togethers and with either a Talk or Film. What's more, you can book the premises for meetings or parties.

. . . Oh! yes, Michael Jones requests a hearing. Will those among you who make tea late of an evening in the Clubroom <u>please wash and tidy up after yourselves</u>. The mess is a bit much to face on a Monday morn . . . not that I've seen it, but I'll take his word for it.

"What's the penalty for being the Senior Check Pilot?" asked an anxious Bill Goldstraw when he was elected for the task at the last Committee meeting.

"Very simple," replied Norman severely. "You get blamed for everything that goes wrong."

"That's what I was afraid of," muttered Bill.

It's a big job, and we all wish Bill Goldstraw every success and support.

There's no doubt the Sea Tiger was the belle of the season. Tiger 'AIVW was ever a most distinguished fellow, having once won the King's Cup, and now she was on floats there was no holding her. (Have I got my sexes mixed? Never mind, I mean well.)

Keith Sissons gave me a check out. We struggled to a reasonable height for a go at stalling.

"Go on," he urged, "close the throttle." I did so and the seaplane stopped. Instinctively I shoved everything forward.

"That's it," said a cheerful voice from the front. "You've learnt," he added reasonably enough, "never close the throttle on her till you've landed."

"Too true," I muttered.

That apart the Sea Tiger on and off water was a dream.

I'm not sure who wrote the Seaplane Section bit that follows. It was probably Tom Freer.

SEAPLANE SECTION: AUTUMN PROGRAMME

Your Seaplane correspondent realises that it is high time he made the effort to put down on paper something definite about the Sea Tiger's plans. It was his intention to inaugurate the season with an announcement that would at least have conveyed some outline of a programme; but always, whenever the moment came, the whole plan fell through and it became necessary to start again at the beginning.

The trouble has been – and to a certain extent still is – our search for a site on fresh water. (The salt corrosion that has resulted from operating in the past at Lee-on-Solent makes it essential that we leave the sea.) Three times this year we have thought we had obtained a fresh water site; but each time the negotiations, after starting well, have run into unexpected difficulties and at a late stage we have had to accept defeat.

If it were not for the fact that we were asked to take part on August Bank Holiday Monday in the Oulton Broad Regatta, the Sea Tiger would probably not have flown this season at all. As it turned out, not only was our contribution to the Regatta much appreciated, but also it led indirectly to an invitation to do some flying on a privately-owned piece of water nearby, called Fritton Decoy.

Fritton Decoy, 6 miles north west of Lowestoft, is owned by Lord Somerleyton. It is a very beautiful lake; the Sea Tiger was received there with an open hospitality such as we have never previously experienced, and we have been asked back again.

Accordingly there will be an opportunity for everyone to fly the Sea Tiger although not as yet solo, in conditions that could not be bettered. Please get in touch with either Keith Sissons or Tom Freer, and if at Redhill watch the notice board at the back of the hangar.

The lake is used by fishermen and others, so we are not to overdo things. We shall therefore ask Lord Somerleyton's permission to fly only on selected weekends, the next one being probably October 23rd/24th.

. . . Of the future, we are uncertain. Our permission to use Fritton Decoy is at present of a temporary nature; and it is, of course, a long way from London and the South-East. But of one thing we are certain. The attraction of Fritton is such that nobody who goes there to enjoy some seaplaning can possibly ever regret doing so.

P.S. Negotiations with the Board of Trade and Industry concerning qualifications for seaplane Instructing are still under way . . . we all have our fingers crossed for good news soon.

In that September I got a letter for the *"Rag"* from Keith Sissons. (And yes, he's still around and flying the B-17 Fortress "Sally B" so superbly.)

"Dear Benjy,
Knowing that you will be making reference to it in *"Tiger Rag"* I would like to say this. It was extremely gratifying to see the terrific enthusiasm which prevailed amongst our members firstly to make the little show a success and secondly to dedicate the time available to getting people in the air. There was no grumbling about the many non-members who were flown on 'diplomatic' grounds or any bickering about some members having more flight time than others and to see so many people pulling on lines, wallowing about in (quite unseaworthy!) rubber dinghies and getting wet in a thoroughly selfless manner was terrifically gratifying to Tom and me after the number of frustrations and setbacks we have had this year. One member came up by train from London and had only 35 minutes flying,

yet no complaint and I feel he would do it again. (Mike Stapp.) His enthusiasm was quite typical. The Southend "Seaplane Handling Services Unit" who refuelled the aircraft at Aldeburgh on the way up and at Bawdsey Ferry later on the return for the BBC's benefit did so completely cheerfully despite the miserable weather on the first occasion and the 3-hour road journey each way. This sort of ardent enthusiasm means one thing basically – that we must keep the Sea Tiger operational almost at all costs. This in turn requires that we get over this ridiculous licence problem somehow for I feel somewhat embarrassed that Tom has no licence at the moment and I've been getting all the fun!

Just for the record members might be interested to know of the following statistics!

The Sea Tiger was erected at Lydd on 18th August.
Since that date until 14th Sept. (4 weeks) it flew 33 hrs 55 mins.
On the Oulton Regatta weekend it flew 12 hrs 15 mins.
On the Oulton Regatta weekend it flew 35 sorties.
On these 35 'sessions' 23 different people had air experience in the Sea Tiger.
The residual 20 hours or so was made up of positioning flights and BBC filming in the Solent.

On the BBC effort the aircraft was based at Denge Marsh Quarry, Lydd (lovely name!) and positioned to the Solent on each of the 3 days flown for the BBC. Michael Jones offered his ocean racing yacht "Mowgli" as a seaplane tender for the final two days 'shooting' and a rendezvous was accordingly arranged 'two cables off Wootten Creek to the nor'east' or something like that. I was advised that the "Mowgli" was a 30 ft sloop with a black hull and flying a red ensign from the stern. In case I had difficulty in identifying the vessel he would hang (you'll never believe this) an inverted bucket from the cross-trees! As those arrangements were being made by telephone I quite naturally asked him to repeat this and he assured me he said "inverted bucket." I said that although I admitted to only a very rudimentary knowledge of lights and daymarks displayed by vessels this would surely cause confusion to passing mariners who would probably take the signal to mean 'I am about to capsize' or perhaps 'I am about to be seasick. Send me some pills.' He said: "If you must know, it means 'I wish to go ashore and need a boat.'"

Altogether another unforgettable weekend!

Thought for the day (in the light of the last Committee meeting): if when taxying a seaplane at night it collides with an unlighted Vice-Chairman's motor cruiser at moorings would this be regarded as bad airmanship or bad seamanship? Sorry I've rambled on a bit but I would like it made known what a grand crowd I think the seaplane section is!

    KEITH SISSONS."

The summer of '71 was for me and my little family something of an adventure. I had purchased a new Broom 30 motor cruiser, and whilst still on her maiden outing had the opportunity to act, as Michael Jones had done previously, as the Sea Tiger's tender. To anchor on the Broad's delightful waters and have, as the day drew in, a real seaplane moor nearby and settle down for the night alongside was, well, an unforgettable experience. Constant food on call, a place for all to gather was 'Benjamina's' lot.

I can sense the raised eyebrow at all this euphoria. Hey, was business that good? In a word, yes. And yes, somewhere along the way Norman had also promoted me Vice-Chairman. Please don't cheer yet, there's a rise and fall in most things, be it Reggie Perrin or the Roman Empire; thank heavens my fall was still some way off, but in the meantime there was a lot of living to do.

DAWN-TO-DUSK, TIMID TURBS, TARMAC REVERIE AND FUNERAL À LA MODE

The Dawn-to-Dusk Competition was growing, catching on fast, with even more original ideas than ever before. David Hamilton provided a concise resumé:

DAWN-TO-DUSK 1971

The Dawn-to-Dusk this year has been one of the most successful so far. The entry list in previous years has varied around 20 with about half the entrants actually starting. This year, however, there were about 30 entrants actually of which some 22 flew. This represents a good increase which is most encouraging.

The weather has always been the major controlling factor and this year it was not kind. The first week provided a large variety of conditions, from heavy rain, low cloud and gale-force winds to sunny intervals, depending on which part of Europe the competitors were keen on visiting. The fact that 8 entrants failed to fly is directly attributable to the initial poor conditions and had the weather been better then it is probable that all would have flown.

The entry list was interesting in that only about a quarter of the entrants had taken part in previous Dawn-to-Dusks. Half the Competitors had less than 100 hrs (P.1) and among them was the holder of a student licence. The aircraft used were spread over a larger number of types than before and included 2 Cessnas, Rallye Clubs, 8 RF.4/5s together with 3 homebuilts and a mixture of other types.

Taking into account the number of differing types and the greater-than-usual number of pilots with limited experience, judging did not prove to be an easy task. The final positionings were close and the pilots would have achieved higher final placing had they not been penalised for careless mistakes which could have been avoided by careful planning. It should be mentioned that a number of entrants failed to read the rules carefully.

Forward planning is the most essential part of the Competition and it has been demonstrated over the years that those who spend time and thought on planning come consistently high in the final placings. There are those, of course, who spend months settling routes and alternatives and cover every conceivable type of weather and there are the few who tend to 'blast off' with the minimum of planning. It is fair to say that those who plan with a couple of alternatives have a greater chance but this must not be taken to mean that two months forward planning is essential. Choice of routes vary infinitely, covering both UK and Europe. The choice of route coupled with ability/experience counts high especially where good reasoning for a route is given. Obviously higher marks are given to the pilot who selects an original route giving reasons rather than the one who gives no reasoning for a mediocre sortie.

Reading and checking the reports carefully has revealed two or three main points which merit mention. Firstly it was noticed early on that the measured (leg) distance varied as compared with the Judges' Navigational Ruler. Further investigations of nine nautical rulers of types currently being sold showed differences of up to 3%. Perhaps the manufacturers should take note of this and certainly owners should check their rulers most carefully. No doubt the Safety Council will wish to consider the problem which is believed to be allied with the manufacture of plastics.

The second problem is fundamentally more serious and can be summed up in one word – carelessness. A large number of pilots, including those with considerable experience (and CPLs) fail to be accurate in their calculations. Probably the most serious of those is the inability to calculate accurately average speed and fuel consumption for each sector of the flight. One report stated that a sector length of 120 miles was flown in 110 minutes and therefore the average speed over the leg was 135! Similarly, fuel consumption calculations were out and in one case by as much as 3 gallons per hour. Either of those could lead to a dangerous situation especially over water and might result in an accident, causing many problems to a whole host of people. The other point which requires watching is the pilot who presses on into deteriorating conditions and eventually becomes a nuisance to the various authorities. One instance of the latter was the pilot who flew VFR in very hilly country (tops 3,500 amsl) with cloud base at about 2,500 amsl and proceeded to attempt valley-flying with the regional ATC contacting him every few minutes to ensure his safety. This should not happen and pilots should be prepared to divert from their original target if faced with these conditions.

The winners this year achieved a very high standard. The routes and reasons were carefully thought out. The Pilot Trophy (Novices) was awarded to Elizabeth Hargreaves who had only 45 hours in command. She arranged for her flight to be sponsored and by flying her brother's home-built Turbulent managed to reach Cornwall and return, raising well over £50 for the Oxfam Relief Fund. Lola Brace and Margaret Dyne (flying as a team) retained the Ladies' (Bonney) Trophy; they planned to follow the route of the 1911 Circuit of Europe which covered Britain, France and the Low Countries. However, poor weather prevailed over the eastern sector of Europe and they diverted to East Anglia to simulate the typical Dutch countryside.

The inimitable Mike Bialkewicz decided to demonstrate the fuel economy of the RF.4 and in sometimes inclement conditions managed to cover 1,255 miles at an average consumption of over 40 miles to the gallon. For the second year running he was awarded the Icarus (Single Seat) Trophy. Alan Perry, who was third, visited all the capitals of the British Isles including Belfast and Dublin.

Alister Mackintosh was runner-up with a flight of 1,150 miles in his Emeraude. He used the prevailing weather to the best advantage in crossing and re-crossing Britain from coast to coast. Lucien Hankart, this year's winner of the Duke of Edinburgh Trophy, went overseas via France, Belgium and Germany to Denmark, returning by way of Heligoland and Holland. Perhaps he has recovered by now from 14 hours in a Cessna 150.

It is possible to elaborate for hours on all the other flights but that would consume far too much space. There are perhaps one or two points in particular that come to mind, from the pilot who ground-looped to Chris Morris (SPL Holder), who returned early to Hatfield (in a home-built Turbi) to ensure that it was checked and serviced for a further competition flight by his fellow owner.

Looking back over the reports it is most pleasing to see the increasing number of original ideas that are being produced and the obvious keenness of all the entrants. But what of the future? The rules are already being re-considered to see whether any further modification is required and it is hoped that there might be a further two annual trophies as from next year. Perhaps the most prized awards are the Annual Dawn-to-Dusk Certificates signed by HRH Prince Philip, Chairman of the Judges, and presented to all finishing pilots. These provide a more permanent memento. The entries promised for 1972 are already high and it could be that the final list might reach 45, a majority of them being more recently qualified and less experienced pilots.

I was recently able to examine the considerable correspondence that flowed between Norman Jones, on behalf of the Tiger Club, and the Palace. It soon emerged that much of the 'ideas' momentum in the growth of the Club's Dawn-to-Dusk contest emanated from HRH The Duke of Edinburgh himself.

For instance, just after the first contest in 1964, originally entitled "Endurance Competition – Turbulent aircraft – Dawn-Dusk, Redhill-Redhill," HRH proposed widening the event's scope to include the entry of other aircraft, but still flown solo. Norman, presumably pushing back unworthy thoughts of a Turb sales promotion down the drain, enthusiastically concurred.

A later suggestion from the Palace that extra prizes be offered was agreed by the Committee, and to reinforce his interest HRH has continued to be the Dawn-to-Dusk Chief Judge to this day in what has become a top European event.

Prince Philip has earned Golden Oldie status within the Club, and during those many years has become a real friend, not only to us, but to the very sport of flying. A vote of thanks wouldn't go adrift.

Anthony Preston, later of the PFA, wrote a cheerful little piece about the Turbulent. His trouble in getting into the tiny machine was a common event. Rollasons later produced 'SAM especially for tall chaps like Anthony but in the meantime the knowledge that once squeezed in all became comfortable was reassuring.

TAKE TWO TURBULENTS

An acquaintance of mine in the Air Force was wont to describe his formation flying as "same way, same day." Last Saturday happened to be the same day for me as it was for Frow. He also happened to like the idea of attempting to go the same way. Two timid Turbulents were seen to be sat side-by-side in amongst the aeroplanes. We approached them with caution. I chose the one with 1500 written on its cowl in the fond hope that this was some significant record of its number of safe manoeuvres and not the number of its victims. The red one had nothing written on it other than G-ARRZ which I took to be a very sinister omen.

As Michael was around I thought a thorough pre-flight check was in order so studiously began by trying to identify minuscule appendages from under the bird droppings. In a surprisingly short time, the wings were located (these can be identified by their resemblance to an aeroplane's tailplane). I also found that these wings have tip handles, no doubt so that one can conveniently tuck the machine under one's arm when tired of flying (or are they in fact a design feature for future Tiger Club formation displays where each pilot links hands with his neighbour's tip?).

During my Ground Check I made the stupid error of checking the engine's compression which wasn't. In fact which wasn't only wasn't but wasn't on all four. I tried to hide my dismay to my sympathetic onlookers by adopting the kind of expression which I find holds me in good stead prior to driving a dodgem-car at the Fair. Unfortunately it did not survive the indignity of trying to fit on the Turbulent which was certainly two sizes too small. Having twice descended gracefully into the cockpit with Bader-like bravado and twice been agonizingly arrested by knees of only too real flesh and blood against the panel, I finally found that I could get it on only by dint of unmanly wriggling and the application of soap and water. Once actually crouched with coccyx lodged against the backrest, knees locked under the panel and feet wedged against the pedals, my eyes fell on a label which intimated something unbelievable about lack of certification. . . . I dared to read that one no further. The one about being bitten I thought to be irrelevant, as in this case it wasn't an aircraft.

Michael at this point must have sensed that something was somewhat amiss for he sauntered over and offered to assist a desperate colleague, who with an expression of disbelief was twirling the prop round like a whisk to absolutely no effect. It wasn't that the fuel had been forgotten – I had driven a motor-mower before, but just that we hadn't located that well-concealed primer. Perceiving my facial expression, control over which I had recently neglected, Michael asked with customary charm whether I had ever flown one before. I admitted that I had but that my memory was unable to summon the finer details of the last occasion. He then with an affectionate and proprietary air proceeded to deal with the prop in a nonchalant but vigorous manner, with which it was clearly accustomed and to which it succumbed with a gorgeous bark from the starboard bow, soon followed by an answering fusillade from the other side.

Suddenly everything seemed to be rather terrific – stub exhausts are an essential ingredient to the good life. Take-off in the toy transforms it into a twitchy thoroughbred, tamed by only the tenderest touch. A short flight in formation soon revived many forgotten joys from service days. Contrary to what I would imagine the average 707 pilot would feel, flying in Turbulents can be great fun – I must ask Frow.

CLUB NEWS: NOVEMBER – DECEMBER 1971

It's still November, but only just, and a short while ago I'd returned home chilled to the bone after a fruitless day as Duty Check Pilot at Redhill. The wind had howled down past the hangar from the NE like a banshee, curling its way into the hangar and causing the aircraft to tremble in its chill wake. We, mere mortals, took to the Clubroom to escape and there to drink coffee. Clubroom – for a Club of our size it must be the quaintest in the business. The description isn't mine, it belongs to a visiting American and neatly sums up the horror-cum-attraction this cosy hole induces. We're often asked why it is what it is, and to be honest, I don't know the answer except perhaps that we've got used to our Clubroom, and in a perverted way even like it the way it is . . . 'sides, there's no room anywhere else.

If a shortage of space forbids us from spreading ourselves somewhat there is one social aspect of our Club that cries out for immediate improvement and that's in the distribution of lunches and teas. We've had a succession of paid helpers, few of whom have stayed the course, so we're going to have to fall back to drumming up voluntary help. Mavis Harriott is asking for wives and girl friends to join her in preparing a duty rota. Alternatively (my idea), what about the Duty Pilot bringing along his wife/girl friend to dole out tea to hungry aviators whilst husband/boy-friend organises the flying? Girls, whether you come along solo or dual please write Mavis and offer to help her.

The seaplane, now derigged after its remarkable debut this summer, put in no less that 66 hours flying. Plans for its reappearance next March are in hand and to keep it company there will be a Turbulent on floats: I'll keep you all posted – methinks the Seaplane section is going to be a lot of fun next season.

"Jacko" Jackson wrote to me as follows:
"As you know my in-tray occasionally gets jammed with historical material and photos, indeed an old friend of mine who died recently has bequeathed me upwards of 10,000 more negs! It goes on all the time and recently with a few more modern ones I received the enclosed Reverie, the covering letter stating that 'some time ago – in 1965 I think – my husband, staying in Surrey, was taken by his host (name not stated) to see the Tiger Club one Sunday afternoon. The enclosed was found recently among his papers and I wondered if it would be of interest to you or the Club magazine.' Members might like to read of the impressions and reaction of an old airman to their doings."

TARMAC REVERIE ONE SUNDAY AFTERNOON AT REDHILL

They stand there, in the splendour of their youth,
Mocking at life, at love, at age, at truth,
Fully alive, the present all their need,
Today a certain now, tomorrow not their heed.
Then, on a hidden impulse not defined,
Breaks up the group, each on his own inclined
To other meetings or a chosen task
Is now unfettered, that is all they ask.
From factory bench or office desk they come
From Stock Exchange or counter every one,
Escapers all from humdrum workday role
To find in flying that which makes them whole.
In phrases strange, staccato, fierce and slick
They talk of 'g' and rate of roll, or flick,
Of Cuban 8s, inverted systems, knots,
Positioning, of spins, of CSUs and slots.
Another, arms in curving gestures, shows
How his own aerobatic sequence goes.
Oblivious to all, yet man to man,
They argue, change, consolidate their plan.
And in a trice to put it to the test
Are in the air, relentless in their zest.
To loop and spin, stall turn and 8-point roll
Nought else in mind, perfection all their goal.
And some of us who stand enthralled, aghast,
Bemused by memory of flying days long past,
When we, like them, were young and gay and bold
And laughed like them at others then grown old,
Recall and yearn to tell, and yet stay mute,
Afraid – (for age can't always talk to youth),
Nor dare to criticise and never blame.
We had so much – they'll never have the same,
So now they fly while we no longer young
Muse on the past and long to join the fun,
Politely shunned – we've had our share of time,
Our flying lives now spent, we're past our prime.
But years before, we realise with dismay,
Did we pay homage? No! So why should they?

This remarkable piece was later to cause something of a furore when authorship was claimed. I recently attempted to turn back the clock and began to probe for an identity, but the nearest, indeed the only name proposed was that of dear old Golding Barrett, our "G.B." But he, if it were he, would have been flying still in '65. It's only a little mystery, but for me the question lingers still . . .

James Gilbert was at this time often given the odd task. His considerable experience coupled with a gift for writing got him saddled on this occasion with a job that was ever floating around, a sorta Safety Officer. His illustrations make fascinating reading today, not because they were penned so long ago but because they're absolutely timeless, as is his good advice. Judge for yourself.

ACCIDENT REPORTS
by James Gilbert

We're going to try publishing occasional accident reports in the *"Tiger Rag"*; not in any way to point a finger of shame at the culprits concerned, for they'll be strictly anonymous. But in the hope that we can all learn from other people's misfortunes, and fly more safely ourselves.

Accidents, even when they stop short of being outright tragedies, are always costly. Rollasons have to fix the bent airplanes, and the Club pays Rollasons, and ultimately you and I pay, in next year's flying rates. So safer flying is also cheaper flying – for all.

And if you think you recognise the pilot in any of these reports, best forget it. It might have been you, Or even me.

Hard Landing in the Fox Moth

Old Warden – always a tricky field, particularly so on display days. "The hedge at the threshold was cluttered by a large number of family cars, adorned with their passengers." Not too much wind, maybe, and two passengers in the Fox's cabin. "Finals were long and shallow, 60 knots reducing to 52 knots over the hedge."

"I was distracted on round-out and flared too high – probably at six to eight feet. The aircraft stopped within 140 yards of the threshold, and was taxied in normally. The passengers said they had heard a crack on landing – I noticed slightly buckled wood below the starboard door."

Cost of repair: £100.

Comment: short landings are a good thing to practise out in the middle of Redhill before you try to do one in anger. A useful thing to do, before you must do a short landing, is to do a gentle approach to a stall while still at altitude. Once you know what the stall speed is, remember that stall speed plus 30% is a generally safe approach speed in most any aeroplane. (This is what the airline pilots use as a rule of thumb.) Below that, sink rate can get out of hand.

Hard Landing in a Turbulent

On the last of four landings "I attempted a full stall landing and made ground contact firmly with no bounce. Upon disembarking I did check the underbelly and the landing gear and found to my dismay that the axles were bent. I reported to the duty engineer, who assessed that no damage had been done to the spar."

Cost of repair: £50.

Comment: hands up all those who have never done a hard landing? Let he who is without sin cast the first stone, for I'll not.

Botched Precautionary Landing in a Stampe
An odd one, this, with some hard-to-understand aspects.

"I took off from Redhill shortly after 18.45 to fly locally with a passenger. In view of the poor visibility I decided to fly to the east of Redhill and remain close to the railway; it would then only be necessary to follow the railway west (into the sun) to return to base." All well and good, but the next thing is he locates himself "just south of Guildford," which is many miles in the other direction. He then follows the wrong railway and comes to the edge of London: "It was fairly apparent from the urbanisation and the lack of a second railway that I was off course."

"Almost immediately there appeared below a small strip on which three aircraft were parked and as it was getting late I considered the wisest course of action was to land on the strip; there was not, in my judgement, sufficient time to further establish my correct position and return to Redhill."

"I landed on the strip. A slight downhill slope that was not apparent from inspection enabled the aircraft to run freely after touchdown; application of the brakes caused the aircraft to veer to starboard, which was almost entirely corrected by rudder, but allowed to continue as it meant that the aircraft was heading for rougher ground and away from parked aircraft."

"I had not observed that the strip was bounded on its windward side by a deep ditch and when this became visible (it was overgrown at its edges by vegetation) it was impossible to take avoiding action. The aircraft hit the ditch at about 15 mph, losing its undercarriage and striking the ground."

Cost of repair: £1,500.

Comment: maps are available from Michael, and the time of sunset from Gatwick Met. Locked in as we are at Redhill by Gatwick and London zones and the TMA, getting lost in our local area is not on. And landing in private fields and strips is generally a risky business unless you have carefully checked them out on the ground first. Stampe brakes are notoriously unreliable, giving to binding in one direction while being non-existent in the other. Perhaps, too, we should practise crosswind landings more often than we do?

The last issue of each year usually called for a light touch. Once upon a time there was a very old flying instructor who taught just about everyone to fly and his name was Wing Commander Cyril Arthur, and he held court at an airfield called Fairoaks.

Dear WingCo, he was a great character with a wealth of flying experience behind him, and in his inimitable dry fashion he wrote "Funeral à la Mode." Enjoy it. I did.

FUNERAL À LA MODE
In the year 1934 I was in charge of the Rangoon Flying School at the Mingaladon Aerodrome a few miles north of that city.

One morning I had a visit from a saffron-robed shaven-headed Buddhist priest or Phoongyi. He had a strange request to make. He wanted to hire one of my aeroplanes to fly the embalmed body of his head priest – who had recently died – around the parish he had ruled over in life. Apparently the custom is that the priest's body is taken about from village to village to enable the local people to pay their last respects.

My visitor, the Phoongyi, thought it would be a good idea to bring the ceremony up-to-date by doing the journey by aeroplane. I agreed to do the business if he would first prepare me a landing ground in the required area, which was about 60 miles west of Rangoon. A date was fixed about a week ahead, sometime during which I would fly out and inspect the landing ground. This I did and found it suitable and complete with white landing ground circle.

I had decided to use a Fox Moth aeroplane which had a small enclosed cabin taking three people. I had the idea that if I took off the two doors I would be able to load the coffin across the fuselage with the ends sticking out of the doorways.

I thought I ought to have a rehearsal, so I borrowed a coffin from a local undertaker and loaded it aboard in the manner I have just detailed. Off I went on what might have been my last flight. I got airborne and rose to about 100 ft; higher the aeroplane refused to go. The point I had overlooked – in my ignorance – was that the protruding ends of the coffin interfered with the airflow over the tail surfaces. I found by gentle experiment that I could just control the aeroplane, and managed to ease it round in a very gentle wide circuit and landed – a rather peculiar wheel landing.

Since I was committed to the charter, and I had no means of communication with the Phoongyi, I had to go ahead with the job. I decided that I would try and persuade my charterers to remove the body from the coffin, in which case I thought it would fit into the cabin quite well.

The day arrived and so did I, overhead the landing ground which presented an amazing sight, being almost completely covered with a crowd of people estimated at about 10,000.

To clear a path for landing I had to dive at the crowd repeatedly until I had sufficient room in which to land, which I eventually did. As the aeroplane rolled to a stop I had to switch off the engine quickly to prevent a serious accident as the people surged around regardless of the whirling propeller. The aeroplane of course, was a very rare object to almost all present.

My Phoongyis agreed to remove the body from the coffin and the ceremony got under way. Two priests were to accompany the body which had been shrunk in the embalming process and was quite small. It was wrapped around with linen bandages from which oozed honey – the embalming medium. This honey was carefully collected and, I understood, would be sold, as it was considered to be very holy.

As the body was loaded into the aeroplane a cannon was fired to scare away the evil spirits.

While all this was going on the police – who had been warned of the affair – managed by dint of beating the people with their bamboo sticks to clear a take-off path. The take-off was hazardous in the extreme, people flashed by a foot or two from the wingtips throughout the take-off run.

The flight completed, I had to repeat the diving technique to make a space in which to land, which was eventually safely accomplished.

The rites of the day ended by the burning of the body on top of an immense pile of wood prepared for the occasion. The burning was accompanied by feasting and merriment, the affair being called – I think – a Phoongyibian – rather like an Irish Wake.

I was asked by the local headmen if I would take people for short flights. This I agreed to do but only managed one flight as I judged the take-off and landing to be too risky, and so, reluctant to turn good money away (I could have done big business) I returned to Mingaladon.

1972

EULOGY, CHRIS WREN, OUR HILTON DINNER
AND THE UNEXPECTED

1972 started with a sense of urgency.

CLUB NEWS: JANUARY 1972

I'm in a hurry, Michael wanted a Newsletter yesterday and with good reason. The big event of the year is nearly upon us, no less an event than the Annual Dinner, to be held at the Hilton on Friday Feb. 11th. Don't forget there is plenty of hospitality available in the London area if you're travelling far. Drop me a line immediately and I'll put you in touch with a warm bed and Tiger friends. WRITE FOR YOUR TICKETS NOW AND BE SURE OF YOUR PLACE AT THE DINNER. The Hilton may be a big hotel, but even they could run out of room.

Committee news is that David Timmis is replacing Don Lovell as Touring Secretary. Don has carried out this duty for many years and with his lovely wife Tessa has led the popular Annual Tours to points all over Europe and has done so with distinguished success. The Club owes Don a great deal. I know you'll welcome David and wish him every success. With Bill Goldstraw looking after the Check Flying, his place as Membership Secretary is being taken by Andrew Chadwick. Welcome, Andrew!

The Kronfeld Xmas party was a great success. There must have been some 50 members present, although I suspect that if the "Rag" had been circulated a little earlier there might have been even more. Our thanks go to Mavis Harriott and Hazel Prosper for organising the food and drink.

I've just seen a copy of the AAA Moth Club newsletter – an extract reads:

". . . The AAA Moth Club was organized in 1963 by Jack Bucher of Hendersonville, North Carolina, who organized it as a rallying point for the many scattered restorers of de Havilland Moth aircraft in the USA. In 1966 it was then chairmanned by Dudley Kelly of Versailles, Kentucky, who performed yeoman service in finding parts and data for the many persons wanting to restore and fly their own Gipsy or Tiger Moth aircraft. In the summer of 1969 the chairmanship was passed to the writer, who has attempted to make the AAA Moth Club into an International Group welcoming all persons in the world wanting to share their common interest in the de Havilland Moth aircraft."

The Chairman is, of course, Club member Ralph M. Wefel.

Can't help reflecting how blasé we made our Annual Dinner sound. At the Hilton no less and, even more inane, they could run out of space. Were we really that confident the Tiger Club knew no bounds? I suspect we were. The Hilton Hotel was then relatively new in Park Lane, rates were acceptable and the management – perhaps as young in spirit as we – permitted a license to our exuberance that would be frowned upon today. An aircraft in the foyer for starters. . . . I couldn't help including the bit about the AAA Moth Club of America which predates our home-grown Moth Club by several years. Isn't it so often the way that real recognition seldom starts in our own back yard?

Heaven knows what got into me for the eulogy on what the Club stood for.

It usually happens around this time of year that I get letters from members in reminiscing mood. An extract from one such letter reads:

"Couldn't help thinking back over the last year and offering up a wee prayer for the Tiger Club. For me it has proved perhaps the greatest directional influence in my life. These are calculated words for within the Club I have found true friends and a way of life that may not have been mine."

He must express a sentiment that many of us feel, and I wondered if the Club meant as much to the newer members as it does to the Golden Oldies (to choke over a well-meant description heard in Committee last night). It must do, for we have just come through our fifteenth year with the Club at its strongest. It's bigger and with more activities going well than any other Club in the world. We proudly lead in National Aerobatics, and have during this last year put Formula I Air Racing on the map. Unique among Clubs is our Legal Fund, ready, able and willing to fight discrimination, and unique again is our Seaplaning. Our Air Displays are still second to none and we've a Glider-Towing Group with an annual tow-rate going into thousands every year. Club members own well over a hundred aircraft – itself a startling revelation of the Club's influence in General Aviation in this country. And did you know that over and above that figure Michael has on charge no fewer than another 73 aircraft? We operate at three airfields in this country and have seven affiliated branches of the Club abroad, and where else in the world is there a Club with so many aircraft to fly and such diverse types? It's a Club that has the resources of aircraft manufacture currently producing racers, tourers and renovating Tiger Moths, and the standard of workmanship and maintenance is in a class of its own. I blow a trumpet and I blow it good and strong. Mark you, I only do it once in a blue moon and after fifteen years it's time we had a blue moon. For me it's the greatest flying Club in the world and its chairman, Norman Jones, is General Aviation's greatest advocate.

Welcome 1972 and, I promise, not another pat on the back till 1987!

Letters from Chris Wren were treasured. Chris, who was a Founder of our Club, was one of nature's most delightful of men. His gift of cartoon illustrations had opened every conceivable face of aviation for him. It wasn't just his artistry that was in a class of its own with his ability to portray the essence of an aircraft in a simplicity of line that left one breathless with admiration, but it was also his genuine wish to embrace all he met with a joyous welcome that made friends of everyone. To this day I can envisage – and still miss – that bubbly enthusiasm and willingness to help.

LETTERS

"My dear Benjy,
Rest assured that your *"Tiger Rag"* efforts are greatly enjoyed, not least by myself. In the current issue, Keith Sissons, in his piece about the Sea Tiger, says that Michael Jones offered to identify his yacht "Mowgli" by suspending an inverted bucket in the cross-trees. This intrigued me so I tried suspending a bucket from a clothes line. I came to the conclusion that the only way this can be done is to screw a hook into the bottom of the bucket, which would ruin the bucket's waterworthiness, or to hang it in a net. I think an explanation is owed by Michael to all your devoted readers. Or to all of us who have never had to suspend a bucket upside down.

All the best,
CHRIS WREN."

CLUB NEWS: FEBRUARY – MARCH 1972

Big event this month – and it's still February as I write this – was the Annual Dinner Dance held at the Hilton on the 11th. Something like 250 members and friends sat down together. Highlight of a good evening, excluding of course that three-hour period when the lights went out, and with it the amplification system, was the great chance to meet, dance and gossip. We missed our Chairman though. Norman was helplessly stuck in Le Touquet, weather-bound with a new Wassmer, and it was left to the Vice-Chairman to welcome our Guest of Honour, Alan Bristow. It's quite on the cards though that no one at the back of that vast banqueting hall heard a word of the proceedings. Martin Barraclough never lets us down when he drags out his beloved toys. This year it was a buzzing, all-lights-flashing Jumbo that caused havoc among the waiters as they scurried about the floor. It was soon joined by another buzzy toy aeroplane, this time decked out as a pylon racer – Fred's, perhaps? By this time the Floor Manager was looking decidedly worried. He became visibly agitated when a mechanical bird flapped its way overhead. He finally lost his cool when Tom Storey produced a massive boomerang and sent it soaring magnificently across the hall. Looking very tight-lipped and red-faced, he moved as fast as diplomacy allowed and confiscated the object, just as one delighted diner was preparing to launch it back again. Even funnier, the Master of Ceremonies: in an attempt to bring a touch of decorum to the proceedings, he fruitily announced the name of our guest, ". . . coupled with our other guests, especially that of Sheila . . ." And he stopped aghast, her surname completely forgotten. 250 guests helped him out. "Scott," they shouted in unison.

My dear Mum used to say of people: "If you can't say something nice, don't say anything at all." (Not that she, bless her heart, wasn't above giving a good slating herself but then she also believed in the principle of "do as I say, not as I do." Heads she wins, tails you lose; and quite right too, she would have agreed.)

Her words come down to me as I ponder that particular Dinner. I wouldn't be my Mother's son if I sat on my thoughts for another twenty-six years. To start with, not all was as I would have readers of the *"Tiger Rag"* believe. Yes, we did have a super time but not with help from our Guest of Honour. If I couldn't find anything nice to say about Alan Bristow at the time it wasn't for the sake of trying. To be fair to him I doubt I tried too hard. (Bristow Helicopters shared Redhill airfield with us and I expect he was invited as much as a notable figure in aviation as in a gesture of friendship. It didn't work that way.)

To rubbish the Club as he did when he arose to speak was unforgivable. It was neither the time nor the place. His address was received in a stunned silence.

As his words registered someone began to slowly tap a spoon on his coffee cup, a solitary echoey ring almost funereal in its cadence, a tapping that gathered in volume as others joined in filling the ballroom with their condemnation. Bristow sat down.

It fell to me, in the Chair for the first time, to thank our guest as best I could. My words were greeted in silence.

And then suddenly, as if the curtain had been raised on Act II, the gaiety returned and our Guest of Honour's rudeness was put behind us.

If I was unprepared for the occasion – I was still at work that Saturday afternoon when Michael phoned to tell me I was to be Norman's stand-in later that evening – it was as nothing to what occurred on meeting Alan Bristow for the first time as I welcomed him along with his fair companion and escorted them to the top table.

He was seated on my right and Lollie the other side of him. Alan Bristow's companion was on my left. My wife, on this her first big occasion, looked bewitching. Bristow took in her fresh radiance and turned to me and suggested we ought to swap partners later on. Involuntarily I glanced at the lady beside me, her open smile showed no embarrassment. If I was thrown at this one-sided exchange, spare a thought for my wife. As she sat down she found she was sitting on Bristow's hand. She stood again and asked him to remove it. Our 250 guests could have had no idea at the goings-on before them. Yet as you now know the show had scarcely begun.

'The last Committee meeting was a classic of its kind. It was after a long discussion on a pilot's rehabilitation that Norman sagely remarked:

"I think we must work on the principle that no one is past praying for."

("Write it down," cried all the other delighted members to me, so I did.)

. . . Recently I received a copy of the New Zealand Tiger Club's *"Tiger Rag."* It's a great pleasure to acknowledge the good work they are doing out there. They have just held their AGM and their *"Rag"* reads much as ours – there is obviously a lot going on. If any member would like the copy of their *"Rag,"* please drop me a line and I'll pass it on. To Bob McGarry, the Editor, my best wishes and condolences.

215

Back home at Redhill the airfield has been fully operational, but conditions have been muddy. I record too that the new Wassmer passed through briefly en route to Fairoaks and, Norman, there are some 100 pilot members anxious to fly it at Redhill! A new aircraft to join the fleet – although I believe only briefly – is the tiny Tipsy Nipper. I can heartily recommend it. Flying it was like strapping a pair of wings to one's shoulders – I've never felt so birdlike. I think I preferred the trip around the peri-track prior to take-off, but boy it sure taxies well. Try it. . . . Incidentally it's the first tricycle aircraft we've ever operated.

And an extract from a letter from Carol Koczon in Toronto.

". . . I hope the American who made his statement about the Clubroom wasn't complaining or being derogatory. If he was, I must come out and say I think that your defence as stated is correct. There is nothing at all wrong with the Clubroom, and if nobody else, I like it just the way it is, cozy and unpretentious, and a character all its own. . . .

If there was a particular strange thing that I cannot explain, it was the strange feeling I had upon my return to Redhill after 3 years. . . . I purposely took the Nutfield train so I could walk from the station and up the hill like I used to do. Everything was exactly like it was in 1967 (save for a few small additions along the road) and when I walked in the back hangar door it was all so unchanged that it was almost as if 3 years had not passed at all. . . . It was the strangest feeling of being gone for 3 years and coming back to find it all as I remembered it. It was a thing that an American rarely experiences, because in this country NOTHING is left alone.

To close, the poem "Tarmac Reverie" was very interesting. I also found WingCo Arthur's little story amusing. Some of the tales one finds in the *"Rag"* really are classic. It's a shame there can't be a book of Tiger Club Tales one day – what a book that would make!"

MACRAE'S AEROS, INITIAL CHECKS, FORCED LANDINGS AND NEIL'S WAY

As ever the start of a new year saw a review of the aerobatics in 1971. Of course I toyed with the idea of including the four pages, but it isn't on the cards, in spite of Frances MacRae's inimitable authorship. A compromise is in order: her delightful resumé will suffice, but if there's anyone out there willing to tackle the subject of "Aerobatics in the '60s and '70s" I'll pass all this excellent stuff on with pleasure.

COMPETITIONS 1971

This year was notable for the arrival of the powered glider in the competition field. RF.4s turned out in force; they tell us that in 1972 the RF.7 will make its mark. We look forward to it. Biggin is taking a very lively interest in the sport. It is particularly pleasing to see these and the Victa Airtourer from Goodwood taking part. At the other end of the scale are the Zlins, and some of the Zlin pilots were equally notable for their absence, which was much regretted. The more versatile risked a shot on the faithful Stampe. The others are waiting for the Zlins to be rebuilt.

The Stampe is a very useful mount – it will do most manoeuvres, given the height – and it was the most widely used. The Tiger is more rarely seen nowadays; but well flown, it is a sure way to the judges' hearts. Bob Mitchell has had fuel trouble with his KZ-8 but when it goes it is worth watching; so is Roy Legg's ubiquitous Jungmeister. It is certainly a healthy and thriving scene.

In the international field, the Akrostar has emerged a winner and competition becomes more exciting and acute.

1971, Frances assures us, was the year the Royal Aero Club instituted an Aerobatics Certificate. She wrote: "Pilots who compete know the value of it – the challenge, the discipline and the satisfaction . . . they will welcome it."

Bill Goldstraw, who had taken on the task of Senior Check Pilot, was not, if my memory serves me, a flying instructor. He was by profession a master at St. Paul's in South London and a competent glider pilot, so his selection was an enlightened, if not a radical, one.

In his initial letter to fellow check pilots he offered a thoroughly workmanlike resumé of our task and, for the first time in the Club's history, points for guidance. His teacher qualities were just what was needed and his written word did much to clarify objectives. So for those who endured that sometimes dreaded Initial Check here's a little background on that forty-minute ride in a Tiger with silent head in the front seat, who if he didn't move didn't mean he wasn't paying attention. There's a fair amount of airmanlike wisdom in Bill's words.

To all Check Pilots

INITIAL CHECKS

The problem we face is to strike a balance between being too lenient and letting into the Club someone who later shows he is not up to Tiger Club flying, or being too strict and keeping out potentially valuable members.

From our point of view we should bear in mind the following:

(i) Rightly or wrongly we as check pilots will inevitably feel upset if one of our 'passes' puts up a boob in his first year or so after joining.

(ii) Tiger Club flying puts a great deal of responsibility on the member. His flying is almost entirely unsupervised and he is able to fly a wide variety of aeroplanes in potentially difficult circumstances. We cannot afford to let in pilots who are unadaptable, show poor airmanship or are unaware of their own limitations. We must be _very_ wary of passing people with the rider "needs to be watched" unless we _personally_ are prepared to do the watching.

(iii) We still need a competent performance on the Tiger Moth. If a pilot is unable to adapt to the Tiger it is probable that he will find difficulty adapting to other Club aeroplanes, _all_ of which are more demanding than the Cessnas and Cherokees in common use elsewhere.

(iv) We are NOT short of members.

(v) A person's flying background should not carry too much weight. What counts is his ability and attitude on Club aeroplanes <u>now</u>.

From the applicant's point of view we must not forget that he will possibly be:

(i) Nervous.

(ii) Unused to the Tiger Moth.

(iii) Used to airline-size circuits.

(iv) Unused to our circuit, airfield and rejoin procedure.

In view of the increasing scarcity of Tiger Moths at other Clubs it is quite in order for an applicant to fly with a willing check pilot before he takes the test.

We can make some allowance for (i). Briefing should cover (iii) and (iv) but it is up to HIM to sort out (ii). (The check flight should NOT be his familiarisation flight on the Tiger Moth.)

<u>Some points on the Initial Check</u>

1. The applicant should have brought with him his licence, log books, a suitable flying helmet and warm clothing.
2. Briefing. Brief fully on aerodrome procedure, booking in and out, booking aircraft, snag book, duty pilot, control tower, entering flying times and intentions book. NO ONE ELSE WILL DO THIS if you neglect it.
   Stress that he is to consider himself in charge of the flight but that he is to keep you informed of what he is doing.
3. The check flight report form covers most points but we should add navigation and precautionary landings in future.
4. Forced landings must be competently tackled and have a good chance of success. Be particularly severe on low airspeed on the approach.
5. Take-off and landing should be safe and show evidence that their success is the result of premeditated action by the pilot. Insist on a proper 3-point landing and a proper wheeler. Intermediate efforts are not acceptable. Make sure he appreciates when each is appropriate. Inelegant landings are OK as long as the pilot appreciates that things are not quite right AND TAKES SAFE ACTION IN GOOD TIME.
6. Engine failure after take-off. I suppose this depends on your nerves but a simulated failure at about 100 ft with a landing ahead on the airfield seems a fair test. Be very ready to take over yourself and don't try it in a severe wind gradient. Some practice on this can be very revealing!
7. The competent pilot usually makes it obvious early on. The marginal ones are the problem. If you would feel unhappy flying with the applicant with you as a helpless passenger then a 'fail' is indicated. If in doubt, get a second opinion. Outright failures may be referred to Rochester or Fairoaks if you think that more practice would bring the applicant up to standard. Let George Young or Ross Skinner know if you recommend this course of action.

I don't recall there being a written list of things to check but we all followed a well-established pattern. The trip usually comprised a gentle climb to 3,000 ft during a series of turns on the way up. There were always stalls and a spin or two, a forced landing (induced by firmly closing the throttle when the poor fellow least expected it) but not below 500 ft officially and, on return to Redhill, some circuits. All very civilised and friendly. We'd check on aeros if requested, but that side of the coin was usually a separate item.

Some earlier forced landing accident, mostly due to a failure to keep the engine warm on the way down and resulting in a real emergency, had prompted a furious debate on the best way to carry out this exercise. Neil Williams, who was always central to debates like this, was adamant his way was best. He'd select a field – a small one for preference, he loved a challenge, did Neil – and dive his Tiger to arrive at the field's threshold doing exactly 100 mph. He'd then throw his mount into a tight circuit which bled off the speed sufficiently to enable him to sideslip neatly in to land, and he added firmly: "It works every time."

To be fair it always worked for me when later on I flew the Arrow Active a lot, and that was a fussy beast if ever there was one, but for some reason or other this perfectly simple and sound idea never caught on. Perhaps it went against the grain to throw away perfectly good height and thinking time so drastically. Neil also contended that the 100 mph speed was good for any light aircraft, but then not everyone was a Neil.

CLUB NEWS: APRIL – MAY 1972

It seems ages since I last wrote the *"Rag"* – all of eight weeks ago – but in that time the seasons have switched dramatically. Redhill is now abloom with light and green and the mud and cold is a world away. I never fail to thrill to that first glimpse of the airfield as the road drops down into that Surrey valley – and I've been making that journey for many years. It is without question the most beautiful airfield I know. And once there I'm happy to report that nothing changes. The hangar is still full of aircraft, mostly old and well-loved, with the occasional new one to excite the pulse. The Wassmer Pacific, that rather sleek newcomer our Chairman is currently assessing, is much admired. I report that it is quiet, easy to fly and very very comfortable, but it is either underpowered or a wee bit heavy, for with three up it takes up an awful lot of runway. I know, I was still groundborne going past the hangars going north; OK, I exaggerate a bit, but not much.

And the new black Crossley Cassutt is a beauty, a welcome newcomer to the racing fraternity. Test flight was carried out by Michael Jones and he reckons it's going to be a fast one. Search the hangar carefully and you'll eventually locate a tiny plastic-sheeted corner in which Robin Voice is assembling a mysterious Ballerina. To be honest it's one I didn't know about, perhaps it was a spare airframe, anyway by all accounts it's reckoned to be flying this summer. Not that I've seen it yet but some of the aerobatic boys are assembling a Pitts Special over at Farnborough, and there's talk of a Fournier RF.4 joining the Club fleet. (STOP PRESS – it's now arrived.)

Our first Air Display this season was at Elstree . . . a well-attended but bitterly cold venue. The standard of flying was very high in trying circumstances of high gusty winds. Especially praiseworthy were the duos of Pete Jarvis and Carl Schofield, and their constant verve and showmanship just about held the display together, and did much to alleviate the disappointment over the missed parachutists and vintage contribution. All in all a good start to what promises to be a very full display season. Incidentally it's time I wrote up a display in full. To give a few lines to record a full two hours' show is an insult to months of practice and preparation.

. . . One of the entertaining aspects of commentating at our Shows is the number of requests for instant plugs. Among the most enterprising was James Gilbert, the new Editor of *"Pilot."* After a sell-out of Spitfire copies signed with Ray Hanna's moniker, he got Manx Kelly to scribble all over the current issue on Stampes. Each move accompanied by a PA announcement! The magazine has taken a decidedly good turn for the better and we all wish him well as Editor. And now may I fly your Jungmeister, James?

PILE-ITS, TURB FRIGHTS APLENTY,
G-BADN AND COLDEST-EVER B.P.

The Club regularly went through a heart-searching period. Like the seasons these earnest offerings alighted on my desk, all full of well-intended warnings to the unwary. Just how many of these contributions were the result of a guilty conscience and the need to seek redemption I'll never know. Whatever the motive there's no doubting the underlying wisdom, every bit as valid today no matter what machinery you fly. John Barnes' list hit some humorous truths smack on the head.

FLIGHT BRIEFING FOR PILE-ITS
(Or: How to Get the Hours in in the Hereafter)

1. Never check the Tiger's fuel system for water (what's good enough for the "water wagon" 707 is good enough for me!).
2. Accept without question the word of the previous pilot that "there's enough for a good hour."
3. Never do up the front straps before you fly alone, smashed front instruments won't worry you 'cos you have a set of your own.
4. Magnets in your pocket help to keep the compass needle steady, so does your cigarette lighter.
5. Never, never check for mag-drop before you fly, think of the time you'll waste while the one on the blink gets a look over.
6. Maps are for amateurs, I know this area like the back of my hand! (Says the chap from East Anglia.)
7. Encourage non-flying passengers to explore the intricacies of the controls in flight.
8. Always carry plenty of rubbish in your pockets when you're doing aeros and for God's sake don't tell anyone if you drop something.
9. Always remember you fly better after a couple or three!

10. If you do get down in one piece, always taxi in fast, it impresses the females and saves time for the next pilot! Always open the throttle as wide as possible when you've taxied in and its tail is toward the hangar doors, the sand does wonders for the finish on the Beta and the rebuilt engines wear in better.
11. Always leave the switches on, it's UP for "off"!
12. Encourage children to play near and on aeroplanes and swing on props, they'll get the flying spirit early.

CLUB NEWS: JUNE – JULY 1972

Summer is belatedly upon us, not that the weather shows that much improvement, but the traditional seasonal things are about us. Things like the Club participation in countless functions all over the place. I sometimes think these small displays are the very personification of all our ideals. A summer fête, that most English of institutions, presents a wondrous backdrop to the spectacle of helmeted man and his flying machine. As a participant I get more kick out of the very amateurism of the whole set-up than a dozen smoothly-run professional shows.

The Wassmer Pacific has now received its C. of A. and may be joining the Club's fleet. Right now it's the Chairman's favourite mount. One that has definitely joined the bevy at Redhill is the Fournier RF.4. Its high aspect-ratio wing takes up a lot of room and it's certainly proving popular, indeed it's seldom on the ground. Get a trip in it, it's well worth while. A visitor to the hangar is a beautiful Bücker Jungmeister, I forgot to ask who it belonged to. I know it's not James Gilbert's, so it could be there will shortly be two of them to roost there. It was great to learn that Norman took second place in the *"Daily Express"* Air Race flying his long-distance Condor and the £300 must have come in handy. The Tiger Club also took the team prize.

An extraordinary item appeared on the Committee's agenda. "'RRZ – not bad airmanship. Formation take-offs in gusty conditions to be approached with care."

Briefly, a formation of three Turbs had scarcely begun a formation take-off northwards past the hangars at Redhill when the number three machine inexplicably tipped onto its nose. The other two cancelled take-off and the pilots later agreed that they had experienced the greatest difficulty in keeping their Turbs from doing the same thing. Indeed the leader confessed it was touch-and-go for him. When the accident was discussed in Committee, Michael Jones revealed that a year earlier a similar accident had occurred, the report of which confirmed identical conditions: i.e. gusty weather and the N. runway. A fascinated Committee touched on every conceivable reason for the phenomena and I report that the current line of thought is that they encountered a sudden wind reversal. Unlikely? We don't know. Anyone any similar experience?

Now that there were seldom less than eight Turbulents sitting on the flight line at any one time (they were cheap to fly hence also very popular), the odds were always going to be an increase in incidents – a much-used euphemism for an accident.

Bill Goldstraw offered good advice:

"Still they do it! Pilots continue to drop Turbs fully stalled onto the ground from wholly unacceptable heights. Result: deflated pilot egos, engineers busy doing heavy landing checks, and one broken undercarriage so far this season.

Don't try fully-stalled landings in Turbulents. They can be wheeled on quite happily and it's much safer. You sit quite close to the ground in a Turbulent, so try and get used to the height before take-off. And don't forget that most Turbs have opaque (or at least translucent) windscreens and the engines don't always work when you open the throttle to try to sort out a sudden sinking feeling."

And a month later Tom Moulson wrote:

". . . In the June/July Newsletter you invite comments on the recent incident of a Turbulent tipping onto its nose on the take-off run.

This happened to me at Redhill, summer of 1970. Yes, gusty conditions, North runway. My recollection is that once the tail lifted there was no stopping it.

This seemed a pretty lame explanation to everyone at the time, including myself. The outcome was a ten-pound fine.

Yours truly,
TOM MOULSON."

(You were lucky – the going rate is now £15. – Ed.)

Couldn't help thinking that with so many Turbs still flying – this in 1998 – items like this must be thought-provoking.

CLUB NEWS: AUGUST – SEPTEMBER 1972

I've just spent the afternoon at Redhill and a more peaceful spot I can't imagine. (The weather was unsettled and warm – it hasn't been a good summer.) Between hopping in and out of all my old favourites – Jodel for the children and the Stampe for me – I tried the RF.4 again. It really is a fine aircraft but not one to taxy around in, for I understand the wee outriggers are prone to buckling. But in the air and cleaned up it behaves delightfully. It is quiet and the visibility is exceptional. The nice new notice in the cockpit drawing one's attention to the possibility of a £100 fine for a wheels-up landing tends to catch one's eye.

Incidentally the latest landmark in the district is the wide tear in the landscape of the proposed southern motorway which conveniently runs hard by the eastern runway.

As I so often do when rummaging around for gossip I turn to the committee notes for inspiration; it never fails me. For instance I spotted the minute: *"10 (1) Pacific discussed. Club would like it."* "Who wouldn't?" I reflected inanely, and then the penny dropped. Norman had offered the Club the use of his Wassmer Pacific and the offer had been accepted with alacrity. I'll keep you posted as to its arrival.

The next Full Display is at Shoreham on the 13th August. (I bet this *"Rag"* comes out too late – it's 30th July now so I'll beg forgiveness in advance.) I do urge members to try and come along. Sometimes I think there ought to be a Club rule that firmly suggests at least one Full Display attendance a year. If ever there was a really traditional Club get-together it's one of these meetings.

The Seaplane Section is well under way: the present site is down at Lydd on a flooded gravel pit. Unfortunately my visit there coincided with thick fog but I know that Keith Sissons and Tom Freer are hard at it encouraging members to get airborne. For my money a day out with this enthusiastic lot is something akin to the perils of sailing and the joys of flying. Believe me, refuelling a rocking Sea Tiger from cans is more precarious than dinghy sailing and there's a similar motion. I recommend the experience to the sailing fraternity amongst you

The Dawn-to-Dusk has now run its course for this year. Out of over 20 entries only eleven finally got going. (A sad mishap during the Isle of Wight races a few weeks earlier put paid to no less than three would-be entrants.) One rumour has it that a contestant flew a hundred miles less engine! Doubtless the RF.4.

Don't forget the Tiger Club International Trophy will be held during 19th/20th August at Rochester. It's essentially a basic aerobatic contest open to all, and even if you don't enter it should prove a good weekend away.

A word of warning. There has been at least one reported case of low flying. No matter what the temptations are, don't do it. Apart from the damage to our good name it could cost the culprit a lot of money. And I refuse to offer the advice: if you must, make it the one pass – its always the second time around that has the sting.

The sleek-looking Wassmers were to be with us for some years to come. I can well recall Michael Jones' indignation at the registration the powers-that-be issued for the first: 'BADN.

"How can I sell that?" he exploded. He was so incensed he got the Registration Board to change it. Reluctantly they did so, but I don't think they ever got the point.

CLUB NEWS: OCTOBER 1972

It's early October and with it the briefest of Indian Summers to set seal on summer '72, the weather for which must have set an all-time low. Indeed it was bitterly cold on September 17th, the occasion of our last Full Display at Fairoaks. The cold grey overcast on that day must have kept thousands away, which was a pity for the actual show was perhaps one of the finest the Tiger Club has ever put on. I used to think that things weren't what they used to be. "No one," I used to assert, "could formate as we used to do," and I wasn't alone in believing that the good times and good flying belonged to yesterday. It simply isn't so. Some of the flying to be seen at Fairoaks was unsurpassed. Mark you, a cynic in me could have pointed out that the presence of a fully-equipped film unit was an irresistible draw to the pilots, who for the benefit of the cameras bore down on the crews in an unmerciful manner. A great day and a fitting final display to an extremely good season.

Our congratulations to Fred "Sausages" Marsh on becoming this year's Air Racing Champion. It's a title that's well deserved for no one has done more for the cause of Formula I racing than our Fred. He and his beloved "Pie in the Sky" Beta has been seen at every race venue up and down the country – and to paraphrase the current police recruiting cry: "Dull he isn't."

Whilst on bouquets, it's time I presented two. The first is to that dedicated team of Air Display helpers led by Roy Davis. Not for them the applause and the hustle for autographs, yet without them the shows could scarcely get off the ground. And there's a great bunch going to the Rollason boys for the consistently high maintenance of our aircraft and their abundant good humour and tolerance. Tolerance? Think of them when you've crept home late one summer's evening and they're still there to welcome you with a grin and to close the hangar doors behind you. (Incidentally I hope you stay behind to help them close up – their dinner is getting every bit as cold as yours!)

. . . This has been the Seaplane Section's year. In the last ten weeks they have flown no less than 95 hours and even better news is that the CAA have granted both Tom Freer and Keith Sissons the authority to check out for seaplane ratings. This is a considerable breakthrough for light flying and will ensure a continuity of pilots with seaplane ratings in a sector of aviating that was nearly allowed to fade away. Currently they are running a series of mid-week sorties off their improbable site down near Lydd in Kent.

. . . The date of the Annual Dinner Dance is established as Feb. 9th and this year it's to be held at the Inn on the Park. Tickets will be £5.50 and available soon. Again this year out-of-towners will be offered hospitality by members in London. There is already a list of willing hosts. Don't hesitate to drop me a line if you're coming down or flying in from overseas and I'll put you in touch. We aim to accommodate everyone, husbands, wives, fiancées and friends – the lot.

I couldn't resist including the cost of a ticket to our big occasion. That included dinner, a nice lady tinkling on a piano in a foyer, and of course the orchestra to dance to (who ever heard of a *band* at a swish hotel?).

LANDING FEES AT REDHILL

It is possible that not everybody is aware that the Club pays a block landing fee at Redhill on behalf of all its members. This means in theory that any member coming to Redhill piloting his own aircraft or even an aircraft belonging to another Club need not pay landing fees at Redhill when visiting on *bona fide* Club business.

Recently we have received a great many complaints from members who have in fact been charged fees and have also paid them, and there is some evidence that members are staying away as a result.

THERE IS NO NEED FOR ANY MEMBER TO PAY LANDING FEES AT REDHILL.

Please would you therefore explain this politely and firmly to the Tower operator when booking in if he is on duty. If he is not on duty mark your entry in the Club movements book: "TC." If you have any difficulty in establishing your *bona fides* to the tower operator on duty, please refer the matter to the Club secretary.

The so-called Tower operator was something of a misnomer. I think his only task was to log landings and take-offs. Of course if the odd punter unused to our ways sought him out the chances were he'd be clobbered for a fee. With hindsight it is now obvious that the then landlords had their eyes firmly on the value of land and were then in the initial stages of a well thought-out campaign to shift us. We innocently flew on.

NOTHING ON THE CLOCK BUT THE MAKER'S NAME
Following disastrous loss of everything right over the judges by a competitor in the Air Squadron:
    "He got so close I could see the whites of James' eyes."
    "First time I knew James' eyes had any whites."
    It *was* quite a moment – in the next judge's chair to James I was an inch clear of the canvas and revising estimates to alternates . . .'
I think the other Judges blamed me for the fright. I was never asked to judge again.

CLUB NEWS: NOVEMBER – DECEMBER 1972
November and it's suddenly only weeks away from Christmas. It's raining hard outside and tomorrow I'm Duty Check Pilot at Redhill. It's a sobering thought – a Tiger in winter, and yet the pilot I'm to check has come from the other side of the world and an important part of his itinerary is this very initiation. I think that we who are close to the Club and within easy reach of the airfield can't comprehend the attraction of our Club to its far-flung membership. It's almost a sort of Mecca. And the Club goes from strength to strength. It's a good moment at the end of the year to tot up its assets. Total membership is now 700-plus, of which around 600 are pilots. The best news of all is that 1973 is going to be the Club's best year. Trouble is I can't mention the reason for thinking so, but will be able to reveal next month. Incidentally it's the Club's seventeenth year coming up.

Even though the weather continues rough, there's been a lot of flying out at Redhill including a series of night-flying schedules. These evenings are great fun and seem to arise spontaneously with someone asking for the goosenecks the moment it seems all the aircraft are bedded down for the night. Just a word of caution however to all Club pilots. In a Club like ours where 90% of flying decisions are left to the individual, a healthy degree of self-discipline is expected. For many years we've run a system of 'do-it-yourself' fines for the odd moment when your flying or actions could have been more considerate. You know the sort of thing: failure to refuel after a long trip, leaving the a/c out of line, or unchecked in threatening weather. Such lapses are judged by your own conscience and the self-imposed fine of 25p has long helped the Legal Fund. What isn't so widely known is that the Duty/Check pilot or a Committee man can clobber the careless aviator with an 'on-the-spot' fine as well. I know it only happens about once in a blue moon but if it does happen to you reflect that a word of restraint may prevent a busted airframe, and anyway the Legal Fund is a most worthy cause. Incidentally the task of running it has fallen to James Baring, who has inherited well over £1,300. The target for '73 is £2,000. Our grateful thanks go to Jack Piercy who retires from the job as custodian after many successful years. If you look like falling foul of legislation and need advice contact James B. immediately. He will keep the Committee informed, and if help is needed the chances are you'll have the support of collective experience and the chance of financial help too.

. . . Our Christmas Party is to be held at the Kronfeld. Do come along and join in. The Kronfeld Club is, as you know, the Tiger Club's London rendezvous, but because of very limited hours of opening it hasn't proved the success it deserves. Late news indicates however a complete change of policy and practically a new Committee to implement it. 1973 should be the Kronfeld's year too, but only with your help. More later when the new committee gets over the initial shock of election and gets down to work.

There's a New Year's Eve Breakfast Patrol at Redhill on December 31st between 9.30 and 10.15 am. It's being run jointly by the Redhill branch of the PFA and the Tiger Club. There's a free breakfast if you can creep in unseen. Everyone's welcome. (Me, I've booked the Active: that should warm things up a bit.)

And that was the coldest-ever Breakfast Patrol. It was so cold that it took half an hour to start the Active. Eventually Jim placed a trestle under the rear of the fuselage and the new position took the engine so much by surprise it started.

A good tip this, it applies to all Gipsy Majors, or so Jim Ellis used to say, and he should know. I imagine fifty years continuous care of those DH beauties ought to make him something of an expert. As ever the Club owed a lot to our maintenance team. A team that was virtually unbroken for our entire time at Croydon and Redhill. There are times a mere "Thank you" is never enough.

1973

'TOO GOOD' FACTOR, REVITALISED KRONFELD, CASTLE WATER AND PARK LANE DINNER

In presenting chunks of the *"Tiger Rag"* in this book I seem to have introduced a 'too-good-to-be-true' factor. I wasn't aware, but Trudi pointed it out as she prepared to type up this new chapter. Was I not living in a dream world? she asked; it can't all have been so wonderful – life isn't like that. Was I, she queried, guilty of painting an unreal picture, because that's what old age prefers to look back on?

It's a good point. If I've a failing as an historian it's that my natural optimism will always push aside the nasty bits – after all who wants to drag them up? But I do believe, with hand on heart, things were as I described them. After all, the Club News excerpts were penned at the time; if it hadn't been for real I'd have faced contradictions. I didn't.

There's no denying that the Club, and life in general, faced its nasty bits. The early seventies were soon to become a time of radical change, mostly political, and much of it a painful experience. Power cuts, fuel shortages, strikes, plus the uncomfortable knowledge that a powerful unionism sometimes ran the country. Since unpleasant facts of life were a universal function of survival, wasn't it a pointless exercise to go on about them? So my philosophy ran.

The Tiger Club always – and this quite unthinkingly – tried to maintain an insular view and kept its collective eye on our ambitions. The Club was about flying, about true friendship, about mutual trust and we shared a genuine belief we were going in the right direction. There was a small downside, but the Club, quite rightly and fully in the traditional British manner, got on with the job. Our world remained buoyant and cheerful.

And nothing could have been more cheerfully positive than the opening report to greet the New Year.

CLUB NEWS: JANUARY 1973
In every walk of life there are firsts. However, once in a while there is an occasion that just doesn't register as a simple first but shouts "great" right out loud. It happened at Redhill on the last day of 1972, on a Sunday that was crisply cold with clear blue skies above a chill haze. The sort of morning it's just good to be alive on. The local Strut of the PFA had organised a Redhill Breakfast Patrol and Neil Williams and his fellow wildmen were firmly in charge. By 9 o'clock 18 frozen pilots and crews vapour-puffed their way into an assortment of aircraft and took off into the wonderful still air to patrol for intruders. Arrival time 9.30-10.15 – with a free breakfast for anyone to get through without being identified by registration.

We took up our positions around the airfield and began searching, scarcely expecting anyone to materialise out of the near-fog that had settled to the north and west. LAP was grounded, so were Fairoaks, Blackbushe and even Booker beyond. But yet they came, and the sky became a hunter's paradise with aircraft wheeling and turning, everyone either a determined McCudden or Richtofen depending on which side they were on. But the best was to come. If there was an indication of something special afoot when I got back to the circuit, it was as nothing to the sight that greeted our eyes when we taxied in. No less than 50 visiting aircraft had struggled through the morning mists to have breakfast with us. To see over 70 colourful aircraft alive in the now bright sunshine was heartwarming indeed. 200 breakfasts back in the Langley canteen where Mavis Harriot and her valiant team turned out eggs and bacon and baked beans and bread and butter and strong tea. It was a wild success, it didn't even matter that two aircraft had foiled our defences, it only mattered that our first breakfast patrol had been such unqualified fun. Had the weather not clamped over so many friendly airfields the total number of visiting aircraft would surely have been around the 100. To that keen local PFA group the congratulations of dozens of us who had forgotten the joys of getting up early and flying, and who were induced to leave warm beds and come along to defend our airfield. That 50 mins in the Active was so blissful I nearly forgot my incipient frostbite.

This Club News, quite rightly I suppose, can still only record the fun of Xmas. There was something special too about this year's Wine and Cheese party at the Kronfeld. I left around 11 pm but I know from one weary barman, i.e. Tony Baptiste, that the party went from strength to strength until 1.30 am. Once again we thank Mavis Harriot and Hazel Prosper for organising the food. I think we ought to award something or other to Mavis, but until then she'll get my bouquet of the month, offered on behalf of all revellers and with grateful thanks.

Neil Williams' brother is an aviation artist of considerable ability, so I have no hesitation in promoting the fact that he is open to commissions in oil for as little as £21.00 including the frame. Historic aviation subjects a speciality. All this I gladly confirm for I am the proud owner of nearly three of his works: nearly, because the Gladiator is still en route!

The Kronfeld Club is closing down on the 3rd Feb. for two months to enable members to redecorate and refurbish. We hope to re-open on April Fools' Day (we're not superstitious) with a great new meeting place for aviation folk and a party to match the occasion. The Club will be open 5 nights a week and with the sort of welcome you'll want to come back to. This Newsletter will be the last chance to publicise the Club's big event, the Annual Dinner Dance. It's at the Inn on the Park on Feb. 9th. Tickets at £5.50 may still be available – phone Michael Jones.

A week before there's going to be an informal film show at the Kronfeld. It's on Sat. 3rd Feb. at 7.30 and the main film is the 35 mm master copy of the Tiger Club show that was filmed at Fairoaks last summer. I've seen a preview and I know everyone will enthuse – it's destined for public release later this year. All are welcome, especially the pilots and crews. I'm told there's room for 60! The bar will be open and, as they say, this could well turn out to be quite a party.

The best news I've saved till last. In the last issue I mentioned that 1973 looked like being a special year, and I can't think of a better way to begin it than to record that our Chairman, Norman Jones, has purchased a wild stretch of reclaimed land just below Rye, within which there is a lake (two in fact): just the place for the Club's seaplane. It's all very premature, and there is a lot of work before the site is ready. On the land between the lakes there's the added bonus of a small firm strip for visitors to fly in on. The site is exciting, not only because it's the first home for those seaplane nomads, but also for those who appreciate the windswept peace of it all.

Finally (and I had nearly forgotten), on behalf of all our members, congratulations to Norman on his much-deserved award of the MBE in the New Year's Honours List.

This issue of the *"Tiger Rag"* was arguably the most newsworthy of any of the previous fifteen years. If worrying bits lurked – and our tenancy at Redhill was getting progressively stressful for starters – it never showed, we simply wouldn't permit it. Take the Kronfeld saga, for instance. The Kronfeld Club was originally born of an idea to provide a London haven for the gliding fraternity. It started up in a damp basement in London's Belgravia close to the Victoria mainline terminal. It was the mid-sixties, but from its inception the membership was never enough to provide either coverage or an adequate income. There were no paid employees, DIY was the name of the game.

Shortly after the Kronfeld started the Tiger Club was invited to join and Norman negotiated a block membership for us. The trouble – and throughout its life it never went away – was that the Club simply wasn't accessible. On the face of it the Kronfeld couldn't have been better situated: reality said otherwise. Few lived nearby and it lacked essential overnight and dining facilities to draw in the out-of-towner. To visit between other commitments was tedious, and car parking was difficult.

That was the down-side, the up-side was our boundless enthusiasm, a ground rental of about six pounds a week and a nigh-on sixty-year lease. Damp it might be but it had several rooms, a fine bar, equipment for films and a small lecture room as well (Heaven knows what the worth of that apartment in Ecclestone Square would be today).

In spite of all the difficulties we decided to give a hand. It sounded grand enough, a meeting place in the centre of London for flying types in a 'social aeronautical atmosphere.' Michael Jones and I accepted directorships and we all set about redecorating the place. It's a sad tale really. Before me I have aged copies of duty rotas, e.g. someone to open up and act as barman. We dragged everyone in to help. But in the end it was to fail. A glorious failure.

Michael Jones was again at his regular stint of the past year's statistics. In 1972 we flew to no less than twenty-three different airfields giving Participation Displays. There were four Full Tiger Club Displays, six

Formula 1 Races, a total of thirty-three displays and race meetings. No mean achievement. There was however a startling statistic revealed in the summary. For the second year in a row just a total of thirty pilots flew the displays. Of course a show, any show, wasn't just about pilots, many others helped, but did so few pilots really fly so much? If one thinks about it it's a possibility, for display pilots, jealous of their skills and hesitant to fly wingtip to wingtip with an unknown, would maintain that safety factor. Even so I was surprised.

CLUB NEWS: MARCH – APRIL 1973

When last I wrote the *"Rag"* sometime back in February the weather was all winter and the Turbs nearly had their snow shoes put on. Today only eight weeks later spring is really with us and Redhill is at its loveliest. And so much has happened in those passing weeks.

The Annual Dinner Dance was a great success. No other word for it. It was held for the first time at the Inn on the Park and every ticket was sold – the first time the demand has exceeded the seat availability. The food was fine and service so good we sought out the management to congratulate them. Everyone had a fine time too, all except perhaps Howard Hughes somewhere upstairs. We did, of course, invite him, not that anyone really expected him to pop down, but we would have liked to have honoured a fine aviator, a fact that is now so often overlooked.

The list of awards is long and worthy.

DAWN-TO-DUSK AWARDS

Duke of Edinburgh Trophy	Lucien Hankart/Mike Bialkewicz
Medallion	Colin Corp (3rd place)
Icarus Trophy	Mike Bialkewicz
Pilot Trophy	Carol Gillam
Bonney Trophy	Jane Goodger
Longest Distance Medallion	Mike Bialkewicz
Enterprising Entry Medallion	John Wilks
Best Log Book Medallion	Lucien Hankart

AEROBATICS AWARDS

McAully Trophy	Mike Watkins
Medallion	Tony Bianchi
Medallion	Ian Senior
Air Squadron Trophy	Roy Legg
Medallion	R.J. Guess
Medallion	Frances MacRae
De Havilland Trophy	Neil Williams
Medallion	James Black
Esso Trophy	Roy Legg
Medallion	Peter Phillips
Clem Pike Trophy	Jack Piercy
De Salis Trophy	Jane Barker
Air Racing Medallion	Roy Berry
Foreign Touring Medallion	Vincent Redding
Glider Towing Medallion	Robert Christie

THE CHAIRMAN'S SPOON

The chairman's hand-carved wooden spoon is specially awarded in 1973 to that member of the Club who entered a number of competitions and demonstrated his ability to be a cheerful losing sportsman.

Winner: Andrew Chadwick.

The team who prepared the ground for this most excellent evening included Andrew Chadwick and David Hamilton. Our thanks to them all, and especially Andrew, for it was he who designed the magnificent table decorations and menu. Let it be known too that he is responsible for the new "Tiger Rag" presentation.

. . . I've been inundated with poster stickers and even franking machine advertising all declaring: 'What in the world is "G.B."?' "G.B." himself must have had even more! It may be declaring the new review at the Westminster Theatre, but to countless Tiger Club members the world over it refers to our beloved "G.B." down there in Gloucestershire. A timely reminder, "G.B.", that you're not forgotten.

Such are the limited facilities at Redhill in the Clubroom these days it would be wise when visiting at weekends to pack a picnic lunch. The 20 or so lunches prepared are quickly booked up and visitors must make do with a slice of Hobson's Choice and a cup of coffee. Sad but true, so come prepared.

Couldn't resist, just this once, including the full list of award winners, and, when you think of it, how better to illustrate the scope of the Tiger Club activities? The Guest of Honour, and this time one we really welcomed, was the ever-popular Rex Smith.

Norman's Wooden Spoon was carved by Norman himself. In later years when he moved away from active Club involvement he busied himself down at Rye carving all sorts of wooden things. I treasure a nut-cracker. It sits before me on my desk as I write, a constant reminder of the Boss's attitude to every challenge. It's engraved: A NUT TO CRACK.

TIMMIS TOURING, WELCOME SECOND SEA TURB, GOODBYE SEA TIGER AND NEW A/C

All this attention to display flying and racing tended to overlook the touring side of the Club. So often more flying hours were put in by this laid-back lot than all the other disciplines put together.

David Timmis, who was then Touring Secretary, put out his wares to tempt newcomers to a completely different way to fly. Reading it today it sounds all too good to be true.

TOURING NEWSLETTER 1973

INTRODUCTION

Each year we plan about six touring events including one or two 'At Homes.' We have long established associations with Clubs such as Beauvais and Osnabrück whom we see each year usually. The rest of the events are always to new places.

On the notice board at Redhill I have put up the events for this year. If you are interested in coming on any of them, put your name up and tick the appropriate column or columns and, if possible, let me know direct.

The touring side of the Club is all very informal and, as far as most of us are concerned, we like the flying and do not feel obliged to spend too much when we arrive at places. Even taxis are quite reasonable abroad when there are four or five people on board.

We do not see many private owners and their aircraft on these events. Please join us on one or more events if you can fit them in.

LILLE 'AT HOME'

The first of two 'At Home' events planned for 1973 will start the season off and take place at Redhill on May 13th.

We first contacted Lille-Lesquin Flying Club in 1972 and this year we have invited them for a one-day visit. They will arrive about midday on the Sunday. We shall probably go to a restaurant for lunch. I would hope for about 10-15 Tiger Club members to join in, so please let me know if you would like to meet the Lille people, as well as others in the Tiger Club who are interested in touring, for a get-together.

ABBEVILLE

As our first 'away' fixture a short flight to Abbeville on the Somme near the mouth of the estuary is about 1¼ hours from Redhill. It is between Berck and Beauvais and about fifteen minutes on from Berck. The date is May 20th, and it is a one-day visit on the Sunday with an opportunity of sampling the local Normandy – or should I say Norman – fare at a hostelry nearby no doubt.

We would arrive at Abbeville about midday and leave about 4.00 pm. You will have to allow for Customs at Ashford or elsewhere. It should be possible to arrange Customs at Abbeville.

OSNABRÜCK RALLY

As a result of a number of proposals and suggestions coming from Osnabrück and the Tiger Club, we are trying something new this year. It is really a development of our 'At Home' events which have been taking place successfully since 1966 at Redhill and Atterheide.

The 1973 rally will take place from 1st-4th June in Germany and involve four Flying Clubs, Osnabrück, Tiger Club, Beauvais and Angers Flying Clubs. The assembly point will be Cologne-Bonn airport, where participants should arrive in the afternoon of the 1st June. From there we shall go to the Steigenberger Hof Hotel in Bonn and a dinner dance will take place in the evening.

There will be some flying competitions and these will start as early as possible on the 2nd June with a flight from Bonn to Kiel. This will take the form of a navigation exercise in which accuracy of flying and the identification of features on the ground will figure prominently. Our accommodation at Kiel will be at the 1972 Olympic Sailing Centre. In order to give non-flyers and passengers a chance in the competitions, we shall then take to boats and do some deep-sea fishing in the Baltic. The biggest catch will decide the winner.

On Sunday the 3rd June the plan is to have the morning free and then fly from Kiel to Osnabrück. This will end with a timed arrival and spot-landing competition at Atter. The last competition will be a non-flying contest and will be an archery competition taking place near the airfield. You will be discouraged from shooting arrows at aeroplanes! In the evening we shall have the final dinner and prize-giving.

Departure for England, if you do not decide to take a week's holiday after all that, will be Monday 4th June. All the Hotels will be booked for us and I do not think that anybody will suffer from boredom.

I am expecting the official programme to arrive about the middle of April, when it will be displayed on the notice board at Redhill. Because there are four Clubs taking part the maximum from the Tiger Club will be 7-8 aircraft. 2-3 are already going, so book early and tell me.

CLERMONT-FERRAND 'AT HOME'

This is not the first time that we have invited the d'Auvergne Flying Club from Clermont-Ferrand to Redhill. However, bad weather has precluded this in the past.

The provisional date this summer is June 30th-July 2nd. This has yet to be confirmed and any change in date will be notified. They will arrive on the Saturday afternoon. We shall receive them in the room we usually have adjoining the hangar. I would like to emphasise how much the Club appreciates the efforts of those who help on these occasions. We need volunteers to make tea, get the room straight, provide transport and organise who goes in which car if a large number of them arrive, to minimise the waiting around. We think it is a good idea, too, if some of the visitors can stay with Club members. It is preferable, as a lot of us know when we go abroad, and gives people a much better understanding of the country as well as being easier on the pocket. Anybody who can do this on the Saturday and Sunday nights – please let me know.

We shall arrange a dinner for the Saturday night near Redhill. Any Club member is welcome. On Sunday we shall take them out for the day in a motor coach to show them some places of interest. They will depart on Monday morning.

ANNUAL TOUR

A week's tour is planned this summer for August 4th-12th inclusive. I am considering going to Scandinavia to visit Denmark, Norway and Sweden. One does not want to be flying necessarily every day and flights of 300 nm are usually enough for one day – so taking it in easy stages. A very interesting route would be as follows:

Flying day 1:   Redhill to North Holland, say Gröningen.
Flying day 2:   Gröningen to Spjald – home of Denmark's vintage flying Club near Ringköbing.
Flying day 3:   Spjald – Gothenberg – Oslo.

Flying day 4:	Oslo – Stockholm or somewhere next to a lake in Sweden like Jönköping.
Flying day 5:	To Copenhagen.
Flying day 6:	To Redhill or stop over in Holland or Belgium.

There would be very little high ground to encounter on this route and I would anticipate that the coastline and island flying in Scandinavia would be fascinating. Of course, you would need radio. A detailed programme and itinerary will be available nearer the time.

David Timmis was something of a Jekyll and Hyde. He was in appearance and fact very much a City man, a quietly-spoken courteous soul; beneath this façade, though, dwelt an unexpected buccaneering explorer's spirit. Put him in a cockpit and this unassuming man became a highly competitive, almost fearless, adventurer. Sadly, many years later, he was to die in a freak flying accident. If bad weather clamped you could trust David to get through, his exceptional skills made him the ideal precision pilot he became. It takes a steely determination to take a tricky biplane – the Arrow Active – *sans* brakes, radio or any but primitive instrumentation, up into the Arctic Circle so he could venture somewhere new. That was David.

SEAPLANE SECTION

There is much activity down at Rye in preparation for the start of the season at the new site that Norman has bought as a seaplane development. The site, now named the Castle Water Estate Co., is adjacent to Camber Castle, on the flat area just south of Rye town.

Entrance by road is halfway along Harbour Road, the road from Rye to Rye Harbour; inside the entrance there is a cottage being refurbished as a Clubhouse, a hangar for the Sea Turbulent (it is not large enough for the Sea Tiger), and a slipway (somewhat soggy) to the water. The main lake is about half a mile to the south-west of the entrance.

The Turbulent is already there, and has made its first flight on the new pair of floats – built like the earlier pair, with great expertise, by John Urmston. The Sea Tiger, in resplendent new colours after an extensive overhaul, will be going down by road from Rollasons during the last week in March, and is expected to make its first flight during the weekend March 31st/April 1st. For details of the ensuing summer programme, contact Keith Sissons or Tom Freer, or see Redhill notice board. The main effort will be directed to enabling as many members as possible to obtain Seaplane Licences.

Committee minutes: March '73

Seaplane:
   1. *All goes well, Sea Turbulent flown.*
   2. *Lambing in progress.*
   3. *Two Tigers in formation over Rye (bad manners).*
   4. *Raft will be ready for use in one week.*
   5. *Sea Tiger next week.*

Norman was already torn between irate farmers, early 'nimbyism,' and a Seaplane Section rearing to go.

. . . New aircraft abound. Robin Voice's beautiful Cosmic Wind "Filly" – he's been building it in the hangar for ages – has flown successfully and indeed Robin is now busy racing in the Formula 1 series. Another racer of considerable interest is Tom Storey's personal Cassutt. He has recently fitted the most remarkable pair of wings to this diminutive machine. They are wafer-thin mahogany, skinned with the sort of glass finish associated with sailing dinghies. Potent isn't the word for it. Ralph Hart's blue and silver Currie Wot is flying well. Another member with a grin from ear to ear is Martin Barraclough, whose new Piper Arrow replaces his Jodel 1050 which I believe has gone to John Urmston whose Puss Moth has gone to Tony Haig-Thomas who's lent it to the Southend Museum – or so the story goes.

One aircraft that hasn't stayed with us is the Sea Tiger, which unfortunately got badly bent recently. Given time and help Tom Freer hopes eventually to get it rebuilt. If anyone has the wish to lend a hand I know Tom would be most grateful. Drop him a line. The Kronfeld Club still goes strongly but has temporarily given ground to the hot weather and is now only open Monday to Thursday. Full five-day opening will recommence in October. It remains the cheapest and best meeting place in London and the new Acting Secretary, David Carroll, will welcome ideas for parties and get-togethers.

How lightly I had skated over the first demise of our Sea Tiger. In a quick reference to committee minutes I noted the Sea Turb had had an early accident in April, and was already out of the picture, and now in July the stark announcement:

Seaplane: 1. Accident reported – not bad airmanship. Badly damaged.
2. Volunteer required to tackle problems as they arise. T. Freer to report progress.
3. Water skiers to be thanked officially.
4. K. Sissons will report on possible improvements to water.

All this was Norman-speak. Interpreted, it read: Tiger hit obstruction in water, water skiers rushed to rescue. Who's going to put it together? (Whole committee look at Tom.) And in case anyone thinks we were having a go at Tom, have Keith do something too. Simple.

The remains of our Sea Tiger were re-positioned to the Redhill hangar where Tom, almost single-handed, rebuilt her. It took a long time. Tom was an airline man, a master navigator of the old school, a practised sailor, but nothing in his CV offered a mechanical bent. His was a lonely and tedious learning curve.

TIGER QUIPS à la Redhill:
B.S. "So I juddered my way around a loop and then rolled straight at the top."
S.T. "We were so low I could tell the difference in ducks on the lake."

"These are terrible, I had three to make sure." Benjy eating mints at Tiger Ball.

TWO-MINUTE WILLOW WREN, CROYDON CLOSES – ALMOST

CLUB NEWS: AUTUMN/WINTER 1973

It's well and truly autumn (it's early November) and all the usual warnings of winter are with us – power cuts, fuel shortages and the odd strike. Once upon a time it was only the onset of the cold weather that heralded the season. How times change! A great deal has happened since the longest and best summer any of us can remember, even now the leaves linger as though reluctant to relinquish their beauty.

Evidence that the longer evenings are upon us is the talk of another New Year's Day Breakfast Patrol. It's organised by the Redhill Strut of the PFA. . . . Book your aircraft early, it's going to be a sell-out of an occasion. The evening film shows have begun again. Take your lead to the programmes from the Redhill notice board. Even the hangar has taken on a new look with a row of fresh offices alongside the Duty Pilot's encampment. Few new aircraft are apparent but then there is so little room for any. True, there was a flutter of interest when the regulars in the hangar were joined by an old Piper Colt en route for Rochester. But alas, it's gone now. Those who did fly it expressed no regret.

. . . Also for sale is what is probably the oldest glider in the country. It's the Willow Wren which is the oldest aircraft on the Tiger Club register but is now surplus to requirements. It has for some years languished down at Rochester and might now fetch around £750. Any offers?

At long last Croydon has closed and the last lingering connections with flying have been severed. Rollasons have been forced to move, some to Redhill and the rest down to Shoreham. It was fourteen years ago that we the Tiger Club moved out of Croydon, leaving the famous field to the developers.

We occasionally get news of Tiger Club branches from abroad. Before me I have a copy of the *"Tiger Rag"* New Zealand-style. It's full of interest and Tiger Moths. Already they have a 100-plus membership. From all of us to all of you down there a Very Happy Xmas and long may your branch thrive.

The Seaplane is being repaired but it will certainly be a long job. Tom Freer again asks for help to put it together. If it's within your power to do some good please give him a ring. The target is flying again on Castle Waters by June '74.

. . . 1973 was quite a year for Air Displays. James Black was the successful director and I know that he is now looking to pilots to begin the necessary practising for the '74 season. If you reckon you have it in you to fly to high standards demanded – yet only need the opportunity – give James a ring. He and his team are on the lookout for new talent. James Baring's party in aid of the Legal Fund was very very good but it was not quite what he expected. All his old friends turned up of course, yet not one newcomer. What an opportunity lost!

Extraordinary as it may seem the aged Willow Wren glider had been in the Tiger Club collection for eight years. A not-far-off guess put its airborne time at about one-and-a-half minutes. Sadly, from the historical point of view, she had to go.

And I got the bit about 'Croydon's lingering connections with flying have been severed' quite wrong. In 1980 I was to spend three months setting up a BIG Tiger Club display there to commemorate Amy Johnson's flight to Australia. It was tight, not more than 400 metres of runway, we were weaving around high-rise blocks, the occupants waving as they looked down on the pilots as they flew by. Anyway it worked and 50,000 spectators had a great day out. I won't spoil future volumes if I reveal that wasn't the last Tiger Club flying there . . .

1974 promised much.

1974

MERRY-GO-ROUND, FUEL CRISIS, WRIGHT FIELD
AND THE REDHILL BATTLE

I start the 1974 chapter armed with a sense of rueful hindsight. It was a year of political turmoil, upsets that touched the Club momentarily and, as if it were the proverbial water off a duck's back, was shrugged away with firm abandon; we had it all before us and nothing was going to come between the Club and that exciting future.

But not everything could be shrugged off that easily. A shrug was fine for the main chance where strength was shared by a huge membership now well over 800 – yet there remained a more intimate reflection, at least in *my* life and that's where the 'rueful hindsight' showed a personal face.

I won't be the first to learn that money born of a devotion to work doesn't necessarily equate with happiness. While my firm, now called Benjamin Knitwear, was even then topping a million turnover, my health and private life was crumbling. No grumbles, but the Tiger Club story I unfold would be the less if I failed to count the cost of just one member's willing commitment to the Club over and above a 25-hour day.

Not that I got off the merry-go round, to do so never entered my mind – I was too busy.

CLUB NEWS: JANUARY— FEBRUARY 1974

I think the item most remembered at the close of 1973 was the effect the fuel crisis had on the Tiger Club. The 50% voluntary cut in flying was, and indeed still is, a most restricting business but the request that we make Sunday a non-flying day has put a lot of us on the spot. It was agreed in Committee that it was both the right thing to do and as a good PR job best complied with, but we are trying to get the request rescinded since it soon became obvious so many of our members had only the Sunday available to them to get airborne. Consequently there is still a wee degree of aviating on Sundays but we urge those who do fly that day to restrain their aviating to quietish aircraft and where possible to make straight in-and-out take-offs and landings with the minimum of circuiting and the maximum of height. Whew!

There, that's put paid to legend, for it had become a standing joke that I always began the *"Tiger Rag"* with a review of the weather and the beauty of Redhill at any given time of the year. Well, the weather so far has been mild and wet, with all the regular glistening wet grass patches to avoid (why does it always seem muddier at the top of a rise?). But for once I report with dismay that the airfield does look different, for a reason I never thought possible. Some heathen butcher has chopped away that lovely apple tree wood that had crept across the neck of the north-south runway to the old pump house. In its place is a rooty stubble of ugliness. In fairness the visibility to the east of the hangar has improved, but oh! at what a cost.

. . . It's sad to begin 1974 with a groan, but even in deepest Surrey we have came up against a potential developer . . . in this case our landlords. Whilst we have every confidence that the remaining seven years of our lease is safe we are forced to protect our interests in the courts, such is the apparent determination to have us moved. All this will cost dearly so the Committee has unreservedly placed the resources of the Legal Fund at the Club's disposal. Although confident of the outcome, the Committee quite rightly takes the threat seriously and should any Club member feel that he is in a position to offer help or advice – perhaps with a word in the right ear, preferably our landlords' – he should contact Michael Jones.

Members, I am sure, will be glad to know that a branch of the Tiger Club has been started in Portugal, the Hon. Sec. being Mrs Anneliese Pinto. It is nice to think we now have branches in Portugal, South Africa, America, Australia and New Zealand.

. . . Michael has asked me to include a notice that, when visiting John Wright's delightful strip at Rydinghurst, pilots are asked to avoid the nearby pub, the Leathern Bottle and the adjoining A281 like the plague. The landlord, it seems, is positively hostile, shame on him!

Even today my face breaks out in a grin at the shenanigans that were daily fare down at Rydinghurst. To start with, John Wright was yet another ripe character and this time an ex-naval one. Not everyone loved him of course, the Leathern Bottle landlord least of all. John, who must have been frightened by a woman when young, couldn't resist unwanted advice to the fair sex; he wasn't always liked in that quarter either, yet he had a depth of understanding and a joyous approach to living, probably the result of having beaten death by his reputed eight crashes, seven of them in wartime aircraft at sea. The only civilian one I can recall was when his two-seat Piper Cub (carrying three) piled up short at Fairoaks.

Nothing ordinary ever seemed to happen to him. In Book One I recounted our hasty departure from his strip pursued by an irate wife. We were off to Baden Baden enticed by his "we'll be alright there, you'll see."

His ongoing war with the landlord took many forms, ideas born of a fertile mind. On one visit he related with glee that he'd crept out and inflated a bladder in the pub's outfall.

"What happened?"

"I don't know yet," he answered. "I only did it last night."

John was hospitable, his farmhouse a rambling place, his second wife a tolerant soul. He kept about three aircraft in tiny hangarage and overnight stays were memorable for gin and massive breakfasts. I once got seventeen eggs on my plate – tiny ones of course. All he'd asked was: "Do you like eggs?" And he'd go rough-shooting day or night at the drop of a hat. We all missed him and his small strip when he upped and went to live in Devon, but memories linger and they lighten the day.

The new year also brought us a letter from our Chairman. Wrote Norman:

"Dear Member,

We are sorry to have to inform you that considerable increases have now got to be made to our subscription and flying rates. Sporting flying is going through uncertain times; we have the present fuel crisis, increased demands for land and premises in the London area, new taxes and the same inflation which affects everybody.

In 1973 we decided to hold all rates to the 1972 levels. This was in response to a general appeal and to lessen the impact of value-added-tax. Unfortunately we suffered not only the normal inflationary increases in costs but also two fuel price increases and in October we had to introduce an emergency surcharge on all flying rates. Now we have a further major rise in fuel prices. For 1974 it has therefore been found necessary to make a substantial overall increase which will incorporate the 5% surcharge already levied and take account of steeply-rising maintenance and other costs. The current fuel situation, if it continues, will have a very marked effect on utilisation and may well cause us to re-examine the rates in a few months time.

To compound our difficulties, we are now also faced with the problem of renewing our lease at Redhill Aerodrome. It appears that not only do our landlords wish to raise our present rental to more than double our existing commitment but also they do not at present consider that they can even offer us the reasonable security of tenure to which we feel that the Club is entitled.

With the support of all our members we will be able to maintain our position and to meet every adversity with good heart."

Having a good heart was a favourite expression of the Boss; it presumably helped with the new flying rates. There were now fourteen different types to sample, fifteen if you reckoned the Super Tiger, as different a machine from the 'Cooking' variety as could be imagined. Fuel shortage or not, we were in clover.

FLYING RATES TO TAKE EFFECT FROM 1ST FEBRUARY 1974
(EXCLUSIVE OF V.A.T.)

TIGER MOTH	£8.16
STAMPE	£8.52
TURBULENT	£4.68
FOURNIER RF.4	£5.64
JODEL DR.1050	£8.52
JODEL D.150	£8.52
JODEL D.140	£11.04
CONDOR 100	£8.16
SUPER CUB	£9.12
SEA TIGER (when available)	£9.12
ARROW ACTIVE (when available)	£9.12
BETA (when available)	£9.12
NIPPER (when available)	£4.68
WASSMER (when available)	£11.28

TOP: Michael Jones, Gavin Dix and a thirsty Tony Haig-Thomas. Lunchtime in the Clubroom at Redhill. Photo: Author's collection.

BOTTOM: Another evocative shot of Redhill's Clubroom at lunchtime. Easily spotted is Tessa Lovell – wearing shades – and Dick Barnby praying to be served next. Photo: Author's collection.

TOP: Could be nowhere but Dunstable. A Club Condor, G-AYFE, at work c.1970. Rollasons built 50 of these sturdy machines, several were converted for towing. Photo: via Michael Jones.

BOTTOM: The Willow Wren – once well-known at Dunstable. The only glider the Club ever had on its books. In its eight years it flew but once, a flight time of under two minutes. Originally built in 1931, it remains the oldest high-performance sailplane in Britain. Photo: via Michael Jones.

TOP: Redhill, looking north-west. A rare sight, for there were few full Tiger Club displays here. It brought home to us all the real size of Redhill. Photo: Author's collection.

BOTTOM: Looking south, Redhill airfield as it is now. A new ATC building replaces the old pumphouse, centre left. Yet Redhill's grassy charm remains. Gatwick looms large in the background. Photo: via Michael Jones.

TOP: Peter Vanneck's own Lord Mayor's Show, November 1977. Neil leads; they are wisely well-spaced as atrocious conditions prevailed. Active, two Tigers and two bucking Stampes. Photo: via Ron Jacobs.

BOTTOM: The Rollason Team – still together after 43 years: John Sarrett, Mavis Harriott, Adrian "Dev" Deverell and the twins Jim and John Ellis, December 1998. Photo: Jim Alderton via Mavis Harriott. (Little-known fact – Mavis and the twins were also qualified pilots.)

The *"Tiger Rag"* was always open to express ideas, wants and sales.

WANT ADVENTURE?

Two Tiger Club members are planning a year-long sabbatical starting late 1975 aboard a new Solaris Catamaran. There is room for two more – 4-way costs and partnership. If you are interested phone the Editor, *"Tiger Rag."*

Someone must have planted the idea in my head that I needed a long break and the thought coincided with having been shown over a new Solaris 40-footer. I flipped. Poor Richard Ball fell in with the idea, but it came to nought, then; we did finally make it in the eighties though, an experience that left us wishing we hadn't.

Once in a blue moon the *"Rag"* published an article that breathed flying. Some folk can describe events – good reporters; some with added feeling – better reporters; but only one ever did so with such total conviction, such total belief, you were there. That man was Neil Williams. No? read Redhill Battle and believe.

THE REDHILL BATTLE

It actually all started on a breakfast patrol in the autumn of 1972. We had gone our independent ways, and some of us had been "shot down," i.e. had our registrations spotted by the defending aircraft. Amid an atmosphere of slight gruntlement we were reminiscing over the inevitable good old days, while we got stuck into our breakfasts. I was in the middle of describing a successful breakfast patrol when we had attacked with a formation of three aircraft when I suddenly thought: "Why not try five?"

Chris, who had flown the Rollason Tiger, was enthusiastic. Others were less so – "If you can't get through solo, how can you hope to do it in a big formation?"

It would obviously have to be carefully planned. We flew back thoughtfully to Redhill, and eventually the project slid into the background. Then came the news – Booker were setting up a breakfast patrol on the last Sunday in January '73. Quickly we made our plans and booked the aircraft. Obviously we couldn't go in low with a big formation, and in any case our normal airshow formations were cumbersome and unmanoeuvrable. We decided to use the battle formations practised by military units, as this would give us maximum flexibility.

Sunday dawned clear and calm, and soon the hangar became alive with voices and the rumble of opening doors. Briefing was at 07.30 and take-off planned for 08.00. But as we watched, the mist started to roll in across the airfield, although we could see blue sky straight up. This was the local Redhill fog, only 100 feet deep. Briefing over, we waited for a clearance, and as the time ticked away, Tony roared off in his car for a visibility check on the south side, which is usually better than in the hangar area.

"Better, but only just," was his report.

The latest take-off time was 09.00 as the breakfast patrol ended at 10.00, and at 08.45 I said: "Right, I'm going."

Individual decisions were made, Pete deciding to do a formation take-off with me and the others going independently. I decided to leave the final take-off decision until I could see for myself what conditions were like on the south side, and a few minutes later five biplanes trundled out into the swirling mist.

Things had improved somewhat near the south perimeter track as I lined up. Thumbs-up all round – once airborne we would have to divert anyway, but all the local airfields had good weather, and all the boys had full fuel and maps.

I dropped my hand and set three-quarter throttle, concentrating on keeping straight. Out of the corner of my eye I could see Pete, neatly tucked in. Ten seconds of basic instrument flying and we were on top in the clear winter sunshine. Pete was sitting happily in the No. 2 slot, his machine gleaming and sparkling in the crisp air. Vertical visibility was quite good, and we could see the blurred outlines of the other aircraft climbing up through the mist, suddenly coming into crystal focus as they broke out. Fifteen-second intervals, as briefed, and twenty seconds for the last man, Mike, in the Active, with his greater climbing speed. In a shallow port turn I could see them in a long line behind my tailplane as they closed in. I rolled out on course and waved Pete out into 'high-level battle'; no R/T here. At least nobody could hear that we were coming! At 1,500 feet over Reigate the formation was established, spread over a quarter of a mile of sky. Tony, the deputy leader, cruised 100 yards off my port wing, beyond him Chris in 'CDC. Pete was holding a steady position on my right; it was hard to believe that he was a relative newcomer to formation. Beyond him the Active hung nose up in the sky, its engine running at only just over half speed. This formation gave us complete cover – I could see all our aircraft and nobody could approach us undetected. The sun was brilliant behind us, silhouetting 'CDC like a painting against the silver morning, but ahead the darkening sky glowered at us, and the wind was against us, and picking up. Anxiously I looked at my watch, gauging the time remaining against our proposed route, allowing for the climb ahead of us, possible evasive action, and contemplating unknown contingencies.

Suddenly a flash of white, low, at two o'clock! A low-flying aircraft parallel to our track. Probably out of Biggin, I thought, searching the sky for the hundredth time. Then I saw it! Low, incredibly fast, streaking towards Fairoaks. At first I thought it was a small jet aircraft; it was only later that I found that it was Manx Kelly in the big Pitts making his first 'kill' of the morning – the aircraft from Biggin. As we cleared the TMA I increased power and lifted the nose. Now the weather was deteriorating – but this meant better cover! Over Blackbushe we wheeled slowly onto 330°, still climbing. By now my knees were shaking uncontrollably with cold – I hadn't bothered to wear a flying suit. Rain was spitting against the windscreen as the clouds lowered. We flew very wide around the defended area and cruised just beneath the airway to the west of Reading. As we cleared the airway we started our final climb, turning over Benson onto 100°. The boys were all huddled in their cockpits against the biting cold, but still steady in formation. Mike was weaving a bit, probably because he had to use more RPM to stop his engine from oiling up. Nine miles to go – still nothing in sight anywhere, surely we must be visible for miles in this great formation. Then I saw them, low, dead ahead, three aircraft, circling. As I watched I saw them pull out of the circle and start climbing. No panic, there's plenty of time. Again I increase power and we start climbing. No Cherokee can outclimb us, but as if they realise it they reduce their climb angle to increase their forward speed so that they can get under us. We have to descend soon, and our registrations are large on the underside of our wings. A flash of wings off to our right – another Cherokee curving in towards us, this one much higher up; this one is dangerous.

It is time – 0957 hours, three miles to go, speed 85 kt. I raise my arm vertically and the boys start sliding in into 'low-level battle.' From a broad short arrowhead to a long slender vee as I press the stick forward and start down. That Cherokee is close now and Mike has weaved again to get into position, swinging out towards the attacker. The three machines below have realised our intentions and are trying to head us off, but it is too late now as the whisper of the slipstream rises to a deep roar and the controls stiffen. Now the nose is really down, the ASI quivers exactly on VNE, somewhere a wire is screaming its protest, I glance in the rear-view mirror, I can see them all holding perfect formation, the dive angle is far too steep for a monoplane to follow, only a biplane could catch us now, and a very special biplane at that, but fortunately he is nowhere to be seen. I swallow hard, clearing my ears, still there is no activity ahead, the airfield is expanding rapidly beyond my shimmering propeller, another glance in the mirror, the boys are still there, even the Tiger, slow in the cruise, but fast in the dive with the aerobatic propeller. As we approach the boundary, I select smoke, as briefed, and the other two Stampes follow suit. I pull out low over the field and as I look back the sky is full of biplanes and smoke, three, four, five, yes, we've all made it! I rock my wings and join the circuit, and the boys join up close. As we run in to break I notice the Biggin Hill Stampe, painted in identical colours to ours. It transpired that Manx had got him in no mean fashion – that'll teach them to copy our colour schemes!

We taxy in and line up wingtip to wingtip. On the drop of a hand we all cut our engines together and climb out. All this just for a free breakfast, you ask? No. It's the fun, the companionship, the team spirit and above all the formation discipline which we have shown, especially away from base. It's the kind of image the Tiger Club used to have. It's real flying. The next patrol is at Shoreham. Anyone for biplanes?

GLOSSARY, CONNED BY D.F.B., REDHILL REMINISCENCES AND TRADITIONAL FOLK SONG

AVIATION GLOSSARY*

AIR TRAFFIC: A concentration of numerous aircraft over a given point, each demanding the same route and altitude and each having a special priority.

AIR TRAFFIC CLEARANCE: A verbal method of snarling the foregoing traffic.

ALTERNATE AIRPORT: The last item of a flight plan. The airport toward which no aircraft has sufficient fuel to proceed to.

BASIC VFR MINIMUMS: Those meteorological conditions under which a chicken can clear a low fence while maintaining satisfactory visibility.

COMMUNICATIONS CENTRE: Draughty, ill-kept, barn-like structure in which people congregate for dubious reasons.

CONTROL TOWER: Ornate glass cage exceptionally good for sunbathing.

FLIGHT PLAN: Piece of paper that arrives in the centre 30 minutes after aircraft concerned has checked over last radio fix.

IFR: Conditions under which colliding 'Birds' do not know for sure what they hit in flight!

* Any resemblance to reality is intentional.

With acknowledgements to Ralf Wefel and the Moth Club of California.

TRUE STORY

A well-known lady pilot of the Tiger Club, whilst visiting at White Waltham in a Turbulent, had occasion to seek help from a bystander. Alone with the task of swinging her prop she asked for a volunteer to sit in the cockpit and operate the switches. The stranger did so and when the engine fired it gradually opened up and there followed a very shaky take-off. Appalled at what had happened she ran trembling to the Clubroom, where she hid. Apparently it took quite a while to convince her it was all a joke.

Every year we all got the Club Calendar for the coming year. No way will I bore you with details but let the numerical aspect filter in.

There were to be eight UK Aerobatic Competitions and four abroad and every one had a healthy Club entry list. There were four Handicap Races and four Formula One races ahead of us, eight races with overwhelming Club participation.

Members would fly to seven European rallies – and then throw in a two-week annual tour. Five Full Displays were promised, and heaven knows how many smaller 'participations.'

CLUB NEWS: MARCH – APRIL 1974

I think the overwhelming impressions at Redhill this last two months have been: 1) the relief that petrol rationing is a thing of the past – we hope – and 2) we're having our summer a bit early. Not once did snow appear – I wonder how many members are aware that sets of skis exist for the Turbulents and the Super Cub and that they are used practically every year? Within the hangar all is bustle with the preparation of the Formula One racers, and then there's a beautiful new red Beta awaiting its baptism of racing . . . its name? "RED BARON." I offered my services to do its acceptance flight but was a bit late, seventeen pilots had volunteered before me. Right up front of the hangar is Pete Channon's delightful pale blue Comper Swift complete with that slow-revving Pobjoy engine. The private owner ultralight contingent is very active right now, what with Ralph Hart's Curry Wot and Ian Maclennan's green Nipper, all of them out on every possible occasion. A bit further back and you will find a Tiger fuselage taking shape under Tom Freer and Fred Underwood's care; it is of course the Sea Tiger coming to life, and all being well it's likely to be airborne again before the summer's out. The waters down at Rye haven't seemed the same without it.

A new Senior Check Pilot has been appointed, and so we take this opportunity to warmly welcome Don Henry to the hot seat. Don has a wealth of flying experience and his easy manner augurs well for this sometimes onerous task. Incidentally it's good to record that Don Henry is an American. I think this is the first time anyone other than a native has joined the Tiger Club's inner sanctum – the Committee. Mark you, in view of our vast overseas membership it's not before time!

A very amusing letter was received from John Wright who, you will recall, has a small popular strip near Cranleigh in Surrey. Because a formation of Turbs happily visited him recently some of the locals got up tight and protested and we were forced to warn members to fly carefully in that area.

He wrote: ". . . then a woman rang up and complained that her children's party had been ruined because, just as the conjuror was pulling the rabbit from the hat, the Turbs went over and all the children rushed to see the planes. She was so rude to me that I told her to "drop dead" and rang off. 15 seconds later the phone went again and a hysterical female voice shouted down the phone: 'And bloody well drop dead yourself!' and hung up!"

CLUB NEWS: MAY – JUNE 1974

So far so good. I mean the weather of course. Warm and dry and Redhill looking as lovely as ever. If there's a wee cloud on the horizon it's the knowledge that our landlords would still wish us out, and we, perforce, must protect our interests. We will win the day of course, but oh! the time, money and effort that will be needed when all three could be put to so much better use.

The season's first display at Rochester went off well, and the second at Elstree on 30th June will be going strong around the time this Newsletter reaches you.

. . . Saw a wonderful TV film on marine life – and whales in particular – featuring Club member Krov Menuhin. He and his lovely wife Ann even graced the front cover of the "Radio Times." It was very well done. And then I received an invitation to join the newly-formed British Aerobatic Association. Anxious to support my friends (they're all Tiger Club of course) I rushed off a hard-pressed cheque. There was an unexpected bonus. The cheque came back – I'd paid too much. They may get off the ground with their flying but they'll never make it pay! We all wish them every success.

Some Sundays ago a noisy stranger crept high past Redhill airfield. We guessed it could only be the Volmer Sportsman amphibian. It so turned out to be and Keith Sissons was flying it. Elsewhere we print a letter from its owner seeking some well-deserved support.

. . . Three of our members were, some days ago, presented with RAeC Awards by HRH The Duke of Edinburgh. The Silver Medal went most deservedly to Tom Storey for his contribution to Formula One Air Racing.

James Baring was awarded the Tissandier Diploma. "Few people," the citation commented, "have given as much of their own time or made so intelligent and knowledgeable a contribution, over the last ten years, to light aviation in the United Kingdom and abroad." All we can mutter is "Hear, hear!" It's a recognition that is long overdue. And to Frances MacRae the Jean Lennox Bird Trophy, a well-deserved gesture to this country's leading woman aerobatic pilot. To them all, our hearty congratulations.

Try if you can to fly, or drive, over to Sywell for at least one of the three days of the big PFA International Rally on July 5th, 6th and 7th. It is believed there could be as many as 400 visiting aircraft. Come along if at all possible; the PFA deserve support for what is now Europe's biggest Air Rally.

Sywell: now that brings back memories. The PFA Chairman was David Faulkner Bryant and very much a Tiger Club man . . . and a wily one at that. He recognised the PR of a good air display for his new and budding annual Rally: that, and he was in need of a few fresh volunteers, so he humbly approached the Committee to ask if they could recommend a new leader for the flying side of the rally. Butter wouldn't have melted in his mouth.

"You've so much experience," he earnestly explained, "and we so wish to learn from you . . . " etc. etc.

Flattered silly, the Committee nodded like a lot of contended oxen and smiled at me. (As if I didn't have enough on my plate.) I didn't think twice.

"Sure," I said.

And so began a seven-year stint as the bloke i/c of all PFA Rally flying and, as David had so craftily reckoned, I was to bring the display teams along with me . . . and in the fullness of the coming years the aircraft followed. From 400 to 1,500, that and a service of fine displays, sleepless nights, followed by utter happy exhaustion. No regrets.

The summer of '74 was great for flying but barren for copy, so I cheated a bit and chose little entertaining items from previous issues. It fitted the *"Rag"* and was well received, memories being so short and all that. . . . Here's a few of the better ones. . . .

JUNE '61: Next time you're on the Redhill circuit take a look in a south-easterly direction about one-and-a-half miles from the airfield. There, on a small rise, is a windmill that still turns, grinding out grain as it has done for hundreds of years. Its owner, an old farmer, still sells his produce at the mill door.

I suspect there can't be more than a couple of other windmills still working in the whole of the country. To catch a glimpse of the great white wooden blades turning over slowly in the sunshine is a breathtaking sight.
(It's still there and still turning. – Ed.)

OCTOBER '62: . . . September was an eventful month with plenty of flying, a fine display and many new credits to mark up to TC members. One such event came as a complete surprise to all of us, for those who saw the Turbulent formation take-off at Fairoaks gasped with astonishment as the No. 4 stayed in place in box and the four were tied together! It is now possible to reveal that James Baring tried out no less than 22 experimental take-offs with Peter Phillips to establish the correct procedure, only to eventually discover that the best way was the perfectly normal one.

Technically, I think this innovation is the most refreshing to come up this year, even though it was the CFS team at Farnborough that first put the idea into James's head: but at least they had brakes!

DECEMBER '62: . . . Just across the airfield from the hangar at Redhill can be seen a little pumphouse. It snuggles down amid some trees right on the edge of the N-S runway – clearly visible but seldom seen, even though everyone taxies by but yards away. Yet right outside the little place is an apple tree and it was only recently spotted. The tree yields a fine crop of Worcesters as so many discovered to their delight this year.

(The pumphouse and tree were moved for good less than a year ago. – Ed.)

CLUB NEWS: NOVEMBER – DECEMBER 1974

. . . I went down to Redhill a couple of weeks ago and plodded about happily in the mud. It has been such a very wet autumn, with much taking off on taxiways and landing short to avoid the mud bath and the gluey patches in the centre of the field. But over hot tea in the Clubroom all soon seems well again. It's a strange place, is Redhill, for if you can ignore the growing concrete 'office block,' it is as though nothing has changed in donkeys' years. It's one of the loveliest spots in Surrey. Nearly forgot to mention that there are two very cheerful new faces to be seen in the Clubroom looking after the food side, namely Margaret and Selina. Long may they care for us and be patient with us!

There was a special reason for mentioning Margaret and Selina Burgess. Eric, Margaret's husband and Selina's father, had died flying the original Beta in a tragic air collision over Tollerton in the previous year. Sadly too another Tiger Club member, Barry Shaw, died in the other aircraft, a Tiger. So now the Club welcomed them, as they us, and together we shared their loss. Both were to play leading parts in the Club.

. . . Even with the rotten weather there has been plenty of flying, but it's a good time to mention the cost of new propellers these days. Currently they come out at around £175. I mention this, for if ever the conditions were prone to prop-snapping it is now. And because of this wildly-escalating cost the Committee have agreed that in future broken props must be paid for. It is a little-known fact, but the Club have never charged for any damage done – albeit pilots have been known to volunteer the costs. Instead a modest fine for bad airmanship has been levied. It has long been a figure around £10-£25 with a never-evoked maximum of £100. So beware, a contrite letter of apology isn't likely to be quite enough in future.

. . . Tom Storey is of course in charge of the Legal Fund – I forgot to mention the fact last month – and it is to him that we earnestly ask that the odd donation be sent. Of the court case there is little to say. At the initial hearing we acquitted ourselves well and the date has yet to be agreed for the next hearing. Our case as tenants at the airfield is naturally a strong one but even so the costs of our defence are considerable, so please do continue to give us your support. Contributions have come from far and wide and, by the way, we have received a generous one from HRH The Prince of Wales for the Dawn-to-Dusk, but we like to think HRH had the Legal one in mind.

TRADITIONAL FOLK-SONG
(found under a runway in Norfolk)

I went to Snoring once on a day
(Heigh-ho! The wind and the rain)
At aerobatics for to play
(And the met. it was a-lousy-oh!).

Taff Taylor, 'e were made Chief Judge
(Heigh-ho! The wind and the rain)
And out of the Clubhouse would not budge
(And the met. it was a-lousy-oh!).

Andrew Chadwick was Secretaree
(Heigh-ho! The wind and the rain)
He postponed eight times between lunch and tea
(And the met. it was a-lousy-oh!).

The aircraft stayed in the hangar stowed
(Heigh-ho! The wind and the rain)
In the end we all went home by road
(And the met. it was a-lousy-oh!).

(JB '74)

1975

REDHILL PATROL, HANGAR, OUR BALL AND MAC'S TROPHY

CLUB NEWS: JANUARY 1975

I'm writing this on New Year's Day. It's evening and the boys are in bed and all is blissfully quiet. Still fresh in my mind is the tremendous fun had by all during our Breakfast Patrol just a few days ago. (Grateful to note that Peterborough recorded it in his column with, I like to think, a degree of approval.) The weather this autumn and Christmas has been wet and mild, and Redhill has been a soggy place indeed. But Sunday the 29th December proved dry and clear but with a steady 25-30 kt wind that whistled up and down the Beaufort scale like a demented dervish. It grounded many of the lightweight brigade – and they were sorely missed – but even so no less than 46 aircraft flew in, a telling testimonial to the reputation the local branch of the PFA have in putting on a Patrol. Visitors came from as far afield as Leicester and East Anglia. Heaven knows what time they all got up, but as a defender myself 8 am at Redhill was early enough; it was barely light. 180 breakfasts were served and a warm vote of thanks goes to all those good folk who fixed so much so well and so cheerfully. Especial thanks to Jackie Wright who was still clearing up at midday. Peter Channon organised the whole thing on behalf of the local Strut, and to him and his gang our thanks for providing a much-needed break from overeating and TV.

'74 may have been a rotten year for much, but without question the '74 Kronfeld party was the best ever. It was nothing short of wonderful. Some 150 guests arrived – there was even room for a few more, but not many! There were more unfamiliar faces than usual and the newcomers were immediately made to feel at home. A great party. (If only the same catalyst could be imported to the airfield where sometimes visitors feel a little left out. This subject has always been a bit of a hobby-horse of mine, so my advice to first-time visitors to Redhill is to go up and introduce yourself or ask the Duty Pilot or Duty Check Pilot for an introduction or two. If nothing else it gives them something to do . . .) To Mavis Harriott and the many helpers, the providers of food and the 'elected on night' bar staff our hearty congratulations.

Elsewhere I've recorded John Dunford's proposed itinerary for the Oshkosh '75 visit in July. It's the sort of adventure that one has to get on. It is also going to cost a lot of money, but if one is determined to get there the money could be found. One club member I know approached his Bank Manager on an early attempt to sound him out and got an immediate promise of help. "It worked, it worked!" he yelled over the phone at me. The other big social event of '75 is almost upon us. It's the <u>Annual Dinner Dance</u> at the Inn on the Park on February 14th, Valentine's Night. Do try and make it. There's plenty of accommodation available for the asking.

The term Strut was beginning to have a new meaning. It was a word coined by DFB (David Faulkner Bryant) to describe a branch of the PFA. Even that description wasn't quite true, for in reality a Strut was, then and now, absolutely independent, a gathering if you like of local enthusiasts within the loose embrace of the Popular Flying Association.

No Club is bigger than its members – even if I say those words out loud my tongue isn't quite lodged in my cheek, for I liked to believe that it was true – and since 1960 I had religiously welcomed the new members by name at the end of each 'Club News.' People mattered, but how trite some of these sayings are. One could just as easily say that no member is bigger than the Club, yet there was an element of truth in either offering. Norman Jones was head and shoulders above the Club, yet the membership did him proud. In truth we all, from Norman down to the most junior passenger member, joined forces to follow the same light, and this unprompted direction had a most unautocratic aspect, no one ever pulled rank. In the cold light of early morning these words sound ridiculous, yet – I cross my heart – it was so. Something happened to each and every one of us the moment we entered that Redhill hangar – we left the rat race behind.

Well, what was the hangar like in the seventies? Prepossessing it wasn't, but for us it had welcome written all over its shabby face. We normally came in by a small back door and, if it were locked, a key hung on a piece of string behind the letter box. Inside we'd find ourselves standing atop a short flight of open stairs; a pause to savour the spread of aeroplanes that interlocked below, then down to the hangar floor.

To the left a narrow space wound around the edges of sleeping machines past drab green lockers leaning drunkenly against the back wall – ever a haven for flying kit, sweaters and secreted seat cushions. A forlorn-looking table-tennis table spent its life defying us not to drop everything upon her, a losing battle of course. A loo, and then loomed those near-vertical steps up to the Clubroom. Further along the wall was a dark hidey-hole of a store-room in which shelfloads of loo paper and cleaning stuffs filled spaces not already occupied by cockpit covers, SOW rigs, picketing gear and collapsible lengths of balsa wood which, when assembled, formed the display hoops beneath which we flew.

The door into Dev's office was at the end of that back wall, through which was Michael's narrow sanctum. Old furniture and an abundance of wartime green paint predominated. Atmosphere? It was better than any film set, no one could have dreamt this place up. And if you thought it couldn't get any more unreal, spare a moment to pull open the battered swing door you came to next. A piece of tired bungee cord banged it to behind you. Here, well-worn work benches held up the walls, and beneath their cluttered surfaces countless forgotten metal treasures hid. This was the engineers' tea room, lunch room, rest room and workshop rolled into one oily lair, a home-from-home for the insiders among us to accept their endless offers of cuppas dished out with honest black finger marks on honest stained mugs. Next door, at the start of the north wall, was where there was just enough enclosed room to work on one fuselage at a time. Cosy.

Of course, if you entered the hangar through its vast sliding doors, you immediately sensed all the human activity buzzing around the pair of offices that drifted from the front down the left side, above which were stored battered bits of aeroplanes. The first served us for booking in and out and was the domain of the "What's going on?" brigade, spurred on no doubt by windows that looked both onto the airfield and into the hangar; the second was secretarial.

No big brother watched here, we did everything in an unfettered way with occasional bursts of energy intermingled with pure idleness. And you know something? I'm told the original hangar format, along with its magic, remain to this very day. Stranger places have had preservation orders slapped on them.

CLUB NEWS: MARCH 1975

The Annual Dinner Dance and Ball was a remarkable success and unquestionably the best occasion yet. Over 160 guests gathered in the warmly luxurious ballroom of the Inn on the Park, ready and willing to enjoy a most excellent meal and to dance the night away. Our Guest of honour was Julian Nott, that intrepid hot-air balloonist who so recently gained for Great Britain the world's altitude record. His brief and very amusing speech was everything one could ask for and, if the dramatic effect of his two crutches lent depth to his exploit, all to the good – that he was in plaster after playing squash added to the laughter.

Perhaps we'll look back on this memorable evening with a touch of nostalgia this time next year. For such is the rising cost of such an occasion your Committee now recognises that it is no longer peanuts to go out on the town in such style, and we must reluctantly seek a more modest venue. In your Editor's humble opinion it is not a real Club evening unless everyone can afford to make it and came along . . . but oh! it was a fine evening we enjoyed. Victor and Joyce Collins came all the way from the States just for the Dinner and so it seemed only right that we invite Joyce to present the year's awards, and she did so and right well too. A bit of late publicity got rave reviews and that was a poster organised by our new PRO, Phillip Falk. A brilliant piece of work by two of his friends. Their cooperation next year is a must.

Flying from Redhill has been a boggy experience during the months of Jan. and Feb. Within the hangar, though, everyone is preparing for the coming racing season working on the Formula One machines. Tom Regan's beautiful new racer he has built (it's based on the Taylor Titch) is just about ready for its initial flight and it will make, I believe, the eleventh F.1 Racer with which to begin the '75 season.

. . . Members will be delighted to hear that the Court case over the tenancy of Redhill airfield went in our favour, but whilst it would be nice to comment further we must stay our hand for the moment since there is the likelihood of an appeal.

A BIG EVENING IS PROPOSED AT THE KRONFELD ON MARCH 12th. We are showing the Chichester film *"The Lonely Sea and the Sky."* It all begins at 7.30 pm. You will recall that the Tiger Club Seaplane was used in the making of this film.

The AAA Moth Club of America were always in touch and Ralph Wefel's howl of indignation that spring mirrored a weaker echo here. I've always stood in awe at the American way of upholding what they saw as their 'democratic' right of speech that was unambiguous – no tippy-toeing here. It was a way of sounding off that could leave the inhibited Briton chilly with embarrassment.

Is it inbred in us not to say clearly what we really think, or is it the so-called British reticence? I suspect Ralph's clarion call – one of many – had, and still has, a continuing bearing on that fine country's freedom to fly.

<u>Always know that the voice of the people of the United States will be heard!!!!</u>

"Yes, <u>YOU</u>, Sam!! Your role in this country is to SERVE the people, not to govern them! And don't you forget it!

And while you are at it, Sam, you might take another look (damn, so many organizations have asked you to) at your Department of Transportation and its ungainly and uncontrolled foster child, the FAA. Both of you as parents have <u>lost control</u>. What does it take to let you know that the majority of the flying and the owning and the spending for aviation in this country is done by <u>GENERAL AVIATION</u>, not the airlines? Perceptive eyes and common sense and flying skill in aviation came far before control towers, transponders, ELTs, landing fees etc. (*ad nauseam*). The GENERAL AVIATION pilot still utilizes these abilities in his flying, whether your heads-up-and-locked airline-oriented FAA planners and irresponsible spenders of OUR tax dollars know it or not!

The use of the air space above the United States will never be denied the U.S. Citizen in General Aviation and it <u>will</u> be kept free for our use – one way or another. It is time you woke up, Sam! This is still and <u>will remain</u> a DEMOCRACY!! General Aviation Pilots fully intend to keep it so and to fly free in its skies!"

QUOTE:
"I've had two pleasant days with this aeroplane – the day I bought it and the day I sold it!" Overheard and repeated by Michael.

CLUB NEWS: APRIL – MAY 1975
The sun is swelteringly hot, beating down on my arms as I sit in my office and peer up into the sky and ponder from whence that Cherokee has come. Just a few weeks ago and that same piece of sky was filled with snow, and for weeks the boggy condition of Redhill was cause for considerable concern. In fact several red-faced pilots reported aircraft bogged down and please could we help.

Action in the hangar has been mainly centred around the F.I racers who by now should have returned from their first overseas sortie down to James Baring country, the South of France: to be specific, Le Castellet. Seven F.I racers either flew or towed there and made the very first F.I race meeting to be seen on the continent. All being well there'll be a report next month. The overseas Tiger Club contingents have been most active. From Australia Bill Hitchcock, who recently founded the Australian Tiger Club, has written. An extract reads:

"Interest is high in this country in the new colourful group, and I feel sure we shall grow. A 'Year of the Moth' formation flight over the large cities of Newcastle and Sydney is planned and an inaugural air show is also coming up. The American Tiger Club and the New Zealand Tiger Club have contacted me also with letters of encouragement.

Enclosed is some material on the Club, plus I have posted magazines to you. Our paper shall be known as 'Tiger Tales.'"

Well, Bill, your cuttings are on display on the Club notice board and all of us wish all of you a great time. Again from down under is the news that Pete Trevan is, as he puts it: 'making a sentimental return trip to the U.K. to give the Stampe a good work-out. . . .'

. . . The Seaplane is nearly ready for its floats to be fitted. What a magnificent job Tom Freer and Fred Underwood have done. Few people can really appreciate the magnitude of the task that faced these two ab initio builders two years ago. Now the big problem is where to fly it from. They are looking for a big lake, preferably privately-owned – and since most of the seaplane team are based in the south, somewhere in the southern part of the country. Anyone who can find such a spot is in for a reward – nothing less than the first flight off its new waters. In all seriousness we do need help and if you can assist in any way ring Tom or Keith Sissons – it'll cheer them up no end.

Denis Kirkham wrote the following explanation of the founding of the McAully Aerobatic Trophy. A report I found very moving, for I too had known Mac. Denis must be one of aviation's quiet folk, quiet in that his important share of the Tiger Club story and the encouragement of real flying in and around Norfolk has been one of the least-recognised features in our scene. Interesting man is Denis. If his contribution to aviation has actively spanned forty years, his other field of both expertise and business has been no less significant; his knowledge of the Broads and every boat on them must surely be unsurpassed for, as *the* insurance man in that part of the country, his cheery presence is as welcome to countless boaters as to his many friends in flying. And a thought for the day. Do you ever wonder why it is that the Establishment pass over so many of the really worthy when they dish out the honours? Sadly sport aviation's harvest of gongs has always been meagre.

THE McAULLY AEROBATIC TROPHY – HOW IT CAME INTO BEING

Elwyn ("Mac") McAully was the Hon. Chairman and a founder member of the Fakenham Flying Group. He had learned to fly at Fairoaks in the late 1950s, and on accepting an appointment as a civilian air traffic controller at RAF Sculthorpe he immediately set about forming a private flying group locally. With a small band of similarly keen fliers and would-be fliers, the group rapidly became established in 1957 with first one and then two Tiger Moths and a Proctor. Initially, a farm field at Docking was the home "airfield," but by the end of 1957 negotiations with the Air Ministry enabled the Group to move to Little Snoring.

In 1958, encouraged and instructed by the late Flight Lieut. Z. W. "Danny" Kaye (the group's honorary CFI) Mac became interested and proficient in the art of aerobatics. He joined the Tiger Club and began to spend more and more time at Redhill flying the new Super Tiger, "The Bishop" (G-APDZ). The names of Leon Biancotto, Charles Boddington and Mike Popoff became known to the other members of the Fakenham Flying Group and close links with the Tiger Club were established as other members of the Group joined the Club. Aircraft from the Tiger Club regularly visited Little Snoring and Norman Jones, "G.B.," "Bish," Margo, Tich and many others rapidly came to expect, and get, a very warm welcome at this somewhat desolate Norfolk ex-Mosquito base. "The Bishop," in its attractive yellow and red colour scheme, soon began to spend more and more time in the air over Norfolk with Mac practising aerobatics during most of his off-duty hours. At the same time, the Fakenham Group was developing rapidly into the biggest (and we would have said the best!) Group in the country, with the addition of Magisters (sorry – Hawk Trainer IIIs) G-AKPF and G-AJHD, Auster G-AHHM and Drone G-AEKV.

During 1959 and early 1960 Mac entered a number of aerobatic competitions and was soon "pushing" some of the top aerobatic pilots already mentioned. He was taking part in air displays, trying for a height record in a Tiger Moth and had flown the Channel inverted. He was also trying to get a Company, to be called Norvic Aviation, formed in order to be involved in flying full-time. At the beginning of May 1960, at one of the then Shackleton Open Days at Kidlington, he was taxying out in a green Turbulent (can't remember the registration!) prior to a demonstration when he was involved in a collision with an Auster. The Auster's prop chewed away the Turbulent's fuselage to just aft of the pilot's seat before stopping. Mac escaped with a bad cut on his forehead and probably concussion. As was his wont, he made light of it and at the end of the day he flew back to Little Snoring in "The Bishop," formating most of the way on Bill Willis and myself in the pale blue Hawk Trainer III G-AKPF. We flew direct to Little Snoring and he left us overhead Swanton Morley, making for our "satellite" hangarage at Foulsham (where the hangar was in better condition and perhaps more secure protection for the beloved "Bishop").

I never saw him again. We had a Committee meeting scheduled for 1930 hours on May 12th at Little Snoring. I arrived at 19.15. At approx. 1900 hours, whilst practising aerobatics over the field prior to the meeting, he was seen to commence an inverted loop: when inverted the aeroplane continued to lose height until it struck the ground simultaneously with a "rolling out" movement. We think he lost consciousness early in this manoeuvre, and that possibly the blow on his head the previous Sunday at Kidlington may have been a contributory factor. In any event he had gone, and with him the tremendous driving force which had created and sustained the Fakenham Flying Group.

I had been Hon. Sec. from the first collective decision to "go." I called an emergency GM, and we unanimously resolved to rename the Group and to strive to carry on. I personally knew that we had no immediate prospect of maintaining the aerobatic standard which Mac had set (although later on, Barry Tempest emerged as a worthy successor, he also having been in the Group from the start). It also seemed to me essential to perpetuate the memory of Elwyn McAully and to try to cement further the close ties which existed between the Group and the Club. I approached a model-making friend who immediately agreed to make a trophy model: G-ACDC was decided upon, being the aircraft on which all Tiger Club members were checked out – and that had, by then, included a number of "country cousins" here in Norfolk.

The Trophy was presented to the Tiger Club, initially for annual competition for pilots of one or the other organisations. This rather limited aim was rapidly extended so that the competition has become what it is today.

So – for those entrants who may wonder why the devil hold the competition in May in the wilds of often-windy Norfolk, I hope that this potted history may explain the reason and (at the risk of being dubbed a sentimental middle-aged chump!) help add to the sense of achievement in winning it. My late mate would like that.

WHIFF OF NOSTALGIA, NEIL'S FLICK
AND WHAT THE OLD PASS ON

From the same issue of the *"Tiger Rag"* there appeared the following evocative piece:

PURE NOSTALGIA

Browsing through the 1934 edition of the *"Flying Clubs and Schools Year Book"* found recently in a second-hand book shop, a fascinating picture of the private flying scene 40 years ago was unfolded.

Sixty-two Clubs are listed, with solo flying rates ranging from £1.3.0 per hour at Marshall's Flying School, Cambridge to £4.4.0 per hour at Airwork's School of Flying at Heston (night-flying was £6.6.0 per hour). However the average rate per hour was about £1.10.0 solo and £2.10.0 dual. The government subsidy scheme helped to achieve these rates by granting £25 for each 'A' Licence gained and £10 for each renewal. The aircraft on the Clubs' books were largely Gipsy Moths, but Avro Club Cadets and Avro Avians were very popular: other planes listed are Desoutter cabin monoplanes, Puss Moths, a few Fox Moths, some Miles Hawks (that is the early Miles low-wing monoplane), a Southern Martlet (an early Miles-influenced biplane), an Avro 504K, a Robinson Redwing and a Spartan Arrow (that was the biplane with interchangeable half-wings so that any section could be fitted in any of the four positions).

Tiger Moths were only available at the de Havilland School of Flying which was run for RAF Reserve training, although members of the London Aeroplane Club could also use them. However, the 1934 civilian version of the Tiger Moth – the Moth Major – was available at the Midland Aero Club and the Scottish Flying Club. The Brough Flying School (also for RAF Reserve training) used Blackburn B.2 Trainers – that was the metal version of the Bluebird – but the most impressive fleet was that of Air Service Training Ltd at Hamble, who listed 26 aircraft, consisting of Avro Avian, Cadets, Tutors, Trainers (that was the earlier version of the Tutor with the Mongoose engine), an Armstrong Siddeley Siskin, an Avian Seaplane, an Atlas (?) and a Saunders-Roe Cutty Sark. The only autogyro training was at the Kent Flying Club, Bekesbourne, which was presumably at the normal Club rates of £2.0.0 dual and £1.10.0 per hour solo.

Since Club flying was predominantly in the hands of the well-to-do, the Clubs also had to provide the normal facilities that people in that station of life were accustomed to. A typical prospectus stated that the "Clubhouse is equipped with a comfortable lounge, billiards and dining rooms. Good meals are served and there is a bar. Accommodation is available for those members who wish to live on the aerodrome." However the Gravesend School of Flying offered, in addition, sailing, riding, golf, badminton and "other forms of recreation" (although these are not specified). Deck tennis was available at the Kent Flying Club, while clay-pigeon shooting was organised at the Liverpool and District Aero Club. The London Aeroplane Club at Hatfield, probably the doyen of them all, had a large swimming pool, two squash courts, lawn tennis courts, and could arrange riding hacks. The Norfolk and Norwich Aero Club sensibly ran a riding club for non-flying days.

Unexpected Club names appear in the annual, from the London Taxi Aero Club (for taxi-drivers) to the upper end of the social scale such as the Old Etonian Flying Club (one aircraft but 3 instructors) and the Household Brigade Flying Club with one Club aircraft but 442 members, of whom 53 held flying licences and 23 owned their own aircraft.

1934 was the last year in which you could still fly solo (but under instruction) within 3 miles of the aerodrome with neither licence nor medical examination.

It was also the year in which the British Air Transport School of Flying was scheduled to move from its temporary home at Gatwick to "the Company's new aerodrome near Redhill," where in addition to the promise of a new Clubhouse, members would "have the use of an attractive Elizabethan house and gardens nearby, which will be used as a residential Club." A lot can change in 40 years.

Couldn't resist including that journey down someone's memory lane. And do you know the original 1934 Clubhouse is still at Redhill? The last time I saw it, it looked very sorry for itself isolated now from the airfield, its long veranda facing nothing but ugly buildings. No line of welcoming wicker seats, no members, just memories.

CLUB NEWS: JUNE – JULY 1975

. . . It's been a questionable sort of period, with good and bad news in equal doses. (The weather was, for a change, lovely throughout.) The bad news, of course, is the ever-rising cost of recreational flying. Unfortunately private flying hasn't the sort of lobby strength to make any impression on a heavy-handed chancellor who firmly imposed a 25% VAT on us, yet the same man hasn't the moral strength to resist a wild cry of protest from rented-TV viewers. Presumably numbers count, not principles. It's all a bit sad. This column has now gone and broken an 18-year rule never to bring politics into the "Rag." Idle reflection: question – is it a sign of old age when the integrity of politicians, like the ever-increasing youthfulness of our police, goes from indifferent to near zero? I _am_ getting old.

Good news of course is that flying does continue, that good friends do still meet at Redhill and visitors flock in to see us from all over the world. To Ralph Hart our sympathy, for it was he who suffered the back-lash of an angry Stampe propeller and broke his arm. We all hope he is soon about and flying again with all that friendliness that's his trademark.

Good news that the 7th PFA Rally at Sywell was everything the organisers wanted it to be, and more. Nearly **600** visiting aircraft made it that weekend. Along with the pilots from all over Europe there were plenty of Tiger Club men to be seen there. It was not only the biggest Rally outside of the States, but it is now FAI-recognised and has been given International status. The sheer weight of movements, over 2,000 a day on the Saturday and Sunday, was but the tip of a logistic iceberg which reckoned accommodation for hundreds, frozen foods in tons and visitors in their thousands. There was a two-day International Convention with delegates from the world over, daily Air Displays, a vast Exhibition arena and near-24-hour catering.

To David Faulkner Bryant, Chairman of the PFA, and his team (many of whom are Tiger Club men), our congratulations for the vision and ability to pull off this magnificent event so successfully. Conspicuous by their absence – for the second year running – was the BLAC.

I'm pretty sure this was the year that the PFA crowds at Sywell were brought to their feet by a completely unexpected piece of brilliant flying. Let me go back a bit. Someone had discovered a fleet of Bücker Jungmanns going for a virtual song in Spain. The Spanish Air Force were putting them out to grass and avid enthusiasts over here were clamouring to get them. The tales and adventures of their journeying to this country – several were wrecked on route – will one day be told, but one in particular was hand-picked, bought and ferried home by Neil Williams, at that time the country's top aerobatic pilot.

He turned up with his new toy at Sywell and I didn't have to lean too hard on him to agree to fly an aerobatic slot in the afternoon's display. I can still see his final approach after a showing that was, in Neil's inimitable fashion, low, smooth and all within a tight envelope; believe me, no eyes left his performance. I thought him a tad fast, a shade high as he levelled out to land, when suddenly he threw in a final 360° flick, his wingtips brushing the grass as he tumbled about, and then with complete assurance sank into a perfect three-pointer.

There was a stunned hush from his audience before a wave of spontaneous elation swept them all onto the airfield. I was unprepared for such a reaction. Sure, I'd read of like happenings, indeed the old newsreels of a black mass of humanity filling the airfield after Lindbergh's landing in Paris are still in my mind, never to leave, but – in staid Northamptonshire?

Neil, who must have watched the approaching horde with some apprehension, not only for their safety but for his beloved aeroplane, switched off, and as his propeller stopped his Jungmann was surrounded. He walked back to my duty caravan, applause and excitement about him. He gave a big grin. I believe he only ever did it once again, and that was at the Oxford display.

. . . .The Le Castellet meeting has been reported in full elsewhere in the *"Rag"* and along with the F.I races and the various participation events, the Oxford Full Air Display, it will readily be seen that it's been all go at Redhill. The Seaplane is finished, and by the time this is read should be floating happily at its new mooring down in Kent. To Tom Freer and Fred Underwood top marks for perseverance over two long years.

After a long spell over here, Don Henry is shortly to return to the States – and we'll miss him. As our Chief Pilot he has done a grand job and it's not going to be easy to fill his shoes . . . so from all of us our warmest regards to him and his wife on their return and may their new home be everything they would wish.

There's a fine new addition to the hangar – it's a Beech Staggerwing. It's owned by Philip Wolf who regularly takes it to displays. I really must ask him for a ride, for it sounds nostalgically like a Harvard.

Chris Wren recently sent me a cutting from the Esso Petroleum Company's news sheet. It seems their Social Club is known, fairly logically, I suppose, as the Tiger Club. Reciprocal membership called for?

WING COMMANDER C.A. PIKE OBE, AFC, CEng., AFRAeS

Members will have heard with regret of the death of "Clem" Pike on June 9th last, in his 76th year. Some will recall a day in August 1966 when, to celebrate the 50th Anniversary of his Pilot's Licence, he visited Redhill to see the Club, meet a group of old friends and fly again in one of his beloved Tiger Moths. I had the honour to be the "Monitor" pilot for this flight in 'CDC and, although "Clem" had not flown for some long time, the old superb skill was still with him and his flying was a delight.

From him the Club received the gift of the "Clem Pike Trophy," awarded annually for OUTSTANDING SERVICE TO THE CLUB, and his interest in our past and present doings was avid and inexhaustible.

It has been said that the actual number of pilots he trained was unknown but vast. (I was one of them. – Ed.) Suffice to say that he had been instructing since the early 1920s up to and through the last war, and was considered by everyone as Master of the Art. His quiet kindly confidence and understanding in everything he did earned him the affection and respect of everyone with whom he was associated, and he will ever be remembered. In the main for de Havillands, 'tho' latterly for the RAF, his involvement with Tiger Moths and instruction thereon was certainly more than anyone else and his love for the aircraft unequalled. It has been recalled that early in the last war at one airfield alone he had under his command a training school having nearly one hundred Tigers and about half as many instructors in constant operation. By chance I actually saw these in action – an astonishing sight.

Thus with his immense Tiger Moth background and experience he was a fitting and honoured member of our Club, and his passing will be mourned by many, both in and outside our ranks.

"G.B." 11/7/75

An obituary will stop my living in its tracks. In the silence it brings there is time to reflect, to regret, and then like a suddenly-released breath the life- and mind-clocks begin to tick again. Life goes on. My time has yet to come.

And isn't there an inevitability about life that will promote events in threes? First Clem Pike, then Hubert Broad, and then the Club's doyen of respected elders, he who had so carefully written of his friends, was himself to join them in the following year: "G.B." Golding Barrett.

But it wasn't the obvious that draws out that feeling of inevitability but a rueful awareness of a bigger pattern than 'threes,' a pattern that contributes and finally outlives itself to be replaced yet again, an ongoing cycle of knowledge that strengthens the object of its favour, in this case our Club. Rueful because I find myself – and this depends on a point of view – at the downside of the cycle.

The Club in its formative years drew on a nucleus of pilots who were of that band of brothers in the Class of '18. They had matured in the 30s and this wealth of collective experience in their latter years gave us the credence we needed in the '50s and '60s. As one Class retired the next took its place, they of the Class '45, now cheerfully on the way out, having in turn given of their knowledge. It's a pattern of giving that should comfort the sceptics because it is ongoing, a pattern built on strength, strength to stay the course.

FAREWELL HUBERT BROAD, PROPS, LEASE RENEWED AND KRONFELD – LIFE OR DEATH

CLUB NEWS: SEPTEMBER – OCTOBER 1975

At last the long hot summer seems behind us, a summer in which so much successful flying was done. The F. 1 racers especially must consider 1975 as their best year ever. There are now no less than 9 Formula 1 racers at the starting grid. To witness these trim craft in angry flight is a sight indeed, and the prospects for 1976 look even better.

A little early perhaps, but I have just heard that the Christmas-cum-New-Year Breakfast Patrol is provisionally booked for December 28th. It is a Sunday, of course, and as before Redhill will be defended by the local PFA Strut/Tiger Club members. Book your aircraft early for they will be in short supply.

. . . Good news from the seaplane front is that it is now flying again and although I am not supposed to mention from where officially, I can say that it is in Kent. (Reluctance to say exactly where is probably due to an oversensitive situation – once the locals get enthusiastic I presume all will be well.) One day someone will tell the story of this remarkable Tiger, its many adventures and of the many many characters whose very lives seem tied up with this ungainly beast. But the winter is nearly upon us and already the problem of a warm home for the seaplane is taxing our minds. So please consider. Do you know of a friendly stretch of inland water that would welcome such a fine old lady to float there, and more, provide a wee plot of land on which to build a shelter? Think on it.

Brian Smith has accepted, albeit reluctantly, the position of Senior Check Pilot. So on behalf of the Committee and members I extend a warm welcome to this occasionally hot seat. It is, of course, an appointment of some significance, for we are as a Club rightly proud of our flying standards, and one of Brian's tasks will be to encourage and promote all flying to an even higher standard, so you will readily appreciate he will need all our support.

And in the September issue, the following obit. . . . and the pattern is complete.

CAPTAIN HUBERT STANFORD BROAD MBE, AFC

The death of Hubert Broad in his 76th year has robbed our Club of one of its greatest protagonists, for he followed our activities with avid interest.

To attempt to record in detail his vast and varied experiences and successes as a Test Pilot, in air-racing and record-breaking, would need a book and no less. Thus it must suffice for the *"Rag"* to remind members of his intimate association with the Moth – the cornerstone of our Club.

He learned to fly privately at the Hall School at Hendon in 1915. Thereafter he served with both the RNAS and RFC, flying Pups and Camels. Credited with six victories, he in turn was shot down and wounded, finishing the war as an instructor.

A period of "joy-riding" on Avro 504Ks and casual test flying preceded his appointment in 1921 as Test Pilot for de Havilland. In the following fourteen years with that company he did the tests and development flying of some thirty separate types of their design. First with the diminutive DH.53 Humming Bird which I saw him loop and roll at Lympne in, I think, 1923, to the original DH.60 Cirrus Moth and all subsequent derivatives of that type. And of course the record-breaking DH.71 – the original "Tiger Moth" monoplane.

But the Moth was his favourite and it is certain that no one knew the type better or loved it more.

Reticent and self-effacing by nature, his contribution to aviation in general and sporting flying in particular was prodigious. Whilst an exceptional navigator, aerobatics were his first love and in his day few were his equal. His book on the subject still makes good sense and reading. In over 30 years of uninterrupted flying his log books show around 7,500 hours on over 200 types.

I knew him well and saw him often. A superb pilot and an equally good friend. Could we have had a more famous and suitable Honorary Member of our Club?

You will wish to join me in this salute to the passing of a great little airman. "G.B." 20/8/75

Another pattern was being aired around this time and it all had to do with swinging propellers. Poor Ralph Hart had busted his arm and others nursed broken wrists and thumbs. A Gipsy Major, especially when hot, was an unforgiving beast. Alan Wilson wrote:

"Please, left arm down by the side, right hand at the propeller tip and follow the swing through, thus carrying hand and arm well clear of that rotating scythe. That's all very well for a L.H. tractor. For a R.H. brute – even racers and the like – I think we really require a race of left-handed swingers! Seriously though, when starting such aircraft particular care should be exercised."

I doubt anything changes and Majors remain unforgiving, only I wonder if the experience, often painfully gained, is around as much today.

FURTHER QUOTES FROM THE SEPTEMBER COMMITTEE MEETING
Tom Freer was discussing the difficulty of readily preparing the seaplane for flight from an unprepared base, and the need to move to something more practical. . . .

"Wheels," muttered Brian Smith.

CLUB NEWS: NOVEMBER – DECEMBER 1975
As 1975 shivers to its end it's nice to reflect on a summer the likes of which we may never see again. Apart from the fact that the long hot spell nearly put me out of business (I produce knitwear, of all things!) it was flying weather all the way. So many long flights were undertaken it was, in spite of VAT, a memorable year.

A log of one such journey will be started in the next issue to inspire others to spend the rest of the winter in planning similar adventures!

Our seaplane has now put in some 26 to 30 hours – hindered only by some radio trouble. That radio is considered necessary at all is in itself remarkable. If Lydd has a movement a week they'd be busy. That's my opinion of course, the seaplane boys are too polite to comment. But now the weather is becoming a bit much even for them, so by now the seaplane will be withdrawn till the spring. Incidentally, Tom Freer is looking for someone to lend the Sea Tiger fuselage a large canvas cover. Anyone able to help?

The Tiger Club has never been noted for a very active social side, but what we do have we thoroughly enjoy, and the social season is about to begin. For starters there's Mavis Harriott's fling at the Kronfeld on Tuesday evening, December 16. It starts around 7.30. Officially this is called the Tiger Club Xmas Party, and so it is, but Mavis and her gang have organised it for so long that it's better known as "Mavis's Do." We charge a modest entrance fee – probably 50p, and from then on till the early hours it's a Great Party.

. . . Yet another item for your Diary is the '76 Annual Tiger Club Dinner and Dance, this year at the Arts Club, and it will only cost you £7.50 (anyway, it's an improvement on last year's Dinner/Dance cost). Write in <u>now</u> for your tickets, there'll only be 150 available this time. <u>Date: Saturday, 14th Feb. 1976.</u>

Years and years earlier we in the Committee reckoned the New Year would always need a booster, something to brighten our days during the dreary winter months whilst we awaited better flying weather. January was a no-no, too many bills, too near earlier hangovers, but February – ah! but that was a tedious month, so why not liven it up with an annual dinner? And Bev Snook, the romantic, chipped in with the suggestion that we make it a St. Valentine's dance as well. '76 St. Valentine's Day fell on a Saturday . . . too good to be true.

. . . Third social event, and a flying one this time, is the yearly Breakfast Patrol traditionally held at the very end of the year when it's all nice and cold and well-attended. Date: <u>28th December '75</u>. Time of assembly, before light! Details from Brian Smith who is i/c defending aircraft. . . . Come along if only to support the home team. Last year there were a couple of hundred visitors and friends. It's a sight to see.

News from the Tiger Club abroad indicates a wildly successful set-up from every quarter. For instance, Club member Ralph Wefel in California has sent me his regular yellow broadsheet and it's welcome reading for those fortunate enough to see it. One item intrigued me – did you know there are something like 533 Tigers still flying? With 115 in the USA, 133 in the UK and 117 in Australia. South Africa, New Zealand and Canada share most of the rest. Ralph even quotes a SWAG total of 605. (SWAG? Scientific Wild-Ass Guess!)

Not to be outdone by Bill Hitchcock's prolific output of Tiger lore for the Australian Club, Dudley Payne has produced a most creditable "Tiger Rag" (puts mine to shame) for the Tiger Club of New Zealand. We can only wish all our fellow members abroad much joy in flying their Tigers. What fun it we could arrange a Great Tiger Club Jamboree one year. Now that would be a get-together to end all get-togethers. Wishful thinking just now perhaps . . . but one day – who knows?

I've left the best news till last. As you know, we have had a long legal tussle with our landlords over the tenure of Redhill. Because it was wise to do so we kept the proceedings in low profile, and because we like it that way we'll continue as we began. But we are glad to tell you that after an out-of-court settlement we are able to confirm an unbroken twelve-year lease from this date . . . with terms and conditions very much to our liking and of course with no hard feelings. We hope we will continue to be friendly and considerate users of our much-loved airfield.

No one can say we, the Tiger Club, didn't do our damnedest to keep the Kronfeld going. In sober vein I penned the following plea in the November of '75.

THE KRONFELD CLUB: Life or death – it's up to you

The Kronfeld has long been our London meeting place, but the Club itself has of later years led a rather chequered career. Once a thriving and busy place it fell into near-disuse some three years ago and at that time several members of the Tiger Club rallied round and attempted to restore the place and its fortunes. And we tried hard. We redecorated and refurbished and then spent lonely and fruitless nights behind the bar awaiting visits from members that seldom materialised; until, tired and disheartened, we again saw this lovely little Club used no more than for the occasional Committee meeting.

So not without good reason the Kronfeld Directors met early this month to face up to the problems of a Club that wasn't. Michael Jones and your Editor, both Directors, pleaded for a year's grace in which to have just one more go to make the Kronfeld viable, and in doing so we have accepted the financial responsibility, should we fail. That year's stay of execution will probably be granted us. We are optimistic of success, for our friends the PFA have now agreed to come in, but they alone may not be enough, and now we seek other such organisations to join us. Not only because they may heed a central meeting place but because they too will recognise the loss to light aviation should this fine place be forced to close through lack of support. Will organisers please contact Michael Jones for details.

To appreciate the Kronfeld's significance is to reflect that the Club (which, incidentally, is virtually Tiger Club-run) has an eighty-year lease at a ridiculously low unchanging rental and it's in Belgravia! Just imagine trying to get such a spot today – much less in later years – in such a position, such a lease and at such a price. As a meeting place it has no equal for it's virtually at the middle of London's transport system. We feel it should remain in our trust for those to follow. The lease is of course of considerable value and disposal is no problem, but we think flying people should have one last chance. What say you? If you feel as strongly as we do, send Michael your name and address, and if there is enough support we'll open it again for a couple of nights a week for starters with perhaps the odd lecture or film show. Passed to you.

When eventually the Kronfeld folded just over a year later I recall Michael and I left the final negotiations for the sale of the lease to the original directors. We made no claim on behalf of the Tiger Club, we considered it had been enough to have shared in such a worthwhile venture. Now, all these years later, I can no longer remember how much that remarkable lease realised, or even where the proceeds went: good causes all, of course. Another way of saying we also missed out.

USE THE "RAG"

Members are reminded that we will gladly open these columns for the odd personal thing or other. So to set the ball rolling again: does anyone want (or can afford!) to buy <u>a smashing home in Kingston, Surrey</u>. It only lacks an airstrip to make it perfect (but Redhill is only 30 minutes down the road). Detached, 5 bedrooms, a pool. Please phone the Editor, Lewis Benjamin, for details.

I spotted this sad little inset in the *"Rag"* with a sorry heart. If a little earlier on I had indicated that my home life was no longer in the same successful ball park as my business, well, this was reality. Lollie and I were to go our separate ways, still the best of friends, but our comfortable home was the first visible casualty.

And, you know, the extraordinary thing was that once on that disastrous roundabout I didn't know how to get off or even save the day. To start with, I'd bought the Arrow Active from Norman; this was an unsociable single-seater if ever there was one, and I spent even more time on Club affairs. Blind? I was in a league of my own. I then went and fell for a petite blonde who'd landed at Redhill to join the Tiger Club after a solo flight in her Cherokee from Denmark. Inge and I planned such adventures.

Can think of no better way to say farewell to another year than to entertain with the following priceless exchange of letters between Frank Price, who ran the American branch of the Tiger Club, and our Chairman, Norman Jones. Neither liked the other, yet an uneasy truce existed and Frank's despairing "I do wish you well and always did," ranks high in the "I tried, I really did" department.

"Dear Norman,
Just sitting here thinking about you for a moment and thought I would say hello.

Hope all is well with you and yours, I'm flying shows this year; because of the Waldo Pepper movie by Universals I did the inverted ribbon pick-up and flew a Curtiss Jenny in one scene.

I still have lots of fun and enjoy life much. Tiger Club here is still pure but small and we will have a nice fly-in of 300 people this coming Sept. 14 and 15. I still don't really feel a part of the other two aerobatic organisations in America even though I'm a founding member of both of them.

I still love flying for what it really is, and will always do so. I know you feel the same in spite of our occasional doubts. I am finally getting around to building my own airstrip and hangars after all these years. Small but nice.

I do wish you well and always did. Hello to all and God speed.
    Sincerely,
FRANK D. PRICE."

"Dear Frank,
Your letters when they arrive come like a breath of fresh air. The Tiger Club over here goes ahead, or at least maintains itself, and its spirit. There are now Tiger Clubs in New Zealand, Australia, South Africa and Portugal, as well as the States. We hope to have one in France. We are doing a film to be called *"The Love of Flying"* which will feature the Tiger Club. Would you like a copy for America? Good luck to your airstrip, any chance of you coming over here soon? I am still

racing mildly and aerobatics go well over here. We are slowly sinking in this country under the dead weight of bureaucracy.

All the best,

Yours sincerely,

NORMAN JONES."

1976

BREAKFAST HAIR-DOWN, G-AIVW, ARTS CLUB
AND CAA TRY-ON

The January Club News heaved us into the new year with a spectacular flourish.

. . . The Breakfast Patrol on the 28th December was one for the book. Do you want the good news or bad news first? Good? OK, here it is. Without question it was a fantastic occasion with over 80 visiting aircraft battling to get in past 20 very busy and determined defenders. The weather was kind, mild with a 2,000 ft overcast. Over 300 breakfasts were provided and I don't think there were more than 9 free breakfasts claimed . . . a fact which must have provided the PFA, who organised the whole thing, with a wee profit. Hardest worked were the cooks. To them, and especially Jane Barker, an appreciative bouquet. (I hear that Jane has just become the part-owner of a Jodel D.9.) That was the good news. The bad was caused by some over-exuberant departures which didn't exactly do our local image much good . . . it must be avoided next year.

And that was putting it mildly. The exuberant activity we were to witness that morning contained a scarcely-concealed wild anticipation. The contest crackled about us from ground-level up as if the confines of Christmas excesses were being cast aside. The pilots, both visiting and defending, freed from family ties now, joyously swept care and restraint aside in an abandoned aerial battle that raged in every direction. It was as if there was an unspoken challenge – let's see how good the Tiger Club is.

I watched from the ground, torn between a vicarious wish to share in the excitement and the sober demeanour expected of the Club's new Chairman. Not that anyone could have curbed what was already in motion. Red Vereys from the duty pistol would have had no meaning except perhaps to have added fireworks to the occasion – the idea was rejected.

The poor Duty Pilot spent his time running in and out of the hangar, torn between attending the noisy mayhem outside and answering the office phone within. No sooner had one call been answered than there was another queuing up to complain. The hangar's strident bell rang incessantly.

"What do I do?" he asked helplessly.

For the first time I understood the meaning of wringing ones hands. "Here, let me take the next call."

The phone rang on cue.

A woman's voice screamed down the line: 'They're flying in the windows."

"But Madam," I began.

"Listen," she shouted, "I'll open them."

She was being strafed, engines roared and roared again. Aghast, I tried to pacify. She put the phone down.

And then they were landing, the moment had passed: breakfast, laughter, and a sort of normality returned. There had been no accidents, no mishaps, but our PR image had taken a beating, and much of it not of our doing. It was a one-off, hair-down experience that was never to be repeated, for later in the year in the November Committee meeting notes there appeared: *"Breakfast Patrol not permitted at Redhill."* More than one head nodded with relief.

1976, and the Tiger Club was 21. If I was figuratively being given the key of the door, Norman Jones the donor, now 71, was feeling his way into a new life. He had married again and in the June of the previous year, Ann, his young wife, had presented him with a daughter, Annabel, a little beauty they'd lovingly nicknamed Tiddler. The new direction they'd found and retreated to was a vast nature reserve of lakes and flat pastures called Castle Water, hard by the old castle at Camber, near Rye in East Sussex.

In passing on the Chairmanship to me Norman had every intention of retaining a hands-on approach to the Club he had founded, but reality spoke differently. Castle Water was a challenge he welcomed but I doubt he initially appreciated how demanding its day-to-day management would be. And if one challenge wasn't enough, there was a family that was soon to grow and would come to fill his days to his complete happiness, and Redhill would seem another and distant world. His move was to be permanent. Of course I speak only of his connection with the Club's flying, for Norman did not relinquish his financial grasp, but that aspect was out of the membership realm and Michael Jones, the Club's manager, wore that worry on our behalf. He did so with an unfailing cheerfulness.

LETTERS

Redhill

"Dear Benjy,

I am surfacing in response to the bait that you "cast upon the waters" of the September/October *"Tiger Rag."* I suggest that you treat this as an anonymous contribution – the *"Rag"* has had enough from me to last it for a lifetime. I enclose two extracts – one from the pen of A.J. Jackson (probably the greatest aviation historian), who related the story of G-AIVW; the second goes part of the way towards explaining the fascination of "flying with floats"! You contradict yourself by references to "this ungainly beast" (NEVER) and "a fine old lady" (MUCH BETTER).

There may have been some "characters" associated with 'VW in her early days, but nowadays I would suggest that the people involved are a bunch of solid citizens performing a moderately difficult operation in a thoroughly professional manner without losing their sense of humour – we all roll about when somebody falls in!

Teamwork sums it up – even refuelling requires a team. The fuel has to be collected in cans, then ferried over to the island in a rubber dinghy, off-loaded and carried by hand to the aeroplane, and then passed up to the hardy soul, perched up on top, to be poured into the tank. As every drop has to pass through a chamois stretched across the funnel the whole operation takes quite a while but we are never short of "volunteers" to go aloft. Verily, it is a way of life that should be sampled by all members at least once. I do wish that more people would avail themselves of this unique opportunity– why not make a resolution to fly a seaplane in '76?

Yours aye,

Fred Underwood."

EXTRACT FROM _"THE AEROPLANE,"_ AUGUST 1973

"SEA TIGER" by A.J. Jackson

G-AIVW was built for the RAF by Morris Motors Ltd., Cowley, during the 1939-45 war as T5370 (c/no: 83135), and was the last of three, G-AIVU, 'VV and 'VW refurbished by the DH Repair Organisation, Witney, for the Newcastle-upon-Tyne Aero Club in 1946. The first two were comparatively short-lived, but 'VW was raced many times, notably by Bill Evans in the _"Daily Express"_ Race from Hurn to Herne Bay on September 20th 1950, at the remarkable average speed of 118 mph, equalled in the 1958 King's Cup Race by Newcastle's airport manager, Jim Denyer, who gave it the distinction of being the only Tiger Moth ever to win this classic event.

Its landplane career ended in a crash landing at Woolsington on September 24th 1959, after which it languished at Rollasons, Croydon, until February 1962 when they acquired it for seaplane conversion. The floats, originally imported from Canada with the Aeronca Sedan, G-AREX, were mounted on specially-made (and very expensive) struts and fittings, the extra drag created being offset by installing a 145 hp Gipsy Major IC engine. The completed seaplane went by road to RNAS Lee-on-Solent where Air Commodore G.J.C. Paul made the first flight on July 20, 1963."

EXTRACT FROM _"FLYING WITH FLOATS"_ by Alan Hoffsommer

Seaplanes, like women, come in a variety of shapes and sizes. Like the female sex, seaplanes can be the cause of great joy or bitter frustration. Seaplanes are a sickness, as any seaplane pilot will testify. Once the pilot, novice or professional alike, has tasted the joys and pleasures of flying his aircraft from the water, he is hooked. Nothing can cure him, except maybe the next flight, and this is strictly a temporary remedy. What is it that makes flying seaplanes so fascinating?

The answers to this question will be many and varied. But whatever the answer is, you can bet your last bilge pump that the seaplane pilot will be as different from the landplane pilot as night is from day. There are many ways to tell a seaplane pilot from his land-based brother. Directions are never given as right or left, but always port or starboard. Tie-downs are never rope, but lines. Instead of the usual boots common to pilots, the seaplane pilot will be wearing an old pair of dirty white sneakers. But the easiest way of all to identify the seaplane pilot is to get him around any sizeable body of water. He becomes glassy-eyed and seems to be leaning into the wind as if making a steep turn from a downwind heading. And if you ever catch an old, old seaplane pilot going around barefooted, you'll find that he's as web-footed as an old pelican. Every pilot is susceptible, and the disease is spreading more each day. Who can say, maybe you'll be next. Join the fun . . . go by floats!

. . . The big event during February was surely the Annual Dinner, held this year at the Arts Club. It was a 'sold out' occasion with something of a waiting list as well. Whilst it's sad we can't accommodate everyone, there is a lot to be said for knowing that an event is going to be financially viable, as opposed to the committed organisers sweating out the sale of paid-for tickets. Not only was the Arts Club an excellent venue – it's a magnificently refurbished house of considerable elegance – but the evening was a most enjoyable one. Our Guest of Honour, Raymond Baxter, proved an entertaining after-dinner speaker, and his presence was the more fitting for knowing that he is also a most experienced pilot. What with the paper aeroplanes and the odd power-model airborne, the laughter, and the fun, it was very much a typical Tiger Club affair. The prizegiving was Top of the Bill. Nothing less than that great variety act, Baxter and Blake, at their very best. Margaret Burgess received the de Salis Trophy, mainly for her devotion to seeing us properly fed at Redhill. To Tom Freer, the Clem Pike Trophy for his work on the restoration of the Sea Tiger. To Mike Crossley, the Air Racing Medallion and, I suspect, in part recognition too of the fact he built his own very successful F.1 racer. The Foreign Touring Medallion went to Fred Williams – who else after that remarkable trip to the Arctic? The Aerobatics Medallion to Mansel Morgan, and the Hamilton Trophy to Mike Bialkewicz. (Neither Raymond or John could resist pointed comment on this award – a rather sharp and lethal looking sword.) The Dawn-to-Dusk went to Tom Foxworth who, with his wife, had certainly travelled the farthest to make the Dinner: New York to be precise. A Special Award was made that night to John Blake for his two-year stint in researching Tom's winning entry. It was only a spell of hospital that made John miss crewing with Tom on that epic Dawn-to-Dusk.

We've already reserved the Arts Club for next year. Our thanks to David Hamilton and Andrew Chadwick for organising it all for us.

Every year there seemed to be a theme, call it what you will, but this time it was inspired by Don Daines' first column as our new Safety Officer, and in it he wrote:

"Now, by way of a start, I would like to draw your attention to prop-swinging – your urgent attention, I might add. One or two members have already written some intelligent remarks on the subject, but may I remind you of the very obvious dangers there are when your feet are on wet grass! Even worse, a very small mud patch. It would be very easy for you to lose your foothold! I have also seen one or two members using two hands to swing. Please, this has got to be very dangerous indeed – don't do it. I may be there when we have to pick up somebody's severed head! It won't be a pretty sight."

I had a feeling that the prop-swinging theme would soon be under way. I wasn't disappointed.

Kelly Aeroplane Ltd, 30 Jan. 1976

To: Don Daines, Safety Officer.

"Dear Don,

Pleased to see in the latest issue of the *"Rag"* that the Club now has a Safety Officer. I was interested in the warnings on prop-swinging but a little bit mystified by the warning against two-handed swinging. Rothmans Aerobatic Team have always been 'two-handed swingers.' We started out in 1970 with 5 Stampes, 2 with Gipsy engines and three with Renault engines. We flew some 3,000 hours on these and probably about 8,000 sorties, involving 8,000 hand-swung starts. The only person who ever got bitten by one of our props was an experienced hand-swinger who was not working for us and not using our technique. With our system of two-handed swinging, one places two hands flat on the blade. The fingers should not be curled round the blade. The feet need to be almost under the disc of the prop so that as one swings one's C. of G. takes you away from the prop disc. Where people go wrong with two-handed swinging is in having the feet well back from the prop disc. This is very dangerous as the head then automatically bows into the disc as the swing is made. The advantage of two-handed swinging is that one can swing through quite high compressions without curling one's fingers round the blade. If one's fingers are curled round the blade a backfire or kickback pulls one into the prop and also damages the fingers and wrenches the arm.

We swing 200 hp Lycomings using the two-handed method. When 'converting' from swinging Stampes to swinging Pitts a good bit of 'dry' practice is desirable because of the different direction of rotation and the fact that the props on Lycomings are usually set so that compression peaks at around the 8 o'clock position. The 180 Lycoming with fixed-pitch Sensenich prop has a propensity for kicking back if hot and has high compression and a sharp trailing edge. I certainly wouldn't like to try swinging it one-handed.

Yours sincerely,

Manx Kelly."

Then Nick Pocock, now over in Texas, wrote:

". . . Secondly, getting back to aeroplanes, I was surprised to read in Don Daines' excellent article on safety a warning not to use both hands for prop-swinging. Then I remembered we were talking about the wonderful 'Gipsy.' Of course this should be swung with only one hand, similarly the Renault Stampe. But, if you have swung, or have occasion to have to swing, an engine without an impulse magneto, which I believe would include your Super Cub, should the battery be flat, one might have to be instructed to use both hands. I still do not find it as easy to swing the 'flats' and radials over here (usually without an impulse magneto) as I used to with a Gipsy. However, I was instructed in the usual practice of using two hands. Another difference in the techniques seems to be that, using two hands, one does not reach up as high when selecting the compression and holds the blade closer to the root, trying to spin the engine as fast and as far as one's strength permits. (THIS is where I have the problem!) Perhaps some 'old-timer' could relate to us how they used to hand-prop some of those enormous engines that had to be swung by several men holding hands, especially how they managed it when the engine was mounted too high to be reached from the ground!!"

And if the theme wasn't sufficiently murky by now, Roger Meadmore urged:

". . . at sometimes muddy Redhill, always do your 'Contact' swing from <u>behind</u> the prop right by the switches, where you can get at them in a hurry if you have to. . . . It's much easier when you get the hang of it and, in my opinion, much safer."

Safer it might have been, but it was far from common practice. In fact I only ever saw the Sea Tiger and the occasional Turb started that way. I can still see dear old "Bish" perched precariously on a float having a go. I don't know who was more relieved when it started, "Bish" or the anxious onlookers.

It was around this time that a NATS paper was being circulated proposing compulsory radio. Our greater safety was the reason, and we were all asked to respond. I still have my indignant letter before me addressed to Lord Boyd Carpenter who was then chairman of the CAA. Strangely enough it was Norman Lamont who answered. I can no longer remember how he got in on the act, but the proposed paper was dropped, as was, eventually, the imposition of a 25% VAT charge on all things aviation, including fuel. Oh! how they like to try it on. . . . Unfortunately our lobby has never been too strong, unlike the Americans, of whom it was said that if the private sector stopped flying in protest the government would plead with them to return.

With the better weather came a more upbeat *"Rag"* for May and June.

. . . And now the real flying season is nearly upon us – the first Full Display is only weeks away – and the air above Redhill is full of animation as teams practise. The Arrow Active is now very much out and about, resplendent in its revised livery and sporting a magnificent old wooden propeller which does nothing for its performance, but does everything for its looks. She recently flew up to Yeadon, Leeds, the place where she was built 45 years ago, to something of a press reception and local acclaim. One enthusiast headline in a Yorkshire paper pronounced the Active as "Concorde's Grandad," for the factory where she was built now make the turbine blades for Concorde. The long-suffering Jodel 140 is in the middle of her C. of A. and in her place as four-seater is the new Wassmer Europa. This fine-looking aircraft was first tried out by the Club a couple of years ago. The current version is somewhat updated and sports a VP prop. It will prove a good touring aircraft and is well worth getting checked out on. Incidentally it is the only tricycle-undercarriaged machine on the Club strength, a fact that will bring a sigh of relief to some.

Members will be saddened to learn of the death of Manx Kelly, who was killed late in April during a display in the USA. We understand that he was flying the Acroduster, a biplane that resembles the Pitts both in shape and performance; during the start of the display the tailplane separated from the aircraft and the remaining structure broke up as a result.

Manx spent most of his career in the RAF flying an assortment of aircraft. After eighteen years service he turned to civil flying, and it was at this time, around 1965, that he became very much involved in the Redhill scene. During the next couple of years his humorous personality was often in evidence and, coupled with his vast experience, he became a much-liked and respected member of the Club. He participated in many displays and this provided him with the basic concept of the Rothmans Team, but it took the kind of drive and tireless energy that Manx had to get the team into the air. The product of his efforts is now a household name.

Display flying apart, Manx was an accomplished aerobatic pilot. He won most of the domestic contests at one time or another, among them the Icicle for three consecutive years. In 1971 he became the British Champion.

His loss to us at the age of 44 is tragic; but it cannot be compared to that suffered by his wife and family. To Judy and the children we can only pass on our deepest sympathy.

From the USA comes a lot of news about the American Tiger Club and all of it sounds good. They are based in Waco, Texas, and although none of the last three Newsletters are signed, I know it's our old friend Frank Price in the middle of it all. One thing I know, there'll be a great welcome for any TC member going out there. The Australian Tiger Club gets bigger and bigger. Bill Hitchcock writes that they had over 10,000 at their Inaugural Air Show in March. There were acts such as the dogfight between the Black Baron and Sir Percy Goodfellow, and how the Keystone Kops rescued Trudy Truelove from the Villains. Aerobatics were by Captain Bent Strut. I like it. Membership is now 230 with no less than 90 Tiger owners.

The Sea Tiger was operating again. But it was far from an established procedure. To start with feathers had been ruffled, and initially Tom Freer and Keith Sissons were flying from one or other of two sites. They would probably have wished to have stayed at Castle Water but the gravel pit lake there was shared by all sorts of people Norman had gathered under his wing – anglers, water skiers, dinghy sailors – and for once the Boss wasn't giving *carte blanche* to the Sea Tiger.

The second site, and the one that was the more peaceful of the two, was Scotney Court; this was another gravel pit not far away but quite unsuited for a permanent mooring. To add to all this uncertainty the seaplane boys had a constant plea; it was for helpers, especially at the beginning of the day. Blessed are those who come in plenty of time, wrote Tom. So for a spell it was a base at Castle Water and circuits and bumps down the road at Scotney. Keen? No, fanaticism was the word I was searching for.

WAC MONEY-RAISING, KRONFELD VANDALISED, PETER VANNECK AND HOME TOURING

CLUB NEWS: JULY – AUGUST 1976

Do you ever get the feeling nothing is changing? Perhaps it's the weather, but visits to Redhill these days all seem on a par – it's almost as though it's been summer for years. No rain and dazzling sunshine all the time. Outside the hangar there's the same line-up of patient old friends to greet you, like faithful hacks awaiting an outing, and then every night Jim or John perform the same miracle of getting them all back into the hangar again (I still don't think anyone else could do it). It's a comforting scene and somehow reassuring, but there's no denying the fact that replacement aircraft to take the place of the lame and the retired are getting few and far between.

Consider. What aircraft would you like to see? The old faithfuls are now becoming as rare as honest politicians, and current costs for like machines are off-putting, to say the least. Currently a Stampe is around £10,000. One alternative would be to use bread-and-butter nose-wheelers, but they aren't our way. They don't aerobat properly or handle as sweetly, and anyway the hard-won skills of so many Tiger Club pilots would scarcely be put to the test with such mundane aircraft, no matter how economically viable they may be to operate. It's a problem, and it's one that is only brought home when an oldie goes on a prolonged C. of A. or gets a bit bent. I suppose all this philosophising was brought on because I miss the Jodel Musketeer, surely one of the all-time greats – and for me, anyway, the new Wassmer isn't the same, for all its swishness and comfort.

We've had two Full Displays so far this year. (Newsflash: Shoreham Full Display on August 8th has just been cancelled.) One was just so-so, and the other was a sizzler. The good one was at Denham, and it had all the best ingredients successfully mixed up, to re-affirm that the Tiger Club still puts on the best to be seen anywhere, notwithstanding the absence of the old acts with which we have grown so familiar. The reason these acts were missing was that the pilots had all been selected for the World Aerobatic Championship and they were out raising money as hard as they could so as to pay their expenses for the journey to Russia. I think it says a great deal for their determination to see the competitors fund-raising, as I did at Sywell, where I saw at least three members of the British Team humping collecting boxes. I wondered three things: (1) How many other competing countries cared so little for those who would represent them? (2) Did the public popping pennies into collection boxes realise it was the actual competitors who were doing the leg-work? (3) Win or lose, I think our pilots have what it takes.

Talking of Sywell. For the second year running the weather was fabulous for this tremendous occasion. Outside of Oshkosh it's the World's Biggest Rally and a truly International one at that. The highlight must surely have been the arrival of

Clive Dunning in the Thorpe 18 he'd built himself and then flown the entire way from Australia. And what an unforgettable and moving reception he got with that spontaneous rendering of Waltzing Matilda. There were over 500 visiting aircraft, many from all over Europe. For the record there were again over 2,000 movements a day over the Saturday and Sunday and all without incident. CAA please note: and we didn't use radio either.

We were glad to welcome Sir Geoffrey and Lady Howe to Redhill recently and that the meeting was a most enjoyable one was in no doubt.

Sir Geoffrey later wrote:

House of Commons, 2nd June 1976

"Dear Mr Jones,

Immediately on my return from Germany, I am writing to extend to you and the other members of the Club warmest thanks from Alec, my wife and I for all the kindness and hospitality which we received on Monday.

Please say a very special thank-you to Messrs Wolf and Benjamin for taking us up in their aircraft and even for allowing our nervous fingers to control the machines under careful supervision!

With best wishes,
Geoffrey Howe."

. . . From Bill Hitchcock of the Australian Tiger Club has just come the detailed news of their Inaugural Air Show. I've pinned up the Newsletter he sent along with some cuttings on the notice board at Redhill; it's excellent reading. I must say the enthusiasm for all things 'Tiger' is most evident. Even the envelope is stamped 'Tigers are Tremendous.'

Sad news for those who have followed the fortunes of the Kronfeld Club's ups and downs for so many years is that the Club is now closed following an invasion by squatters who, before they left, vandalised the place, breaking or stealing everything within sight. The Tiger Club have long been the main supporters of this Club and indeed Michael Jones and your Editor are Directors, but even we have had to face the inevitable fact that even before the vandals the Club got very little support from anyone and its end was close. Although the Club as we know it is finished, the Directors are prepared to offer the lease to a suitable aviation-minded organisation, and eventually to offer the proceeds to some worthwhile charity.

The Osnabrück visit to Redhill went well, with especial thanks to Phil Irish who lent his strip during their tour of Devon. Unfortunately they found for their return to Germany the only bit of wet thunderstorm we've seen in ages!

We hope the following word of caution will be taken in the right spirit. A member very recently force-landed a Stampe after running out of fuel. It is reported that the gauge at the time read half-full. Whilst we have every sympathy for his predicament, this definitely constitutes Bad Airmanship. We contend that a pilot is <u>always</u> ultimately responsible for ensuring there is sufficient fuel for a flight.

So do check up, and remember that float-type gauges are notoriously unreliable. If in doubt, refuel. It's as simple as that.

The *"Rag"* published a letter from Peter Vanneck. Peter, who, as he explained, was a Founder Member, was also Lord Mayor of London Elect, if that's the right expression. His Lord Mayor's Parade in the following year was an event and a half. . . . I'll cover it later, it's too priceless to miss.

"Dear Benjy,

On reading the May/June No. of the *"Rag,"* I thought, as a Founder Member, I must chime in on the subject of the formation of the Club. Really Jim Denyer and Norman Jones have it pretty well right between them, but for the record it was just before the Auxiliary Air Force flying squadrons got the chop, which as I well remember was on January 10th 1957, when I flew a last happy hour of solo aerobatics in a Meteor.

We talked about the idea at the National Air Races in the summer of 1955, and then with Norman in the chair at a table at the Racing Dinner in the autumn the whole thing gelled. Right at the beginning I seem to recollect three of Norman's six Tigers being kept in 601 Squadron's hangar at North Weald and we, in his old Squadron, certainly raced them the following year.

How successful this simple idea has grown, and in so many aspects of sporting aviation. We all owe so much to Norman with his well-deserved MBE for his imagination as well as invaluable service to his ideals.

Enough puffing up of the Chairman! In my 20 years in the Club I have never met such an interesting and varied group of individuals with one unifying thought – enjoying themselves in the third dimension. *Floreat* the Tiger Club!

PETER VANNECK."

CLUB NEWS: SEPTEMBER – OCTOBER 1976

Really do apologise for the long delay in getting down to this Newsletter, but your Editor, having sold his home, has been living out of a suitcase for the last two months, first on a boat, warm and dry, and then the last three weeks in a new home, weather wet and windy, *sans* carpets, curtains, hope or money. So understandably the *"Rag"* got put back a bit!

The *"Tiger Rag"* was always a personal sounding-board for all of us. We really were interested in 'people' as well as aeroplanes, it all helped to keep such a diverse and widely-spread membership together; the gossip was friendly, encouraging, never ever malicious – no one was ever put down, – in fact it tried to be everything an idyllic family would like to be, so the opening extract wasn't in any way unusual.

But since I'm writing this book and explanations can bring a smile to the reader's face, here goes.

For starters I soon sold our home in Kingston and with what was left for me (Lollie of course had half for her new home) I bought a big 50 ft wooden displacement motor cruiser of great charm. It came to me with a sad story.

The first owner had it built to the most demanding of standards, and the interior panelling would have delighted Onassis, it certainly bowled me over; anyway, on the day the new owner stepped aboard he was so overwhelmed with happiness he had a heart attack and kicked the bucket. I was heartless enough to burst out laughing when Bill, Broom's friendly sales manager told me, but he assured me it was true, so I superstitiously touched wood and bought her.

Her strange name was "Famdor" and it was in her that my new Cherokee-flying girl-friend Inge and I proposed to sail across the North Sea to Denmark. But first Inge had to return briefly to Denmark on business.

"Please," she asked, directing her bright blue eyes at me, "don't do anything silly whilst I'm away."

As if I would.

She hadn't been gone a day when I drove down to Chichester – where we had together brought "Famdor" around from the Broads – intending to work on her. As I passed through Fernhurst I spotted a hand-written notice on the roadside advertising a new home for sale in two acres of land. To this day I don't know why I stopped, but in doing so I discovered a gem of a place literally constructed in solid oak and decked out with antique brick and slate – lovingly assembled and all in splendid isolation. That's mine. And inside a week it was. Oh! yes, and to pay for it I sold the boat. No, Inge didn't leave me, but it was close.

. . . That long, parched summer came to a sudden end in September, yet within two weeks of rain the countryside miraculously became a glorious place of green again. Gone was the dry desert and Redhill, along with the rest of Surrey, bloomed. '76 was very much a flyers' year – still is, of course. From every quarter came tales of memorable flying, of cloudless skies that blessed every conceivable event. Perhaps the most important one for us was the convincing performance of our British Aerobatics Team in the World Championships. To them all, team, judges, and ground-crews alike, all the congratulations from the rest of the Tiger Club (I believe that without exception every International team so far has been 100% Tiger Club). I shouldn't wonder if Norman Jones didn't allow himself a modest grin of satisfaction, for it was undoubtedly his early and unstinting support of aerobatics that gave the impetus and original training to our team.

Redhill has been so often visited by overseas members that it's a rare day that doesn't greet cheerful faces from the great beyond. And they come great distances. A few weeks ago I actually witnessed an American who, with his niece, made the not-inconsiderable detour to London and hence to the airfield, just to fly Tiger 'CDC. Not bad for someone en route from New York to Florence. Phili Voice tells me that this isn't at all unusual. I'll not be alone in expressing my deep admiration – long may we have 'welcome' written all over the mat.

My postbag is currently full of information from Tiger Club outposts; from Bill Hitchcock in Australia (just what did happen to that visit, Bill?), from the irrepressible Frank Price down in Waco, USA. An extract from his newsletter – the American Tiger Club version – takes some beating for downright get-up-and-go:

". . . Beer keg and cokes waiting after the show for Club members and then off to Mexican food for those remaining who think they are still Tigers. Camping space at Sid's and parking space has been vastly improved. Strip is 2,700 ft long and smooth grass, and Ramada Inn has courtesy car from Sid's and McGregor. Rental cars available. McGregor is about 6 miles SW of Municipal and Sid's is 5 miles on the 70 Degree off the VOR. Sid says: 'If you really need a VOR, come over by bus. Remember to book your own room and pick up your own trash after the show and I won't have to take time off work to do yours.' Snoopy has been grooming for his part in the show for a month. Great show at Tulsa, Okla. last week. Always enjoy those folks up there, they are just like us. Greenwood, Miss. and the Stearman Annual Fly-In at Galesburg are all the shows I have left to do, so if you want to promote one in your place, hire me. Old men need to eat too!"

. . . A new division of David Timmis's long running and successful Foreign Touring Section is Home Touring. It's aimed at the pilot who would like to join a gaggle of fellow members on short trips, usually over a weekend, to explore some of those strips one hears about but never seem to get around to visiting. Organising genius is Richard Ball. Phone him or David for news of the latest destination. I gather the concept is nice and basic, slow and economic. Will keep you closely posted on this development for it promises to be a lot of fun. And the organisers would like to hear from members with such strips we could fly in to. Local bed and breakfast, a pub for dinner that night, and some transport, is all that is needed.

Perhaps Home Touring wasn't such a new idea but the way it was propounded ensured an instant success, a sort of forerunner of today's Fly-In but more relaxed, and every visit took one to new strips, new friends and a way to fly that was, and still is, timeless.

DISPLAY EXPENSES EXPOSÉ, FAREWELL "G.B." AND FINALE

As I shuffled through that file of papers for the end of '76 I came across what I believe was the first attempt anyone had made to clarify how much the pilots should charge for a Tiger Club participation in someone else's show, usually a fête, race meeting, or anything else our pilots were game to attend. Many venues of course had no provision for a landing so the show was a pre-timed affair. Eyes up, applause, eyes down, and the team either flew on to another venue or came on home, or better still stopped for tea on a friendly strip. Mobile phones would have worked miracles.

The reason for this price list was that an element of entrepreneurship had begun to creep in, with the occasional undercutting of a fellow flyer, and not a little poaching. The paper was entitled 'Expenses for Display Acts,' with the emphasis on expenses. Since we had no wish to be considered sordidly commercial – it would have attracted the unwanted CAA in search of corresponding licenses, licensed airfields and attendant paper work, to say nothing of lurking taxmen – we flew for love and hours and hoped our halos didn't slip too much.

I've reproduced it now as a pragmatic way of life. Remember too, all arrangements were made by individuals, teams or pilots and not by the Club. The Club only benefited by the aircraft hire. Even in those days some backs got scratched more than others . . . oh! but what fun.

EXPENSES FOR DISPLAY ACTS BY THE TIGER CLUB – 1977

ACT	COST
1. **TIED BIPLANES**: Three aircraft tied together with colourful bunting carrying out formation changes, wing-overs, loops and culminating in a Prince of Wales Feathers burst, whilst emitting smoke.	£130 by arrangement if aircraft on site
Additional Acts if Tied Biplanes Booked:	
(a) <u>Dog-Fight</u>: Simulated aerial combat with use of smoke to indicate a 'kill.'	£50
(b) <u>Streamer Cutting</u>: Dropping and cutting of long streamers synchronised to all points of the area.	£50
(c) <u>Flour Bombing</u>: Use of flour bags to strike a stationary or moving target well clear but in front of the crowd (prior arrangement only).	£50
(d) <u>Balloon Bursting</u>: Coloured balloons released at ground level, burst in a spirit of competition between pilots.	£50
2. **DUO STAMPES**: Two biplanes flying formation, synchronised and opposed aerobatics including flick manoeuvres, and featuring the mirror formation. All figures picked out in continuous smoke.	£250
Additional Acts if Duo Booked:	
(a) Dog-Fight	£40
(b) Streamer Cutting	£40
(c) Flour Bombing	£40
(d) Solo Aerobatics	£90
(e) Balloon Bursting	£50
3. **SOLO AEROBATICS**: A Stampe biplane flying aerobatics to a high international competition standard and emphasising the sequential pattern with smoke.	£150
4. **STANDING ON THE WING**: A girl stands on the wing of a Tiger Moth at 60 mph at low level, waving to the crowd and obviously enjoying the experience.	£180
5. **STANDING ON THE WING PLUS TURBULENTS**: The above act with the girl leading two Turbulents, one on each side, by bunting strips tied to a wingtip and holding the other ends in her hands.	By arrangement if aircraft on site

6. FOUR TURBULENTS: Four tiny aircraft with   £220
   Volkswagen engines maintaining a close formation
   with wingtips tied together. Includes:
   (a) Synchronised Streamer Cutting
   (b) Limbo Flying under man-held hoops
   (c) Balloon Bursting
   (d) Flour Bombing (prior arrangement only)   £50

7. THREE TURBULENTS: Very similar content to the above.   £170

8. ARROW ACTIVE DEMONSTRATION: A vintage   £190
   biplane first flown in 1928 and now the sole survivor,
   performing graceful aerobatic manoeuvres and low-level
   display flying.

9. FOURNIER RF.4: An optimum-design, low-power,   £100
   high-performance, long-wing aircraft, flying a
   sailplane-like routine with style and grace.

10. FORMULA ONE RACER: A demonstration of high-speed £150
    (200 mph) manoeuvring within a limited airspace such
    as a display arena. Currently contending the Formula
    One Championship of the United Kingdom. The high rate
    of roll (faster than a Gnat) is featured.

11. PITTS SPECIAL S.1: World Championship class By arrangement
    of aircraft in aerobatics. An exciting combination
    of artistry, speed and power exploring all corners
    of the flying spectrum.

12. COMPER SWIFT: A famous prewar (1939-45)   £120
    racer of distinctive lines and sounds, showing off
    its very good paces and including aerobatics.

13. DIAMOND NINE: Tribute to the Red Arrows. By arrange-
    A formation of five biplanes and four monoplanes ment if
    flying a figure nine pattern. aircraft on site

14. MINI DISPLAYS: Combinations of any of the above
    acts can be arranged at a package-deal price, probably
    with bonus acts thrown in as make-weight. The visual
    impact of a 'circus' of aircraft displayed on the ground or
    flying in the vicinity of the display site should not be
    underestimated.
    (a) Individual requirements can be easily catered for if
    a time or budget indication is made.
    (b) 100 nautical miles radius is the normal radius of
    ferry from Redhill. Longer distances will be undertaken
    at extra cost.

15. <u>SEAPLANE TIGER ON FLOATS</u>: Unique fly-past.   £175
By arrangement depending on suitable water landing sites.

<u>NOTE</u>: Figures include all expenses including flying costs and **VAT**. All display acts subject to pilots' and aircraft availability.

<u>Committee Notes: Oct '76</u>
<u>Seaplane</u>: Seaplane now out of water. 1976 season – 78 hours, 29 pilots, 11 passengers. Attended 4 airshows. 3 new licences issued, 3 nearly there.
<u>Any other business</u>: "G.B." was ill. Committee all wish him well.

Wing Commander Arthur Golding Barrett – "G.B." – died in the November. There was a funeral and a simple fly-past; a moving moment. Veryan, his widow, wrote later: "Wouldn't the old buzzard have loved the fly-past?" She loved the old buzzard dearly, we all did.

Sometimes I think we sense our coming death – "G.B." surely did. Shortly before he died he wrote me a long letter. Be patient with me if I reproduce some, for "G.B." was one of the Few, one of the pioneers that gave us flight. His link with the past gave meaning to so much of what we did in the Club, of which he was integral part.

". . . I was mildly surprised – and much entertained – by your assurance that I was not forgotten.

In a lifetime involved with flying I made few enemies and friends aplenty. Today, it is my 72nd year. I wield the pen more than the joystick in the interests of flying, but I still manage to keep my eye and hand in as opportunity offers. I am not dead yet. Only one of the few left. I seem endlessly to be writing obituaries. I often wonder who will write mine – if any. I'll bet they get it wrong. I have never sought fame. Perhaps they'll remember that in all those years dedicated to the Tiger Club I never broke an aeroplane! Nor in fact ever elsewhere. The last year or so have seen so many of us 'old uns' make their take-off. Old pals from what is known as "the good old times." "Toc H" George Lowdell, Clem Pike, Latimer Needham, Thurston James, Frank St. Barbe, Hubert Broad, Gordon England. We should lament their passing – but I deplore the inexcusable loss by disposal of their records. One or two have left me their log books and I am presently busy or sorting 'effects' and diverting photographs, log books etc. to appropriate Clubs and associations for safe keeping. But alas! so few are really interested. (Stop – for pen refuelling.)

The saying that old men forget may generally be true – but not wholly. Names, dates, places, yes. But not occasions and experiences. I've seen so much in a long life. Saw powered flying born and – in its early interpretation – almost die. No longer an art – it's become a science, dispensing vastly with use of hand and eye. I sat in Concorde the other day, P.1 seat. So much instrumentation on floor, walls, and ceiling – and nigh impossible to see out of the windows! And as I sat there I recalled a long-forgotten early solo flight(s) in an Avro 504 with an 80 hp Renault engine ('EBPJ?). It did have an altimeter which used to stick at various readings –

and remain so until taxying after landing. The oil gauge showed around 50 lbs/sq. in. on t/o and slowly sank to zero – a signal to land at once. With an ASI u/s the stalling speed was never known, just when it went all quiet. So times have changed somewhat.

Now all the lights have gone out – pause for investigation. Ah! well, nothing wrong inside – must be fault in pylons. So a 'Tilly' lamp is in action.

. . . Can't consider TC Dinner . . . much beyond finances of OAP on fixed income. So shall remain here – and as you rightly envisage me, aged, forgotten and stagnating (not true. – Ed.) – just living with my memories! Yet somehow coping – and leading a pretty full life – constantly in touch with many sincere friends in and out of circulation. Ha! There goes the telephone – I wonder what this is? Who? Why? What fun? I'll answer it. Sheila Scott – from whom or of whom I hadn't heard for ages – wanting to know anything I could remember of Mrs Elliot Lyn (Lady Heath) way back 40 years in 1930/2. So more research – another letter – ah! well, it all helps to break the sad monotony of my 'sunset years.'"

Another twelve months had slipped by, a year full of events. If, in reporting only the highlights on this season, the details of now annual displays have been put to one side – like eating porridge every morning for breakfast too much could only induce a diminishing interest in its taste – the year 1976 was, in a practical sense, our biggest and best.

A total of twenty-six displays with Club aircraft were given, four of them abroad. That was only the public face; even more flying was going on in glider-towing, aerobatics and touring sections, quite apart from the Club's favourite activity, just turning up at the never-ending garden party going on across the grassy spaces of Redhill, where in our memories the sun always shone, there to enjoy getting airborne simply to feel the wind in our face.

I promised earlier to mention Founder Member Peter Vanneck's elevation to Lord Mayor of London. True, it occurred in the November of '77, a year beyond the scope of this present volume, but it was such a significant event for Peter, for the Club and myself I can't resist the temptation.

For some unaccountable reason I was easily breathless so I sought out my doctor who, suspecting the cause, sent me to a heart specialist.

Nice bloke. "You've got angina," he said, "heart trouble."

"No way," said I; "I'm as fit as a fiddle."

He, the tell-tale, told my doctor who, having tried unsuccessfully to get me to take the condition seriously, resorted to shock tactics.

"You can't go on flying."

Even if I hadn't shown it, the message got through and I confided my worries to Cliff Robertson who was staying with me down in Surrey during another session of filmmaking.

"Go and see Edward Diethrich, he's a great friend and the best heart man in the US."

I flew over to Phoenix, Arizona for an opinion.

"You need a bypass, like yesterday," said Edward.

On my return to England there was a letter from Peter thanking me for offering to organise a flypast on his big occasion and accepting with alacrity. What Peter didn't know was that we had also planned a big surprise for his Lord Mayor's Show; we kept it a surprise for another reason, we didn't reckon the CAA would have approved a five-plane tied-together formation, complete with smoke, 500 ft over the heart of the City.

I revisited my quack and asked if he recommended I go through with the US bypass. He was adamant.

"Straight away," he urged.

"Can't," said I; "at least not before the 12th." – some two weeks away.

"Why not ?" he asked with asperity.

I told him.

". . . and I'll lead in the Arrow Active," I added.

The breath left his body and he sank back in his chair.

"Let me get this straight. You intend to fly low over the centre of London tied to other aeroplanes over thousands of people?"

I nodded proudly.

Before you could say Jack Robinson (alright then, Cliff Robertson), my license had been revoked and Neil Williams had taken my place in the Active.

The occasion was a great success but it was such a violent, windy day that the tapes would never have remained. It was as much as James Black, Brian Smith, Carl Schofield, Peter Jarvis and Neil could do to stay in the same piece of sky. Perhaps it was as well I was blissfully unaware, recovering in the Arizona sunshine. There's a sad postscript. It was Neil's last display. He died a couple of weeks later in the Spanish mountains whilst ferrying a He.111 back to Blackbushe.

The second book is finished, yet I sense there's a certain something that's needed to round off the story. I sit back and review the twenty years of the tale so far – a halfway point in the Club's present life. Isn't there more to it than just the logic of a potted history served up in convenient mode, a decade at a time? Wasn't twenty years also a generation, and wasn't 1976 therefore a significant year, a turning point? So it was to be.

I reached for my concise O.D. *"Generation"*: 'whole body of persons born about the same time.' And then the penny dropped. A new generation was taking over from the old, from those founding stalwarts we irreverently labelled our Golden Oldies. And now in the wake of all those others of his era men like "Bish" and "G.B.," Norman too was retiring.

Today, that generation cycle is at it again. Who would have thought that one day I and those contemporaries of mine would in turn become the Oldies?

No complaints, just content our Club still thrives in the hands of many a Golden Oldie-to-be . . . and proud to have taken part.

APPENDIX 1

TIGER CLUB: DISPUTES WITH LANDLORDS (BRITISH AIR TRANSPORT) RE REDHILL AERODROME

The dispute with the landlords that came to a head in 1966 was about landing fees, and in this connection the interpretation of the wording of the lease.

The Club maintained that 'landings' meant 'arrivals' since the lease only required us to keep a record of 'arrivals and departures.' However, also under the lease the landlords were entitled to charge the Club for 'landings' over and above '1,000 per annum.' The Club argued that these 'landings' in fact meant arrivals from other airfields, not local flights. The problem for the landlords was that the onus was on them – for charging purposes – to keep records of all landings. So what in fact happened was that, unbeknown to the Club, logs were secretly kept over various periods by people employed by the landlords and the Club was suddenly presented with a very large and unexpected bill.

Needless to say, the Club refused to pay and the matter came to Court. Unfortunately the Court ruled that the landlord's interpretation of the lease was correct and Norman settled the bill. This however left open what was to happen in the future since the lease had come to an end and both parties, surprisingly, wished to renew it. The landlords were tacitly quite happy with the way that the Club was running the airfield; they had no wish to employ people to keep records of landings, and having themselves run flying Clubs at the aerodrome in the past, both before and after the war, they were not in favour of air traffic control. However when the Club arrived at the airfield in 1959 they did not anticipate that it would expand in the way it did, both in terms of membership and flying activity. Consequently after some skilful negotiating by the Club's solicitors it was agreed to amend the lease in the matter of landing fees by adopting a new formula, and that was that the Club would pay an annual *per capita* charge of £2.12.0 per member. At the time this sum appeared extremely onerous, since it amounted to a very substantial proportion of the annual subscription, which consequently had to be doubled overnight. However, in the long term this agreement proved very favourable to the Club, since not only were all worries over landing fees removed at a stroke but also it applied to the growing number of members who owned their own aircraft. . . .

The dispute with the landlords which occurred in 1973 again coincided with the renewal of the lease and was potentially much more serious than in 1966. Since then the landlords had sold the airfield to a large financial conglomerate with aviation interests – British and Commonwealth Shipping Co. (With hindsight it might have been a good idea if the offer made to the Chairman to buy the aerodrome several years earlier had been accepted!) British and Commonwealth, now the Club's new landlords, also by now owned Bristow Helicopters, who had moved to Redhill as an independent company in 1960. They now claimed that they required the Club's hangar for Bristows and offered the Club two years to get out at a grossly inflated rent.

After protracted and fruitless negotiations, including a change of solicitors by the Club, the dispute finally came to Court in October 1974 and in January 1975, and it was not finally settled until November 1975 when the landlords withdrew their appeal against the result. This turned out very favourably for the Club with an award of a 12-year lease at a rent which was affordable and the landing fee agreement intact at the existing rates. In achieving this result, the Club were extremely fortunate in that, despite the fact that Bristows were heavily involved with North Sea oil at the time, the landlords failed completely to make out a proper case for wanting the Club's hangar. Secondly the Club had obtained at very short notice the services of an extremely able and energetic surveyor, and finally, it was lucky that the Judge knew a thing or two about flying Clubs and Tiger Moths and recognised the difficulty of finding another home.

Needless to say as everybody knows the landlords did not let the matter rest there. . . .

CONFIDENTIAL
THE TIGER CLUB: RENEWAL OF LEASE AT REDHILL AERODROME APPLICATION TO LEGAL FUND

REPORT

The Club's lease at Redhill Aerodrome runs from 29th September 1959 to 29th September 1980 but is determinable at the 7th and 14th years. The end of the 14th year fell due on 29th September 1973.

The Landlords, Redhill Aerodrome Holdings Ltd, have given the Club notice to quit with the offer of a two-year lease at double the existing rent. In making this offer they have stated that their associated company, Bristow Helicopters Ltd, may want the hangar at the end of two years.

The Club's solicitors have tried to negotiate with the landlords and attempts have been made to negotiate with individuals on the boards of Redhill Aerodrome Holdings and Bristows – but so far without success. Meanwhile the Club has rejected the Landlords' offer and under the Landlord and Tenant Act, which entitles an existing tenant to a new tenancy for a term not exceeding 14 years, has applied to the Court for a new lease. This application has been supported by counsel's opinion that the Club has a very good chance of obtaining a longer term than offered by the Landlords.

On the question of rent, once the period of tenancy has been determined it is hoped to decide this on the basis of comparable rents for hangar space in the London area. The Landlords have mentioned a figure of 50p per sq. foot for a long term whereas the present rate is only 16p.

A complicating factor is that the solicitors acting for the Club in this matter also acted for the Chairman in the matter of renewing the lease of the Fairoaks Aero Club and, although they were a different set of circumstances they were unsuccessful, with the result that the Fairoaks Aero Club has been thrown off Fairoaks Aerodrome, having been established there for about 30 years. As a result there has been a breakdown of confidence and also the firm has asked for the very high fee of £2,000 to handle the case of the Tiger Club. In view of this, it has been decided to engage new solicitors with a fresh approach and for a lower fee, which is now estimated at not exceeding £1,000 total.

At the December meeting of the Committee, it was decided that the Legal Fund would give unlimited support to this case, although it is strictly outside its terms of reference, and it is hoped that this report will put members of the Committee and any other interested members fully in the picture.

The case is due to be heard at Reigate on 19th February and it should perhaps be realised that unless the Club is successful in obtaining a longer term, 1974 could well be the last full year of the Club operating in its present form, and also possibly the last full year that Redhill Aerodrome will be available for light aircraft.

The British Light Aviation Centre have promised to give their full support to the case.

Negotiations are still being attempted with members of the Landlords' board and the board of Bristow Helicopters, and if anybody has any special influence they can exercise in this respect, it would perhaps be helpful to make approaches. The key personnel are Sir Nicholas Cayzer, who is Chairman of British Commonwealth and Shipping Company and Chairman of Redhill Aerodrome Holdings, Hon. Anthony Cayzer, Deputy Chairman of British and Commonwealth and director of Bristow Helicopters and also a Vice-President of the BLAC. He has already been approached but is unable to be of assistance. There is also George Russel Fry who is a director of Redhill Aerodrome Holdings and Managing Director of Bristow Helicopters, and who has been a member of the Tiger Club since 1960. He has promised to do all he can. Finally there is Alan Bristow himself who may be able to help but has not been approached directly as far as is known. There are various other directors of both companies and a full list is available if required.

As far as the question of comparable rents for similar hangar accommodation in the London area is concerned, if any member has any reliable information on specific aerodromes, it would be appreciated if this could be communicated to the Secretary without delay.

D.M.J. Jones
Secretary
5.1.74

CIRCULATION: Committee members past and present.

APPENDIX 2

TIGER CLUB AIRCRAFT OPERATED DURING 1967 - 1976

Tiger Moths
G-ACDC
G-AIVW (seaplane)
G-ANMZ
G-ANZZ
G-AOAA
G-ASKP

Puss Moth
G-AHLO

Fox Moth
G-ACEJ

Stampes
G-ASHS
G-ATKC
G-AVCO
G-AWEF
G-AWIW

Jodel D.140
G-AROW
G-ATKX

Jodel DR.1050
G-ARUH
G-ATLB
G-ATJA

Jodel D.150
G-AVEF

Condors
G-ARVZ
G-AVCZ

G-AWSS
G-AXGS
G-AYFD

Turbulents
G-APNZ
G-ARJZ
G-ARLZ
G-ARRZ
G-ARZM
G-ASAM
G-ASDB
G-AWPA

Piper Cub
G-ARAM
G-AVPT

Arrow Active
G-ABVE

Beagle Husky
G-ATMH

Beta
G-ATLY
G-AWHV

Fournier RF.4
G-AVHY

Wassmer WA.51A Pacific
G-AZYZ

Wassmer WA.52 Europa
G-BDSN (ex-G-BADN)

APPENDIX 3

TIGER CLUB MEMBERS JOINING BETWEEN 1967 AND 1976

A

Michael Abott	1967
Arthur Adair	1967
Michael Alexander	1967
Derek Arlow	1967
Michael Austin	1967
H.M. Alliott	1968
Anthony Atkinson	1968
Mrs M. Austin	1968
Olaf Ahnstrand	1970
William Archer	1970
Michael Astor	1970
Ronald Ashford	1971
Edward Acres	1972
Eric Afleck	1972
John Armstrong	1972
Ulf Abrahamsson	1973
Ronald Austin	1973
Rosemary Alliott	1974
Kim Ardron	1974
Keith Agate	1975
Una Allman	1975
Sheena Anderson	1975
Edgar Adams	1976
Ian Aitken	1976
Eric Armstrong	1976
Marianne Ashraf	1976

B

Margaret Bailey	1967
Mrs B. Barnes	1967
Ann Barnsley	1967
David Barrett	1967
Mrs M.J. Barrow	1967
John Batt	1967
Charles Beauchamp	1967
Vivian Bellamy	1967
J. Billyack	1967
Michael Bishop	1967
Mrs Blackburn	1967
Clive Boarder	1967
Bruce Bonner	1967
Mrs R. Bonner	1967
S.S. Bosley	1967
Royston Box	1967
Hubert Broad	1967
Barry Brown	1967

Peter Bugge	1967
Derek Burn	1967
Donald Butterfield	1967
P.J. Barclay	1968
John Baudrier	1968
J.J. Baynes	1968
Barry Bell	1968
H. Bialkiewicz	1968
Alan Boyle	1968
Jan Breman	1968
Jennifer Bridges-Adams	1968
John Brockman	1968
D. Bryant	1968
Alexander Burne	1968
Carl Badgett	1969
Peter Baxter	1969
Neville Birch	1969
Roy Booth	1969
R.D. Brown	1969
R.J. Burgess	1969
Norman Burley	1969
Mrs M.D. Burn	1969
W.J. Burrough Jr.	1969
Anthony Baptiste	1970
John Bennett	1970
Edmund Bewley	1970
Thomas Bidwell	1970
John Bright	1970
Roger Brookhouse	1970
Christopher Bryant	1970
Peter Bubbear	1970
Martin Butcher	1970
Stephen Barnes	1971
Alan Beckett	1971
Anthony Beckton	1971
Derek Bishop	1971
Alan Brown	1971
Peter Brown	1971
Angus Buchanan	1971
Eric Burgess	1971
Mrs Lynn Burt	1971
Patrick Bangerter	1972
Jane Barker	1972
Edgardo Bartoli	1972
Roy Berry	1972
Christopher Bevan	1972
Ladislav Bezak	1972
Deane Brandon	1972

John Breese	1972	Wendy Cook	1967
Suzanne Brooks	1972	Thomas Crane	1967
Josh Burner	1972	J. Crawford	1967
William Baird	1973	D. Culver	1967
Alain Ballini	1973	David G. Campbell	1968
Carole Baptiste	1973	David N. Campbell	1968
Richard Barnby	1973	John Carter	1968
Michael Beach	1973	David Champion	1968
Michael Beasley	1973	Richard Chandless	1968
Charles Berridge	1973	Michael Charlesworth	1968
Josef Blomeke	1973	Robert Christie	1968
Robert Brewer	1973	D.J. Clark	1968
Nick Bristow	1973	Michael Coburn	1968
Margaret Burgess	1973	James Cox	1968
Selina Burgess	1973	A.H. Cruikshank	1968
Edmund Burke	1973	James Cumming	1968
Richard Butler	1973	Angus Clydesdale	1969
Frank Ball	1974	G.C. Collett	1969
Richard Ball	1974	Michael Conron	1969
Gordon Banner	1974	Jean Couronne	1969
Caroline Barker	1974	Frances Crampton	1969
Barry Bell	1974	D.A.M. Cresswell	1969
Bertram Binnewald	1974	Maurice Cronin	1969
John Boxall	1974	Gerald Chisum	1970
Derek Bray	1974	Roger Constable	1970
David Brown	1974	Peter Cordery	1970
Robert Buckels	1974	Werner Cramer	1970
Carl Bury	1974	Kenneth Cunningham-Brown	1970
Sybil Barnby	1975	Alan Curry	1970
Rowan Beach	1975	Christopher Card	1971
Brian Bennett	1975	John Carrodus	1971
Lynne Boreham	1975	George Chamberlin	1971
Stephen Brearley	1975	David Cheetham	1971
Julie Brewer	1975	G.W. Cleven	1971
Ralph Brooker	1975	Graham Coe	1971
Tim Barnby	1976	Margaret Cope	1971
Peter Beck	1976	Michael Caverley	1972
Christine Bellhouse	1976	Arthur Cansick	1972
Christopher Bellhouse	1976	Rhoda Cansick	1972
John Boys	1976	David Carroll	1972
Warwick Brown	1976	Peter Channon	1972
		Douglas Clyne	1972
C		Thomas Coleman	1972
Arve Caspersen	1967	Graham Costello	1972
Inger Caspersen	1967	Dennis Cresswell	1972
Sheila Chapman	1967	Michael Crossley	1972
S. Cherry-Downes	1967	George Campbell	1973
Minnie Churchill	1967	Peter Carr	1973
Mrs A.B. Clarke	1967	Roger Connellan	1973
R.G. Collis	1967	Trevor Conway	1973
Sheila Combs	1967	George Cordery	1973
Priscilla Corbett	1967	Nicholas Cranfield	1973

John Cranfield	1974	Thomas Dehn	1976
Michael Carlton	1975	Marcelo Demaria	1976
Judith Chisholm	1975	Michael Dentith	1976
Robin Coffey	1975	Anthony Dillow	1976
William Colson	1975	Christopher Donne	1976
Beverley Connell	1975		
Ian Cummings	1975	**E**	
Clayton Cunningham	1975	Richard Elliman	1967
John Cunningham	1975	Euan English	1967
Janet Canvin	1976	Martin Emery	1968
Mark Carless	1976	David Faulkner Bryant	1968
Edna Carr	1976	Inga Forss	1968
Per Cederquist	1976	Peter Eggett	1970
Peter Chinn	1976	George Ellis	1971
Gary Cufley	1976	J.R.F. Espir	1972
		Anthony Easton	1973
D		John Edgley	1974
John Dauncey	1967	James Emptage	1974
Burden Davidson	1967	David Edmundson	1975
Mrs V. Davidson	1967	Richard Earnshaw-Brown	1976
Richard Dent	1967	Gordon Edmiston	1976
Sydney Docwra	1967	Peter Eglington	1976
Mike Denham-Till	1968		
Miss P.B. Delaney	1969	**F**	
Betty d'Erlanger	1969	Keld Fenwick	1967
James Dixon	1969	David Fogden	1967
Rodney Dean	1970	Peter Ford	1967
Robbie Dorsey	1970	Rutger Forss	1967
David Doyle	1970	Mrs G.H. Frankel	1967
James Dufour	1970	Neville Freeman	1967
Geoffrey Dunster	1970	Enid Frow	1967
John Dyson	1970	Anne Freeman-Cowan	1968
Thomas Delany	1971	R.P. Fairfield	1969
Andre Delcroix	1971	Phillip Falk	1969
Ivan Dickenson	1971	Michael Fenton	1969
Baron Michael Donnet	1971	Erith Fjeldberg	1969
Peter Downing	1971	W.N. Floyd	1969
Kenneth Dowell	1972	R.A. Fowle	1969
Adrian Droog	1972	Richard Fisher	1970
John Dunford	1972	Amanda Forse	1970
Brian Dunlop	1972	David Fox	1970
Sylvia Dyer	1972	David Fidler	1971
Colin Dyne	1972	William Flener	1971
Margaret Dyne	1972	Gordon Franks	1971
Donald Daines	1973	Jocelyn Freeman	1971
George Donaldson	1973	Alan Foreman	1972
John Drabelle Jr.	1973	Gordon Fraser	1972
Paul Drumheiser	1973	Michael Fraser	1972
Ronald Dixon	1974	J.H. Fraser	1972
Michael Dunkerly	1974	Sheila Fennell	1973
Patricia Ditzel	1975	Colin Ford	1973
Anthony Docherty	1975	Leonard Foster	1973

Mrs C.E. Fricker	1973
Ingemar Florell	1974
Graham Francis	1974
Spencer Flack	1975
Ragnar Fredriksson	1975
Peter Furlong	1975
George Field	1976

G

William Gamblen	1967
Andrew Gibson	1967
Raymond Golby	1967
Ian Graham	1967
Peter Garrison	1968
Charles Goodhew	1968
B.J.S. Grey	1968
Carrolyn Griffiths	1968
Frank Gathercole	1969
David Gill	1969
Prince William of Gloucester	1969
Reginald Goldsmith	1969
David Gardiner	1970
Timothy Gardiner	1970
Ernest Green	1970
Roger Gulliver	1970
Torbjorn Gustafson	1970
Maximo Gainza	1971
Leonard Gallagher	1971
Christopher Geary	1971
Peter Gibbs	1971
Nicholas Goff	1971
Jonathon Goldwater	1971
James Green	1971
Timothy Griffith	1971
Robert Grimstead	1971
Matthias Gsell	1971
Stephen Gamblen	1972
Peter Gell	1973
Christopher Gibbs	1973
Norman Gibbs	1973
Paul Gliddon	1973
Nicholas Grace	1973
John Glanville	1974
James Golliday	1975
Kenneth Gollop	1975
Jean Gorton	1975
David Gough	1975
Robert Graves	1975
Derek Griffiths	1975
Erica Griffiths	1975
Pamela Glanville	1976
Hugh Gordon	1976

H

Vincent Hallam	1967
Michael Hardy	1967
Mrs L.A. Harries	1967
D. Harry	1967
Daphne Hart	1967
Terence Henderson	1967
Don Henry	1967
George Hilder	1967
Norbert Homeyer	1967
John Horley	1967
V. Hounsfield	1967
Ronald Howard	1967
Keith Hyde	1967
Julia Haig-Thomas	1968
David Hamilton	1968
Lucien Hankart	1968
Michael Harries	1968
A.A.T. Headon	1968
John Hemmington	1968
Peter Hill	1968
K.J. Hoban	1968
Mike Holtby	1968
Heather Holtby	1968
Clewin Hughes	1968
Alan Hyatt	1968
Georgina Hamilton	1969
Ray Hanna	1969
John Hayes	1969
Roy Heath	1969
Eric Hill	1969
John Hodgson	1969
P. Hollander	1969
J.L. Humpert	1969
Timothy Harding	1970
Ian Hay	1970
Paul Hill	1970
Raymond Hoggarth	1970
Francis Humblet	1970
James Hanamer	1971
Elisabeth Hargraves	1971
Anthony Harold	1971
Skitch Henderson	1971
E.A. Hines	1971
Maureen Holcroft	1971
Graham Horder	1971
Alan Howkins	1971
Denniss Hulme	1971
John Hall	1972
John Havers	1972
Richard Haydon	1972
Stephen Haye	1972

Martin Heal	1972	Gordon Jones	1972
John Heath	1972	Clifford Jacobs	1973
Jonathan Hodgkins	1972	Rudolf Jakma	1973
Brian Huggins	1972	Edward Jeffery	1973
John Harper	1973	Janine Jeffery	1973
Joan Hawkins	1973	Anthony Joss	1973
Robert Head	1973	Glen James	1974
Ian Hill	1973	Robert Johnson	1974
Peter Hill	1973	Raymond Jones	1974
Frederick Hinchley	1973	Terence Jones	1974
Patricia Holmes	1973	Anthony Jover	1974
Kenneth Horn	1973	Inge Jorgensen	1975
David Howden	1973	David Johnson	1976
Kenneth Hoy	1973	Leslie Jones	1976
Michael Hallam	1974		
Ormond Haydon-Baillie	1974	**K**	
Peter Holman	1974	Edward Kirk	1967
Richard Howard	1974	Stefan Kleckowski	1967
Trevor Howe	1974	T.A.King	1969
John Hardie	1975	Bernard Kirby	1969
Jeffrey Harris	1975	D.S. Knudsen	1969
David Hayler	1975	Hugh Kavanagh	1970
Stuart Hoare	1975	Richard Keen	1970
Michael Hood	1975	Seamus Kelly	1970
Anthony Hutton	1975	Bruce Kemper	1970
Lars Haakensen	1976	David King	1970
Edward Hack	1976	Mary Knapp	1970
B.A. Hammeken	1976	Christopher King	1971
John Harrison	1976	Robert Kowal	1974
Douglas Hartong	1976	Gavin Keegan	1975
Richard Hathaway	1976	Malcolm Kember	1975
Clive Hawes	1976	Benjamin Kershaw	1975
John Hemington	1976	Thomas Kewin	1975
		Marwan Khalaf	1975
		Michael Kimber	1975
I		Alec Kirk	1975
Linda Innes	1969	Sandra Keegan	1976
Douglas Iles	1973	John Kirwan	1976
Michael Ireland	1976	Peter Krause	1976
J			
Brenda Jacobs	1967	L	
Pat Jarvis	1967	Betty Lees	1967
David Jarvis	1967	Margaret Lewis	1967
Philip Jebb	1967	Peter Liversidge	1967
Audrey Jenkinson	1968	William Lowe	1967
P. Jameson	1969	Alan Lowe	1968
Neil Jensen	1969	Christopher Leach	1969
Philip Joyce	1970	Roy Legg	1969
Robert Jordan	1971	Geoffrey Lemon	1970
A.R. James	1972	Wallace Lumb	1971
Christopher Jenner	1972	John Lunan	1971
Chris Jesson	1972	Roderic Lloyd-Kirk	1972

Jonathan Legat	1974
Jock Lowe	1974
Frank Laessle	1975
Richard Lane	1976
Keith Longden	1976

M

Alastair Macintosh	1967
Doreen Mackenzie	1967
Henry Mackinnon	1967
Mrs A. Martin	1967
Gertrud May	1967
Robert McClintock	1967
Brian Middleton	1967
Loraine Mimpriss	1967
Lorna Minton	1967
Richard Mole	1967
Isobel Morris	1967
N.K. Manley	1968
Susan Margarett	1968
D.A.C. Marshall	1968
Edwin Martin	1968
Geoffrey McBreen	1968
Fiona McDougall	1968
Cecil McKinney	1968
Peter McLennan	1968
Philip Meeson	1968
Krov Menuhin	1968
Annie Menuhin	1968
R.E. Mitchell	1968
Ian Macclennan	1969
Arthur Markl	1969
Philip Mayne	1969
Iain McClelland	1969
Andrew McClymont	1969
Richard McCowen	1969
Clive Miln	1969
N.J.R. Minchen	1969
Daniel Montgomery	1969
Thomas Moulson	1969
Russell Munson	1969
Jane Munson	1969
Iain Mackay	1970
H.J. Mackintosh	1970
Don Mallinson	1970
Valerie Martin	1970
Michael McRobert	1970
George Mears	1970
Alexander Mitchell	1970
Bo-Lennart Modee	1970
Alan Morris	1970
Arthur Myers	1970

George Macpherson	1971
Margaret McClymont	1971
Walter Mears	1971
Julius Meinl	1971
Richard Millward	1971
Alan Milton	1971
Caroline Morris	1971
Leonard Martin	1972
Hans Martinus	1972
Hans van der Meer	1972
Warren Mills	1972
A.S.B. Moss	1972
Mathleen Moss	1972
Stuart Munro	1972
Carolyn Mansfield	1973
Roger Meadmore	1973
William van Meter	1973
Dennis Moss	1973
Rodney Murdoch	1973
Donald Macleod	1974
Peter McNair	1974
Mansel Morgan	1974
Kurt Mortensen	1974
John Moyse	1974
Niall Mandal	1975
Patrick Mason	1975
Nicholas Mathias	1975
Ian MacFarlan	1976
Geoffrey Masterton	1976
John McBoyle Reid	1976

N

Toni Nielsen	1967
Jack Norton	1967
Christopher Norman	1968
John Neumeister	1969
Dick Nesbitt-Dufort	1970
Robert Noble	1970
John Nurse	1970
Stelio Nardini	1971
K.P. Nathan	1972
Robert Newton	1972
Kenneth Nicholson	1972
Dennis Neville	1973
John Nichols	1973
Jennifer Nelson	1974
Hubert Norton	1975
Nina Neuschotz	1976

O

Morten Olsen	1967
Lene Olsen	1967
M. Owen	1967

Thomas O'Brien	1968	Leif Petersen	1976
R.G. Olsen	1968		
Patrick O'Rourke	1969	**Q**	
John O'Callaghan	1970	Gordon Quinnell	1970
Robin Owen	1970		
John O'Loughlin	1972	**R**	
Peter van den Hoek Ostende	1972	Robin Rackham	1967
Brendan O'Brien	1973	Thomas Radford	1967
John O'Hara	1975	Jeremy Ray	1967
Per-Olof Olsson	1976	Glyn Richards	1967
		David Rimmer	1967
P		Brian Robinson	1967
Ian Palmer	1967	David Ronayne	1967
Donald Parker	1967	Jean Rose	1967
Lois Parker	1967	Clive Rose	1967
Anthony Poirrier	1967	Ian Runnalls	1967
Ann Procter	1967	Vincent Redding	1968
Timothy Pryor	1967	Nick Rowe	1968
Trevor Pegram	1968	Eva Radwanski	1969
Mark Preston	1968	Robert Ranscombe	1969
John Proctor	1968	R.I. Rea	1969
Stuart Peterson	1969	M.H. Reid	1969
Robert Pfaff	1969	John Ramshaw	1970
Tim Philips	1969	Thomas Reagan	1970
Robert Powl	1969	Bo Martin Rex	1970
Richard Pearson	1970	Susanna Rose	1970
Nick Pocock	1970	Iona Radice	1971
James Prankard	1970	John Rhodes	1971
David Pratt	1970	Eric Rowley	1971
Roger Pratt	1970	John Russell	1971
John Parkin	1971	Brian Rea	1972
Clifton Parsons	1971	Willem van Rijk	1972
James Parsons	1971	Thomas Rose	1972
James Pembleton	1971	Nicholas van Rozelaar	1972
Keith Pogmore	1971	Harold Randall-Cutler	1973
David Perrin	1972	Paul Robinson	1973
Peter Perry	1972	Robert Rundle	1973
John Parkhouse	1973	Issy Rondel	1974
John Percy	1973	Sidney Reay	1975
Celia Pickard	1973	Melvyn Rice	1975
Norman Pocock	1973	Alan Rowell	1975
Clive Ponsford	1973	Denis Rowland	1975
Nicholas Parkhouse	1974	Stratton Richey	1976
Allen Parsons	1974	Graham Rushworth	1976
Donna Peck	1974		
Nicholas Parsons-Smith	1975	**S**	
Magnus Pedersen	1975	Roger Sherron	1967
John Pelham Burn	1975	Joseph Smith	1967
Christopher Perry	1975	Mary Smith	1967
Arnild Petersen	1975	Pauline Snook	1967
Graham Plumbe	1975	Robert Snook	1967
Bo Vincent Petersen	1976	Michael Somerton-Rayner	1967

Mrs M.A. Spence	1967		Barry Smith	1974
Stephen Stephens	1967		Kenneth Smith	1974
Mrs R. Stringer	1967		Colin Stevens	1974
Fred Stringer	1967		Michael Stow	1974
John Saffrey	1968		Lief Sabro	1975
James Sheppard	1968		Angela Sampson	1975
Rex Smith	1968		Paul Singer	1975
J.F. Smith	1968		Charles Smith	1975
Brian Stevens	1968		Stanley Sollitt	1975
Stephen Stewart	1968		Ernest Sweeney	1975
Angela Smith	1969		John Schwarzmann	1976
Angus Stewart	1969		Pauline Senior	1976
Darrel Stinton	1969		David Shepherd	1976
Geoffrey Sykes	1969		Mary Sherron	1976
B.F.J. Seares	1970		Frank Smit	1976
Keith Sissons	1970		Gerald Steer	1976
Frederick Sparshott	1970			
Milos Safranek	1971		**T**	
Joyce Safranek	1971		Diana Tempest	1967
Geoffrey Salt	1971		Victor Townsend	1967
Anne Salt	1971		Julia Turner	1967
Patrick Schipp	1971		Robert Twitchell	1967
Patrick Schofield	1971		William Thomas	1967
Robert Silverthorne	1971		Jenny Timmis	1968
Brian Skillicorn	1971		I. Todd	1968
Martin Sobel	1971		Ray Turner	1968
Gordon Spencer	1971		Robert Trees	1969
Michael Stapp	1971		Charles Tutt	1969
Alexander Stenhouse	1971		Douglas Twyman	1969
Patricia Schlesinger	1972		Hilary Trice	1970
Richard Schwenker	1972		Robert Turnbull	1970
Theodore Secola	1972		Janet Tabor	1971
Richard Seeley	1972		John Toone	1971
P.J. Sellar	1972		Nicola Toone	1971
Richard Sherwin	1972		Ann Tovey	1971
Douglas Smith	1972		Elspeth Trees	1971
Ronald Smith	1972		John Turner	1971
Christopher Sperou	1972		Philip Thwaites	1972
Mary Steer	1972		Ann Tilbury	1972
David Scallon	1973		Peter Trevan	1972
Bruce Schneider	1973		Joe Turner	1972
Ian Senior	1973		Christopher Taylor	1973
John Setter	1973		Perry Taylor	1973
Hans Seubert	1973		James Thomson	1973
Freydis Sharland	1973		Sue Taylor	1974
John Smith	1973		Alan Thelwall	1975
Anthony Sobey	1973		Neil Thomason	1976
Leslie Steward	1973		Anthony Tringham	1976
John Strong	1973			
Andrew Stuart	1973		**U**	
Robert Swansborough	1973		Frederick Underwood	1967
Leif Simonsson	1974		Allan Usherwood	1968

Anthony Unwin	1970	Michael Woodley	1970
Jack Upchurch	1976	Evelyn Woods	1970
		John Woods	1970
V		HRH Prince of Wales	1971
Miss A. Vincent	1967	Robert Wallis	1971
C.A. Vettiger	1969	Eric White	1971
Peter Vinson	1970	John Wilks	1971
Wally Voice	1976	James Woolford	1971
		Mike Wallis	1972
W		Edwin Williamson	1972
F. Walker	1967	Peter Williamson	1972
P. Warcup	1967	Philip Wolf	1972
Werner Werdenberg	1967	Kenneth Wood	1972
Donald White	1967	Joseph Wright	1972
Robin Wilson	1967	Mark Wakem	1973
C. Winch	1967	Anthony Webber	1973
Reginald Wise	1967	Peter Wiggins	1973
Richard Wojcechowski	1967	William Wilks	1973
Patricia Wolfson	1967	W.J. Wratten	1973
F. White	1968	Jacoba Wright	1973
Mrs P White	1968	Wendy Webber	1974
Arthur Wignall	1968	Ronald Weidner	1974
John Wilkinson	1968	John Whibley	1974
Frederick Williams	1968	Kenneth Whitehead	1974
Michael Wilson	1968	Bart Woodall	1974
Roger Wilson	1968	Graham Wrightson	1974
Derek Wood	1968	Audrey Wall	1975
Christopher G. Wren	1968	Nicholas Warner	1975
Roy Watling-Greenwood	1969	Leon Whelchel	1975
Ralph Wefel	1969	Alan Walker	1976
Miss C. Wentworth	1969	Bob Wedan	1976
Mrs Lesley Wilson	1969	Doris Wrightson	1976
Gwendoline Wood	1969		
Alistair Worters	1969	**Y**	
William Wells	1970	Darrel Yoder	1969
Iain Weston	1970	John Young	1969
Brian Wheeler	1970	George Young	1970
T.M. Wilding-White	1970	Paul Yarnold	1971
Brian Woodcock	1970	Anthony Young	1976

NAME INDEX

A

Adair, Robin	64
Alexander, M.	96, 142
Allan, Dave	14, 63, 97, 98, 160
Almond, Richard	49
Ames, Sally	67, 107
Ames, Simon	17, 67, 106
Andrews, Mike	18, 19, 20, 21
Anning, Charlotte	117
Anning, Jill	117
Anning, John	117
Arthur, W/Cdr. Cyril	209, 215
Ayres, John	40, 41, 59, 83, 98
Ayres, Rose	40

B

Ball, Richard	241, 277
Bannister, Paul	107
Barber, Ambrose	85, 86
Baring, Alexander	155
Baring, James	34, 36, 37, 42, 43, 51, 62, 63, 84, 105, 107, 111, 126, 155, 156, 188, 226, 236, 246, 247, 252
Baring, Nini (née Fisher)	107, 140, 155, 156
Barker, Jane	230, 266
Barnes, John	220
Barnes, Roger	174
Barraclough, Martin	69, 126, 127, 131, 151, 214, 235
Baxter, Raymond	269
Bedford, Bill	37
Bellamy, Viv	76
Benest, Peter	139, 142
Benjamin, Lewis ('Benjy')	35, 48, 75, 94, 105, 130, 151, 200, 214, 235, 264, 267, 274, 275
Benjamin, Juanita ('Lollie')	33, 34, 35, 44, 51, 85, 94, 110, 116, 162, 188, 215, 264, 275
Benjamin, Robin	33, 51
Benjamin, Toby	110
Benjamin, Trudi	24, 227
Berliner, Don	92
Berry, Roy	230
Bialkiewicz, Mike	156, 183, 203, 230, 269

Bianchi, Tony	230
Biancotto, Leon	254
Bigger, Frank	45
Birch, A.E.	82
Bishop, Gladys	65
Bishop, C. Nepean ('Bish')	35, 52, 59, 63, 65, 67, 82, 98, 129, 155, 156, 254, 271, 282
Black, James	14, 23, 25, 27, 42, 57, 79, 96, 97, 98, 101, 102, 106, 121, 127, 134, 142, 156, 183, 230, 236, 282
Blake, John	17, 45, 50, 55, 76, 103, 128, 140, 142, 149, 160, 177, 269
Blech, Robin	42, 59, 89, 93, 190, 191
Boddington, Charles	33, 96, 98, 116, 121, 122, 130, 135, 138, 157, 170, 254
Boddington, Diana	170
Boesman, Jan	18, 19, 20, 21
Boesman, Nini	18, 19, 20, 21
Bonnet, Pierre	142
Booth, Roy	108, 135, 154
Boyd Carpenter, Lord	271
Brace, Lola	183
Bramson, 'Bunny'	64, 82, 101, 144, 150, 156, 194
Bramson, Miriam	82, 194
Bright, Bill	156
Brissenden, Ken	109
Bristow, Alan	214, 215, 285
Broad, Hubert	129, 259, 260, 280
Browning, Neville	102, 158
Bucher, Jack	212
Burbridge, D.	96
Burgess, Eric	247
Burgess, Margaret	247, 269
Burgess, Selina	247

C

Campbell, Donald	16, 40
Carroll, David	235
Carter, Nick	25, 34, 52, 101
Caspersen, Arve	153
Caster, David	23
Cayzer, Anthony	285

Cayzer, Nicholas 285
HRH Prince Charles 176, 248
Chadwick, Andrew 96, 97, 139, 142, 157, 176, 177, 212, 231, 248, 269
Chadwick, 'Chad' 196, 197
Channon, Pete 244, 249
Chesson, Bill 14, 84, 93, 111, 117, 126, 155, 161, 162, 191
Chichester, Sir Francis 35, 36, 173, 189
Christie, Robert 230
Churchill, Winston 57, 103, 147, 160
Clarke P.F.W. 107
Clutton, Cecil ('Sam') 46, 47, 54
Coburn, Mike 158
Collins, Joyce 251
Collins, Victor 251
Cook, Wendy 75
Conyers, Paul 116
Corp, Colin 230
Cottelarda, Andre 142
Cottelarda, Madeleine (née Deleroix) 142
Crabb, Gordon 64, 93, 161, 171, 184
Crane, Tom 116
Cronin, Maurice 55
Crossley, Mike 269
Crucifix, Georges 40
Culver, Dennis 63, 103
Cunningham, John 82

D

Daines, Don 269, 270
Davis, Duncan 195
Davis, Roy 49, 127, 191
Davidson, Jinny 193
de Havilland, Geoffrey 24, 61
Denyer, Jim 268, 275
d'Erlanger, Elizabeth 103
d'Erlanger, Robin 22, 23, 61, 93, 97, 98, 103, 104, 126
Delaney, Philomena (later Voice) 127
Deverell, Adrian ('Dev') 25, 29, 30
Diethrich, Edward 281, 282
Dix, Gavin 53, 177
Donghi, Steve 96
Doyle, John 153
Dunning, Clive 274
Dunsford, John 249
Dyne, Margaret 203

HRH Duke of Edinburgh 23, 34, 92, 147, 176, 204, 245

E

Eggett, Terry 177
Eggleston, Angus 138
Ellis, Jim 53, 141, 226, 273
Elliott-Lynn (later Lady Heath) 281
Emery, Dick 57, 105
England, Gordon 280
Evans, Bill 268
Evans, Peter 155
Eyston, George 23, 129

F

Falk, Phillip 251
Fane, Edmund 18, 19, 20, 21
Faulkner Bryant, David 246, 249, 257
Ferguson, Janet 75, 79, 111, 112, 130
Firth, John 79, 96, 99, 106, 139, 142, 156, 160
Fisher, Nini (later Baring) 34, 64, 67, 94
Fisher, Zaza (later Barraclough) 67
Forss, Roger 116, 142
Foulds, Harry 166
Fox, Freddie 156
Foxworth, Tom 269
Francis, Clive 14, 26, 34, 48, 49, 50, 85, 86, 89, 105
Francis, Jean 48, 85, 102
Freer, Tom 23, 89, 121, 183, 189, 200, 223, 234, 235, 236, 244, 253, 257, 261, 269, 272
Frow, Ian 205, 206
Fry, George 285

G

Gairns, Robert 88
Gardner, Charles 128
Gaster, David 139, 142, 156, 157
Gilbert, James 40, 42, 52, 61, 63, 149, 162, 208, 220
Gillam, Carol 230
Giroux, S/Ldr. 167
Golding Barrett, Arthur ('GB') 23, 24, 25, 45, 64, 65, 69, 104, 138, 156, 183, 185, 207, 231, 250, 254, 259, 261, 280, 282
Golding Barrett, Veryan 280

Goldstraw, Bill   139, 142, 161, 199,
              212, 217, 222
Goodyer, Jane   230
Griffiths, Barry   56, 57, 61, 105, 119,
              120, 126, 151, 159, 162
Griffiths, Elspeth   159
Guess, R.J.   230

H
Haig-Thomas, Hanna   117
Haig-Thomas, Julia   117
Haig-Thomas, Tony   30, 31, 32, 33,
                      61, 67, 96, 98,
                  106, 117, 126, 139,
                      142, 190, 235
Hamblett, Jack   197
Hamilton, David   103, 126, 127, 138,
                  142, 164, 166, 202,
                      231, 269
Hamilton, Georgina   103, 127
Hankart, Lucien   204, 230
Hanna, Ray   108, 154, 191, 220
Harding, Lloyd   63
Hargraves, Elizabeth   203
Harriott, Mavis   63, 106, 141, 206,
              212, 228, 249, 261, 262
Harrison, Neil   134
Hart, Ralph   177, 235, 244, 257, 261
Hartas, Dennis   14, 84
Heller, Dagmar   42
Henrick, Crown Prince   137
Henry, Don   138, 245, 258
Herring, Paul   42
Hickley, Brian   23
Hindle, Alan   152
Hitchcock, Bill   253, 262, 272, 274,
                      276
Hoffsommer, Alan   268
Holmes, 'Titch'   184, 254
Holtby, Mike   190
Hoseason, Jimmy   32, 33
Hoseason, Leslie   32
Howe, Lady   274
Howe, Sir Geoffrey   274
Hounslow, Bob   127
Hounslow, Lottie   107
Hounslow, Frank   107, 127, 154
Hughes, Clem   96, 139, 142, 158
Hughes, Howard   230
Humphreys, Arthur   61
Hunt, John   156

I
Iles, Brian   118, 130
Iles, Pat   118, 134
Innes, Bill   50, 51, 93, 103, 127
Innes, Linda   93, 103
Irish, Phil   274

J
Jackson A.J. ('Jacko')   24, 25, 206,
                      267, 268
Jacobs, Ron   75
James, Thurston   280
Janney, Gordon   84
Jarvis, Pete   50, 51, 59, 84, 96, 101,
              106, 126, 127, 128, 137,
          142, 167, 188, 190, 220, 282
Jensen, Neil   126, 190
Jewkes, Jim   71
Jolley, Judy   37
Jolley, Mike   23, 34, 37, 50
Jones, Ann   267
Jones, Annabel   267
Jones, Michael   14, 42, 53, 54, 61,
              70, 83, 89, 91, 102, 103,
              106, 107, 108, 111, 117,
              130, 135, 139, 140, 147,
              148, 149, 150, 153, 155,
              160, 166, 171, 173, 183,
              184, 188, 193, 199, 201,
              205, 209, 212, 215, 219,
              221, 223, 228, 229, 239,
              252, 263, 267, 274, 285

Jones, Norman ('The Boss,')
    Tiger Club founder.

*With mentions on every other page,
the author could suggest no greater
tribute to Norman than to offer him
the unique status of being unindexed.*

Jorgensen Inge   264
Judge, 'Pee Wee'   34, 37, 50, 71, 74,
                      77, 170

K
Kahle, Peter   134
Kaye, 'Danny'   254
Kelly, Dudley   212
Kelly, Judy   272
Kelly, 'Manx'   93, 96, 97, 126,
                  139, 142, 154, 156,
                  157, 159, 199, 220,
                  242, 243, 270, 272

Kerridge, Major 146
Key, Sam 93, 104
Kingsley, Jerry 155
Kirkham, Denis 116, 253
Koczon, Carol 216

L
Laffy, Peter 185
Lamont, Norman 271
Langstone, Peter 160
Legg, Roy 96, 116, 139, 142,158, 177, 189, 190, 217, 230
Lindsay, Pat 126
Liversage, Peter 152
Lodge, Angela 15
Lodge, Tim 15
'Lollie' – see Benjamin
Lovell, Don 25, 26, 27, 34, 134, 164, 189, 212
Lovell, Tessa 15, 25, 27, 40, 42, 189, 212
Lowdell, George 280
Luckin, M. 167

M
MacGillray, Father 135
MacKintosh, Alister 204
MacKenzie, Charles 63
MacLennan, Ian 244
MacRae, Frances 93, 96, 97, 98, 101, 106, 141, 142, 143, 157, 177, 191, 216, 217, 230, 246
Masefield, Charles 37, 126
Masefield, Peter 105, 106
Masefield, Mrs Peter 106
Marsh, Fred 32, 79, 82, 102, 111, 156, 223, 224
Martin, Vicky (also see Storey) 117
McAully, Barbara 32, 116
McAully, Elwyn 32, 61, 254, 255
McBreen, Geoffrey 81, 106
McCowen, Ian 157
McGarry, Bob 215
McKellar, Margo 81, 254
Meadmore, Roger 271
Meeson, Philip 139, 142, 156, 157, 161
Meeson, Ian 157
Menuhin, Ann 245
Menuhin, Krov 245
Merrill, Dina 15
Millward, Dick 178, 180, 181, 183
Mimpriss, John 15, 81

Mimpriss, Lorraine 15, 81
Minton, Paul 54
Mitchell, Bob 96, 97, 139, 142, 156, 158, 217
Moffatt, Hamish 45, 46
Monk, Geoffrey 25
Moore, Anna 78, 103, 151
Moore, Michael 78, 103, 151
Morgan, Dave 95
Morgan, Mansel 269
Morgan, Peter 95
Morris, Chris 204
Moulson, Tom 222

N
Needham, Latimer 280
Neilson, Toni 102
Neumeister, John 157
Newbury, Jack 167
Nott, Julian 251
Nurse, John 177

O
Ogilvy, David 185, 186, 187
Olsen, Lene 89, 137
Olsen, Morten 89, 93, 137
O'Rourke, Patrick 152

P
Page, Maurice 42
Parker, Lankaster 129
Pashley, Cecil 69, 195
Paul, Chris 117, 129, 268
Payne, Dudley 262
Penrose, Desmond 61
Perrin, David 190
Perry, Alan 204
Prince Philip (see HRH Duke of Edinburgh)
Phillips, David 35
Phillips, Peter 37, 43, 44, 84, 94, 98, 126, 127, 171, 178, 179, 180, 182, 184, 190, 199, 230, 247
Phillips, Sue 37, 94, 116, 126
Phillips, Tim 155
Piercy, Jack 23, 26, 63, 64, 84, 161, 226, 230
Piggott, Derek 122, 124, 125
Pike, 'Clem' 258, 259, 280
Pinto, Anneliese 239
Pocock, Nick 98, 160, 270

Pooley, Bob 24
Pooley, Yvonne 24
Popoff, Mike 102, 116, 254
Preston, Anthony 204, 207
Preston, 'Mossy' 195
Price, Frank 264, 272, 277
Proctor, Roy 156
Prosper, Hazel 212, 228

Q
Quill, Jeffrey 154

R
Radice, Iona 177
Radwanski, 'Rad' 184
Redding, Vincent 230
Reed, Miss 134
Regan, Tom 251
Reid, Dicky 160
Reynolds, John 135
Richards, Dicky 195
Richards, Glyn 50, 150, 156
Riley, Mike 96, 101, 106, 134, 142,
156, 157, 183, 190
Robertson, Cliff 15, 110, 111, 121,
281, 282
Rose, Clive 134
Rose, Howard 71

S
Sarratt, John 53, 141, 273
Saunders, Beryl 27
Schnabel, Hubert 42, 106, 156
Schofield, Carl 96, 97, 98, 101, 126,
127, 140, 142, 155, 167,
188, 190, 220, 282
Scott, Sheila 25, 49, 50, 87, 94,
111, 140, 155, 214, 281
Scott-Hill, Ian 34, 167
Senior, Ian 230
Shaw, Barry 96, 142, 184, 247
Short, Oswald 129
Simpson, Bernard 38
Sissons, Keith 173, 183, 189, 199,
200, 214, 223, 234, 235,
245, 253, 272
Slessor, John 50, 77
Slovak, Mia 111
Smith, Anthony 118, 134
Smith, Brian 135, 137, 142, 183,
190, 260, 262, 282
Smith, Ken 59, 93

Smith, Rex 231
Snook, Bev 34, 62, 93, 150, 167,
183, 184, 262
Snook, Pauline 184
Sole, Dennis 177
Somerleyton, Lord 200
Somerton-Rayner, Mike 155, 191
Southam, Jill 102, 118, 141, 160
Southerland, Bridget 116
Southerland, Tony 32, 116
Spurrell, Ralph 51
Stapp, Mike 201
St. Barbe, Frank 280
Stenhouse, D. 139, 142
Stevens, Brian 126, 190
Stewart-Wood, John 51, 103
Storey, Eleanor 173
Storey, Tom 15, 47, 63, 64, 81,
84, 94, 104, 111, 117,
120, 130, 147, 173, 194,
214, 235, 245, 247
Storey, Vicky 120, 173
Strecker, C. 152
Swire, Adrian 93, 154, 160, 190

T
Taylor, Danny 197, 198
Taylor, John 34
Taylor, 'Taffy' 23, 98, 102, 128, 129
Tempest, Barry 32, 96, 157, 255
Thompson, Steve 88, 142
Thompson, 'Tommy' 61, 106
Tidmarsh, Vivian 51
Timmis, David 23, 212, 231, 234, 277
Travan, Pete 253
Treadaway, Peter 130
Trice, Hilary 166
Trudi – see Benjamin
Turley, Alan 37, 38, 42, 43, 88, 116
Turley, Dawn 38, 42, 43, 88, 116
Turner-Hughes, 'Toc H' 280
Turner, Julia 111
Turner, Michael 134
Turner, Ray 96, 97, 102, 116, 139, 142
Turvey, Nick 102, 151, 152
Tyrrell, Arthur 56, 57, 148

U
Ugarte, Manuel 76
Underwood, Fred 244, 253, 258, 268
Urmston, John 93, 234, 235

V

Vanneck, Peter 132, 275, 281, 282
Vaughan, Roger 171
Voice, Philomena 173, 188, 276
Voice, Robin 23, 35, 42, 48, 74, 102,
104, 105, 108, 117, 126,
127, 134, 135, 136, 137,
154, 164, 173, 174, 188,
190, 219, 235

W

Wales, Vivian 111
Watkins, Mike 230
Watts, Mike 32
Weber, Jurg 87, 88
Wefel, Ralph 212, 244, 252, 262
Welsh, John 42
White, 'Chalky' 30
Wilkinson, Julia 67
Wilks, John 230
Wilkinson, John 126, 160
Williams, Burch 170
Williams, Fred 96, 269
HRH Prince William
of Gloucester 176, 183
Williams, John 126
Williams, Neil 14, 23, 24, 25, 28, 34,
50, 51, 52, 57, 63, 79,
88, 96, 97, 98, 103, 106,
134, 142, 157, 158, 160,
184, 191, 219, 227, 228,
230, 241, 257, 258, 282
Wilson, Alan 261
Willis, Bill 254
Winter, Bob 15, 83, 98, 101, 106, 138
Winter, Nicola 15
Wise, Reg 94
Wolf, Philip 258, 274
Woodward, 'Baggy' 196
Wren, Chris 213, 214, 258
Wright, Jackie 249
Wright, John 239, 245

GENERAL INDEX
(a selective guide)

A

Aircraft (a listing of Club aircraft
where registration is shown, plus
all listings of Club-owned vintage
'one-offs.'):

Arrow Active G-ABVE 22, 23,
25, 29, 50, 70, 71,
127, 154, 175, 219,
226, 234, 240, 242,
264, 271, 282
DH Fox Moth G-ACEJ 22, 23,
24, 28, 29, 51, 70,
107, 140, 147, 167,
168, 175, 208
DH Puss Moth G-AHLO 22, 23,
25, 28, 29, 51,
63, 70, 93, 107,
134, 140
DH Tiger Moth G-ACDC 14, 23,
68, 69, 83,
118, 127, 258
DH Tiger Moth G-AIVW
(Seaplane) 35, 36, 70, 129,
173, 175, 183, 189,
199, 200, 202, 206,
223, 229, 234, 235,
236, 240, 244, 252,
253, 258, 260, 261,
267, 271, 272, 280
DH Tiger Moth G-ANMZ 93
"The Canon"
DH Tiger Moth G-ANZZ 93
"The Archbishop"
DH Tiger Moth G-AOAA 55,
"The Deacon" 63, 74,
93, 127, 176
DH Tiger Moth G-APDZ 61,
"The Bishop" 254
DH Tiger Moth G-ASKP 35, 45,
47, 55, 61, 176
Jodel Musketeer G-ATKX 30
Piper Super Cub G-ARAM 54, 88
Rollason Luton Beta
"Forerunner" G-ATLY 140
Rollason Luton Beta
"Blue Chip" G-AWHV 140
Rollason Sea Turbulent
G-ARJZ 89, 92, 93, 121,
133, 173, 175, 189,
234, 235
Rollason Turbulent G-ARRZ 204,
221
Rollason Turbulent G-ASAM 204
Rollason Turbulent G-ASDB 42
Wassmer WA 52 Europa
G-BDSN (ex-G-BADN) 23

Airfields (frequently-mentioned
ones only):

Blackbushe 52, 101, 143, 176, 227
Castle Water
(Seaplane base) 229, 234,
236, 267, 272, 273
Challock (Gliding) 108, 109, 176
Denham 35, 36, 273
Elstree 44, 185, 186, 198,
219, 245
Fairoaks 173, 176, 189, 190,
198, 210, 223, 227,
228, 246, 254, 285
Goodwood 82, 94, 140
Little Snoring 22, 32, 116, 254
Rochester 22, 35, 36, 42, 84,
134, 140, 161, 162,
164, 173, 175, 176,
223, 236, 245
Shoreham 48, 50, 51, 71,
85, 108, 120, 126,
170, 171, 173, 222,
273
Sywell 35, 36, 48, 67, 246,
257, 273
Australian Air Race 133, 134, 154,
155, 156

Awards:

Air Squadron
Aerobatic Trophy 22, 96,
106, 142, 156, 184,
225, 230
Bird Trophy 23
Clem Pike Trophy 23, 63, 184,
230, 258, 269

Dawn-to-Dusk Awards   10, 23,
              34, 42, 106, 128
         156, 160, 164, 183,
              202, 204, 223,

**Dawn-to-Dusk Trophies
and Medallions:**
Best Log Book Medallion   230
Bonney Trophy (Ladies)   184,
                  203, 230

Duke of Edinburgh
   Trophy   183, 230
Duke of Edinburgh
   Medallion   230
Enterprising Entry
   Medallion   230
Icarus Trophy
   (single-seat)   156, 183, 230
Longest Distance Medallion   230
Pilot Trophy   230
de Havilland Trophy   22, 23, 96,
         142, 156, 199, 230
de Salis Trophy   23, 59, 106, 156,
              189, 230, 269
Desandier Trophy
   (RAeC)   184, 246
Esso Trophy   23, 52, 96, 134,
         138, 142, 156, 170,
              184, 230
Hamilton Trophy   164, 165, 173,
              176, 269
Icicle Trophy   97, 142, 156, 157,
              204, 272
Leon Biancotto Trophy   52, 134
Jean Lennox Bird Trophy   246
McAully Trophy   22, 23, 96, 106,
         116, 142, 156, 184,
              230, 253, 254
Tiger Club
   International Trophy   106,
                     223

Tiger Club Medallions:
Aerobatics   269
Air Racing   106, 156, 184,
              230, 269
Chairman's Spoon   230
Foreign Touring   23, 150, 156,
              184, 230
Spot Landing   25

B
British Aerobatic
   Championships   199, 272
D
"Daily Express" Air Race 248, 269   221
Duty Pilot   53, 54, 79, 206,
              225, 249, 266

E
European Aerobatics
   Championships   142

F
Formula One Air Races   92, 111, 147,
         166, 198, 213, 224,
         230, 244, 245, 259
Full Displays   15, 35, 36, 48, 50,
         51, 91, 105, 108, 120,
         121, 126, 127, 170, 171,
         190, 198, 219, 222, 223,
              245, 273

I
Isle of Man Rally
   and Race   45, 47, 111

K
"Kent Messenger" Race   166
Kronfeld Club   16, 17, 28, 30, 59,
         94, 102, 140, 173, 199,
         212, 226, 228, 229, 235,
         249, 252, 261, 263, 274

L
Lockheed International
   Competitions   40, 68
Legal Fund   26, 64, 65, 66, 81, 84,
         103, 107, 161, 213, 225,
              236, 239, 247

N
National Air Races   42, 43, 82,
         84, 106, 161, 275

O
Overseas Clubs listed:
   Abbeville   232
   Beauvais   38, 162, 164, 189
   Berck   26, 34
   Clermont-Ferrand   233

Lille   232
Osnabrück
    (Atterheide)   38, 232, 233

R
RAeC Air Racing Dinners   17, 245
Rochester Air Races   42, 84, 161
Rollasons   28, 53, 64, 67, 69,
                107, 117, 154, 184,
                191, 208, 236, 268

S
Shobdon Air Races   134

T
Tiger Club Dinner Dances   23, 25,
                   67, 93, 102, 104,
                   140, 156, 173, 175,
                   183, 184, 212, 214,
                   224, 230, 249, 251, 262
Transatlantic Air Race
    ("*Daily Mail*")   111

W
World Aerobatic
    Championships   22, 97, 98,
                141, 160, 273, 276

WOULD YOU LIKE TO KNOW THE WHOLE TIGER CLUB STORY FROM THE BEGINNING?

If you have enjoyed reading this book, a limited number of copies of VOLUME I are still available:

THE TIGER CLUB – A TRIBUTE, VOLUME I: 1957-1966

To receive a copy by return of post, send a cheque for £11.45 (£9.95 plus £1.50 p/p) to:

CIRRUS ASSOCIATES, KINGTON MAGNA, GILLINGHAM, DORSET SP8 5EW.

What some have said about the book:

The Jodel Club: "Your Editor admits to frequent and usually uncontrollable fits of nostalgia. When something as priceless and unputdownable as this turns up, he has to write about it . . . Benjy has produced a masterful record of the true rebirth of genuine Sport Flying in the UK."

"No aviator's bookshelf can be without your book."

". . . The greatest bit of nostalgia ever to hit paper . . . You really succeeded in capturing the fun and enthusiasm which, combined with competence and trust, made the Tiger Club unique. What a good thing it has been recorded so that future generations can learn the proper way to achieve things."